FREE-LANCING

A Guide to Writing for Magazines and Other Markets

Ronald P. Lovell
Oregon State University

For information about this book, write or call:
Waveland Press, Inc.
P.O. Box 400
Prospect Heights, Illinois 60070
(708) 634-0081

ISBN 0-88133-752-8

Printed in the United States of America

7 6 5 4 3 2 1

Table of Contents

Preface

Free-lancing: A Guide to Writing for Magazines and Other Markets represents an attempt to give students a realistic picture of a glamorized, yet often frustrating, part of journalism: free-lance magazine writing. The freedom and challenge of working for oneself is an attractive alternative to holding a staff position. But venturing onto such shaky career ice should not be done without knowledge of the risks involved—and a sturdy lifeline to solid ground at the edge of the pond.

Throughout the book, I have presented the advice of talented and successful free-lance writers and magazine editors on both coasts. I have thrown in the sometimes cruel lessons I have learned during 30 years as a magazine staff writer and free-lancer, as well as a university professor teaching courses in magazines and magazine writing.

Part I, Joining the Ranks of the Occasionally Unemployed, covers the joys and sorrows of magazine free-lancing and gives readers a basic understanding of magazines, past and present. The different kinds of magazines are reviewed in chapter 4, while editors and the editing process are examined in chapter 5.

Part II, Subjects Without End: The Kinds of Magazine Articles, forms the core of the book. Its seven chapters explore the principal kinds of magazine articles free-lancers usually wind up doing: those about people, subjects in the news, things that happen to them, places, how-to-do-its, and long articles. It ends with a chapter on writing reviews. Each chapter includes articles written by accomplished free-lancers and analysis indicating how and why each was written. Suggested markets for each kind of article are noted. There are special sidebars on important subjects like selling interviews as interviews, becoming a stringer, and writing for trade publications.

Part III, Before Pen Strikes Paper (Or Cursor Strikes Screen), gives readers information on such vital subjects as conducting research, cultivating editors, setting up a free-lance business, writing query letters and interviewing. Sidebars in these chapters indicate the best books for a reference library and how to interview scientists and doctors. This section also includes the beginning of a unique feature of this book: a multi-chapter segment, Lessons in Free-Lancing, in which I take a reader through the ins and outs of researching, interviewing for, and writing an article. I hope that this feature will give readers a valuable insight into what it is like to take an idea and turn it into a publishable article.

In Part IV, Writing Magazine Articles, the chapters describe how to write leads, transitions, and articles themselves, and how to submit manuscripts and ancillary items to editors.

Part V, Keeping the (Proverbial) Wolf from the Door, makes readers aware of two general problems free-lancers face and offers solutions. The first problem is making enough money to survive and the solution for free-lancers is to supplement their income by doing public relations writing, computer writing, and writing books. The second problem area concerns such legal concerns as libel, invasion of privacy, and copyright violations. The solution for free-lancers is to learn the definitions and laws pertaining to each of these concerns and to write their articles within these limits.

The book ends with a glossary of terms and a list of other books about magazines, magazine writing, and free-lancing.

As I often do in the books I write, I imposed on my friends first: the men and women I have known and worked with in a long career in journalism and journalism education. I value the time and insight given to me by: Jack Fincher, Robert Goldberg, Susan Hauser, Bill Ingram, Robert Kenyon, Bill McKibben, Mollie Mondoux, Peter Ogle, Rob Phillips, Hilda Regier, Wendell Smith, and Randy Wood. I appreciate the time of Geoffrey Morris of National Review, Hearst Magazine editors Rebecca Sawyer and Irene Copeland, and most especially Sally Lee of *Redbook* and Frank Vizard of *Popular Mechanics*. I also wish to thank Lauren Galliker of the Hearst public relations staff for arranging the latter interviews.

Kevin Miller, a former student and old friend, deserves special mention. His courage as a person and a writer, revealed so well in chapter 11, is unequalled. I thank him for sharing it with me—and the readers of this book.

I also wish to thank the publishers and free-lance writers who allowed me to reprint their articles in this book, particularly Pauline Kael, Gael Greene, and Mike Moore.

A computer-phobe like me could probably not get a job in journalism if I was starting out today. I have a real attitude problem when it comes to computers. Happily, for this and other books, I have had the help of Treena Martin, who can tell her own stories of "joy and sorrow" in dealing with my first draft. I wish also to thank Verna Lovell for continuing faith and support.

This book would still be mere words on a proposal but for the support of Neil Rowe, publisher and owner of Waveland Press. For the second book in a row, I have had the pleasure of working with Laurie Prossnitz, associate editor. My sincere thanks to them both.

This book will succeed if it guides readers through the perilous, swiftly moving rapids that magazine free-lance writing has become. As they take the plunge in an oft-leaky and careening boat, they need to know that successful navigation of the stream may be difficult, but is not impossible.

—Ron Lovell

Acknowledgments

Chapter 1 Interview material for Jack Fincher, Robert Goldberg, Susan Hauser, Bill McKibben, Rob Phillips, and Hilda Regier is used with permission.

Chapter 3 Robert Kenyon interview material is used with his permission.

Chapter 5 Interview material for Irene Copeland, Bill Ingram, Sally Lee, Geoffrey Morris, Peter Ogle, Rebecca Sawyer, and Frank Vizard is used with permission. Selection on pp. 59–66 is reprinted with permission, Medical Tribune, Inc.

Chapter 6 Selection on pp. 77–80 is reprinted with permission of Noreen O'Leary. Selection on pp. 80–84 is reprinted with permission of Joanne Kaufman. Selection on pp. 85–87 is reprinted with permission, Medical Tribune, Inc.

Chapter 7 Selections on pp. 95–100, 101–106 are reprinted with permission, Medical Tribune, Inc.

Chapter 8 Selection on pp. 110–122 is reprinted with permission of Kevin Miller and *The Register-Guard*, Eugene, Ore. Selection on pp. 122–125 is reprinted with permission of Susan Hauser. Selection on pp. 126–128 is reprinted with permission of Wen Smith.

Chapter 9 Selection on p. 129 from *The Old Patagonian Express* by Paul Theroux. Copyright © 1979 by Cape Cod Scriveners Co. Reprinted with permission of Houghton Mifflin Co. All rights reserved. Selection on pp. 135–140 © 1992 by The New York Times Company. Reprinted with permission. Selection on pp. 140–145 excerpted from "Stranger on a Train," *Sunrise With Seamonsters* by Paul Theroux. Copyright © 1985 by Cape Cod Scriveners Co. Reprinted with permission of Houghton Mifflin Co. All rights reserved.

Chapter 10 Frank Vizard interview material is used with his permission. Selection on pp. 153–157 is reprinted with permission of Frank Vizard.

Chapter 11 Interview material for Jack Fincher, Bill Ingram, and Rob Phillips is used with permission. Selection on pp. 163–171 is reprinted with permission of Rob Phillips. Selection on pp. 171–185 is reprinted with permission of Jack Fincher, from *Smithsonian*, January 1989.

Chapter 12 Selections on pp. 193–196, 197–199, and 203–206 © 1992 by The New York Times Company. Reprinted with permission. Selection on pp. 201–203 is excerpted from *Kiss Kiss Bang Bang* (1968) by Pauline Kael. Reprinted with permission of the author. Selection on pp. 207–209 is reprinted by permission; © 1992 Edith Oliver. Originally in *The New Yorker*. Selection on pp. 211–214 is reprinted with permission; © 1992 James Wolcott. Originally in *The New Yorker*. Selection on pp. 215–218 is reprinted with permission of Robert Goldberg. Selection on pp. 219–222 is reprinted with permission of Gael Greene.

Chapter 13 Interview material for Jack Fincher and Hilda Regier is used with permission.

Chapter 14 Interview material for Jack Fincher and Rob Phillips is used with permission. Guidelines in Box 14.1, p. 234, are reprinted with permission. Copyright © 1992 The Nation Company, Inc. Press card on p. 244 is used with permission of Medical Tribune, Inc.

Chapter 15 Interview material for Jack Fincher, Susan Hauser, Sally Lee, Bill McKibben, Rob Phillips, and Hilda Regier is used with permission. Selection on pp. 253–254 used with permission of Mike Moore. Selections on pp. 254–255, 255–256, and 256–257 are used with permission of *Redbook*.

Chapter 18 Selection on pp. 287–297 reprinted with permission, Exxon Company, USA.

Chapter 19 Interview material for Randy Wood is used with his permission.

Chapter 20 Selection on pp. 314–315 is reprinted with permission of the Oregon State University Department of News and Communication Services. Selection on pp. 317–319 is reprinted with permission of the Oregon State University College of Liberal Arts. Interview material for Mollie Mondoux is used with her permission.

PART I

Joining the Ranks of the Occasionally Unemployed

More than fame, more than money, that may be free-lancing's richest reward: the bracing burst of adrenaline that only pure terror can command.

—Bill Barol
in *Newsweek on Campus*

1

The Joys and Sorrows of Free-Lancing

Free-lance. The term dates back to medieval times when knights unpledged to any king offered their lances for hire. Substitute pen, typewriter, or word processor for lance as the service offered and add the word "writer" and you have a segment of journalism that many people long to enter but few people really prosper in or remain in for any extended period.

A free-lance writer offers his or her skills to research and write articles for magazines and, to a lesser extent, newspapers on a kind of piecework basis. Free-lance writers work on assignment or because editors accept their article ideas—outlined in query letters sent beforehand. Free-lance writers get paid by the article. If they are lucky, they get reimbursed for travel and other expenses. Period. No guarantee of future work or health or retirement benefits or monthly paychecks.

The precise number of free-lance writers in the United States is impossible to calculate. The American Society of Journalists and Authors (ASJA), a national organization of what it calls "independent nonfiction writers," has 800 members, all of whom have met standards of professional achievement. There are more free-lance writers than this, of course, but many are not joiners of this or any group where they can be counted. Some people call themselves free-lance writers when they are between full-time jobs or even to camouflage the fact that they aren't working at all. Others say they are free-lancing but really make most of their income by doing other things. Typically, people who free-lance also work regular jobs, primarily as editors, teachers, lecturers, and as public relations practitioners. An ASJA statistic that is disheartening to anyone hoping to have a career in free-lance writing is low pay. The average gross income of free-lance writers in 1981 was $17,500. No comparable figures were available for the 1990s but an educated guess would make the range of incomes from $20,000 to $30,000 a year, with $35,000 to $40,000 possible in a big market like New York. A lucky handful of Eastern writers working for *The New Yorker* make considerably more. The magazine pays as high as $30,000 for a 20,000-word article.

These facts are not presented to deflate those contemplating a free-lance writing career or to deter them from even considering such a choice. They are simply offered in the interest of truth. Free-lancing is not for everyone, but it might be for you—as long as you face reality.

The Joys of Free-Lancing

There are many reasons a writer would want to pursue a free-lance career.

- *Being your own boss.* The chance to set your own hours and seldom dress up appeals to many people who choose free-lance careers.
- *Picking your subjects.* Never having to do a distasteful assignment (except for money) or writing to fit a certain style every day are other positive considerations.
- *Enjoying the variety of subjects and publications.* A successful free-lance writer will never get in a rut. When the subject of one article gets boring or a particular editor a bit overbearing, the writer can switch to something more enjoyable.
- *Thriving on challenge.* For someone able to overcome the drawbacks, free-lance writing—especially for magazines—offers the ultimate challenge and ultimate psychological "high." Except for trying to make a living as a poet or a painter, few jobs are as challenging.
- *Avoiding office politics.* Virtually no office in the world can avoid what is commonly called "politics": who is in favor with management, who is in disfavor, who is having romantic liaisons, who is not getting a raise, who is rumored to be resigning—or about

to be fired. If you only answer to yourself (best not to talk to yourself), most of these distractions can be avoided.

- *Having the chance to make more money than when on a fixed salary.* In theory, at least, free-lance writing offers the chance to make an almost unlimited amount of money. All it takes is hard work, ability, and a great deal of luck. The theory may not always be borne out in practice but it is possible to make money commensurate with the number of assignments carried out. For example, a skillful free-lance writer may be working on articles for major magazines at the same time he or she is completing a book and doing a monthly public relations newsletter. In theory.

The Sorrows of Free-Lancing

Sadly, there are just as many reasons a writer would decide against free-lancing full-time.

- *Dwindling magazine markets.* The 1990s recession has taken its toll on advertising revenues and magazines have cut their editorial pages accordingly. This means fewer and fewer chances for free-lance writers to place their proposals and get assignments. (The bad economic times have benefited free-lance writers on some magazines, however, because companies are laying off full-time staff writers and using free-lancers simply because they don't have to pay them any benefits.)
- *Stiff competition from other writers.* In a slow economy there are large numbers of free-lance writers chasing the few markets remaining. Only the most creative writers—or the ones with the most cunning survival skills—endure.
- *Editor indifference.* With so many free-lance writers beating on the door, editors can afford to be very selective. Editors on most national consumer magazines get several hundred unsolicited manuscripts every week. It takes a good idea and a lot of persistence for a writer to break through and get attention and action.
- *Editor rudeness.* This buyer's market means that editors are slow to respond to queries and very reluctant to take a chance on an unknown writer. At best, an editor may ask a writer to do an article "on speculation"—in other words, write the article with no promise that it will be published when it is completed. "If it meets our needs, we'll consider it," is a common refrain. That's hard for a free-lance writer to justify in a field where every minute counts. If you aren't writing and placing articles, you aren't making any money.

- *Slowness of payment*. Even when a writer gets the approval to proceed on an idea and completes the article on time, he or she may not be paid very quickly. Even though editorial business offices *should* know how close to the edge most free-lance writers teeter, they still put payments on a 30-day cycle or longer. This means that fees and even reimbursement for expenses can be delayed interminably and received long after the writer's own bills are past due.
- *Lack of benefits*. A free-lance writer has no retirement plan or health plan, and has to pay Social Security taxes. Little things a staff writer takes for granted are missing too, like unlimited telephone use, free copy machine use, and free postage.
- *Too much solitude*. When you work alone, there is no one with whom you can bounce ideas around or to read passages of your articles. Even if you are well-disciplined and self-motivated, you might get lonely and nervous about the lack of assignments and income. If you do, you won't make it as a free-lance writer.

Free-Lancing Without Tears

There are ways to ameliorate the situation just described. The main purpose of this book is to present a realistic picture of what a career in magazine free-lance writing is all about. Anyone contemplating the plunge into the dark, murky depths that is modern free-lance writing should consider a few basic points about himself or herself and a few tips for survival that will be expanded upon in later chapters.

The self-examination should begin with a few questions:

- Do I have the self-discipline to start working every day at the same time, even though no one is really making me do so, and to stick to some kind of regular schedule, day in and day out?
- Do I have the diligence to study carefully the magazines I am interested in writing for and to come up with ideas that both fit the format and haven't appeared in a recent issue?
- This done, do I have the creativity to come up with unique, salable ideas that will interest editors?
- After getting the assignment, do I have the kind of writing ability that will make me stand out from the pack of other creative and gifted writers so that the editor will like the article and use me again?
- Can I meet deadlines, no matter what, with no excuses?

- Am I willing to gain the knowledge necessary to specialize in several subjects or a region of the country so that I can set myself apart from other writers?
- Am I willing to swallow my pride on occasion and pursue busy and sometimes abrupt editors who have turned me down once, but who I think will like my latest idea?
- Am I willing to become very industrious and try to sell the same story ideas to noncompeting publications to get more mileage out of my material?
- Am I willing to do other, less glamorous writing—such as for public relations or technical publications or as a ghostwriter for others—to keep money coming in while I concentrate on my real love, magazine writing?
- Do I have the right kind of personality to succeed as a free-lance writer? Am I too nervous or easily worried about lack of money? Am I self-reliant enough?

Only you can answer these questions and they all don't have to be answered affirmatively. They do need to be considered, however.

Eavesdropping on Free-Lancers

Lest this chapter be considered too discouraging to those interested in one of the most stimulating and challenging careers in journalism, it will close with some words from people who are doing very well as free-lance magazine writers.

> Even the frustrations are fun in this business. I used to think free-lancing depended entirely on merit. It depends a lot on people who know people who know people. The key is perseverance. You've got to be indestructible. Free-lancing is so changeable. You really do need to stretch to fit the editor's need. That's the real strength you have. If you love words, love communicating, you proceed with every opportunity. On a recent assignment, I interviewed Steve Forbes, the editor of *Forbes* magazine. "You're free-lancing," he asked me. "Do you sleep at night?"
>
> —Rob Phillips, a free-lance writer who works for airline and aviation magazines

The trick is having steady, regular customers. I do regular work for *The Wall Street Journal, People*, and have recently been contacted by *The New York Times* to write for the Sunday magazine and Sunday travel section. I get frustrated with working for *People* but need the money so I put up with it. Trying to succeed at free-lance writing is a little like waiting for a big break on Broadway. A friend told me, "*People* is your waitress job."

Why do I free-lance? Free-lance writing is a constant learning process. Another reason is access, especially if you work for well-known publications. I can call anyone and say, I write for *The Wall Street Journal* and they'll talk to me. For example, I was the first journalist ever allowed in [Nike president] Phil Knight's home because he wanted to be in *People* magazine. Ego plays a role too: I like for people to see what I've done. You feel a lot of hero worship, such as in talking to college classes. There is also the opportunity for travel, even when you're not doing travel stories.

In spite of all the "pros" to free-lancing, there are "cons" as well. I'm at the point where I'd like to get into book writing, be a little more relaxed. I wake up nights worrying about my income, about whether I'm making enough to pay the bills. Even though I've been fairly successful, I worry that I'll get stuck with the kind of writing I'm comfortable with and make the same level of money. I guess I have a real lack of self-confidence at times. I worry if I can do what I want to do. I stick a query in the mail slot with several clips of writing I'm proud of attached and think, "Is that good enough?" I worry that my outlook is not fresh enough or that up and coming writers will replace me. I guess I worry too much.

—Susan Hauser, a Portland, Oregon free-lance writer (who recently quit working for *People*)

A magazine I was editing went out of business and I soon got a call to edit a medical book. Then word got out that I was available and I started getting magazine assignments from people I knew on another magazine I worked on. I got to thinking, "Hey, maybe I can do this." I would never have set out to do this. I don't have the personality for it. But I've learned that one of the benefits of free-lancing is that you are able to relax. There is a lot less pressure than in a staff job. People have said I look more relaxed. It is probably easier to work in New York because it is a marketplace for a lot of work. A lot of medical writers also compete in this marketplace, of course. Today, with things like fax machines, it is possible to be a free-lance writer elsewhere, especially with an established medical background.

—Hilda Regier, a free-lance medical writer
who lives in New York

I like the freedom of free-lancing, although it's an illusory kind of freedom. Instead of one boss, I have two or eight or ten. If I get up and don't feel like writing this morning, I can read this morning. I wear old clothes. I come and go as I wish. Every once in a while I put on a suit and get on a plane and go out and be Mr. *Reader's Digest* for a week. I do happy, positive stories for them so the people I meet are at their best. They wine and dine me. Then I go home, climb into my old clothes and write at my own pace. To do what you love. That's the circumstances that are best for me. I'm at my best when I'm given a task and can then go out and do it. I'm not a leader of men—or a follower either.

From a broader point of view, I think journalism is a great way to appreciate what is going on in the world. It's a front row seat at history. In an interview, which I consider a contract with the person being interviewed, they either see you and want you to make them look better than they are or, if possible, see how what they did was great. There is no better way to approach people. All I wish is that free-lancing paid more regularly and paid better.

—Jack Fincher, former staff writer
at *Life*, free-lance contributor to
Reader's Digest and *Smithsonian*

Free-lancing is only an occupation for people able to cope with large amounts of uncertainty. Working at *The New Yorker* for five years gave me good credentials. People know you and that gets your foot in the door just once. If you foul up, that's it. You've still got to turn your copy in on time so it is ready to go fast. That's the key. The few times I've edited things I've come to realize this. In ideal times, an editor would get high quality material only. That world does not exist. More common is to get copy they have to beat their brains over [improving].

I went into free-lancing because I decided to live outside of a big city. There aren't many options. There is not a magazine staff job you can do a long way away. I have an independent streak. I would be hard pressed any more to work normally. But, as a free-lance writer you have to accept the fact that it is a poor way to make money. If you're going to do it, you've got to figure out how to live on less money instead of trying to make more.

—Bill McKibben, free-lance writer of books and magazine articles and a resident of upstate New York

If you really want to make money, you should go to law school. Free-lancing is a lucrative profession for very few people. Even if you're doing well and get top dollar, you've got to consider how long it takes to do a piece, write it, revise it.

From the inception of the idea to the time you get your check, a lot of time passes. You come up with an idea and go out and research it. You send out query letters. Let's say you take a week to write up and send out the proposal. If you're lucky you hear back in three to four weeks that an editor wants you to do a piece. You get the assignment and research it fast—another two weeks. Equally fast you write the whole thing in a week. Let's say you send it in to an editor who is doing five other things, which all editors certainly are. The editor asks for revisions and that takes another two weeks. You get a firm OK after that. Then, how long will it take to move your fee through the accounting department? You'll probably still have to wait another month to get paid.

And how much are you getting paid? A dollar a word is the standard "good" rate. An early piece will probably not be 3,000 words, but maybe 1,500. At $1 a word, that's $1,500. This whole process has taken 16 weeks, four months. Who can survive on less than $400 a month? You can make more working at McDonald's. That's the down side of free-lancing.

Of course, you will eventually be able to cut days off of that. When you're known, for example, you won't need a query letter. You can just phone the editor and try out your ideas. You'll cut days off when you get faster as a writer. This speeds up the process. You also write longer pieces and this brings in more money.

Eventually you learn the secrets of free-lancing: juggle more than one assignment. While you're writing one article, you have a query in for a second, you're doing a final revision on a third, and you're waiting to get paid for a fourth. And what really helps is to have a steady gig, a regular column. I'm lucky enough to have a regular TV column in *The Wall Street Journal.*

The upside of free-lancing is that you're always learning. Each week you're off to do new, exciting things. One week you travel to Detroit to do a piece on the Tigers for *Sport Magazine*. Then you're in L.A. to interview Tom Hanks for *Connoisseur* or Timothy Hutton for *Vogue*. If you're lucky, you'll go to Paris to do something or other.

It can be a lot of fun. But make no mistake, free-lance writing is a business, an often exhausting business. Most people fail at it because they don't approach it like a business. You need to dream, to imagine your byline on amazing stories, to think about traveling around the world. You need to do all of these kinds of things to get yourself going—but to succeed, you need to run your free-lance career like a business.

—Robert Goldberg, New Jersey based free-lance writer, book author, and TV critic for *The Wall Street Journal*

2

The Golden Age of Magazines

Magazines did not become an established segment of American journalism until long after the United States became a nation, although two had appeared within a few days of one another as early as 1741. Benjamin Franklin had intended to get his *General Magazine* in print first, but Andrew Bradford's *American Magazine* appeared ahead of it. Neither stayed in business very long but now share the distinction of being the first magazines to be published in what is now the United States.

In total, five magazines were launched during the Revolutionary War, but only one, Robert Aiken's *Pennsylvania Magazine*, endured for very long. It contained literary works and political analysis, including the writing of Tom Paine.

Other magazines published in this period contained a similar mix of the literary and the political, their largely gray pages broken up only occasionally by engravings of portraits or nature scenes. In general, magazines resembled books more than they did newspapers, their closest journalistic competitors.

People turned to magazines when they needed something more than the often sensational and usually superficial newspapers of the day, which were aimed at the masses rather than at people who were more educated and thoughtful. Indeed, it was the rapid spread of education and the reduction of illiteracy—along with improvements in printing processes and the growth of big cities—that caused the great expansion in the number of magazines early in the 19th century. Journalism historian John Tebbel (1974) notes that the number of magazines increased from less than 100 in 1825 to about 600 by 1850.

Tebbel considers the most important development of the period to have been the rise in the number of general monthly magazines. One of the first such ventures was *The Casket: Flowers of Literature, Wit and Sentiment*, brought out by Samuel C. Atkinson and Charles Alexander in 1826.

By the 1830s, magazine publishers were joining with such noted authors of the time as Washington Irving, James Fenimore Cooper, Nathaniel Hawthorne, and John Greenleaf Whittier to raise the quality of the writing offered to readers. Two of the more successful ventures of this kind were *Graham's Magazine*, first published in 1840 by George R. Graham, and *The Knickerbocker Magazine*, founded in 1833.

The first hint of the specialization that characterizes the magazine business today began in this same period with the introduction of magazines aimed at women. The first successful one was Sara Josepha Hale's *Ladies Magazine* (1828), noted for its campaign for women's rights. This magazine was all but eclipsed two years later by Louis A. Godey and his *Godey's Ladies Book*. The publisher spent a great deal of money to make his magazine look good, with hand-colored fashion engravings and good quality printing to enhance the fiction, poetry, and non-fiction articles. The results in terms of circulation and profits were unheard of at the time. By 1839, the magazine had a circulation of 25,000; this number had increased to 150,000 by 1860. At his death, Godey left an estate worth more than $1 million.

In 1850, the New York book publishing firm Harper and Brothers started *Harper's Monthly*, continuing the tradition begun by *Graham's* and the *Knickerbocker* of publishing high quality writing, well-illustrated by woodcuts up to then seen only in books. *Harper's Monthly* was soon publishing the works of British authors Charles Dickens and Anthony Trollope. Mark Twain sold his first published story to the magazine. By the outbreak of the Civil War, *Harper's Monthly* had reached the then unheard of circulation of 200,000. The magazine is still in business today, the oldest in this country's history. (In 1857, the same publisher introduced *Harper's Weekly*, which was less literary, more news-oriented, and resembled a newspaper in its format.)

That same year, a new rival was brought out in Boston with a similar look and content. *The Atlantic Monthly*, which also is still being published, was started by Francis H. Underwood and Phillips, Sampson and Company, following two days of meetings at the

Parker House. Others at the bargaining table included Ralph Waldo Emerson, Henry Wadsworth Longfellow, Oliver Wendell Holmes, and James Russell Lowell. Lowell became the magazine's first editor.

This cadre of New England's finest writers—soon joined by Henry David Thoreau, Nathaniel Hawthorne, and Harriet Beecher Stowe—established the magazine's reputation early. Initially, however, the publication's aim was to "bring the literary influence of New England to aid the anti-slavery cause." Its circulation at the start was 15,000, but its seriousness kept it well below the high levels reached by the more spirited *Harper's*.

Other similar magazines came and went during this period: the *Century* (1881), *Scribner's* (1886), the *Forum* (1886), the *Arena* (1889) and the *Literary Digest* (1890).

In 1879, Congress gave a boost to the magazine business by passing legislation to establish cheap postage rates. According to journalism historian Edwin Emery (1972), this caused some magazine publishers to try to reach mass readers for the first time. Cyrus H. K. Curtis founded the *Ladies Home Journal* in 1883. Under editor Edward W. Bok it soon reached a circulation of 500,000. Curtis also bought *The Saturday Evening Post* for $1,000 in 1897 and hired George Horace Lorimer as editor. This venerable magazine traced its lineage to a publication bought by Benjamin Franklin in 1729. Subsequent investigation has debunked that claim, however, and sets the year of the *Post's* founding at 1821.

Many of these early magazines adopted an editorial mix that remains largely unchanged today—for example, *Harper's* and *The Atlantic*. Likewise, a publication not everyone in the business likes to admit is a magazine had its forerunner as well. *Frank Leslie's Illustrated Newspaper* resembled today's *National Enquirer*. From the first issue in 1855, this publication attracted attention by its wide use of pictures and sensational news. It also was noteworthy for its timeliness: news taking place as recently as two weeks before might be in its pages.

Leslie's Illustrated Newspaper ignored the sober public affairs coverage of other magazines to concentrate on popular serial fiction and stories about music, drama, fine arts, racing and other sports, and books—all appearing in designated departments like today's news magazines. Leslie would occasionally use his publication to crusade against abuses of the public trust—such as when he printed photos of the filth in dairies supplying New York City with milk. These revelations led the New York Legislature to pass a law prohibiting the sale of so-called "swill milk."

During the Civil War, Leslie sent artists to record the scenes of various battles, which he then reproduced as woodcuts. *Harper's*

Weekly followed this practice too. This was another innovation that readers enjoyed and marveled at, because they had not seen anything like it before.

As the 19th century entered its last 15 years, the older and more staid high quality magazines began to face formidable competition from three periodicals aimed at a more popular audience and selling at a lower price: *Cosmopolitan* (1886), *Munsey's* (1889), and *McClure's* (1893). They were later joined by *Everybody's*, which also published distinguished articles.

Of the three, *McClure's* has had the most enduring fame because it was the first to publish articles by that remarkable group of writers called the "muckrakers." President Theodore Roosevelt gave the magazines and their writers the name, intending it as a slur as he likened them to the "Men With the Muckrake" in John Bunyan's 17th century book, *Pilgrims Progress*, who even ignored the offer of a celestial crown to continue to "rake to himself the filth of the floor." This figure, Roosevelt went on, typified those writers who ignored what was lofty and concentrated only on what was "vile and debasing" and he assailed them as "potent forces for evil" in society.

History has ignored Roosevelt's admonition, however, and the term has come to signify a remarkable period of investigative reporting in which many of the evils of society were exposed in magazine articles and corrected by subsequent legislative action.

McClure's led the way in these crusades when it began to publish the writings of Lincoln Steffens, Ida Tarbell, Ray Stannard Baker, the novelist Upton Sinclair, and others.

Steffens' series of articles on corrupt municipal governments set the tone of excellence:

> Go to St. Louis and you will find the habit of civic pride in them; they still boast. The visitor is told of the wealth of the residents, of the financial strength of the banks, and of the growing importance of the industries, yet he sees poorly paved, refuse-burdened streets, and dirty or mud-covered alleys; he passes a ramshackle fire-trap crowded with the sick, and learns that is the City Hospital; . . . he calls at the new City Hall, and finds half the entrance boarded with pine planks to cover up the unfinished interior. Finally, he turns a tap in the hotel, to see liquid mud flow into wash-basin or bath-tub. . . . (Steffens, 1904)

He later chronicled political corruption in Minneapolis, Cleveland, New York, Chicago, Philadelphia, and Pittsburgh. In 1905 and 1906, he turned his attention to corruption in several state governments.

Tarbell's "History of the Standard Oil Company" took five years to research and ran in *McClure's* for 15 months, detailing how John

D. Rockefeller had been unscrupulous in amassing his great fortune:

> . . . If Mr. Rockefeller had been an ordinary man the outburst of popular contempt and suspicion which suddenly poured on his head would have thwarted and cursed him. But he was no ordinary man. He had the powerful imagination to see what might be done with the oil business if it could be centered in his hands. . . . (Tarbell, 1904)

Baker's writing on the problems of the working class, blacks, and child labor had great impact because these groups had never before been examined:

> One thing impressed me especially, not only in this court but in all others I have visited: a Negro brought in for drunkenness, for example, was punished much more severely than a white man arrested for the same offence. The injustice which the weak everywhere suffer—North and South—is in the South visited upon the Negro. The white man sometimes escaped with a reprimand, he was sometimes fined three dollars and costs, but the Negro, especially if he had no white man to intercede for him, was usually punished with a ten or fifteen dollar fine, which often meant that he must go to the chain-gang. . . . (Baker, 1908)

The novelist and journalist Upton Sinclair did some of his best and most vivid writing during this period. His novel, *The Jungle*, exposed the terrible practices in the meat packing industry, a subject he also wrote about for magazines:

> In the course of the testimony before the court, the chief man of Armour & Co. admitted that the "canned roast beef" which they furnished to our soldiers during the Spanish War had first been boiled to make "extracts"; and we see that the Federal inspection is powerless to prevent that. I have charged, and I charge here again, that the so-called "potted ham" and "deviled ham" sold by Armour & Co. consist of the old dry waste ends of smoked beef, ground up with potato skins, with the hard cartilaginous gullets of beef and with the udders of cows, dyed to prevent their showing white. The Federal inspection has no power to prevent that! . . . (Sinclair, 1906)

Such articles were remarkable and readers had not seen anything like them before. Their impact was quickly felt, as outraged readers put pressure on legislators. Congress passed the Pure Food and Drugs Act of 1906, which regulated the activities of manufacturers. Reform of municipal governments, begun in a sporadic way in the 1890s, was probably accentuated by Steffens' articles and subsequent book, *The Shame of the Cities*.

An ironic side effect of Tarbell's articles on Standard Oil and John D. Rockefeller was their role in the eventual emergence of the modern public relations business and the trend for wealthy people to set up foundations. After the negative impact of her work and the killing of miners and their families at a company-owned coal mine in Ludlow, Colorado, officials hired publicity man Ivy Lee to improve the Rockefeller image. His techniques worked so well that other business leaders employed him—and others who soon followed—to do similar wondrous things for them. Later, the Rockefeller family established a foundation which has given millions to worthy causes over the years and helped improve the family image.

Historian Arthur S. Link (1956) notes that the *McClure's* experiment proved the public would buy a magazine devoted to serious discussion of contemporary problems. This success, however, led to the adoption of the muckraking technique by publishers and writers of dubious integrity who exploited their subjects merely for financial gain. Muckraking turned into yellow journalism in 1906, in Link's view. Although the public was at first interested, it soon grew tired of exposé after exposé. By 1908, the muckraking movement had been discredited.

McClure's, the magazine that had started it all, benefited from the muckraking boom while it lasted. Its average monthly circulation rose from 100,000 in 1895 to 414,000 in 1906. By 1912, McClure was forced to sell the magazine, whose quality declined without the strong hand of its founder. Although S. S. McClure regained control of his beloved magazine in 1924, he was only able to publish it from May through August of that year before he ran out of money. It was again sold and went through several format changes—as a romance magazine and then as a men's magazine—before dying completely in 1930. S. S. McClure himself died in 1949.

A totally different kind of magazine was gaining influence and enjoying wide success during the early 1900s. After its purchase by Cyrus H. K. Curtis in 1897, *The Saturday Evening Post* began a steady rise to dominance of the general magazine field. With its blend of popular serial fiction, articles on Hollywood stars and prominent people, and Norman Rockwell covers, the *Post* soon became an American institution. So important was it to readers that its dimensions were used by the U.S. Postal Service to determine the size of rural mailboxes.

Editors boasted that a typical issue had enough editorial material to hold the attention of an average adult for three hours a day, seven days a week, until the next *Post* appeared. In the 1920s, single copies at 5 cents each ran to as many as 272 pages and weighed two pounds. After school every Thursday, youngsters in cities and small towns delivered a new issue of what humorist Will Rogers called "the great American nickelodeon."

Other kinds of magazines prospered in the 1920s—those like *Vanity Fair* and *The Smart Set* that mirrored the hedonistic good life, or those that tried to shock readers out of their complacency, like H. L. Mencken's *American Mercury*.

But the 1920s were not all escapism and avoidance of serious issues. *Reader's Digest* began its phenomenal success in 1922 by giving readers something they hadn't seen before: condensed versions of articles from other magazines in a small, easy-to-read format. In 1925, *The New Yorker* first appeared and emphasized quality fiction and nonfiction writing.

Henry Luce's introduction of *Time* in 1923 was an even more significant event because of its influence on journalism and readers. Luce and his friend, Briton Hadden, decided that the public would read a weekly compilation of national and international news in a convenient format. Although early issues contained little more than stories rewritten from *The New York Times*, *Time* had an immediate impact, both because of its novel content and format and its style of writing.

With Luce handling the business side of the new enterprise, Hadden developed a distinctive *Time* style, which conferred unusual titles on people (child star Shirley Temple, for example, was a "cinemuppet," and MGM president Louis B. Mayer, a "cinemogel") and favored energetic verbs and compound adjectives. Sometimes sentences were written in an unusual order and with an unusual cadence, prompting the writer of a later *New Yorker* profile of Luce to note: "Backward ran the sentences until reeled the mind."

Luce gained sole control of *Time* after Hadden died in 1929, and turned it into the single most important magazine of the 1930s, 1940s, and 1950s. The exaggerated style was gradually toned down and eventually dropped, and the staff expanded greatly to do original reporting. In 1936, Luce founded *Life*, another innovation in magazine journalism: the first weekly news picture periodical. He had started *Fortune*, a business publication, in 1930. "The March of Time" newsreel series was also influential during the 1930s and 1940s, bringing film footage of news events, particularly World War II, to the nation's theaters. In this period before nightly television news, such newsreels had quite an impact.

Luce's magazines were widely copied: *Time* by *Newsweek*, founded in 1933, and *Life* by *Look*, founded in 1937.

Magazines in the United States, thus, have a rich and colorful history. Although changed greatly in format, content and numbers of readers, magazines have maintained their place in the literary and cultural life of this country.

References

Baker, Ray Stannard. 1908. "Following the Colour Line." *McClure's*.

Emery, Edwin. 1972. *The Press and America*. Englewood Cliffs, NJ: Prentice-Hall.

Link, Arthur S. 1956. *American Epoch*. New York: Alfred A. Knopf.

Sinclair Upton. 1906. "The Condemned-Meat Industry: A Reply to Mr. J. Ogden Armour." *McClure's*.

Steffens, Lincoln. 1904. "Five Days in St. Louis." *McClure's*.

Tarbell, Ida. 1904. "The History of the Standard Oil Company." *McClure's*.

Tebbel, John. 1974. *The Media in America*. New York: Mentor Books.

3

The Golden Age Slightly Tarnished

The Magazine Business Today

Periods of excellence—whether of nations, individuals or even magazines—come to an end sooner or later. For magazines, the slow decline in the dominance of general magazines began in the 1960s. Up until that decade, *Reader's Digest*, *Life*, and *The Saturday Evening Post* had more readers separately or together than any magazine before and since. Today, only *Reader's Digest* exists in its original format. A close examination of *The Saturday Evening Post* and *Life* explains a great deal about the current situation.

The Saturday Evening Post

By the 1960s, the *Post's* largely rural audience—still receiving their weekly copies in their specially designed mailboxes—was no longer one advertisers wanted to reach. The United States had turned into a nation of urban dwellers and big city residents got their escapist entertainment from television, not from the short stories and serial fiction in the *Post*. As a result of this change in reader taste and advertiser action, the *Post* began to have financial trouble. By 1968, its annual number of advertising pages fell to about 904 (compared to 4,425 in 1950).

A succession of publishers and editors failed to find an alternative format that worked. One attempt, which the magazine called "sophisticated muckraking," actually began the magazine's ultimate slide to disaster. A 1963 article, "The Story of a College Football Fix," accused a former University of Georgia football coach of fixing that team's game with the University of Alabama the year before. The coach sued the *Post* for libel and a jury awarded him over $3 million in damages, an amount later reduced to $460,000. Other libel suits totaling $27 million were filed against the *Post* during the same period.

In 1968, Martin Ackerman became president of the *Post's* parent company, Curtis Publishing, and tried to turn the magazine into one with "class" rather than "mass" readers as a way to attract the advertisers who had been put off by all the rural readers. Accordingly, he dropped 3 million of the Post's 6.5 million subscribers.

This was the first indication of a new trend in the magazine business. No longer was it profitable to have more readers than any competitor, as had been thought before. It was more important for subscribers to be the right kind of readers—of a certain age bracket, income level, and education level—whom advertisers perceived as buying their products.

Another factor was important as well. With 6.5 million subscribers—many gained through cut-rate offers that did not pay the true costs of getting the magazine into their hands—a magazine had to print and mail 6.5 million copies each week and both printing and mailing costs were going up. Ackerman felt he could both save money and attract more desirable readers if he dropped half his subscribers. Unfortunately, the pruning was done by computer according to whether the address seemed to be rural. Jettisoned by this method was the governor of Arkansas (a Rockefeller) and even the mother of the magazine's editor. All of this generated a lot of ridicule and did not solve the magazine's problems.

After corporate losses of $62 million over an eight-year period, much of it due to the *Post*, Curtis closed the magazine in 1969. (The magazine was revived as a quarterly in 1971 to capitalize on the interest in nostalgia. It is now published monthly from Indianapolis and gives readers fiction reprinted from the old *Post*, along with general interest articles.)

Life

The demise of *Life* in its old weekly format was equally sad. Soon after it began publication in 1936, the new picture magazine altered the way Americans saw the world. No longer were even rural readers isolated from world events. *Life* photographers regularly covered everything of significance in any given week and editors made a special effort to get their photos in print as quickly as possible. Readers waited eagerly to see how *Life* would cover the big news stories of the week. Newspapers would have reported the same stories on a daily basis, of course, but in the years before television news programs, the only way the public could actually see what happened was to read *Life*, along with the good writing which accompanied the photos.

The end of the Depression, World War II, and post-war America; important discoveries in medicine and science; history, nature, famous people—all of these subjects filled the pages of the world's most popular magazine, and their stories were told through photographs by the best photographers then working, along with paintings and illustrations commissioned for the occasion.

From its first years, the magazine spared no expense to be first into print with its photos. Staff members regularly chartered airplanes to get film to New York. Editors paid high prices to free-lancers for exclusive use of their photos.

This penchant for supremacy is best exemplified by the 1965 coverage of the funeral of British statesman and author, Sir Winston Churchill. *Life* paid for the outfitting of a chartered DC-8 aircraft to fly 34 staff members from New York to London, where they picked up the film shot of the funeral, and then flew to the Chicago plant where the magazine was printed. On the way to Chicago, staff members developed the color film, wrote copy and headlines, did the layout, and checked facts using reference material on board. The magazine even brought along a British officer familiar with the royal family and other notable people at the funeral so he could identify them for caption writers.

The trip to cover the Churchill funeral was *Life's* last major spectacular, defying all odds to get a story into print. Competition from television required no less than an all-out effort. Nevertheless, time was running out for *Life*. Even with this kind of herculean and costly effort on the part of staff members, the issue reached readers a full week after they had seen the funeral on television, albeit in black and white. After applause for the feat had died down, *Life* editors could only pause to contemplate the losing war they were fighting, even with a few impressive battle wins from time to time. A photo news magazine with extended deadlines could not compete with network television news departments, able to cover events as they happened—just as a magazine containing a lot of escapist fiction like *The Saturday Evening Post* could not equal the entertainment of television. Another factor weighing heavily against *Life* as a weekly was the enormous task of covering the world in the magazine's traditional manner. No expense was too great—an attitude that was fine when the magazine made money but less possible to justify after losses were posted.

Life editors noted the changed situation in the late 1960s and began to include a lot of text: long articles, a number of groundbreaking exposés, excerpts from books, and reviews on many subjects. The magazine remained in the circulation numbers race, even taking 1.5 million unexpired *Saturday Evening Post* subscriptions. By 1970, *Life* had reached a circulation high of 8.6 million. Unfortunately, advertising revenue had peaked in 1966, when the magazine sold 3,300 pages of advertising for nearly $170 million.

It is a fact of journalistic life that a publication cannot prosper on circulation alone. It costs a great deal of money to print and mail each issue as noted in the previous discussion of the *Post*. It costs more money still to seek new subscribers to replace those who eventually leave. At its point of highest circulation, for example, *Life* subscribers were paying as little as 14 cents a copy. People who buy a magazine at such low rates do not always stay with it when their initial subscription expires.

Life officials eventually realized their mistake of thinking more was better and, following the example of the *Post*, actually trimmed the number of subscribers to 5.5 million. But it was too late. Production costs were too great. Postage increases of 127 percent that began in 1972 only added to the magazine's woes, even though they were spread over five years.

The magazine's fate was actually sealed by advertisers, who decided that *Life's* readers were not buying their products. Advertisers determined that they could reach a mass audience more cheaply through television. Ironically, the large number of subscribers hurt the magazine because its ad rates were based on that number and high page rates drove advertisers away.

Life, which lost $30 million over its last four years, could not be saved. The December 29, 1972 issue was its last as a weekly.

Life returned as a monthly in 1978, aimed at a more affluent audience and a more modestly sized one (700,000). Readers were also asked to pay a more realistic price ($1.50 a copy, $18 a year). Unlike the old days when 96 percent of its circulation went to mail subscribers and 4 percent to newsstands, *Life's* new version sold 70 percent via newsstands and supermarket checkout counters. The new formula seemed to work: *Life* survived, still featuring good photos (most now in color) and well-written articles, and printed on high quality paper. But readers of the old *Life* might demur in extolling the virtues of the new incarnation. A great, great American institution was gone and readers would never again see its equal.

The Rise of the Specialized Magazine

The combined fates of *The Saturday Evening Post*, *Colliers* (another general interest magazine very similar to the *Post*), *Life*, and *Look* (another picture magazine appearing every other week), sent shudders of doom through the tightly-knit magazine world of New York. If these great institutions had fallen victim to changed economic realities, which magazines would be next?

The great soul-searching and hunt for causes and scapegoats ultimately produced an easy solution: specialization. If mass readers were not the answer—given high costs of printing and mailing and lack of advertiser interest—small segments of them might be, with both editorial and advertising more carefully focused than before.

Publishers began to come up with ideas for specialty magazines at a rate much greater than ever before. There had always been such magazines. Many, such as those aimed at women, were staples of American journalism. What happened in the 1970s is that economic factors accentuated their rise.

Three subject areas illustrate this point—running, science, and computers.

In the mid-1970s, several publishers introduced magazines for runners, lured by a sudden public interest in running. *Runner's World Magazine*, for example, increased its circulation from 70,000 in 1977 to 233,000 one-and-a-half years later. In 1978, *The Runner* appeared with a target circulation of 50,000.

These publishers were interested in runners for their great demographics—age, income, and education mix important to all magazines because of the attraction they hold for advertisers. In this instance, the statistics were very tempting. A Gallup Poll reported that 11 percent of all Americans—about 25 million people—ran or jogged regularly. The same survey found that runners tended to be young, college-educated, single, and in upper-middle income brackets.

A *Wall Street Journal* story on running magazines quoted a New York importer of Perrier, a bottled water from France, on why he chose to advertise his product in these periodicals. He replied that the readers were health conscious and would thus be appreciative of his product, a statement he probably could not make about general magazines with greater numbers of readers with more diverse interests (Zonana, 1978).

During this same period, science-related national events like the accident at the Three Mile Island nuclear plant, a series of crashes of the DC-10 airplane, and toxic waste disasters like Love Canal created a desire for more information. *Scientific American* and *Science* had long catered to a more limited segment of the market, the scientist and science educator. But now, publishers rushed to serve a general public eager to know how science influenced their daily lives.

In a short time, *Science Illustrated*, *Science 80*, *Omni*, and *Discover* appeared and did well, along with *Popular Science* which had existed for a number of years. Hearst revamped its long-standing *Science Digest*. These magazines were helped along by television, both in its coverage of science-related events like the space program and regular shows like "Nova" and "Cosmos."

By 1983, the circulation numbers were beginning to reveal the astuteness of the move to science publications: *Popular Science* had a circulation of 1.8 million, *Discover* had 904,647, and *Omni* had 802,528.

Computers were another field where specialized magazines thrived. As sales of personal computers increased in the early 1980s, the number of computer magazines grew as well. The demand for timely, unbiased information about computers, written in plain English so the lay reader could understand, seemed unending. Advertisers followed the readers and within a year more than 600 journals, magazines, and newsletters were in business, with a combined circulation of about 12 million.

But this success began to diminish the following year. Even though more than 750,000 personal computers a month were being sold throughout much of 1984, circulation totals for computer magazines were leveling off and advertising was down dramatically, as much as 20 to 30 percent for some publications. There was also a lack of good story ideas. There are apparently only so many subjects to cover when the topic—personal computers—is so limited. Slowly, many of these magazines began to cut back, combine, or go out of business. Only the hearty remain today.

But reader taste and advertiser interest were not the only factors affecting the magazine industry as it attempted to cope during the 1970s. In the early days of the Nixon Administration, postage rates were increased dramatically and the costs to magazines were staggering. For example, the annual postage bill for *Reader's Digest* increased from $7 million in 1969 to $16 million two years later; *Time's* postage costs rocketed from about $4.5 million to $14.4 million in the same period. This seemed to publishers to go against the intentions of the founding fathers who created the less-expensive second class mailing rate for newspapers and magazines for the purpose of spreading education and increasing literacy for all Americans. Lobbying efforts in Congress eventually got the rates reduced somewhat.

Another example of the changed situation was a move on the part of publishers to make their magazines cheaper to mail. They began to use lighter-weight paper and even narrower margins to get more words on a page. Some even changed their overall dimensions. For example, *Esquire*, *McCall's* and *Fortune* all reduced their size from a large, or *Life* size, to 8 3/4 inches by 11 inches.

Publishers also started to concentrate on newsstands sales rather than trying to get as many people as possible to buy long-term subscriptions so expensive to mail. More magazines aimed their sales at supermarket checkout counters. This caused a subtle change in subject matter depicted on covers as editors found out what readers wanted and would buy on impulse: photos of pretty girls sold better than politicians, for example.

Time, Inc. illustrated the truth of that trend and the lesson it had learned from the failure of *Life* when it launched *People* in March 1974. From the start, it concentrated on newsstand sales rather than paid subscriptions. *People* started with a circulation of one million. Its shrewd mix of celebrity news and photos caused the magazine to break even after only 18 months, when it was selling 1.8 million copies a week.

Such success in the 1970s magazine industry was not unusual, though certainly not guaranteed. In that decade, anywhere from 200 to 359 new magazines were announced, all of them with a specialized slant. For every *Runner's World*, *Ms.*, and *People* that succeeded, however, there was a *New Times*, *Media People*, and *Your Place* (for apartment dwellers) that did not. In the 1990s, the morality rate was still bad, given the sluggish economy. Every year, 200 to 300 new magazines are started, but only 10 percent survive, according to industry figures.

In the 1970s and early 1980s, it took $75,000 to get started on plans for a new magazine because that was the cost of a 100,000- to 250,000-person direct mail test to determine likely readers. A 3 percent to 5 percent affirmative response was considered good enough to draft a prospectus explaining the magazine to potential investors and delineating costs and revenues for the first five years. At that time, it cost about $1 million to start a national magazine. Now the cost is even higher: an estimated $4 million to $5 million. If everything goes well and the original premise was valid, the publication should break even within two years. That's the biggest reason so much money is required: to sustain the new magazine for the time it takes for readers to find it and decide they like it.

If not? The history of the modern magazine business is filled with the forgotten names of periodicals that did not succeed, whatever their solid backing and thoughtful premise. Their loss reduces diversity for readers and possible outlets for the work of free-lance writers.

Magazines in the 1980s

On the surface, at least, the magazine industry went into the 1980s with many of its past worries put to rest. Competition from television had been met by a move away from a general format to more specialized ones. The impact of rising postage rates had been eased by reduction in size and weight of paper, and the greater reliance on newsstand and supermarket checkout counter sales.

A look at any large magazine rack in 1980 gave the impression that business was thriving, given the "something-for-everyone" formats and healthy heft of so many individual publications. Magazine advertising revenues in 1981 totaled $3 billion and circulation hit 289 million.

Behind this facade of well-being, however, a few problems remained. The recession of 1982–1983 cut into both advertising revenue and circulation growth. There was some worry that the growth of specialized magazines, which saved the industry in the 1970s, might decline because of competition from cable television, which aimed at similar special interest programming and advertisers.

Robert E. Kenyon Jr., then executive director of the American Society of Magazine Editors, did not join the doomsayers. In a 1983 interview, he indicated that the most encouraging trend in the industry was the increase in good writing. "Certainly in competition with TV, a magazine's major attribute is its writing," he said. "As cable TV becomes more pervasive, magazine writers should make even greater efforts for excellence. Editors can be counted on to aid and abet this trend" (Kenyon, 1983).

Kenyon also cited the increased attention magazines were paying to design and visual presentation. "The category in our National Magazine Awards in this area used to be called visual excellence," said Kenyon. "Now, however, the category is called design and the award goes to the magazine whose design has contributed to the attainment of its editorial objectives. The purpose of good design and presentation is to help readers get the most benefit from a magazine" (Lovell and Geraci, 1987).

Kenyon did not think that cable TV would supplant magazines altogether, a belief time has vindicated. "Some people feel that with so much cable, the printed page will become obsolete," he said. "I doubt it. The value of the printed page is too great to be demolished by TV in any form. Just remember that when movies came along, many people thought reading would go down the drain."

Magazines in the 1990s

The bad economic slump that hit most magazines in the early 1990s actually began in the mid-1980s, as publishers were plagued with declining advertising revenue and circulation numbers and increasing costs. Even big and successful corporations like the Washington Post Company was forced to close a specialized magazine (*Inside Sports*) and Dow Jones, publisher of *The Wall Street Journal*, decided to kill plans for a magazine.

These early hints of trouble grew into large-scale problems when the recession of the early 1990s worsened. When publishers gathered in Florida in 1991 to celebrate the 250th anniversary of the American magazine, the outlook was fairly grim. Advertising pages had fallen 10 percent overall in 1990 at the 171 magazines tracked by the Publishers Information Bureau. (They would fall 8.7 percent in 1991.) Declines in advertising were continuing, causing one magazine company, Family Media, Inc., to close, along with individual titles like *Business Month*, *Woman*, *California*, and *Fame*. Admittedly, none of these periodicals were industry giants, but their demise did signal that not all specialized markets could be served by a magazine. Even magazines that were holding their own were having to lay off employees.

Despite the bad news, the industry did show areas of strength, according to a report on the publishers meeting in *The Wall Street Journal* (Reilly, 1991a): Family-oriented publications, practical fix-it magazines, and some fitness-related magazines were doing well. Women's service titles were holding their own as well. The *Journal* story noted that publishers were changing the way they did business: reducing ad rates slightly, and raising newsstand and subscription prices to lessen their reliance on advertising revenue.

The decline in business at a few key industries in the United States was responsible for the advertising slump. In 1990, for example, six major airlines spent $220 million on advertising. In 1991, the six were either in bankruptcy, planning to file for bankruptcy, or out of business. Even those companies still flying had cut their ad budgets. The banking industry also had problems with bad loans and falling profits. A wave of mergers meant fewer banks to advertise.

All of these declines affected magazines, other media, and ad agencies, causing all of them to lay off employees.

At the National Magazine Awards luncheon in 1991, many of the award winners were suffering from the worst financial situation in years. *The New Yorker*, for example, was a finalist in five categories and the winner in reporting. Its ad pages fell 35 percent in the first quarter of 1991. *Esquire*, the winner in fiction, was down 31.5

percent in the same period. *New York* magazine, the winner in personal service, was down 17 percent. *Conde Nast Traveler*, the winner in design and general excellence, was down 16 percent.

Magazines that did well in the same period, according to another article in *The Wall Street Journal* (Reilly, 1991b), were those with a regional orientation or those with a highly specialized content. For example, the ad pages of *Outside*, an environmental magazine, were up 10 percent. *Parenting* was up 23 percent in ad pages.

"The quarterly tote board on magazine advertising is closely watched because ad revenues make up 60 percent to 85 percent of most publications' revenue," noted the *Journal* story. "Because many publishers discount subscriptions to readers, ad revenue is even more vital to a magazine's survival."

By the spring of 1992, the situation was turning around slightly. Magazine ad pages were up 3 percent from the year before. A few publications enjoyed double-digit increases: *Newsweek*, 22.6 percent; *Entertainment Weekly*, 25.1 percent; *Conde Nast Traveler*, 15.6 percent; *Cosmopolitan*, 11.2 percent; *Parenting*, 39.8 percent; and *U.S. News*, 15.8 percent.

By June of 1992, the economic situation had improved even more. Advertising pages in the 175 magazines counted by the Publishers Information Bureau rose 7 percent from June of 1991. The Magazine Publishers Association was predicting a gain in ad pages of 3 percent for 1992, the first since 1989.

Given what they had been through, publishers at a July 1992 Washington conference seemed to be preoccupied with the bottom line and keeping profits up and costs down. This translated into worries about increased postage rates and higher paper costs. It also meant fewer staff members, with the industry as a whole employing 10 percent fewer people than even two years before.

Kenyon, now retired from his post at the American Society of Magazine Editors, has some thoughts on what this means to the magazine industry and to those who work in it, like free-lance writers.

"The ad business has changed and advertisers are going for sales promotions, in-store promotions and via direct mail rather than traditional media," he says. "Agencies are trying to bring back clients to media advertising. The recession has also been a big factor. When times get tough, the first thing to go is the advertising budget" (Kenyon, 1992).

The changed economic climate has caused magazines to depend more on circulation revenue than ever before. Any rise in circulation rates is tricky, however, because it could cause numbers of readers to decline and, since ad rates are based on circulation, this could lead to lower ad revenue. "If it falls the right way and you don't lose dedicated readers but the high cost, cut-rate circulation, you are ok," he says. "You revert to the hard core."

The result of the 1990–1991 slump has been cost cutting and staff cutting. Ironically, troubled times are better for free-lance writers than boom periods, in Kenyon's view. "This means fewer people to pay salaries and benefits to," he continues. "Using free-lancers is a less expensive way to fill pages. The question is, are there enough good writers? It's often been said that an editor's greatest asset is his Rolodex."

Bad times or not, the magazine business is still dominated by specialized magazines as it has been for the past 20 years. Now, however, it's called "niche publishing," according to Kenyon. "Things have improved for special interest magazines. Many have a field all to themselves. They've got a homogeneous editorial and advertising package," he says.

In Kenyon's view, good writing is still the most important thing about magazines. "It's the payoff for magazines and that means a continuing need for good free-lance writers. People watch television and listen to radio but they *read* magazines. The written word is still very important."

The future in the view of this longtime magazine expert? "Leaner and meaner. Magazines have to develop their own niche to survive, whether it's news weeklies or women's service magazines or whatever. They have to find out what readers are interested in and shoot for that. Magazines will always be around but will be more specialized and will rely more on circulation and less on advertising. It's already happening. *Ms.* magazine carries no advertising, charges $50 a year, and is doing well. In time, I think magazines will depend less on expensive photography and heavy paper. They'll be printed more economically and get back to the written word. That's the important thing."

For free-lance writers, these magazine industry trends have a mixed meaning. The improved advertising revenues could mean more work for them, especially if there are fewer people on staff to fill the suddenly fatter issues. Or, just the reverse could be true. The mixture of pure terror and adrenaline noted earlier will probably continue to prevail.

References

Kenyon, Robert E., Jr. 1983. Personal interview with Ronald Lovell.

Kenyon, Robert E., Jr. 1992. Personal interview with Ronald Lovell.

Lovell Ronald P., and Philip C. Geraci. 1987. *The Modern Mass Media Machine*. Dubuque, IA: Kendall/Hunt.

Reilly, Patrick M. 1991a. "Not the Best of Times: Magazines Turn 250." *The Wall Street Journal*, July 12, p. B8.

Reilly, Patrick M. 1991b. "Magazines Get Honors Amid Bad News." *The Wall Street Journal*, April 19, p. B7.

Zonana, Victor F. 1978. "Publishers, Lured by 'Great Demographics,' Push to Put Out Magazines for Joggers and Runners." *The Wall Street Journal*, April 28, p. 36.

4

Magazines Up Close

Magazines are the segment of journalism most associated with free-lance writers. Newspapers use free-lance contributors to write analysis pieces, reviews, and feature stories. It is to magazines, however, that free-lance writers must turn most often as markets for their article ideas.

Both tradition and necessity dictate this situation. Newspaper editors have long relied on full-time staff reporters to fill pages. They buy material from free-lancers only occasionally. With magazines, just the reverse has been true both historically and today. Editors are accustomed to relying on free-lance writers for good ideas and good writing.

Even though times have been economically tough for magazines in the 1990s, something has to fill all of those editorial pages. And, except for those publications that are exclusively staff written, that "something" is usually the work of free-lance writers. There is always a scarcity of good writers who know the needs of editors and are able to meet them with well-written copy turned in on deadline.

Despite the economic slowdown, the wolf is hardly lurking at the editorial door. Total advertising revenue for the top 164 magazines in 1991 totaled $6.5 billion, down from $6.7 billion the year before, according to Magazine Publishers of America (MPA).

The impact of editorial content in magazines can be illustrated by the total annual combined circulation per issue of all magazines surveyed by MPA. In 1991, 364,747,479 people read magazines in the United States. This means that if you write for magazines, a lot of people are going to read what you have to say.

Distinguishing Features of Magazines

A magazine is not published on newsprint. It does not appear every day. Those characteristics describe a newspaper.

A magazine does not broadcast its content over the airwaves as does a television or radio program, although both of those mediums regularly describe programs in a longer time format as "magazine shows."

Instead, a magazine is a printed publication that comes out weekly, biweekly, monthly, bimonthly, or quarterly. A magazine is printed on quality paper and bound in a separate cover, usually of slightly heavier paper. The content of magazines varies widely, depending on the intended audience. In many cases, both the editorial pages and those containing advertising are aimed at that intended audience. For this reason, many magazines take on their own personalities in a way a newspaper seldom does. People actually look forward to receiving their favorite magazines, while reading a newspaper is more often viewed as a duty.

The format of magazines allows more extensive treatment of subjects than is found in most newspapers, and the infrequency of distribution allows staffs more time to prepare material. Magazines also look better than newspapers because their high quality paper enhances photographs and illustrations and overall page design. It is also easier to design a page measuring 8 x 10 1/2 inches than the more unwieldy 14 x 20 inch size of most newspaper pages.

There is a permanence to magazines that does not exist in newspapers or broadcasting: because a new issue will not be arriving for a week or a month, people tend to keep magazines around longer than the highly perishable newspaper. Broadcast programs, of course, can be kept on videotape and played back on videocassette recorders, although not everyone does this.

Robert Kenyon, former executive director of the American Society of Magazine Editors, adds to the definition: "Magazines are the easiest, most effective, least expensive way to process information of a particular kind for a clearly identifiable audience. The trick is to get hold of a subject and convert it into information that is valuable to people who want it, thereby making the medium valuable to advertisers who want to reach that audience" (Lovell and Geraci, 1987, p. 158).

To succeed, a magazine needs a distinct personality, a unique mix of editorial content and advertising that will appeal to readers. Once it attracts readers with that concoction, a magazine must never lose sight of what those readers want and expect.

It is a magazine's editors who keep it aimed precisely at that goal. "An editor is a gatekeeper who knows better than the reader the kind of material that best serves the reader's interests as well as the magazine's editorial objectives," continues Kenyon. "And there's the element of surprise. A reader loves to find something totally unexpected in a favorite magazine. A magazine edited by readers instead of for readers would not survive very long in my opinion. A reader who wants to select material of interest only to him or her should rely on reference books" (p. 170).

This distinct personality is the element that sets magazines apart from both newspapers and broadcast news, which depend more on the flow of daily events than they do on trying to show readers and/or viewers that they have something different to offer. People buy a daily newspaper to find out what happened during that day or the previous day, to catch up on sports scores or stock market listings, or to determine what is on sale at the supermarket. People turn on television news to see an instantaneous and abbreviated version of the day's events or to see the weather forecast.

None of this comes from a magazine.

What magazines contain instead is material that is well-written and well laid out with a pleasing combination of type, photos or other illustrations, and presented over an adequate number of pages to provide complete coverage of a subject. If readers don't find what they want in the first magazine they pick up, there are many others available to consider. The quest for the ideal combination of subject matter and design is what makes the magazine business interesting—for both readers and editors.

Some parts of the magazine editing process resemble that of newspaper editing. Magazine reporters and editors follow most of the same practices as their counterparts on newspapers; that is, they get assignments from editors, interview sources, and write their articles. The articles are edited and sent into the system to be set into type. Galley proofs or complete page proofs come back for correction. As writers have been working, graphic artists have been designing and laying out editorial pages. Up to this point, the process is about the same as on newspapers.

The similarities, although present, are deceptive.

The first major difference between the two mediums exists because of frequency of publication. Putting together a weekly, biweekly, monthly, bimonthly, or quarterly magazine is not as hectic as publishing a daily newspaper. Deadlines, while still tyrannical, aren't daily.

Some aspects of magazine publishing are not as convenient, however, or as modern. Few magazines have their own printing plant. Instead, it is considered more cost effective to contract with large printing companies—usually located in other cities—to print the weekly or monthly run, along with a lot of other magazines. This means that it is more difficult to make editorial changes after the issue has been transmitted to the printer. In newspaper publishing, a reporter or editor has only to walk to the printing department in another part of the building and make changes up until the presses roll. On a magazine, subsequent changes have to be made via fax machine or over the telephone. One designated staff member of a magazine might also spend several days at the printer to make last minutes alterations. This reliance on distant printers heightens the importance of deadlines. If the material from one magazine has not arrived, the printer will simply start working on another and the first will be delayed and not finished on time.

Until recently, many magazines were not as computerized as newspapers. This has changed in the past few years, but magazine computer systems are still not as sophisticated as those of newspapers.

Magazine writing has its differences too, when compared to newspapers. For one thing, most magazine articles are written in the present tense. They contain more colorful description of people and events and, increasingly in recent years, the opinions of the writers. Although blatant editorializing is not permitted on magazines any more than it is on newspapers, prohibitions against it are less stringent. Another difference exists in the tolerance on magazines of varied writing styles. Except for features, newspaper stories are generally written to reflect the single "voice" of the newspaper. Magazines allow a wider variety of styles.

Space in magazines is allocated a bit differently too. A newspaper advertising department places advertisements on pages a day or two before the editorial department finds out what spaces remain for its stories, headlines and photos, except for the front page and the first pages of all section fronts which have no ads. Space for stories is divvied up in a daily meeting of editors.

On magazines, a similar ad placement is completed by that department, but more whole pages are left blank for editorial content. The smaller overall dimensions of most magazines makes this allocation easier than on the large newspaper pages. At a point early in the publishing cycle, editors then meet to *break the book*; that is, to decide how to parcel out editorial pages and determine which pages can be *closed* (completed) early and sent to the printer.

Another difference between magazines and newspapers is the preparation of the cover. A newspaper has a front page that contains a number of stories whose placement there denotes importance and depends on newsworthiness. Except on big city tabloids, however, headlines and picture selection for page one does not normally affect sales.

On magazines, just the reverse is true: the cover story is an extremely important element. The subject of the cover—and story inside to accompany it—is one that has a lot to do with the success of the issue. Subscribers are less the target here—they've paid in advance and are stuck with the issue no matter what the cover—than newsstand sales, especially in mid-town New York near the offices of the big advertising agencies whose staff members decide where to place their clients' ads. Those agency people select the so-called "hot" or successful magazines after finding out how they sold on stands located along Madison Avenue near their offices. The belief here is that the impulse purchase of a newsstand browser is a better gauge of a magazine's ability to generate interest than the number of subscribers who are locked into getting copies for at least a year.

Some magazines use their cover subject as a way to promote themselves. *Time* carefully guards the selection of its annual "Man of the Year" for just that reason. The person chosen is then announced with great fanfare a few days before the issue is printed. For magazines like *People*, which depend so heavily on newsstand sales, the choice of a cover subject has economic consequences. Even on magazines not so oriented or dependent on cover success, the cover story is usually planned more carefully than other stories and allowed to run over more pages. An increasing number of magazines are also using the cover to tout other articles inside in bold headlines only slightly smaller than that for the cover and the nameplate of the magazine.

Other elements make magazines—and working for magazines—unique. Articles usually look better because magazines are printed on higher quality paper than newsprint. More time is devoted to designing pages, which usually include the element of "white space" to enhance the headlines, text, photos and illustrations. Those photos and illustrations are also planned carefully and are often in color.

The additional time between issues of a magazine places more of a burden on the staff to prepare a good product that reflects the added care in designing and editing. A reader might tolerate an occasional typographical error or blurry photo in a newspaper, but not in a magazine. The space devoted to articles and the greater time allowed to prepare them place more responsibility on editors and reporters too. It isn't that all newspaper stories are hastily put together. It is just that people expect more of magazines. And, if the magazine does not live up to expectations, people won't buy it on newsstands or renew their subscriptions. With a newspaper, readers seldom have another choice so will buy it flaws and all.

Staffing Magazines

The frequency of distribution usually determines the number and kind of staff on a magazine. Weekly and biweekly magazines tend to employ a large number of full-time staff members because of the greater number of issues and pages. Most weeklies use only staff written material and do not run the work of free-lance writers except on rare occasions when generally "big name" writers are assigned to write something specific. Free-lance writers who submit material to weeklies, especially newsmagazines, will receive a rejection slip fairly quickly. (This is not true of all weeklies, of course. *The New Yorker* runs material from free-lance writers but they are usually from a small and select group the editors have dealt with for years.)

Newsmagazines have added a new layer between reporters and editors: researchers. These people double-check every fact in an article by looking it up in reference books or talking to other experts. Weekly newsmagazines are rewritten and edited more heavily than monthlies or even other weeklies. This approach began out of their initial desire for the articles to speak as one voice and has continued. In recent years, newsmagazines have included bylines, but the stories are very much a group effort.

Monthly magazines have fewer full-time staff members because the less frequent publication means fewer pages to fill. Thus, monthly magazines are often a better outlet for free-lance writers. Although the few full-time editors do more writing themselves, they spend a lot of time answering writer queries and editing copy. Some monthlies still employ their own writers. There is no set rule.

Another important difference between magazines and newspapers that also affects staffing is the geographic area covered. Except for truly national newspapers like *The New York Times*, *Washington Post*, and *The Wall Street Journal*, most newspapers are responsible for what happens in their immediate geographic area. They get their national and international news from wire services like Associated Press. A magazine, on the other hand, deals with its subject matter on a national basis or, at least, a regional or state one. This aspect increases the scope of the magazine and attracts more readers and advertisers. It also adds to cost—for travel by staff members and reporting by long distance telephone. A reporter for a national magazine deals with a wide range of sources all over the country (or region) on a variety of subjects. In time, these reporters and their editors will have to acquire the proper amount of expertise to give readers the depth of information they desire. Staff members must seek out good sources to help them gain this knowledge.

Planning for a magazine begins several weeks or months before its appearance. Editors work backwards from the printer's deadline to establish dates when articles, illustrations, and layouts are due. A free-lance writer must become accustomed to writing about Christmas in July or summer vacation in February. A writer can do well by looking ahead at upcoming events or anniversaries and suggesting stories accordingly.

Magazine Advertising

No discussion of magazines is complete without taking a look at advertising. A magazine succeeds or fails primarily on its ad sales. Numbers of readers—the right kind of readers—are important, especially those who will buy the advertisers' products. A magazine is lucky to break even on subscriptions and newsstand sales although many magazines are charging more and allowing fewer cut-rate subscriptions than in the past. It has to sell ads to survive. The average issue of a magazine contains a ratio of 48 percent advertising and 52 percent editorial, according to the Magazine Publishers Association.

Magazines come into the world determined to crack the multimillion dollar cache that companies spend to advertise their products. Some have greater success than others. The quest for profits can be tricky because of the need to achieve the necessary balance between 1) gaining enough of the right kind of readers to attract advertisers, and 2) having so many subscribers—some whom advertisers perceive as not buying their products—that profits are eaten up by high production and mailing costs.

Magazines sell advertising through use of a sales force headed by an advertising manager. These salespeople deal with ad agencies hired by companies to evaluate media and prepare advertisements for magazines, newspapers, television, radio, or direct mail. As a result, magazines are not only competing with one another for ads, they are competing with other media. They gain their customers by their *page rates* (established by total circulation) and by agency perception of how ads in that particular magazine will aid the client (the so-called "hot book" phenomenon noted earlier). The agencies also pay for research information showing use of product, reader demographics, magazine reading time, how long a magazine is kept in a home or office, and the amount of *pass along readership*—

that is, people who read a magazine who did not actually buy it. All of these factors determine the success of a magazine's advertising efforts.

In recent years, magazines have gotten more sophisticated in gaining new advertisers. A very successful innovation has been the introduction of regional and demographic editions. A regional edition contains pages that appear only in a certain part of the country. This attracts an advertiser who might not want—or be able to afford—to advertise nationally, but who can see the value of doing so regionally. A demographic edition, on the other hand, is aimed at readers of certain income levels and occupations. It may have special ads and even editorial pages that only reach these certain people. In both cases, extra pages have to be added at the printer but the additional ad revenue evidently is worth the extra expense.

The range of companies that advertise in magazines is wide. In 1991, automotive accessories and equipment were the leading advertisers in magazines, followed by direct response companies, toiletries and cosmetics, foods, business and consumer services, apparel and footwear, travel and resorts, computer and office equipment, drugs, publishing and media, and cigarettes, according to the Magazine Publishers of America.

Kinds of Magazines

Although magazines may look alike when they are grouped together on a large rack in a supermarket or airport, there are vast differences in format and content once readers open their pages. This variety is what sets magazines apart from other kinds of media.

The 2,276 consumer magazines in the United States today may be divided into broad categories for a better understanding of this variety. These categories include general, newsmagazines, class, city and regional, celebrity, political, specialized, Sunday supplements, trade, and public relation.

General Magazines

Such magazines are practically nonexistent. Only the *Reader's Digest* (1991 circulation 16.2 million) really qualifies for inclusion in this classification due to its broad subject matter. Two other magazines are somewhat specialized in content but have large enough circulations to people in all demographic niches to be considered general magazines: *TV Guide* (1991 circulation 15 million) and *National Geographic Magazine* (1991 circulation 9.7

million). The magazine with the largest circulation of any American magazine—*Modern Maturity* (22.4 million in 1991)—has also to be placed in this general classification by size and varied content even though it goes only to members of the American Association of Retired Persons. All of these magazines use free-lance writers.

Newsmagazines

These magazines reach large numbers of readers with a review and analysis of the week's news. *Time* (4.1 million in 1991) is the biggest, followed by *Newsweek* (3.2 million in 1991) and *U.S. News & World Report* (2.2 million in 1991). Two of the three (*Time* and *U.S. News*) have faced changes in ownership and corporate restructuring in the past five years leading—in *Time's* case—to massive layoffs of editors and writers. All three were affected by a decline in advertising in the 1990–1992 recession. All three have been written off for years as dying dinosaurs unable to compete with the public's hunger for information more instantaneously. Still, they persevere, offering more analysis than newspapers and more depth than television. None of these magazines use a great deal of non-staff written material, except for a few regular columnists.

Class Magazines

The oldest and most respected of periodicals, class magazines are more likely to have financial difficulties because of their smaller circulations and advertising base from which to draw support. They aim at readers with higher income and education levels than other magazines. Two of the oldest magazines in the United States are in this category: *Harper's* (founded in 1850) and *The Atlantic* (founded in 1857). Both magazines were saved from extinction by new owners in 1980—*The Atlantic* (473,000 in 1991) by a Boston real estate millionaire, and *Harper's* (190,000 in 1991) by the MacArthur Foundation. *The New Yorker* (1991 circulation 623,000) went through a great upheaval with a change in editors in 1992 brought about by financial losses and a feeling by its owners, the Newhouse family, that the editorial mix needed fixing. Only *Smithsonian* (1991 circulation of 2.1 million) remained strong, and it has the backing of the venerable Smithsonian Institution in Washington, D.C.. All of the magazines in this category publish articles by free-lance writers.

City and Regional Magazines

City and regional magazines have become particularly popular since the 1960s. For readers living in the cities and states served by them, these magazines are indispensable guides to urban living: articles on politics, crime, culture, coping with life, saving money on major purchases, where to dine, and what to do for entertainment. The first successful one was *New York* (1991 circulation 423,000), which began in the 1960s as the Sunday magazine of the *New York Herald-Tribune*. Other successful magazines in this category include *Los Angeles* (174,000), *Philadelphia* (143,000), *Chicago* (200,000), *Washingtonian* (166,000), and *Texas Monthly* (300,000). Even more successful have been magazines that concentrate on lifestyles: *Southern Living* (1991 circulation of 2.2 million) and *Sunset* (1.4 million in 1991). The magazines in this category, all of which publish the work of free-lance writers, have been successful because they cater to affluent readers who tend to buy the expensive products advertised in each issue.

Celebrity Magazines

Such magazines are a mixed lot, ranging from the reasonably high quality *People* (1991 circulation 3.3 million) and *US* (1991 circulation 1.2 million) to the sensational, often unethical, and distasteful but nevertheless successful *National Enquirer* (3.7 million) and *Star* (1991 circulation 3.1 million). Sold primarily at supermarket checkout counters and thus saving money on postage, these publications promote their mix of stories on famous (and infamous) people, bizarre events, sex, medicine, and the occult with a great deal of advertising on television. Another magazine in this classification, although decidedly better than all others, is *Vanity Fair* (1991 circulation 991,178), first published in 1914 and reintroduced in 1983. Its former editor, Tina Brown, was rewarded for her successful mixture of celebrity profiles and provocative covers by being named editor of the more prestigious *New Yorker* in 1992. All of these magazines accept articles from free-lancers.

Political Magazines

Politically oriented magazines have always had trouble surviving. Some are subsidized by wealthy benefactors (*The New Republic* and *National Review*) who believe in the opinions expressed and the causes promoted in their pages. These magazines do better when their political philosophy dominates in Washington. For example, both *Human Events* and *National Review* thrived during the Reagan presidency. *The Nation*, a magazine with a liberal philosophy, is one of the oldest in the country; it was founded in 1865. All of the magazines in this category use a great deal of free-lance material, although they pay less than their so-called "slick" competitors and writers need to pay strict attention to the political viewpoints they express in their articles. Their circulations range from 50,000 to 160,000.

Specialized Magazines

Specialized—also called *niche*—magazines are still the fastest growing segment of the market, serving more readers in total than any other category. To achieve their success, these magazines have adopted the approach of trade publications in aiming their content only at certain readers, and then attracting advertisers who want to reach those readers. All offer good markets for free-lance writers willing to specialize in one or more subjects. Because of their specialized nature, these magazines must be divided into sub-groups.

Home

Always successful, these magazines feature articles and a lot of color photos on ideal homes with the underlying message to readers: your home can look like this especially if you buy our advertisers' products. Biggest in this category is *Better Homes and Gardens* (1991 circulation 8 million).

Women's

Magazines in this category are very profitable and quite varied in their subject matter. The biggest is *Good Housekeeping* (1991 circulation 5.1 million) which holds to the same goal to "produce and perpetuate perfection—or as near unto perfection—as may be attained in the household" as it did when it was founded in 1885. Other magazines in this category include: *McCall's* (1991 circulation 5 million) and *Ladies' Home Journal* (1991 circulation 5 million), *Family Circle* (1991 circulation 5 million), *Redbook* (3.8 million in 1991), and *Cosmopolitan* (1991 circulation 2.7 million) which concentrates on young career women and contemporary male-female relationships.

Fashion and service

Here is a classification where advertisements are equally important to articles because readers want to see what fashions are going to be popular in the upcoming season. These manufacturers are happy to oblige and the magazines are as thick as Sears catalogues used to be. Biggest in terms of circulation are *Glamour* (2 million in 1991), *Seventeen* (1.8 million in 1991), and *Vogue* (1.2 million in 1991).

Business

The original business-oriented readership has now broadened to include anyone wanting to understand how the American economy and the companies which comprise it operate. Most successful are *Money* (1991 circulation 1.9 million) and *Kiplinger's Personal Finance Magazine* (1.1 million in 1991), followed by *Business Week* (887,150 in 1991) and *Nation's Business* (859,340 in 1991). Also included in this category are *Fortune*, *Forbes*, and *Inc.* Though not in the top 100 magazines, these three are still considered very successful.

Farm

Magazines in this area focus on the business side of farming as well as specialized areas. Biggest of the general farm magazines is *Farm Journal* (800,000 circulation in 1991). Others are divided into such categories as equipment, crops and soils, dairy, livestock, management, and a number of regional publications. *Writer's Market* has a complete listing of the varied titles.

Outdoor and sports

This category comes the closest to being a "men's" category, although magazines in it certainly have many women readers. *Sports Illustrated* (1991 circulation 3.2 million) is the largest, followed by *Field & Stream* (2 million in 1991), *Outdoor Life* (1.5 million in 1991), and *The American Rifleman* (1.2 million in 1991). Also included here is *The American Hunter* (1.1 million in 1991), *Golf Digest* (1.4 million in 1991), *Golf Magazine* (1.1 million in 1991) and *Car and Driver* (1 million in 1991).

Mechanics and science

These periodicals are aimed at a wide range of readers, from the garage tinkerer to the science aficionado. Included here is the original men's service magazine, *Popular Mechanics* (1991 circulation 1.6 million), first published in 1902. It was the first magazine to present mechanical and scientific material with a popular approach. Similar magazines such as *The Family Handyman* and *Home Mechanix* (both with 1991 circulations of slightly over 1 million) have also been successful. At the science end of the spectrum are *Popular Science* (1991 circulation of 1.8

million) and *Discover* (1991 circulation of 1.1 million), both aimed at a popular audience, and *Scientific American* (1991 circulation of 600,000), a lavishly designed magazine that is difficult to understand.

Miscellaneous

Separate categories could probably be formed for some of these magazines, but they are being combined into one group for simplicity. Many have high circulations and should not be overlooked as free-lance markets. They range from *Playboy* (3.5 million in 1991) and *Penthouse* (1.3 million in 1991) to *The American Legion Magazine* (2.9 million in 1991) and *V.F.W. Magazine* (2 million in 1991). Also included in this varied lot are *Parents Magazine* (1.7 million in 1991), *Soap Opera Digest* (1.4 million in 1991), *Rolling Stone* (1.2 million in 1991), *Sesame Street Magazine* (1.1 million in 1991), and *Weight Watchers Magazine* (1 million in 1991).

Sunday Newspaper Supplements

Sunday newspaper magazine supplements have been a part of newspapers since William Randolph Hearst put his full-color *American Weekly* into the *New York Journal* in 1896 as another weapon in his circulation battle with Joseph Pulitzer. The idea caught on, and many big city daily newspapers still have their own Sunday magazine. Most use the gravure printing process which enhances the quality of color photos and advertisements printed on slick paper. The magazine format also enables newspapers to present editorial material in a slightly different manner than they normally do. Although Sunday magazines often contain the work of staff members of the newspapers themselves, editors often like to vary the mix by accepting the work of free-lance writers. *The New York Times Magazine*, founded under another name in 1914, is the most durable and successful. The *Boston Globe* has also published a magazine for many years. Both the *Washington Post* and *Los Angeles Times* have started very similar magazines in recent years. *Parade* follows another approach: it is sold to a number of newspapers. Although bland and boring in subject matter and atrociously designed (ads get the most prominence, articles often seem like a buried afterthought), *Parade* is successful (35 million circulation in 1991) and buys 90 percent of its material from free-lance writers. Another successful Sunday supplement (16.4 million circulation in 1991) is *USA Weekend*, which used to be called *Family Weekly*. Since its purchase by Gannett in 1985, it has been totally redesigned.

Trade Magazines

There are 4,452 trade magazines in the United States, covering almost every profession and trade imaginable. Their main aim is to help readers keep up with developments so they can do their jobs better. At first glance, trade publications do not look all that different from their consumer counterparts: they are magazines, newspapers, and newsletters with cover stories and color photos and headlines and bylined articles. From front cover or front page to back page, trade publications—also called business publications and technical journals—contain news stories, feature articles, and advertising devoted exclusively to a particular profession or job. No one outside the subject area would be interested in reading the publication. Indeed, in most cases, such publications do not want readers from other fields and may prevent them from subscribing. Publishers want to tell advertisers that they reach only chemists or purchasing agents or construction engineers. In this way, readership is not diluted by anyone outside the field. Most trade publications use a great deal of material from free-lance writers. (Box 4.1 discusses trade magazines and newsletters in more detail.)

Public Relations Magazines

Magazines in this category may look like their counterparts in other categories, but that superficial view can be deceiving. Few contain advertising. All have a content controlled by their publishers: the companies desiring to put forward a certain image-building message to audiences within and outside of the company in a manner not otherwise possible. Such magazines are usually distributed free to anyone who wants a copy. The best PR publications are as sophisticated, well-written, and well-displayed as any consumer magazine because their sponsoring companies realize that high quality will project the desired image. The worst are too parochial and shrill and do little for the images of the companies paying the bills. Because few public relations magazines employ more than a full-time editor and, occasionally, a graphic designer, the market for the work of free-lance writers is broad. Not only does this approach enable a company to avoid the expense of having a number of employees on the payroll, but free-lance writers also offer variety of content and point of view. Editors of PR magazines often prepare guidelines for writers detailing the kinds of subjects they are interested in. They also assign articles to writers. The good ones pay fees equal to consumer magazines and often pay travel expenses as well. The one limiting factor in writing for PR

Box 4.1 Trade Magazines and Newsletters

The most unknown part of this mass media is also one of the largest, most successful, and influential. Trade magazines are also an excellent source of work for free-lance writers. According to estimates by their trade organization, American Business Press (ABP), there are 4,452 trade and business publications. The most common pattern of ownership is for large companies to publish trade publications in a number of fields.

ABP considers postgraduate education the fundamental purpose of trade and business publications. The guiding idea behind these periodicals is the fact that half of what a person learns in college is outdated in 10 years. Trade and business publications fill this information void.

The high regard in which readers hold many trade publications stems from two factors: their specialized content and their timeliness. Trade publications devote all their attention to one subject, in both editorial matter and advertising. Everything else is excluded. Readers know they will find articles and ads on that subject that they cannot find in any other publication. They also know that they will often get the latest information on their subject before it appears in the general media.

For free-lance writers, trade publications are invaluable sources of employment. In the first place, there are more such periodicals than there are those directed at consumers. Their specialized subject matter enables free-lancers to specialize and thrive, as long as they can handle technical material. Although they usually don't pay as well as consumer magazines, trade publications offer both a good market and a good apprenticeship.

Newsletters are another sometimes unknown outlet for the work of free-lance writers. There are an estimated 5,000 of them published in the United States today. In some respects, newsletters are like trade publications because they most always deal with one subject. The resemblance ends here, however. Newsletters are fairly primitive in design—two to 12 pages of copy, broken only by headlines or boldface lead-in sentences with no photos or other illustrations except an occasional graph or chart. They contain no advertising and get their revenue from a high annual subscription rate (typically starting at $100 and going as high as $400).

People buy newsletters because of the information contained in them, not the way they look. On a good newsletter—and only the good ones stay in business very long—readers get "inside" detail not available in any other publication. Newsletters are usually directed at professionals and businesses whose livelihood depends on receiving quick, accurate, impartial reports on subjects they work in every day. Most newsletters deal in material the general reader does not care about. Indeed, the arcane nature of many newsletters make their subscription lists short. One hundred people is considered the minimum number of subscribers to make a newsletter profitable. That small number also explains the high cost.

Free-lance writers can get assignments to write whole newsletters regularly or contribute specific articles. The same need to specialize and be able to handle technical material that applies to working for trade publications applies to newsletters.

magazines is the absence of any "bad" news. Anything negative about the company involved is generally cut, especially if it adversely affects image. Some essentially PR magazines make it so well financially that they outgrow their original purpose. A perfect example of this is *Modern Maturity*. As noted earlier in this chapter, it is the official magazine of the American Association of Retired Persons. Two other similar magazines mentioned earlier make the top 50 magazines—*The American Legion Magazine* and *V.F.W. Magazine*, as does *Discovery* (1991 circulation of 1.6 million) which is the official publication for members of the Allstate Motor Club.

Airline in-flight magazines represent a sub-category of PR publications. Distributed free on most U.S. airlines, these magazines buy articles on a wide range of subjects from free-lance writers. They differ from other PR magazines because they contain advertising. Leading magazines in this category include: *Delta Airlines Magazine* (410,000 circulation in 1991), *Continental Profiles* (400,000 in 1991), *TWA Ambassador* (300,000 in 1991), and *American Way* (280,000 in 1991).

Reference

Lovell, Ronald P. and Philip C. Geraci, 1987. *The Modern Mass Media Machine.* Dubuque, IA: Kendall/Hunt.

5

Editors and the Editing Process

> An editor does not add to a book. At best he serves as a handmaiden to an author. Don't ever get to feeling important about yourself, because an editor at most releases energy. He creates nothing.
>
> —Max Perkins

Mention Max Perkins and people who know anything about the process of editing think "consummate editor." Although Perkins was a book editor, he is often thought of as the perfect editor in any medium. Not only did he inspire his authors to produce the best that was in them, but he was a friend, confidant, and at times, a career counselor and money lender. According to his biographer, A. Scott Berg, Perkins aided his authors in every way. "He helped them structure their books, if help was needed; thought up titles, invented plots. . . . Few editors before him had done so much work on manuscripts, yet he was always faithful to his credo, 'The book belongs to the author' " (Berg, 1978). By the end of his long career at Scribners, Perkins had become almost as legendary as the major novelists he worked with: F. Scott Fitzgerald, Ernest Hemingway, and Thomas Wolfe.

The magazine business has not had editors who are as famous today as Perkins still is, but great editors have guided important publications and the writers who work for them for over a hundred years.

The Legendary Editors

An early tendency in magazines was for owners to name their new progeny after themselves. Of those, only *McClure's* is remembered today, principally because it was the vehicle of expression of the muckrakers. As he assembled his remarkable team of journalists and writers, McClure imposed only two standards: accuracy and readability.

Wrote one of his best, Lincoln Steffens:

> S. S. McClure was a good journalist, one of the best I ever knew, and he knew it, and he knew why. One day when I returned to him a manuscript he had asked me to read and pass upon, he picked up, glanced at, and dropped unread into the wastebasket a long memorandum I had written. "What's this?" he demanded. "A review? I don't want your literary criticism of a manuscript. All I ask of you is whether you like it or not. . . .
>
> "Look," he said. "I want to know if you enjoy a story, because, if you do, then I know that, say, ten thousand readers will like it. If Miss Tarbell likes a thing, it means that fifty thousand will like it. My mind and my taste are so common that I'm the best editor." (Steffens, 1931, p. 393)

McClure was always full of ideas for his writers, but gave them a great deal of freedom in doing their work. He also gave them generous financial support, for travel and the writing itself. Although then, as now, magazine work would not make a writer rich, it provided a comfortable living. And, during most of his reign as editor and publisher of the magazine, McClure was in a constant scramble for money to keep his enterprise afloat.

If the owner/editor as entrepreneur had advantages for writers in terms of the freedom to decide what to publish and what to pay, there were disadvantages too. McClure seemed always to be on the verge of ruin, a position that put his magazine and its writers constantly in jeopardy.

An editor can feel more secure and convey that feeling to writers if the money paid as fees belongs to someone else. No early editor better exemplifies this truism than George Horace Lorimer, editor of the *Saturday Evening Post* from 1899 to 1937. Lorimer had been hired by Cyrus H. K. Curtis after he bought the Post for $1,000. Curtis' editorial philosophy was "get the right editor and you'll have the right magazine."

Curtis was also willing to spend money to give the magazine a new start. The first year, he spent $1.2 million on his new venture, $950,000 of that on promotion. In Lorimer's first year as editor the *Post* had a circulation of 97,497 and $59,338 in advertising income.

Advertisers were slow to sign on and the high costs nearly bankrupted Curtis.

Before long, the editorial mix that Lorimer concocted was attracting both readers and advertisers. By 1905, circulation had reached 696,044 and advertising income $1,058,934. The *Post* was launched as the leading mass magazine in the country.

Given editorial freedom, Lorimer set out to bring readers the best in fiction and nonfiction and he was happy to pay well for what he wanted, especially to fiction writers. Writers like F. Scott Fitzgerald and Ernest Hemingway kept afloat between books by the fees the *Post* paid them for their short stories: $1,500 to $2,500. Lorimer did not pay nonfiction article writers quite as much, but gave them more than most had earned previously for their work.

"Under Curtis' exuberant, free-spending management," wrote *Time* (1969) in its obituary of the magazine at its death, "the *Post* grew up with the century. It was the expansive age of oil and railroad fortunes and of Horatio Alger; young, middle-class men everywhere were ambitious, eager to make money. The *Post* captured their readership with such articles as 'How I Made My First Thousand Dollars' and with the masculine fiction of Kipling, Bret Harte, and Jack London."

Another legendary magazine editor who was given the power to spend an owner's money to create an excellent product was Harold Ross, who founded *The New Yorker* in 1925, with the financial backing of Raoul Fleischmann, heir to the margarine fortune. Ross had been editor of the military newspaper *Stars and Stripes* during World War I and met writers Franklin P. Adams and Alexander Woolcott, who were also on staff.

After the war the three set out to create a magazine that was both humorous in its short pieces and cartoons, but also covered the more serious issues of metropolitan life and public affairs of the day. Its sophisticated tone would make it different than anything ever published before and it would not be aimed at what Ross called, "the little old lady from Dubuque."

Ross himself was rather unsophisticated to be presiding over a group of writers as distinguished as E. B. White, James Thurber, Ogden Nash, and S. J. Perelman, and cartoonists Peter Arno and Charles Addams. He was renown for having hundreds of questions about the articles and short stories he edited. He once asked a colleague, in all seriousness, "Is Moby Dick the whale or the man?" (Gill, 1975, p. 9).

But Ross knew what he wanted in his magazine and he remained obstinate until he got it. "One was constantly tempted to turn a professional difference of opinion with Ross into a quarrel," wrote longtime *New Yorker* writer Brendan Gill in his book about the magazine, "because as an editor his posture was that of a belligerent. With a few notable exceptions, of which I was not one, Ross suspected writers of trying to put something over on him. He knew reporters—after all, he had been a reporter himself, and a conspicuously raffish and incompetent one—and he was convinced that they would always get away with murder if they could. Again and again in his notes about a piece he would type: 'Given facts will fix,' and the impression conveyed by those words was, and was intended to be, that a sorely tried man of superior skills was consenting to improve the work of someone who was at best lazy and at worst an imbecile. . ." (Gill, pp. 9–11).

When noted humorist and *New Yorker* writer James Thurber was talking to Ross about joining the staff, he told the editor he wanted to write. "Writers are a dime a dozen, Thurber," he had replied. "What I want is an editor. I can't find editors. Nobody grows up. Do you know English?"

When Thurber said he did, Ross was not convinced. "Everybody thinks he knows English, but nobody does. I think it's because of the goddamn women schoolteachers" (Thurber, 1957, p. 5).

Thurber reported in his memoir, *The Years with Ross*, that the editor was forever trying to come up with the perfect editing system:

> From the beginning Ross cherished his dream of a Central Desk at which an infallible omniscience would sit, a dedicated genius, out of Technology by Mysticism, effortlessly controlling and coordinating editorial personnel, contributors, office boys, cranks and other visitors, manuscripts, proofs, cartoons, captions, covers, fiction, poetry, and facts, and bringing forth each Thursday a magazine at once funny, journalistically sound, and flawless. . . . Ross's mind was always filled with dreams of procession and efficiency beyond attainment, but exciting to contemplate (Thurber, pp. 7–8).

A more benign view of the great editor was given to Gill by William Shawn, who succeeded Ross after the editor's death in 1951. "Every issue of *The New Yorker* represented hundreds of editorial choices, hundreds of decisions," said Shawn. "Ross chose, and Ross decided. Somebody had to say what went into the magazine and what stayed out; Ross was the one who said it. He read proofs of everything that went into the magazine, and respectfully 'queried' anything he thought was questionable; his queries, in the course of time, influenced writers and other editors, set technical and literary standards, established a canon of taste, and laid the basis for a tradition of good writing that still flourishes. . . ." (Gill pp. 389–90).

Shawn became something of a legend himself during his years

as editor of *The New Yorker* from 1952 to 1987. His death in 1992 brought forth a virtual flood of tributes printed in a special section of the magazine.

The image of the irascible yet caring editor conveyed to writers by Harold Ross was quite different than the editorial style being developed on another precedent-breaking magazine, *Time*, first published in 1923. *Time* was founded by two Yale classmates, Henry Luce and Briton Hadden, and the two were co-editors and co-owners. In the beginning, the two had shared duties, with Luce handling the business side and Hadden the editorial end. To be truly innovative and camouflage the fact that each issue of *Time* contained little more than articles rewritten from *The New York Times* and not much original reporting, Hadden knew he had to put a distinctive slant to the fledgling publication.

"Hadden's editorial ingenuity was devoted to the slicing, trimming, flavoring, coloring, and packaging of the news to make it more interesting and more salable than it was in real life," wrote W. A. Swanberg in *Luce and His Empire* (1972). "Seizing and running off with an old Pulitzer maxim that people in the news should be more than mere names, he began draping them with jazz-age versions of the Homeric epithets he had learned in Greek. . . ." (pp. 59–60).

Swanberg noted that Hadden began to use forceful verbs. People in *Time* rarely said anything, they barked, snapped, gushed, muttered, or growled. He also employed unusual combinations of adjectives and adverbs to describe those being written about, some of them not very flattering. "A trim-figured, keen-brained politician who strode in and unfolded his policies had no complaint against *Time*," continued Swanberg. "But a flabby-chinned, gimlet-eyed candidate who shambled and snarled was apt to lose votes. . . ." (p. 60).

Such writing seems corny and dated when read today, but it was different enough to attract the kind of attention Hadden desired. He continued to use it and force other editors to do so too. Even after his death, the magazine followed this approach, much to the horror of English purists and the bemusement of rival publications which ridiculed what was called "Timestyle." The approach was modified over the years and eventually dropped.

After Hadden's death in 1929, Luce took over both halves of the magazine. He was never the hands-on editor that his old friend had been, however. Luce was more interested in using the magazine to promote his pro-business, Republican views than in worrying about clever adjective/adverb combinations to describe the subjects of *Time*'s stories.

Swanberg wrote that Luce "moved ever further away from

dealing in news as news and had become the world's most powerful unacknowledged political propagandist." He quoted Luce as telling his editors in a memo that the cause of *Time* was to apply the morally correct "fundamental attitudes to the reporting of the news." In Swanberg's view, this meant that the magazine had to interpret and slant the news, "blending it with opinion and editorializing so that the reader got not mere news but a proper understanding of what it really signified and what his own attitude toward it should be" (pp. 141–42).

More Earthbound than Legendary

The tales of magazine glory days and the great editors who made them glorious need to be tempered with large doses of reality in the 1990s. Hundreds of good editors work in the magazine industry but there are few "legends" among them. This fact has less to do with ability or personality than business and economic factors. Editors today have no time to be legendary. They are too busy trying to keep readers happy by filling each issue of their magazines with stimulating articles. This, in turn, attracts advertisers trying to sell their products to the same readers. The cycle ends with happy publishers and magazine owners who feel the right editorial "mix" is making them rich.

Because of the low fees involved, literary agents usually do not handle a writer's dealings with magazine publishers. Thus, for the free-lance writer, editors are the key ingredient to success or failure, indeed, the "feast or famine" scenario that so often characterizes the business. One editor or a layer of editors will make a number of decisions that affect the welfare of writers. From the decision to accept an idea or offer an assignment, to the actual editing of copy and the level of final payment, an editor will be involved. Although opinions differ markedly from editor to editor and writer to writer about what makes an ideal editor (see Box 5.1), a close examination of how two very different editors operate reveals a great deal about the fascinating and sometimes infuriating world of magazine journalism.

Redbook is a magazine that targets what it calls "jugglers, the next generation"; that is, career women 25 to 44 with young children. The magazine was established in 1903 as *The Red Book*, so named because its first editor thought red was "the color of happiness." At first, it contained only short fiction. Its content was broadened and its named shortened to *Redbook* in 1929 after its purchase by the McCall Corporation. Beginning in 1951, the magazine was aimed at young married couples and tackled

Box 5.1 The Ideal Editor

In General:

- Is open to new ideas, as long as they are adequately researched and pertinent
- Knows what she or he wants and is prepared to assess a free-lancer's ideas and how they fit into the magazine
- Appreciates the diversity free-lance writers can offer the magazine
- Fights for an adequate editorial budget, both in terms of space for articles in the magazine and funds to pay both staff and free-lance writers
- Gives clear direction to writers and knows what she or he wants
- Is well-organized and doesn't forget that something has been assigned or loses a writer's copy once it comes in
- Resists pressure from the business side to slant copy toward advertisers or run stories just because they are about advertisers

With Copy:

- Is not a compulsive editor
- Assists a writer in improving copy, not making it her or his own
- Edits for style, grammar, spelling, and theme only
- Shows galley proofs of final version to writer before publication and listens to suggestions on editing changes, headlines, artwork

controversial issues. In the 1970s, both ownership and management changed as did the target audience: young mothers. After Hearst Magazines acquired *Redbook* in October 1982, this focus stayed the same. It evolved into its current form after a new editor took over in early 1991, and its target audience changed slightly: working women with young families.

As a senior editor responsible for filling many of the editorial pages not containing fiction, Sally Lee loves free-lance writers. "Except for fashion, beauty, and food copy which is written in-house by staff members, 95 percent of our articles are submitted by free-lance writers," she says. Although she has what she terms a "stable" of free-lance writers—"the old reliables," she calls them—Lee is always on the lookout for new talent, unlike many editors who seem to return again and again to a small group which outsiders find it difficult to break into. "Every editor has a mandate to find good free-lance writers," she continues.

Lee's idea of a "dream writer" is a good stylist with fresh ideas and consummate investigative reporting skills. "There is a real dearth of them. Ideas are probably more important than stylish writing. We have good editors in-house who can polish and fix copy. But with the market so competitive, ideas that are creative and—more important—exclusive are crucial to us. We don't want things you see in *People* or *USA Today*. Once something has been in a national market, it's a dead issue for us. There are parts of the country that are under reported. We really need material from Seattle, Texas, and the heartland. A good free-lancer with a great idea and some access from there would do well. I don't care if a writer is new or untried. If his or her idea knocks our socks off, I'll give it a chance."

Lee's greatest source of frustration are writers who send in query letters or finished manuscripts on subjects the magazine never covers. "I have a whole file drawer full of submissions from people who are completely oblivious of who we are and who our readers are. They haven't picked up a *Redbook*—ever. If they would take a little time to look at several issues, they might figure out what we want by seeing what we've done and not done." Lee says the magazine has a few staple subjects that are dealt with in most issues: "We usually run at least one article on sex, several on relationships, a profile of a mother, and articles on issues like the rise in hate groups or growth in middle class poverty."

Redbook gets hundreds of unsolicited manuscripts a month, and Lee says "70 percent to 80 percent are way off." When they arrive, they are all read by assistants, then only the most promising are passed along. Out of the 1,000 or so unsolicited manuscripts submitted each year, *Redbook* runs only three or four. Either Lee or one of her assistants responds to every submission.

An equal number of query letters arrive as well. Lee has definite ideas about this standard part of a free-lancer's business. "They don't have to be limited to one page," she says. "A writer can take as long as necessary. I can tell in the first paragraph if I'm interested. I prefer the first paragraph of the query to be like the first paragraph of the article. That way, I can get a taste of the writer's voice and see if it hooks me. There also has to be some evidence that the writer has done research to support the subject and that he or she has uncovered some news or a fresh angle. We also look to the writer's sources. We are expert sensitive around here. We know the easy targets, the experts every magazine goes to every month. If the writer gives me the generic expert and the generic line on something, that tells me something about the writer."

Lee prefers writers to attach clips of past work to the query, but not a résumé. The idea and the strength of the proposal, and her assessment of the writer's ability to deliver what has been promised will make the assignment. (Query letters are covered in greater depth in chapter 16.)

When the assignment is made the deadline and fee are set at that time in a writer's contract. Lee has no set word or page rate as do many other magazines. "It depends on the writer's experience, the type of article, and on the demands involved," she says. A typical article runs 2,000 to 2,500 words, but a writer might get $2,000 for a 1,000 word article and $1,500 for a 2,500 word article. Lee decides when the contract is drawn up.

Once someone has been accepted into the *Redbook* free-lance "stable," Lee takes good care of them. She talks over issues with the writers in advance, talks to them on the telephone or in person constantly. She collects material for them when she sees it in articles or books and sends it to them for their use.

In the end, of course, the difference between a writer's success or failure depends on that writer. "We are very demanding and have very high standards," says Lee. "They have to be good. There is only so much I can do as an editor."

But Sally Lee will never stop looking. The magazine is growing and she says she has to fill its pages. "I can always use more articles. No one has a monopoly on good ideas. I have a philosophy that every person has one good story in them. I keep looking. I've got my Rolodex of writer's names here on my desk, but I need to look for new talent too."

Three thousand miles away in his office in San Francisco, Peter Ogle has a very different philosophy. As chief editor of the technical magazine *Diagnostic Imaging* and editorial director of the medical unit at Miller Freeman Inc., Ogle has more specialized needs. Because his readers are interested in the latest developments in radiology, he must look for writers who understand that complicated subject well enough to both assess story ideas and write about them competently. In these circumstances, Ogle has found it best to rely on a small group of free-lance writers he knows and trusts.

"I feel strongly that the use of free-lance writers is one of the greatest strategies an editor has to improve quality," he says. "I probably get 75 percent to 80 percent of the free-lance material I use from three people. The other 20–25 percent comes from six to eight people and these are constantly changing."

Ogle does this for a very simple reason: "They are expert on one subject and they know what I want."

Ideally, Ogle likes to work with free-lance writers who have worked on a magazine staff. Some have previously worked for him. Given the specialized nature of the magazine, Ogle does not get many personal phone calls or even query letters from free-lance writers who do not know the subject. "If letters are addressed, 'Editor, *Diagnostic Imaging*,' I'll throw them away," he says.

He keeps in constant touch with his small group of writers, talking to them on the telephone, taking them to lunch or dinner, trying to get to know them both personally and professionally.

Diagnostic Imaging pays from 30 cents to 50 cents a word for the free-lance articles it publishes. The average article is 1,500 words long and the typical payment is $600 per story, plus expenses.

What is Ogle's view of the ideal free-lance writer?

"Somebody who has worked for a publication and appreciates the dynamics of putting out a magazine," he says, "someone who is trained in one field the magazine addresses or is versatile enough or intelligent enough to learn quickly. I need someone who meets deadlines and turns in good copy. What I need is more than words on paper. I need someone I can depend on to be flexible enough to help me on short notice, to give me what I want, without a lot of direction from me."

Eavesdropping on Editors

A lot of editors assign stories to free-lancers that they don't have time to do. Then, when the writer hands it in, the editor has a preconceived idea about how it should read, what should be in it. So, they're never satisfied until you turn in their story to them. A good editor lets the writer chase the story where it goes. A good editor tries to leave the writer's voice in it. This is not committee journalism.

—Frank Vizard, electronics and photography editor, *Popular Mechanics*

Free-lance writers are very important to us. The whole magazine is written by free-lance writers. I wouldn't encourage writers to submit anything to us without having read the magazine. They need to study the magazine to know what we do. It makes no sense to send the same thing to different magazines. We are all so different. Writers need to be able to research a subject. We want new material, not just their ramblings.

—Irene Copeland, senior articles editor, *Cosmopolitan*

A good editor is one who knows when to leave well enough alone, one who understands a substantive change, a stylistic change, and a personal opinion change. A good editor tries to keep up a good relationship with writers, talking to them frequently on the telephone, taking them to lunch when they are in New York. It is also important to give writers galley proofs to read so they can make changes. For writers, they've got to understand that this is a business, a marketplace. It is not enough that their name is on the article, it's got to have something substantive in it. You can't be a concert performer unless you've got an audience. There is so much ego involved in the way writers view themselves. They think that the world is waiting to read what they've written just because their name is on it.

—Rebecca Sawyer, features editor, *Country Living*

The ideal free-lance writer is someone who meets deadlines, is accurate in reporting, is dependable, has good sources, and is a good writer. A good editor is someone who can question a piece in terms of sources, references, factualness. A good editor is able to turn bad copy into good copy. We depend on a regular pool of 15 free-lance writers. Writers get into this "pool" by establishing themselves with us because of their ideas, their reporting, and their knowledge of a particular subject.

—Geoffrey Morris, executive editor, *National Review*

The ideal editor brings out the best in a writer. Lets the writer's voice shine though. I spend a lot of time exploring issues with writers, sometimes bringing in the voice of common sense if they get carried away. A good editor makes a writer feel challenged, enthusiastic, and valuable. An editor is only as good as her writers.

—Sally Lee, senior editor, *Redbook*

> A good editor is somebody who takes time to communicate with writers, who gives clear direction and makes reasonable demands in terms of deadlines, turnaround time. A good editor is someone who is organized enough to know what he wants and has been at the job long enough to know that what he asks for is "do-able" and will work in the magazine.
>
> —Peter Ogle, editor in chief, *Diagnostic Imaging*

An Editor at Work

Bill Ingram is editor-in-chief of both *Medical World News* and *Medical Tribune*, specialized publications aimed at doctors. A veteran writer and editor who has worked in New York for 35 years, including a stint at the fabled *New York Herald-Tribune*, Ingram knows what he is talking about when it comes to crafting sentences out of someone else's words.

In the article reprinted here, Ingram had assigned a free-lance writer to prepare a cover story on exercise. The impetus for the cover piece came from an American Heart Association (AHA) study warning that physical inactivity is now a major risk factor for heart disease. The article was aimed at the 100,000 primary care physicians who read the magazine with the message that they might want to set up exercise programs for their patients.

Medical World News highly values the services of free-lance writers, using them about 30 percent of the time. The rest of each issue is filled with staff written materials. Only budget limitations prevent it from commissioning more free-lance pieces.

Here is the reasoning behind Ingram's editing of this article:

"We assigned this to a young woman, a free-lance writer who had not worked for us before. I indicated the approach I wanted and gave her the name of at least one doctor I wanted her to interview, the president of the American Academy of Family Physicians. (She wound up not talking to him, for some reason. These writers get stubborn and want to do things their own way.)

"The lead of the article she submitted took the wrong approach for our magazine. It emphasized the medical problems women can sometimes get by too much exercise. It went on to talk about going into any health club and seeing women lifting weights and working out on nautilus machines and continued by discussing karate and self-defense. None of this had anything to do with this story.

"I started my editing by cutting back the emphasis on women. The story shouldn't consider any particular sex. We have both male and female readers. What she submitted belonged more in a women's magazine. I could see that angle as a sidebar, but we wound up without the space for it."

AN EXERCISE PRESCRIPTION: PATIENT PROFILING TAKES SHAPE

When I [Ingram] looked at the story, I decided that anything that got in the way of telling the family practitioner or the internist exactly what he or she could do to profile patients for exercise should be eliminated.

1 Since the end of World War II, researchers have been steadily building an impressive body of knowledge about the benefits of exercise. More than 50 major epidemiological studies of thousands of men show that regular physical activity has many salutary effects, especially the capacity to delay the onset of heart disease.

The way it turned out, I rewrote the piece to lay the groundwork for exercise and the AHA study conclusions. It took me longer than I wanted—the third page—to get to the main thing I wanted the article to say: the five things doctors can do to set up exercise regimens for their patients. Why did I delay this so much? I ran out of time in rewriting this article. As it stands it's ok, but it doesn't have the succinctness I like. It kind of dog paddles around for the first two pages. We did get everything summarized in the rest of the article. It could have used more structure. I really wanted to see something harder with more punch than the original that was turned in.

2 The long-term benefits of exercise are particularly compelling: it lowers triglyceride levels, raises the level of high-density lipoproteins and reduces elevated blood pressure in certain hypertensive groups. Many studies have also shown that exercise can improve the survival rates of patients after a heart attack.

3 In short, regular physical activity has been shown to lower the risk of dying from heart disease substantially.

4 The beneficial effects of exercise are not just limited to the heart. A number of studies now strongly suggest that exercise protects against colon cancer and the development of non-insulin-dependent diabetes.

5 Regular aerobic activity also helps control obesity and contributes to a sense of well-being, although studies in this area are not well-controlled. Some researchers believe exercise helps thwart depression, reduce tension and improve sleep, acting as a kind of natural tranquilizer.

6 At one time, endorphins, the body's opiates, were thought to be responsible for a feeling of euphoria because blood levels of endorphins rise during vigorous exercise. However, more recent evidence suggests that the compounds do not cross the blood-brain barrier. Nevertheless, the impact of exercise on psychological well-being is an emerging area of research.

7 Despite the evidence that exercise can make a significant impact on overall health, Americans are not physically active. In fact, an astonishing 20% to 30% of adults in the United States are considered sedentary, according to epidemiological studies.

8 "That amounts to 35 to 50 million individuals at increased risk for developing coronary heart disease," said Steven Blair, P.E.D., director of epidemiology at The Cooper Institute for Aerobics Research in Dallas. "Physical inactivity is clearly a major public health problem."

9 Last month, the American Heart Association finally took a stronger stance on the role of exercise in lowering the risk of heart disease by making physical inactivity a "major risk factor" for heart disease.

10 At a press conference in New York to announce its new position, AHA president Dr. Edward Cooper, of the University of Pennsylvania School of Medicine in Philadelphia, said, "The body of research is now of sufficient strength to identify a sedentary lifestyle as a risk factor comparable to high blood pressure, high blood cholesterol and cigarette smoking. Exercise improves lipid and cholesterol profiles, tends to prevent diabetes and obesity and can help blood pressure. We are talking about an easy, inexpensive way to prevent cardiovascular disease."

11 As the strength of the data on exercise's benefits continues to build, organized medicine has decided to issue a strong message that adequate exercise is an intrinsic part of patient care. Physicians are beginning to talk about a "prescription" for exercise, much like any medicine. "Exercise should be used like a drug; it has benefits and risks and you have to weigh those against a particular individual and their particular needs," said Dr. Gary Balady, director of cardiac rehabilitation at Boston University Medical Center.

12 Physicians active in sports medicine stress that an exercise prescription can be a relatively simple procedure that is not overwhelmingly time-consuming.

13 Many of those sedentary Americans will pass through the offices of the nation's primary-care doctors.

14 But is it reasonable to expect doctors in family or general practice to spend the time to assess the fitness of every patient, especially those who are apparently healthy?

15 Dr. Cooper and other experts say that primary-care doctors have a special role to play in promoting exercise.

16 "I think family practitioners are the premiere group to do that function," said Dr. Bernard Keown, a family physician who is taking a one-year fellowship at the Sports Medicine Center in Omaha, Neb. "An exercise prescription is not a terribly complex procedure, and family practitioners see the widest range of individuals," Dr. Keown said.

17 However, before an exercise regimen begins, doctors should develop a comprehensive step-by-step patient profile that includes:

- conducting a thorough history and physical
- deciding whether to conduct more tests, particularly among older patients
- evaluating body-fat distribution
- taking skin-fold measurements
- assessing the patient's exercise habits.

After the bulleted list, we could have had bulleted boldface lead-ins—conducting a history and assessing exercise habits—or subheads. These are subtleties that help readers understand the points you are making.

18 The first step is to take a fairly thorough history and physical to determine whether there are any preexisting conditions that would preclude an exercise program. At the minimum, an easy-to-fill-out form called Par Q & You can be used to assess a patient's readiness to begin an exercise program.

I really wanted to take a pot shot at the AHA in this article because it came out

19 The importance of a good history should not be overlooked. Drugs such as beta-blockers and insulin can alter the body's response to

with a blithe, sweeping statement that made it [their ideas on the importance of exercise] official. But doctors who are considered the spine of American medicine—family practitioners and internists—have no idea from the AHA how to do this.

exercise, and special problems like arthritis would obviously prevent patients from engaging in running sports or other high-impact aerobic exercises.

The piece still suffers from this vagueness and we wound up not telling the doc where to find the guidelines. We leave it up to them to collect the pertinent information.

20 "This part of the history should be as important as questions concerning cholesterol levels, family history and smoking habits," said Dr. Ileana Pina, director of the cardiac rehabilitation center of Temple University School of Medicine in Philadelphia, and one of the authors of the AHA's new position statement on exercise.

We probably should have gotten to the doctor sooner and made these major points earlier than we did, but at least they're there.

21 Once the physical and history are done, then a physician has to decide whether more tests are necessary. In general, the American College of Sports Medicine recommends that any apparently healthy individual can begin moderate exercise, meaning 40% to 60% of VO_2 max, without the need for exercise testing. Moderate exercise also means that the patient can sustain the exercise comfortably for up to 60 minutes.

Once you get the doctor involved, it becomes a matter of elegant repetition. After the list, the article repeats the major points [grafs 18 to 44]. Here is where bold face lead-ins would have helped.

22 Some doctors also feel that an exercise test is not necessary for cardiac rehabilitation patients, provided that the patient starts at a low level—45% to 50% of maximum heart rate—and progresses gradually to higher levels of exercise.

It's a measure of any story's success to qualify, refine, and repeat the major points. If you do it right, it becomes symphonic and not a lot different from Tchaikovsky or Beethoven as you go on a recognized major theme. You'll have a good piece of music if you have got a good beat at the beginning.

23 Advancing age, however, is a determining factor of whether an exercise stress test should be done, particularly if the patient wants to exercise vigorously, according to sports medicine experts. Men over the age of 40 and women over 50, regardless of risk factors, should get a stress test if they are going to exercise at more than 60% of their capacity. And anyone who has one or more major risk factors for heart disease should be tested, says Dr. Tedd Mitchell, director of the Cooper Wellness Program at the Cooper Aerobics Center in Dallas.

24 But any apparently healthy individual who wants to exercise at a moderate pace can do so without the need for an exercise test, according to the ACSM.

25 Nationwide, the Bruce protocol for treadmill testing is the most widely used measure of fitness, providing essential information on underlying blood pressure and response to exercise. At the Cooper Institute, Dr. Mitchell said that strength and flexibility testing, and body-fat measurements are all part of fitness evaluations.

26 Indeed, fat distribution is an important parameter of general health. Studies have shown that patients with fat distributed in their abdomen, the android pattern, are at higher risk for diabetes and heart disease than patients with a gynoid pattern of fat concentrated in the hip and thighs.

27 An easy way to measure obesity is by measuring the ratio of the waist-to-hip circumference. When it is above 0.9 for men and 0.8 for women, the health risks associated with obesity rise sharply.

28 Skin-fold measurements with calipers also can be used to evaluate obesity, but Dr. Mitchell warns that it takes practice on at least 50 patients before a physician becomes proficient with the technique. He said it is worthwhile to take the time to learn the caliper technique because "many patients need the numbers to make them do something."

29 Whether or not physicians get any special training in preventive medicine, including the use of treadmill tests and other techniques to measure fitness, depends on the individual teaching program. However, most medical schools do not incorporate nutrition and exercise education into their curricula. Preventive medicine is usually described as a step-child of organized medicine. But many observers believe that this situation will have to change.

30 "It will have to change because the health-care costs are skyrocketing and companies are realizing that healthy employees cost them less money," Dr. Keown said. "Exercise prescription will take off when the insurance companies finally reimburse physicians fully to do a wellness exam. And the family practitioner can do it cheaper than anyone else."

31 And as studies continue to probe the effects of exercise on the body, it is clear that the impact that regular activity has on the heart and other organs can be gained without expensive equipment or even a huge time commitment. The minimum requirement is three times a week for 20 to 60 minutes each session.

32 "From the point of view of someone who just wants to be healthy, if they exercise three times a week for 20 to 30 minutes at 50% to 60% of their maximum heart rate, they will achieve maximum aerobic benefit," said Dr. Keown. "If you put in more time, you won't necessarily live longer or lower your risk of heart disease," he advises.

33 Regular exercise increases maximal oxygen uptake (VO_2 max), the maximum amount of oxygen that can be taken up, delivered and used by the body during physical activity. By boosting the volume of blood ejected by the heart and increasing the body's ability to extract oxygen from blood, exercise makes the heart work more efficiently.

34 VO_2 max declines 5% to 10% per decade for both men and women after the age of 25. But someone who exercises regularly can maintain a higher maximal oxygen uptake than is expected for any given age. It is now known that regular activity can prevent the decline in oxygen uptake that occurs with aging.

35 The American College of Sports Medicine recommends 20 to 60 minutes of continuous aerobic activity at 60% to 90% of maximum heart rate or 50% to 85% of VO_2 max, three to five times a week. Three sessions a week is the minimum amount of exercise required to gain health benefits.

36 Continuous, rhythmic exercise that uses the large muscle groups is considered the best kind of physical activity, according to the ACSM and sports medicine experts. Examples include walking, jogging, bicycling, swimming, stair climbing and skating.

37 The ACSM also recommends moderate strength training as an integral part of an adult fitness program. The recommendation: one set of eight to 12 repetitions of eight to 10 exercises that involve the major muscle groups at least twice a week.

38 It is also essential that physicians find out what their patients like to do, said Arthur Weltman, Ph.D., an exercise physiologist at the University of Virginia in Charlottesville. "To get them started, tell them to find the time when they know they can do an activity and integrate it into their life," he said.

39 Walking is widely considered the most reasonable activity for many people because it does not require any special equipment, clothing or skills. "I rarely see a patient who is so sick that they can't walk," said Dr. Paul Thompson, director of preventive cardiology at the University of Pittsburgh Heart Institute.

40 Dr. Thompson said that he tells patients "to walk with a purpose, as if you are going some place." And he said that if physicians just ask what kind of exercise their patients get, and set an example in their community by walking or riding a bicycle, it would be a big step.

41 As the graying baby-boom generation enters its middle age, regular exercise can help increase the number of years that people remain healthy. Physicians can talk to their patients about a "healthy life expectancy," according to exercise physiologists and sports medicine specialists.

42 "When you are healthy, you maintain your independence," Dr. Mitchell said. "Most people are not afraid of dying but of losing their independence."

43 Realistic goals, however, are essential. "A lot of people start an exercise program and assume you have to run to get in shape, but that is a misconception," Dr. Keown said. "Thoreau said there is a great art to sauntering and I think he is right on the money from a wellness point of view," he said. While an exercise prescription is a "wonderful concept," Dr. Keown acknowledged that "getting the rubber to the road is a different story."

44 Although there is much data on the effects of exercise on the cardiovascular and other systems, researchers are still unsure exactly how much exercise, and at what intensity, is needed to prevent premature morbidity or death. More research needs to be done on the effects of physical activity in women and minorities and on what happens when middle-aged sedentary people become active.

45 Clearly, a blanket exercise prescription for the entire nation is beyond the purview of general and specialty medicine right now.

46 "We know that exercise is good, but we are no longer out there recommending that everybody pound the pavement every day," said Dr. Mitchell, an internist. "There is such a wealth of data on exercise, and now everybody is trying to figure out specifically how much is good for each individual and how much is too much," Dr. Mitchell said.

47 However, many primary-care physicians would be hard pressed to find the time to do a full fitness evaluation. "You really do need to set aside time with the patient," Dr. Mitchell said. "We try to emphasize that if you are trying to create a preventive medicine aspect to your practice, you really need to pay a lot of attention to the people who appear healthy."

48 But Dr. Mitchell conceded that it is a problem of busy physicians. "Primary-care physicians are so inundated with acute-care patients that it is hard to justify spending an hour with someone who is healthy and really talk to them about lifestyle habits that are detrimental," he said.

You hope to have a good windup, a climax. Ours was not that great. I like to leave the reader with something to think about. We did, but it was not good enough. In the last graf, a doctor is saying that primary care physicians might find it hard to spare the time to set up these exercise plans.

But we didn't go far enough and get into the obvious question of who pays for this. Medicare won't pay. Medicaid won't pay. So, you are discriminating against the old and the poor. It's sad. We didn't level with doctors about this.

In general, I'd say this was a good idea. We achieved about 79 percent of what I hoped to achieve.

Continues Ingram on the subject of magazine editing in general: "In analyzing magazine writing in general, I have to conclude that constructing a long story—a cover story—is really pretty daunting. In magazine writing, the old rule from newspapers that it is easier to write longer does not hold. Short pieces can often be done by simple formulas for less time with a simple beginning, middle, and end. Longer stories must be artful and packaged for maximum impact with a lead and a type structure that helps readers understand the subject. After that, you consider the authenticity of the expertise of the people quoted—their reputations and titles. The rest is refinement.

"I think you also need sidebars and charts and graphs. An unrelieved stretch [of gray, unbroken magazine pages] is a killer for readers. All of this gives readers a reason to keep the issue around for a couple of weeks before throwing it away.

"Other rules of editing I think about include giving readers something they are not likely to get anywhere else and playing it in a way to make reading the article a riveting experience. If that's what you are trying to do, you have to have solid writing, good organization, good images, solid science and a feeling for the readers. In short, you want to give them a complete meal and not an empty clam shell. Everybody can recognize a satisfying meal and a satisfying article. The test is really whether the article pulls together careful research and reporting and is then written, revised, and reorganized to make a solid piece that readers enjoy and learn from.

"The cover story is very important to newsmagazines. It is the hallmark of *Medical World News*. It is the only medical magazine that gives a third of its space to the cover story. The success or failure of the magazine depends on the cover story. This puts tremendous pressure on cover graphics and presentation and the handling of the story."

References

Berg, A. Scott. 1978. *Max Perkins: Editor of Genius*. New York: E. P. Dutton.

Gill, Brendan. 1975. *Here at the New Yorker*. New York: Random House.

"The Saturday Evening Post." *Time*, Jan. 17, 1969, p. 48.

Steffens, Lincoln. 1931. *The Autobiography of Lincoln Steffens*. New York: Harcourt Brace and Co.

Swanberg, W. A. 1972. *Luce and His Empire*. New York: Charles Scribner's Sons.

Thurber, James. 1957. *The Years With Ross*. Boston: Little, Brown and Co.

PART II

Subjects Without End
The Kinds of Magazine Articles

The real burst of energy from the outside a publication gets from free-lance writers is important. You usually know what you are getting from inside staff writers, but not from outside. You hope to get a good, new writer on the way up as opposed to an experienced writer who is over the hill and expensive.

—Bill Ingram, editor-in-chief of *Medical World News* and *Medical Tribune*

6

Writing about People

People seem to like to read about other people more than any other subject. People make news, of course, so government officials, rock and movie stars, and sports heroes are forever of interest to others. Such articles are often called *personality profiles*. People are also fascinated by people they can identify with in a "there but for the grace of God go I" kind of way. As a result, the *human interest* story has long been a staple of both newspapers and magazines.

The Role of the Personality Profile

Since the mid-1970s, *People* and several copycat publications—and television programs—have capitalized on the public's almost insatiable appetite for stories about the famous and infamous. The word "famous" is often stretched to its maximum definition, proving the truth of the late painter Andy Warhol's observation that everybody would be famous for 15 minutes at one time in life.

People has become thick with ads and long on subscribers and readers (3.3 million in 1991) by providing a steady diet of short, readable stories and large photos of notables and those who become noteworthy because of their involvement in an event beyond their control. At the other end of the quality spectrum is *The National Enquirer* which, for postal service reasons, also is classified as a magazine. It has made a lot of money and attracted numerous readers (3.7 million of them in 1991) with a constant stream of stories about Elvis Presley, the children of the late Princess Grace of Monaco, the Kennedy's, TV sitcom star Roseanne Arnold, and women who give birth to alien children after time spent on flying saucers.

Beyond such flamboyance lie a number of publications, both newspapers and magazines, which run profiles of people. From *Vanity Fair* to *The New York Times Magazine* to more specialized periodicals such as *Sierra* and *The Columbia Journalism Review*, there is a market for stories about people whom other people might find interesting.

The Human Interest Story

Long a standard element of all newspapers, the human interest story has made its way into magazines. "Human interest," as the term implies, involves writing about people who may be of interest to others, either because of something they've done (heroic deed, infamous crime), or are currently involved in (job, hobby).

Newspapers probably run more human interest stories about everyday people than magazines because they have more space to fill and are also looking for a means to lighten the readers' way through a steady flow of hard news stories that often deal with negative, depressing subjects. Human interest features often appear on the front page for that reason and are boxed for easy identification. The box says to the reader, "This is something different and you might want to try it."

The subjects of human interest stories do not have to be famous. They just have to have done something interesting or quirky or funny or sad or even bizarre. Writers probably encounter such people every day. The challenge is finding out who they are, what their particular story is, and getting an editor interested in the article.

How to Discover What Makes People "Tick"

In writing either the personality profile or the human interest story, you have to get to know your subjects. The trick in gathering the material for, and eventually writing articles about people, is getting them to open up and tell you a great deal about themselves. Your skills as an interviewer will be put to the ultimate test in doing people stories because many people do not like to talk about

Box 6.1 Selling Interviews as Interviews

A variation of writing the usual profile is to interest a magazine in an interview with a person that is run as an interview. The format looks like your notepad: the questions are printed (usually in boldface type to set them off), and the answers follow. This approach enables people to read the words of your source directly, unfiltered by you. They can judge for themselves how someone has answered your questions. In some respects, this Q and A format closely resembles a television talk show or a press conference.

Playboy magazine long ago pioneered the interview as interview. Indeed, many of its interviews have become famous; for example, when former President Jimmy Carter said he had "lust in his heart" during a session with the magazine's editors just before he took office in 1977. Many magazines and newspapers use this Q and A format as a sidebar to a major article, getting a source to expand upon a topic in greater depth and in her or his own words.

Q and A pieces rarely stand alone, unless they are a standard part of a publication's content. Two rules govern their use. First, the person has to be well known (either temporarily or long-term) to an extent that others will be interested in what she or he has to say. Second, the interview must be carefully constructed so that the questions and answers follow in some kind of logical order. To be ethical and honest, you really shouldn't move things around or eliminate anything. A Q and A should run "as is."

themselves in an introspective way. In other kinds of stories people are telling you about something else—a news event, a technical development, a trip, or a place. In a well written people story, subjects have to open up to you, and through you, to thousands of readers.

Interestingly enough, famous people are easier to interview than people not used to the limelight. Many are ego driven and accustomed to adulation. Many have been in psychoanalysis so long that it is easy for them to talk about their problems and feelings. The problem with the famous is not getting them to talk, it is getting to them for the interview through the phalanx of public relations people or agents or security guards.

Once there, you might be intimidated as you sit before this larger than life person. You can guard against becoming tongue-tied in front of a famous person by:

- being extremely well prepared with background information gained from library and computer searches, good questions,

questions written down in advance;

- not trying to "wing it" and breeze through the interview by asking whatever comes into your head;
- thinking through your article in advance to establish a possible theme in order to determine what you really want to find out; you must, of course, change course during the interview if things follow a path other than you expected;
- remembering that this famous person is still a human being with a mortgage, a family, a cat and a dog;
- imagining, as famed television journalist Edward R. Murrow said he did, how the person would look sitting there in underwear; and
- practicing your questions out loud with a friend to hear how they sound and see if they make sense.

With everyday people, just the reverse is often true. They may be intimidated by you because they are not accustomed to being interviewed. You can avoid the problems of interviewing those who fear interviews by:

- trying to put them at ease right from the start of the interview;
- explaining why their story is of interest to you and your readers;
- "shooting the breeze" for a time before asking questions pertaining to your story;
- being willing (deadline permitting) to go back several times, first to get acquainted and gain trust, later to conduct the formal interview;
- talking about yourself a bit more than usual to search for common ground;
- resorting to flattery; and
- noting the good that will come from publication of a story.

Observing Details and Using Them

A good people story involves more than quotes from your main source. These quotes are only the beginning. Equally important are details that you observe and record the minute you enter an office or home or wherever you are conducting the interview. In the profile of Charles Kuralt reprinted later in this chapter, the writer tells us that his office is "tiny" and that he has so many Emmy Awards around that he uses several as hat racks. We learn too that his desk is so piled high with papers that he must sit at a small table.

The writer of this profile got these details simply by observing them during her interview. She then used them in the article in such a way as to convey Kuralt's personality. You can do the same thing if you keep your eyes open and write notes to yourself. If something puzzles you, ask your source about it.

These same powers of observation are important in noting details about the person you are talking to. Be alert to body language, ways of speaking, and how a person looks. You may or may not use the material later, but you should write it down in case you want to do so. In the same profile, the writer called Kuralt "balding" and said he had a double chin. This went well with her theme that he and his program, "CBS Sunday Morning," were an unconventional success.

In the profile of novelist John Grisham, also reprinted in this chapter, the writer never describes his physical characteristics or his office or home because she interviewed him in the office of his New York publisher. Instead, she uses his manner of speaking, his Mississippi drawl and overall "expansive folksiness" to fit into her theme that underneath the country demeanor is a hard-driving novelist determined to succeed.

Talking to Others

A profile written after only one interview with the subject is seldom adequate. Although you will feature the subject prominently in your article, it is much better to expand this rather one-dimensional portrait by talking to family members, friends, coworkers, and even enemies. This is not always easy to do. With a cooperative subject, you can usually gain that person's assent at the end of your interview and even ask for names. If it looks as though this cooperation will not be forthcoming, however, you should probably talk to friends and associates of your subject *before* the main interview, before the subject "puts the word out" to refuse to see you.

Enemies of your subject should be handled with caution. They may dish out plenty of dirt but you need to be extremely diligent in verifying the accuracy of what they say. At times, you may need to worry about libel as well. It is best to verify most negative material with one or two other people.

Sometimes, the subject of a human interest story or profile is not available for interviews. The centerpiece to my profile of an imprisoned doctor (reprinted later in this chapter) was his wife, because the doctor was unavailable. All of the material for the story came from her because she was the only person with the necessary details. And, because of deadline pressure, the interview had to be conducted over the telephone, not always the best choice for this kind of article where details gained by personal observation are important.

Box 6.2 Suggested Markets

People Profiles/General:

- *People*
- *Vanity Fair*
- *New York Times Magazine*
- *New York*

People Profiles/Specialized:

- *Redbook*
- *Money*
- *Smithsonian*
- *Sierra*
- *American Journalism Review*
- *Rolling Stone*

Human Interest Stories:

- *Reader's Digest*
- *Saturday Evening Post*
- Local newspapers
- Regional magazines

Weaving in Broader Concerns

There is usually a good reason to write a profile of a person beyond her or his apparent fame. There normally has to be a news peg for you to attract an editor's interest. That news peg may be as simple as the publication of a book or the release of a film. Your subject may be an authority on a topic that is dominating a political campaign, such as abortion, sexual harassment, or nuclear weapons. It may be an anniversary of an important event in which the person was involved.

That compelling reason will probably dominate your questions and provide the theme for your eventual article, even though you will be concentrating on one person. In March 1992, for example, *Time* published a cover story, "Fighting the Backlash Against Feminism," which focused on two authors with best-selling books on the subject, Susan Faludi and Gloria Steinem. The main theme of the article was the backlash, but the two women and their books were used to personalize the subject. Steinem was the subject of a sidebar profile within the article and both women were interviewed in a separate Q and A format at the end. A similar approach personalizing a broader subject formed the basis for an April 1992 article in *The New York Times Magazine* on the opening of the East German secret police files. The story was told through the experiences of those whose lives were ruined by the police and their accusers, in one case a woman's own husband.

Personality Profiles and a Human Interest Story

The first profile, from the Arts & Leisure section of the Sunday *New York Times*, was written by a free-lance writer who works full time on another publication. It is a good example of how to write an entertaining and informative article without going to great lengths to travel and interview a large number of people. (It also shows free-lancers what a good market Sunday newspapers are, given additional pages to fill and looking for bylines and viewpoints other than those of their regular staff reporters.)

The second profile was written for the Leisure and Arts page of *The Wall Street Journal*. It involves an interview with the subject, novelist John Grisham, and time spent observing him at a book signing in New York. The piece is an interesting profile that is cleverly conceived and probably reported without a lot of effort. It is pegged to the publication of Grisham's new novel, *The Pelican Brief*. She lets her subject do most of the talking.

The human interest story reprinted here is one I wrote for *Medical World News* in 1970 from several telephone interviews. The magazine was interested in writing about doctors involved in events beyond medicine. When the editors discovered that only one doctor was being held prisoner in Vietnam, I was assigned to do an article about him. I had only one source, the doctor's wife, who I tracked down by calling directory assistance for the state I knew she lived in. She was cooperative from the moment I identified myself and gave me most of what I wanted in the two long telephone interviews. Publicity, of course, was was important ally for her in her fight to get him released.

Personality Profile #1

THE UNLIKELY HEROIZING OF CHARLES KURALT

—by Noreen O'Leary

The article is about Charles Kuralt and his program, "CBS Sunday Morning." The writer began by describing a typical program: bird watchers and paintings, and 3.3 million viewers. In the lead, she strikes the theme: the show is an unlikely hit.

1 Last Sunday morning, a group of people in straw hats went bird watching, some rhododendrons bloomed in the Great Smoky Mountains, a Kandinsky painting just hung there, and approximately 3.3 million Americans sat contentedly in their living rooms and watched.

In her transition sentence to the second graf, the writer informed readers that a program of such unlikely content is celebrating its fourteenth anniversary (the vague news peg for the profile, probably used by the writer to sell the piece to *Times* editors in the first place). She goes on to describe the host, Charles Kuralt, with words viewers of the program immediately recognize ("balding," "quiet presence," "double chin"). We learn that he is also a kind of "cult hero."

2 In an age when a long-awaited television series can come and go within weeks, "that show about deer running through the woods" (as some young CBS News staffers call it), otherwise known as "CBS Sunday Morning," is sailing smoothly into its 14th year. Its host, of course, is Charles Kuralt, a balding 57-year-old whose quiet presence and double chin are far from the stuff of anchor stardom. Yet he is the object of such devotion that some see him as a cult hero.

In graf 3, the writer supports her theme: the program leads in its time period.

3 "Sunday Morning" dominates its time slot (in New York, 9 to 10:30 A.M.), drawing some of its highest ratings on the West Coast, where it airs as early as 6 A.M. Slicker, newer competitors, like NBC's "Sunday Today," which went on the air five years ago, have yet to make a dent in its audience share.

In graf 4, she repeats this theme, calling the show "an improbable success," and characterizes the rest of the news business that contrasts starkly with it: news as entertainment, budget cutbacks, anchors as stars.

4 By current standards, "Sunday Morning" is an improbable success. It is flourishing in an environment in which news has become entertainment—next season more than 10 percent of the networks' prime-time lineup will be produced by their news division—and ratings increasingly dictate the tone. As network news operations grapple with cutbacks and budget pressures, many say the emphasis is shifting from news gathering to news packaging and bemoan the ubiquitous celebrity chat, exposé and anchors as stars.

In graf 5, she authenticates the theme yet again by quoting several longtime fans of the program.

5 "There are a lot of us who are forgotten when it comes to entertainment these days," says Kevin McCarthy, a retired accountant in Lafayette, La., who tapes "Sunday Morning" segments for his 5-year-old granddaughter. "We've been watching 'Sunday Morning' for years. We seldom miss it unless we're out of town." One of Mr. McCarthy's former employees, Modine Landry, spent a recent vacation in Dannebrog, Neb., a town she knows only from the program. "Big busloads of tourists" were there, she reports, for the same reason. Dr. Elliot Davis, a Manhattan dentist and Kuralt admirer, says: "There's a feeling of tranquility to the show. Charles Kuralt is very comforting."

In graf 6, she notes how advertisers are responding by quoting an advertising agency official.

6 Advertisers like hearing that. "We think of 'Sunday Morning' as prime time for a certain demographic," says Arnold Semsky, executive vice president and director of media and programming for BBDO New York, an agency that buys air time for marketers like General Electric, DuPont and Apple Computer. "A lot of business leaders, professional managers and upper-income viewers are available at that time of day, and may be more focused than in the evening."

The writer uses graf 7 to let several current and former staff members note their experiences with fans and the success of the program. This again reinforces the article's main theme.

7 CBS research confirms that "Sunday Morning" has the greatest number of those viewers in its time slot, but data also show that half the program's audience have only a high school education or less. A former "Sunday Morning" media critic, Ron Powers, remembers being surrounded by a group of menacing young men at a Philadelphia movie theater. Instead of being mugged, as he feared, he was politely questioned about his work on the show. John Leonard, his successor, tells of a Miami book fair where 500 Kuralt fans turned up, eager to meet anyone from the show. Mr. Leonard obligingly signed copies of Mr. Kuralt's latest book. "I understand celebrity," he says. "I don't understand this kind of affection."

In graf 8, she gives readers background on the program and its host, calling him a

8 "Sunday Morning" was conceived in the late 1970s, when Bill Leonard, then president of CBS News, wanted a news program for people

protege of the legendary CBS correspondent Edward R. Murrow.

who didn't watch television. He tapped the producer Robert (Shad) Northshield to design a show that would unfold in much the same way as a Sunday newspaper, with long news features, criticism and leisurely segments on the arts. But credit for the program's success, and its following, must be shared by its host. Mr. Kuralt, who was an Edward R. Murrow protege at CBS Radio, may be one of television's last ties to Murrow's legacy of understatement and verbal elegance.

By graf 9, readers are finally introduced to the subject of the profile, Charles Kuralt himself. The writer brings them into his office, describing it as "tiny" and noting the Emmy statuettes and notebooks for story ideas scattered around. Readers also hear from Kuralt as he "muses" (something he would no doubt do rather than "saying" something). Her description makes readers feel they are there.

9 A disdain for television convention is apparent in Mr. Kuralt's tiny office on West 57th Street in Manhattan, a place where Emmy Awards are used for hatracks and story ideas are scribbled in dogeared, dime-store notebooks. "People talk too much on television, and things go too fast," mused Mr. Kuralt, sitting at a small table because his desk was piled high with papers. "We knew Sunday morning was a different time of the week, and it gave us the excuse to do what we wanted to do anyway: a slower-paced, more thoughtful kind of news program. Viewers aren't rushing off somewhere, and we can get away with a more unorthodox TV format."

In graf 10, the writer introduces a discordant note about the failure of a similar program to succeed on weekdays and in prime time.

10 The formula doesn't seem to work on weekdays. In the early 1980s, Mr. Kuralt was briefly a host of "CBS Morning News." And in 1988, when he teamed with Mr. Northshield for a prime-time effort, "Try to Remember," it died an early, some said merciful, death.

By grafs 11 and 12, the writer continues her theme by noting the show's spare set and unique mix of correspondents. She also mentions the number of Emmy Awards it has won. Her phrase "anti-television television" nicely summerizes the program.

11 "Sunday Morning" is often described as anti-television television. There are no quick edits, and the "set" consists of an easel and a few plexiglass panels. On-air critics like John Leonard deliver essays full face to the camera, with an effect no less startling than the face of a raccoon caught in the glare of headlights. Some correspondents, like David Culhane, are longtime CBS reporters; others, like Mr. Leonard and William E. Geist, had never spent time before a camera before.

12 "Sunday Morning's" unconventional issue-oriented cover stories have won more Emmy Awards than anyone on the staff has ever bothered to count, but it is the other segments, more literary than electronic in nature, that viewers say they can't find anywhere else. Every other week, for instance, the show's "human interests" reporter, Roger Welsch, takes viewers to Dannebrog, population 320, for a tour of windmill factories or a pickup-truck ride to the nearest voting booths. Mr. Welsch, a former University of Nebraska professor, often wears overalls for the occasion.

The writer uses graf 13 to talk about the program's "end piece," arguably its most unique segment: a nature scene without music or narration.

13 Then there is the "end piece," a 2 1/2-minute meditation on nature, with no background music and no sound effects except those found in nature (water lapping against rocks, birds calling, wind blowing). Recent subjects have included the ospreys in Honeymoon Island, Fla., and melting snow. In a medium of sound and movement, "Sunday Morning" can make the claim of having aired more silence than any other show and perhaps the greatest amount of video devoted to inanimate objects like paintings.

The last paragraph continues the "improbable hit" theme established in the lead. The writer notes that NBC is hoping to overtake the CBS program by hiring a "young Charles Kuralt type."

14 The formula defies conventional wisdom. But over at NBC, the competition, "Sunday Today," is gearing up for a revamping next month. One of the new hosts, who comes from National Public Radio, has been described as a young Charles Kuralt type.

Number of interviews for this profile: 7, including Charles Kuralt, plus background research and viewing of the program.

Personality Profile #2

LAW AND AUTHOR: GRISHAM'S NEXT CASE

—by Joanne Kaufman

The writer sets the scene nicely, bringing readers with her into a bookstore on Wall Street along with "150 lawyers and paralegals" lining up to have their books autographed by what

1 About 150 lawyers and paralegals lined up last week at the Wall Street Waldenbooks to admire one of their own: John Grisham, the Mississippi attorney who made himself over into a spectacularly successful novelist. Some of the crowd even turned up again the next day at the midtown B. Dalton for another big

she calls "a spectacularly successful novelist."

welcome, a warm handshake and several more signed copies of Mr. Grisham's new legal thriller, *The Pelican Brief.*

For graf 2, she uses an unusual and effective transition: she has looked over Grisham's shoulder to see what he is writing. She also hears what the people say about the author's last book (having them "gush") and how the author responds.

2 "To Nancy. Best wishes, John Grisham." "To Ed. ["Ed, that's a good short name," he says as he writes.] Best wishes, John Grisham." Nancy and Ed and a lot of other people gush that they loved Mr. Grisham's previous book, *The Firm* (1991). LOVED it. "Hope y'all like this one too," Mr. Grisham says with a broad grin. "Thanks for stopping by."

By graf 3, the writer is filling readers in on Grisham's background and describing what she calls his "aw shucks" personality.

3 It is tempting to accept this expansive folksiness at full face value until one remembers that Mr. Grisham, 37 years old, once considered a career in politics, even served in the Mississippi House of Representatives. It is tempting to see a bit of Southern-boy bemusement at outrageous good fortune here, until one considers that over the past year Mr. Grisham has been doing the "aw shucks, this isn't going to change me" maneuver with enough skill to risk losing his amateur standing.

In graf 4, the writer discusses the novelist's previous success and the positioning of the new book on the best seller list. She also quotes the novelist, taking the readers from the signing to his publisher's office.

4 But it's all good for business—that's how Mr. Grisham unabashedly describes his career as a novelist—and good for building an already substantial constituency. With the success of *The Firm* (525,000 hard-cover copies in print; 2.2 million paperback) and *The Pelican Brief* (Doubleday, 371 pages, $22.50), which debuts Sunday at No. 1 on *The New York Times* fiction best-seller list, Mr. Grisham is making a bid to become the Tom Clancy of legal thrillers. "All I aspire to do now is write . . . a high quality of commercial fiction," he says, sitting in an office at his publisher's. "That's all *The Firm* and *The Pelican Brief* are.

In graf 5, she gives readers a summary of the plot, having it "center on the assassination of two ideologically disparate Supreme Court justices"—a terse, but complete description.

5 *The Pelican Brief* centers on the assassination of two ideologically disparate Supreme Court justices, and a pretty law student's surprisingly successful attempt to identify the culprit. What the novel lacks in style and nimble dialogue it comfortably compensates for in narrative drive and its satirical portrayal of high-ranking politicians.

In graf 6, she lets Grisham expand upon how he writes his books by using his legal background. In this case, the good quote makes the transition without anything else needed.

6 "When I was a lawyer," Mr. Grisham explains, "I spent a lot of time in courtrooms and thought about killing judges . . . he says kiddingly," the author adds hastily. "The good thing about writing fiction is that you can get back at people. I've gotten back at lawyers, prosecutors, judges, law professors and politicians. I just line 'em up and shoot 'em."

In graf 7, readers get some biographical material on the author and more quotes from him.

7 The son of a construction worker, Mr. Grisham grew up all over the South, majored in accounting at Mississippi State University and got his law degree at Ole Miss. "In the early days I think I was a really good lawyer," says Mr. Grisham, who specialized in criminal defense. "But you get tired of helping a lot of people and not getting paid for it. And I found myself a lot of time representing people I didn't really like in cases that were boring. And once I started writing the first book, the law couldn't measure up."

In grafs 8, 9, and 10, she lets Grisham tell how his experiences and those of his cronies led him to write his first best seller, *The Firm*.

8 Mr. Grisham wrote that first book, *A Time to Kill*, a courtroom drama set in a small Southern town, over a three-year-period whenever he could eke out time from his practice. And he began to read the offerings of the best-seller lists. "I wanted to see what the public would buy," he says. "I was shocked. I was amazed at the truly bad books. I would read something and I would say, 'This is awful. I can do better than this.'"

In graf 9, she responds to the quote in the previous graf ("maybe so") before going on to mention the failure of his first novel.

9 Maybe so, but the public wouldn't buy *A Time to Kill*, which was published quietly and buried quickly. Mr. Grisham persevered and began writing another novel, taking as his inspiration the experience of some law school cronies. "They were top students—I was not," he says. "And they went through the interview game with big firms and it was fun to hear them compare offers and perks and talk about how they didn't really know the people who were recruiting them."

10 The result was *The Firm*, a novel about a hungry Harvard law school graduate who accepts the high-octane offer of a Memphis law office only to learn he's been married to the mob. "It took two years," says Mr. Grisham. "I sent it out Labor Day of 1989. And then all hell broke loose."

By graf 11, readers find out about the novelist's phenomenal success since: movie deals, interviews . . .

11 First came the movie deal with Paramount, then the sale to Doubleday. Reporters began converging on Oxford, Miss., a place best known to non-Mississippi readers as William Faulkner's hometown. In those first interviews, comparisons were made between Mr. Grisham and Scott Turow, the then reigning novelist-lawyer hyphenate. "If you want to compare me to a guy who can command a first printing of a million hard cover, I'm flattered," Mr. Grisham told them.

. . . and the downside of success, dealing with people at cocktail parties (graf 12) and . . .

12 Until Mr. Grisham and his wife pared down their party-going, they had to suffer long conversations with strangers about how Kevin Costner would be perfect as Mitch McDeere, the protagonist of *The Firm*. Or Patrick Swayze. Or Tom Cruise, Mr. Grisham's personal choice.

. . . needing an unlisted telephone number (graf 13) and a fence around his property.

13 Until he unlisted his phone number, Mr. Grisham logged calls from, among others, a Texas lawyer who wanted to discuss selling the film rights to a novel he was about to start. Until he fenced in his property, Mr. Grisham had to endure being one of Oxford's prime tourist attractions.

In grafs 14 and 15, the writer lets Grisham reflect on his success some more.

14 "There is no way to anticipate any of this," he says. "It's almost surreal. *The Firm* was a one-shot to the top. I didn't labor for years writing novels, gradually expanding readership and suddenly I'm on the best-seller list."

15 In Mr. Grisham's case, he was on it and on it and on it. Go ahead, ask him about his position on a regional or national list on a given week in a given city. He'll tell you, for example, about the week last summer when the reissued *A Time to Kill* put in an appearance on the *Publishers Weekly* trade paperback best-seller list, the week in February when *The Firm* was No. 13 on *The New York Times* best-seller list and No. 3 on the paperback list. "The next thing we're watching," he says, "is if there's a chance *The Pelican Brief* will be No. 1 on the hard-cover list the same time *The Firm* is No. 1 in paperback. I watch that. I think about it a lot."

In graf 16, she picks up a word from the previous graf ("thinking") to make her transition.

16 He's also thinking about *A Time to Kill*, which will be issued as a mass-market paperback this summer. "There's a chance when it comes out it will be on the best-seller list," he says, "and I'll have three there at once."

In graf 17, she notes what he has done with all the money he has made and reveals that he still accepts a few cases so he won't be cut off from the law that is the basis for his books.

17 Mr. Grisham, who won't talk about money except to say—several times—that it isn't particularly important to him, used the proceeds from the sale of film rights to *The Firm* (reportedly $600,000) and his advance from Doubleday (reportedly $1 million) to build a house and a pool and to buy a 70-acre thoroughbred farm, a Chevy pickup truck and an oak desk where he does his writing—always thoroughly outlined—and works on the two or three legal cases he still accepts. "There's a kind of fear about getting totally cut off from the law because that's where the ideas come from," he says.

Grisham talks in graf 18 about future book plans.

18 "Right now the ideas and words are coming fast," adds Mr. Grisham, who just signed a three-book contract with Doubleday. "I want to get them while I'm thinking about them. I look at this like Bo Jackson's career," he says, pointing to a poster of the athlete. "One of these days Bo won't be playing professional sports. I think this career will be over too. It may be five years, it may be 25 years, but I can't see me doing it when I'm 70."

In the final graf (19) the writer adds a cautionary note, indicating that critics may be "gunning" for him this time, after praising his first novel and how he responds.

19 Some of Mr. Grisham's caution is based on a realistic fear that the critics who were pulling for him when he was a rookie will be gunning for him this time around. "A lot of folks can't wait to carve me and the book up," he says. *The Pelican Brief* has already been trashed in Detroit and Chicago. But my skin is pretty thick. As long as people are buying the book that's all that matters. Why should I care about one person's opinion in Detroit?"

Human Interest #1

THE PRISON CAMP PRACTITIONER: A CAPTURED ARMY DOCTOR TREATS FELLOW AMERICANS

—by Ron Lovell

I wrote my lead to emphasize the doctor's distinction as the only American military doctor then imprisoned in Vietnam. I used a colon to enhance the cadence and power of the sentence. I went on to note where he was being held and the irony that he did not even know about advances in medicine. I also featured his wife's efforts to supply him with needed first aid supplies.

1 Maj. Floyd H. Kushner holds a distinction he would just as soon surrender: He is the only American military doctor to be captured in the Vietnam war. Confined in the vacuum of a Vietcong prison camp in South Vietnam since December 1967 and unaware even that doctors have succeeded in transplanting a heart, he still manages to practice medicine, according to his wife, Valerie. And she is so determined to dramatize his situation that she recently flew half way around the world with a 17-lb package of drugs furnished by the AMA.

I expanded upon details of his capture in graf 2, using his name and age as a means of transition . . .

2 The 28-year-old Kushner, a flight surgeon, was a passenger aboard a helicopter gunship that crashed into a mountainside during a monsoon rainstorm in late November 1967. On December 2, a Vietcong unit found him wandering in the jungle.

. . . and noted what his life is like in confinement in graf 3 and how he tried to treat fellow prisoners.

3 According to information Mrs. Kushner has obtained from released prisoners, her husband spends much of his time treating fellow prisoners at a camp near the demilitarized zone. "There is little soap so it is difficult to keep clean," she says. "Many of the men have skin sores which my husband must constantly lance."

Given the professional audience, I detailed the ailments he was treating in graf 4.

4 Whatever he does must be accomplished with little more than basic first aid equipment provided by the Vietcong, particularly in instances where men have been critically ill from dysentery or wounds. "I am told the VC get upset when they learn someone is going to die, and the necessary drugs suddenly appear," she says.

By graf 5, I needed to talk about the dramatic journey his wife made to Cambodia to try to bring him drugs to

5 When she heard her husband was short of supplies, she decided to take the package to Cambodia and try to get it delivered. She asked the AMA to provide and pack the drugs, handle

help him treat fellow prisoners.

publicity, arrange a liaison in Cambodia, and pay for the trip. The organization agreed to all but the last request, saying it had no funds to do so.

In graf 6, I went into detail about these drugs and noted the assistance she got from the American Medical Association. Because of the medical readership, I did not need to define any of the drugs or equipment noted in this paragraph.

6 The AMA package contained antibiotics, antidiarrheals, antimalarials, aspirin, multivitamins, food supplements, and fungicide ointment, plus a scalpel, stethoscope, hemostat, surgical scissors, and bandages. The AMA also sent its Saigon-based refugee health coordinator, Dr. Don Erben, to Cambodia to assist Mrs. Kushner, who arrived in Phnom Penh last November with only a letter of introduction to a Cambodian Red Cross official. She had avoided official channels because she had heard that the Vietcong would not see her if it thought she was there in an official capacity. "The VC take great pride in not dealing with the U.S.," she explains.

I used grafs 7, 8, and 9 to give details of her trip and her difficulty in delivering the drugs.

7 Mrs. Kushner and Dr. Erben were received by Nguyen Hoang Kinh, a second secretary at the Vietcong embassy, five days after her arrival. He was cordial during the meeting but would not take the medicine and drugs because he said he could not guarantee delivery. He did take letters to two other prisoners, a picture of Dr. Kushner's son, born after his capture, two pairs of eyeglasses for Kushner to replace ones broken in the crash, and a Merck Manual.

I slipped in and out of quotes to let her tell the story whenever possible.

8 During the session, held in the parlor of a converted French villa, Kinh "congratulated me on my son," and "even tried on a pair of glasses to check the refraction," recalls Mrs. Kushner. "He didn't lecture me," but when he urged her to demonstrate against the war, "I told him I was a wife and mother, not a politician."

9 Kinh would not tell her when her husband might be released or even confirm that he was alive. "I don't resent this or the fact that he was taken prisoner, but I cannot understand their not providing a doctor with medical supplies," she says. "The profession of medicine goes beyond politics."

By graf 10, I begin to end the story with a look at the prospects for the doctor's release. I switched gears

10 But the doctor's fate probably rests with political decisions at the peace table or haphazard Vietcong release procedures. In the meantime, he will continue his primitive

here by using "but" as the transition.

prison-camp practice. "The released prisoners report that he talks medicine all the time, as much to remind himself that he is a doctor as anything else," says Mrs. Kushner. "It will be a problem, away from medicine so long."

In graf 11, I included details about the doctor's medical training I hadn't been able to fit in before. It went well with his future plans.

11 Dr. Kushner, who hopes to specialize in the ear, nose, and throat, graduated from the Medical College of Virginia in 1966 and interned at Tripler Army Medical Center, Honolulu. He had no residency, though volunteering for Vietnam instead and treating both G.I.s and civilians there.

I ended the story by letting the doctor's wife have the last word, using the phrase "for her part" as my transition. I ended with a strong and stirring quote from her about the value of publicity. When the doctor was eventually released, I felt my story had played a small part in that happy event.

12 For her part, Mrs. Kushner still hopes to get a package of drugs to him. She will also continue to publicize the plight of all prisoners in any way possible. "Publicity is our strongest point," she says. "Public indignation is all that is left to us."

7

Writing about Subjects in the News

It occurs in thousands of places and happens to thousands of people. Sometimes the people affected aren't aware of that in which they're involved. At other times, the enormity of the event changes the lives of all it touches, leaving no doubt that something significant has taken place.

News is very different from ordinary, everyday events.

Those with enough training and experience recognize it instantly for what it is: an event that will affect the lives of more than one person and be interesting to others. An additional element is necessary as well. To be considered news, an event must be reported. The biggest story in the world will not receive that designation if nobody knows about it.

As a free-lance writer, you won't be dealing with news as much as if you were a newspaper reporter, of course. But there will still be times when the ability to report and write about news will pay off, if you know how to handle it. You will have to learn what news is before you can place articles with a news orientation.

The process of learning to recognize news begins in school. From that point on, you learn by experience—your own and the work of other writers. In time, it is possible to develop the proverbial "nose for news." That is, you will gain the ability to know immediately when something is newsworthy. Another aspect to consider is the fact that the mere selection of a topic to write about can make a subject newsworthy. If the publication that accepts your article is an important one, and that publication gives your article prominent placement, the subject will become newsworthy.

Reporting and Writing News

Going Beyond the Obvious News Peg

Rarely will a free-lance writer be the first to break a news story. Only in exceptional cases—usually involving extensive investigation that is beyond the resources of most free-lance writers—will an article make news. The secret in making news pay off is to go beyond the obvious news peg when you propose and write an article. This kind of article is called a *news feature*.

Your selection of a topic starts with a thorough knowledge of what is going on in your area. As you read local daily and weekly newspapers and watch local television news, you need to remain alert to stories that will be of interest to the audience of the magazine or magazines with which you regularly work, whether they be local, regional, or national. You must constantly ask yourself, is this a story I can sell to my editors? (A rarer source of ideas will come from tips your sources give you. The rarity comes because they may not think to call you because they won't consider you a "news" reporter.)

Next in importance comes the sustainability of the story, the element that producers of plays on Broadway call "legs." How long will the story last? If it is news now, will it remain newsworthy long enough to report, write, edit, and get it into a magazine that won't be out for a month?

Proximity also plays a large role in your ability as a free-lance writer to handle a news story. Normally, a magazine will not send a free-lancer great distances to cover such an event. Instead, editors will pick someone nearby to do the job because of the expense involved. If you are gathering enough material to write a query letter—or, even rarer, write an article on speculation—you won't want to spend a great deal of money on travel or long distance telephone calls.

How, then, do you make news a salable commodity?

Look for subjects that are nearby geographically, have some national interest over an extended period of time, and are "doable." Your "nose for news" will develop over time as you observe the news events around you and respond to occasional tips from sources.

Box 7.1 The Elements of News

- *Proximity.* If an event happens close to readers geographically, it is news. Usually, this means in the same town, state, or region.
- *Impact on numbers of people.* Events that affect a large number of people always make news. The more people affected by a story—for good or bad—the more news interest.
- *Accidents, crime, natural disasters.* Death often constitutes news, but so do robberies, train wrecks, airplane crashes, and such natural disasters as tornadoes, hurricanes, snow storms, and forest fires.
- *Unique, bizarre people or events.* People never get tired of reading about the unusual. This kind of story is of the classic "man bites dog" variety.
- *Nostalgic, humorous, sad, or ironic people or events.* Readers like to read about "the little guy" who becomes newsworthy by accident. The public can identify with such people and laugh or cry with them.
- *Prominent people.* Readers always seem fascinated by the activities of a small group of notables with power and money, who do strange and bizarre things. Readers may not want to trade places with movie and rock stars, European royalty, African tyrants, or the family of whoever is president of the United States, but they love to get vicarious thrills by reading about their exploits.
- *Governments at all levels.* As daily life in the United States becomes ever more influenced and controlled by government, stories about officials of these governments are newsworthy.
- *Wars and threats of wars.* No matter how obscure the conflict, war is always newsworthy. Readers sometimes have a great deal at stake (the Gulf War) or little chance of personal involvement (Bosnia or Somalia), but they still are interested in the horror, death, and displacement of war.
- *Timeliness.* Any of these elements will cease to be newsworthy if no new details emerge. Readers want to know the latest developments about a subject, and they will quickly scan and leave unfinished a story that doesn't offer anything fresh. News has to be new.

Personalizing a News Event

A good approach to take in both querying and later writing about news is to personalize it. Readers will more readily identify with an event, no matter how great or small, if they see it through the eyes of others. This enables them to put themselves in the shoes of the people who experienced the event.

Thus, your first step in searching for more information about a given news event is to find people who participated in and were affected by that event. You can find these people by reading the news clips of the event. Which people are mentioned in the stories? You can usually reach them through their place of work or by calling directory assistance or consulting the phone book or city directory.

At other times, you may have to use your own ingenuity to track down people who might be affected by an event but are not mentioned in the news accounts. Here, you need to become sleuth-like in your quest for people. Who is likely to be affected by this event? Residents along the coast near an oil spill? People present when a bank was robbed? Relatives of a person running for political office? The list is endless. The point is simple: for every news event there are people affected by it about whom other people—readers of magazines—will be interested.

Adding Information and Detail

Once you have selected a subject and found people to talk to, the key ingredient in your success will be your interviews. The questions you ask and the answers you get in return will make or break your article.

Preparing for this kind of interview is not as easy as getting ready to talk to someone who has recognized expertise and a published body of work to consult (as noted in chapter 15). It is easy to jot down a list of questions when you can refer to other articles. In the kind of interview examined here, the person may never have been interviewed before, and may not at first see why you want to talk. Such people may resist an interview out of fear or shyness. Such cases require extra persistence.

As a result, you may go into an interview with only the vague details of this person's involvement in the news event that prompted you to contact him or her in the first place. You will have to improvise as you go along, beginning with broad questions and then using details from one answer as the basis for other questions.

The trite question many television reporters ask after even the most tragic events—"how did it feel?"—comes to mind as the worst way to begin an interview with reluctant and scared sources. Ironically, however, that is precisely what you are trying to determine. You want to discover the innermost feelings of your interviewees, along with as much detail as you can possibly gain. A variation on the "feel" question might be, "When did you realize you were part of a significant event and what was your reaction?"

From here, the easiest approach is probably a chronological one.

Box 7.2 Suggested Markets

- Sunday newspaper magazines or feature sections
- *Modern Maturity*
- Public relations magazines
- Trade magazines
- Specialized magazines

Guide the person through a step-by-step account of what happened. As the story comes out, you'll need to interrupt constantly for details: sights, smells, colors, impressions, time of day, what others said. Because it is hard to think of everything as you go, you will need to leave an opening with your source so you can call again for clarification.

Giving Readers a New Slant

The ability of any writer to see a story in a subject— news or otherwise—is what makes that person a writer. Most people are readers (or viewers) not writers. Many subscribe to newspapers and magazines (and watch television) in order to be informed and entertained. As the person writing the articles, you are providing a special service and, hopefully, you can earn a living or extra money by doing so. The knack for seeing something interesting in a subject others generally ignore (until it is pointed out to them) is a special gift. It comes from experience and ingenuity and intelligence.

Any time you approach a subject you need to first spend some time thinking about it and the manner in which it should be handled. This thought process will usually result in a list of who to talk to, what to ask them, and how your article will tell the story. You should also endeavor to come up with a new slant on the subject. In order to intrigue editors with your query and readers with the final article, you must gain insights and information they haven't seen covered before.

The Roundup Story

The roundup or survey story is a kind of news story free-lance writers can work on profitably. These kinds of articles are, as their name implies, a "roundup" or "survey" of opinion on a given subject. They are not to be confused with public opinion surveys scientifically conducted by polling firms. Rather, the roundup or survey story reports opinions of various sources on a given topic.

This kind of article has long been a staple of trade magazines. McGraw-Hill World News bureaus around the United States in the 1960s and 1970s regularly received survey assignments from the New York editors of various magazines to call "10 purchasing agents in your area" (*Purchasing Week*) or "five chemical company presidents" (*Chemical Week*) and "ask them the following questions." Reporters in the bureaus covering whatever beat the topic fell into would then spend a day or two doing the interviews. Sometimes, for variation, the reporters would do the interviews in person. After they had gathered the material, the reporters could send the raw transcripts by teletype to New York where an editor on the magazine would write the article.

Business Week used its bureaus in a similar way for broad stories about the economy or politics or international trade. *Time* and *Newsweek* also started getting its bureaus to gather material on a variety of topics, especially those appearing in cover stories. All three of these magazines run such informal surveys regularly, although in no set pattern. The work is usually carried out by staff members.

The Wall Street Journal is the only national newspaper publishing this kind of story on a regular basis. They are called "roundups" and appear several times a week on a variety of subjects. The work is carried out by staff members.

There is a role for the free-lance writer in the reporting that goes into surveys and roundups. If you can get the designation of stringer (see Box 7.3), you will probably do a lot of this kind of story. The more regions of the country such an article includes, the more credible it is. Using your services as a stringer is a fairly inexpensive way for the magazine to appear truly national even if it isn't really.

For your part, the telephone calls and transcribing of your notes can be done fairly quickly (if you don't put it off) and you don't have to slave over a lead or transitions. The editors just want a selection of raw quotes.

It is also possible to suggest roundup ideas to any editor on any subject. Most magazines can incorporate this kind of article within their formats and editors might welcome such a variation from the norm. The topic needs to be just as appropriate to the overall mission of the publication as a more conventional one- or two-source story, of course. Instead of that typical approach, however, you will propose that you call a number of sources to get quotes on a general topic. Then, instead of submitting the results to an editor, you will

Box 7.3 How to Be a Stringer or Contributing Editor

A "stringer" is a part-time employee of a news organization who is paid for material submitted. Although not a regular employee, a stringer can usually count on having material used frequently and, as a result, get paid with some regularity.

News organizations employing stringers (or "correspondents" as some call them) usually have set procedures for what kinds of stories they want, how they are submitted, and what the pay will be. Some will pay by the inch or the story, others will put a stringer on a retainer. Stringers seldom get company benefits. Some publications will list them in the staff box which may help impress other prospective employers or sources who want "proof" of a stringer's link to the magazine or newspaper.

Stringers usually keep track of news developments in a geographic area for the publication and attend press conferences. They often submit material for roundup stories too. When it comes to really big subjects, however, the magazines or newspapers in question usually send in a regular staff writer from headquarters. The stringer will make the arrangements for the interview and little more.

Being a stringer is a good way to make some extra money and get items in print, but it is not something on which to build a career.

An entirely different issue is being named a contributing editor. This is more than an honorary title, but not much more. Magazines use this designation in its staff box for people who write regularly for it but are not full-time staff members. A listing there guarantees that editors will read your queries carefully and often approve them, certainly to a greater extent than people unknown to them. They may also give you an occasional assignment. For your part, you can show the staff listing to dubious sources and use it in query letters to other publications. You will not, however, get any benefits or even a retainer.

probably write the final article. It is, after all, your idea. One caution: because you will probably be calling sources all over the country, be sure to ask for sufficient expense money to cover your telephone bill.

Two News Features

Both of the articles reprinted here are examples of news features. They are based on broad issues in the national news at the time, which I then made more personal by interviews and the approach I took. The stories also illustrate how a free-lance writer can "mine" a region for ideas and gain the interest of editors, not because they are about cutting edge issues but because they take interesting slants on familiar topics. Both stories were for medical publications, yet are not really about new surgical procedures, or cures, or breakthrough drugs. Instead, they deal with problems some doctors have had to cope with and how they did so.

The national news peg in the first article is widespread unemployment among loggers in the Pacific Northwest. In this piece for *Medical World News*, however, I needed a medical slant so I proposed something on the high rate of crippling and sometimes fatal accidents among loggers. To report the story, I traveled to the southern Oregon coast and a town in the heart of the timber industry. The second article written for *Medical Tribune*, uses the national controversy over the spraying of herbicides as the news peg for an article about how two doctors in a small town on the Oregon coast are coping with the problem on a local level.

News Feature #1

TREATING TRAUMA IN TIMBER COUNTRY

—by Ron Lovell

I begin with a favorite device: an italicized section to set the scene. In it, I describe two typical kinds of logging injuries.

A "powder monkey" is blowing stumps to build a road. He places a stick of dynamite under a stump to blow a small hole that he can then pack with nitrogen fertilizer and more dynamite. Unfortunately, another worker has already packed the stump with the larger charge. The "monkey" lights the fuse expecting to ignite one dynamite stick, and steps back. The impact of the double charge sends him flying 150 feet—70 feet in the air—injuring his knees, breaking one leg, and tearing the ligaments in the other as he hits the ground.

A truck driver is unloading logs. The restraining chains have been released and he violated the cardinal rule of men in his occupation: never turn your back on a pile of logs. The 40-ft-long, 4-ft-diameter "peak" or top, log suddenly rolls off and strikes him across the legs. Doctors later amputate both of them, one above the knee, the other below.

In my actual lead, however, I do not refer to the preceding section. I just note

1 For doctors in Coos County, Oregon, trauma has a special meaning.

that trauma has a special meaning to doctors.

To emphasize the horror of logging accidents, I use words like "crippling" and "crushing."

2 True, it still means automobile accident victims and people who have mishaps in their homes. More often than not, though, trauma to doctors in this remote area on the south Oregon coast means dealing with victims of some of the most crippling and crushing accidents imaginable: the loggers and mill workers who make their living in the timber industry.

In graf 3, I let a source pick up the idea to authenticate what I've just said. I also reveal his place in the story: he is an emergency room physician in a hospital that gets these injuries from over a wide area.

3 "When guys get hurt in the woods, they usually don't sprain an ankle, it's more serious," says Dr. Richard E. Imm, one of the emergency room physicians at the new $6.7 million Bay Area Hospital in Coos Bay, which serves over 55,000 people between the California border and Florence, 150 miles up the coast, and inland 15 miles to the Coast Range. This facility gets nearly all major accident victims because it is better equipped to handle them than the three smaller and older hospitals in this remote area.

The physician and an emergency room nurse elaborate on the serious nature of logging accidents and bolster the theme set down in the lead.

4 "Many of the injuries are very severe," says Dr. Imm, "especially accidents out in the woods. Mortality is high—many don't reach doctors." Adds Sherry Martin, the emergency room supervising nurse: "I've never seen trauma like this. They come in totally traumatized, often with more than one thing wrong."

In grafs 5 and 6, I switch gears and explain why logging is so dangerous using statistics of a typical tree to show how heavy and formidable it is.

5 By its very nature, logging is dangerous work that has to be conducted in almost inaccessible areas on rough, uneven terrain. The men who work in the woods must live every day with the knowledge that all or part of a 200-ft-tall tree with a 3-to-6-ft diameter might fall on them.

6 Even the mills, which turn raw logs into various wood products, are dangerous. Here, trees, cut into 36-ft logs with 3-ft diameters, move along conveyors and encounter saws with blades as tall as a man. "One of those blades and one of those logs sound like a freight train roaring toward you," says a local doctor. A common problem among workers is splinters—not the kind a parent removes from the finger of a child, but several inches long that rot in the hand and become infected if not removed.

In graf 7, I indicate that timber companies try to avoid accidents. A good article should present as many sides to the story as are needed to paint a complete picture. Thus, in graf 7, I talk about the safety precautions that timber companies take.

7 The large companies that dominate the industry have stringent safety rules and better safety records than those of the smaller, independent loggers who used to prevail. All field supervisors and some loggers at Weyerhaeuser, for example, are trained in first aid. Safety engineers for each region have had emergency medical training and all sites are equipped with two-way radios. The minute an injury takes place, the process of getting the man to a doctor begins. Depending on the severity of the injury, the supervisor decides to send the man by ambulance, four-wheel drive vehicle, or obtain a Coast Guard or sheriff's department helicopter.

In grafs 8 and 9, I get into the medical aspect for the first time: how the injured are treated. "In the vernacular of" provides an expedient bridge from the technical description to an explanation in layperson's terms. I again let a source carry the story along for me with his quotes.

8 After initial treatment in Bay Area's emergency room, Dr. Imm and two other emergency room physicians usually call one of several specialists on the staff. Dr. James A. Holbert, an orthopedist and chief of surgery at the hospital, gets many of the calls. "You've always got a broken body case in varying stages of reconstruction," he says. In the vernacular of Coos County trauma, a broken body case is a combination injury. "It involves injury along the spine and the head or the chest and in the abdominal area—all in the same patient," Dr. Holbert says.

9 "Every doctor knows that you have to approach a broken body case systematically, first creating an airway and adequate oxygenation or you won't have a patient," he continues. "The next problem is to control the bleeding and then you can sort out the individual injuries and see which are important and which can wait."

In grafs 10 and 11, I let the doctor lead readers to a discussion of the worst kind of injury of all: a "widow maker." This phrase, used for years by doctors in this area, is a writer's dream: It is so descriptive and colorful. Because this article will be read by other doctors I don't have to define words like "plexus."

10 But even more vexing than this is dealing with what are known in the area as "widow makers," tree limbs that fall without warning and hit the men working below. The size doesn't matter, says Dr. Holbert, because "even a small limb can be damaging if it falls from 100 feet up."

11 Widow makers do most of their damage by hitting the shoulder with tremendous force, driving the shoulder down, injuring the nerve plexus, and affecting with varying degrees of severity all muscles and senses in the upper extremities. "If it breaks the plexus off at the root and tears it off at the spinal cord, there's no way to recover," says Dr. Holbert. "The man then has what I call a 'flailed out extremity.'" Dr. Holbert recommends amputation "if every nerve root is pulled off and all is gone." If not, he says the men "spend the rest of their lives using one arm to move the other one."

12 Despite the seriousness of many of these accidents, Dr. Holbert thinks the improved safety standards of the industry have reduced the number of accidents from what they were 15 years ago when he arrived from the Mayo Clinic to begin his practice. Another area doctor has seen even more change in the trauma situation.

In graf 13, I bring in someone who had been a key source: a retired doctor who had been working in the area since 1936. (Indeed, I had gotten the details for that italicized intro from him.) I heard about him from other sources after I got to town and was delighted to get so many good quotes from him.

13 Dr. Raymond M. McKeown, 72, retired two years ago from a practice he began in the area in 1936. The former AMA treasurer and trustee first worked in the logging camps of the region as a boy of 14. "I saw men killed and badly injured all around me," he says. Things hadn't improved much when he returned from the Yale Medical School at the end of the Depression. "Men broke legs and had their necks broken regularly by cables," he recalls. "Once, the man next to me had his head knocked off by a cable, I turned around, vomited, and went on."

In grafs 14 through 17, I let this very colorful source (the kind any writer hopes for) tell his story.

14 Although trained in obstetrics and gynecology at Yale, Dr. McKeown found the economic situation grim in Coos County when he arrived. "People were using wooden money for barter because they didn't have any of their own," he says. "I became a GP fast because I couldn't make a living as a specialist." A company doctor handled most of the cases in the woods, but frequently there were too many for him so Dr. McKeown was called in.

15 "There was one x-ray machine in the hospital and no orthopedists," he says. Luckily, Dr. McKeown had had good training in orthopedics and written a number of papers on the healing of fractures. "We had been taught to feel a break and, by the sense of touch, to know when we had it right."

16 At that time, when an accident happened, the supervisor would blow five blasts on the camp whistle and men with a stretcher would immediately be sent out to the injured man. If the telephone was working, a call would go out to the doctor. If not, a runner would be sent to notify him about the accident. Once alerted, the doctor would set out over dirt roads to the camp, some 60 miles away.

17 "How fast you got to them and instituted supportive treatment until they got to a hospital was important," says Dr. McKeown. "The longer the delay, the more disastrous it could be. The strong survived; the weak didn't make it."

I make the transition into graf 18 by using a phrase ("physical stamina") to sum up what the previous quote had discussed. I then bring readers back to the present and continue to discuss treatment procedures in grafs 19 through 22.

18 The physical stamina of the men affects their recovery. Because loggers work outdoors all the time, they are generally in good enough health to withstand the rigors of their injuries. Says RN Martin: "They are amazing people. I've never seen a group of individuals as stoic. I'm sure that's why they survive."

19 Today, though, physicians do not always go to the scene of the accident. Dr. Holbert flatly refuses: "If you go to the site, it takes you X amount of time. When you get there, you usually have the wrong thing because the description from the person who called you is inaccurate. So you've wasted time getting there. The time loss could cost you the patient. It would be detrimental to the patient to send a doctor out. There's a reason why the house call is dead."

20 Dr. Holbert says he would go to the site only in the event of a major spine injury where a wrong move might injure the patient severely. He prefers to rely on helicopters or onsite ambulances. But Dr. Imm thinks even the much-heralded helicopter has its limitations. "It's not a universal answer," he says. "Because of the foggy rainy weather, it's limited. Also, it can land only in certain areas because of the steep, uneven terrain."

21 He uses a recent instance to prove his point: A man with a crushed leg had lost a great deal of blood by the time the helicopter arrived. He had been given first aid to stop the bleeding and a tourniquet had been applied. The helicopter was too small to accommodate his stretcher, however, so he was lashed to one of the external pods of the craft and covered with a canvas tarp. Out there, exposed to the wind and rain, he went into shock and bled to death by the time the helicopter got to the hospital.

22 Says Dr. Imm: "If he'd been cared for on the ground right there, he might have survived." Most trauma victims are luckier and do survive, although rates of permanent disability are high.

I use graf 23 to illustrate why things are better today: young doctors and specialists are treating the cases.

23 The presence of young emergency-trained doctors like Dr. Imm and specialists like Dr. Holbert probably make the biggest difference now over the situation in the past. Dr. Holbert still worries about the lack of a neurosurgeon for the bad head cases. The hospital is trying to attract one into the area permanently. Now, those cases must be sent over the mountains to Eugene, 116 miles away. Several times, Dr. Holbert has talked on the telephone to a Eugene neurosurgeon who instructed him in the proper procedure for drilling holes in a skull to relieve intracranial pressure. The severity of the man's condition precluded a trip.

24 With all the improvements and hopes for further changes, the doctors live with the realization that the situation can never end because of the way men make their living in Coos County. There will be broken body cases and victims of widow makers as long as men go into the woods.

The last paragraph is the only place I hint at a news peg: injuries are down because of the recession in the timber industry.

25 Recently, accident cases have fallen off—but for an ironic reason. Because of the slowdown in the economy, particularly housing, a lot of loggers have been laid off and haven't been going into the woods. They're in the unemployment lines instead.

News Feature #2

I again used one of my favorite devices to begin: an italicized paragraph to set the scene. Unlike the previous article, however, the lead does not stand alone. You would have to read the "scene setter" to understand the lead. I let one of my sources bring readers right in with her quote.

ON HERBICIDE SPRAYING IN OREGON

—by Ron Lovell

In rural Lincoln County, Ore., on the Pacific coast, a controversy boils over the health effects of aerial herbicide spraying by the U.S. Forest Service and timber companies. While the chemicals remove forest brush, opponents argue they may also be responsible for a higher-than-normal rate of neural tube defects—especially anencephaly and hydrocephaly—among newborns there over the past decade. In 1977, FPs Chuck and Renee Stringham were alerted when they treated 20 demonstrators who had been sprayed during a protest; headache and nausea were the complaints.

1 "In trying to help these patients, I discovered I knew nothing, and that no one knew very much [about herbicides]," recalls Dr. Renee Stringham. "In the process of doing research, I became an expert in the side effects of spraying.

I lay the groundwork for what is to come by taking readers back to the beginning of involvement by the two doctors who were my principal sources.

2 To find out more about the possible health hazards of herbicides, the Stringhams attended a conference in June, 1979 at the University of Oregon School of Medicine in Portland. There they heard experts on the subject like Dr. Samuel Epstein, professor of occupational and environmental medicine at the University of Illinois School of Public Health, citing the possible dangers of herbicide use. On the second day, foresters and farmers talked about their need for herbicides.

In grafs 3 through 9, the story continues. Again, these kinds of sources and their good quotes are a writer's dream. They truly allowed me to let the story tell itself.

3 "We left with the feeling that these things could be dangerous," said Dr. Chuck Stringham. "The conference also gave us the knowledge that we were not just isolated people in the hinterlands worrying about what no one else knows."

Because of the medical readership of *Medical Tribune*, I could use medical terms without defining them. If the article had been

4 The Stringhams became more persistent in their study of the problem. They noticed, for example, that of the 300 babies they delivered during their first four years in Lincoln County, seven had major neural-tube defects: three

aimed at the general reader, I would have had to insert brief explanations.

hydrocephalics, two anencephalics, one encephalocele, and one had a porencephalic cyst.

5 "I called the CDC to see if this rate was high and the person I talked to asked if I was near Benton County, which he called one of four hot spots for anencephaly in the country," said Dr. Renee Stringham. Benton County is the next county to the east and includes major portions of the Siuslaw National Forest. The Stringhams also noticed that one out of three pregnancies of patients they treated ended with spontaneous miscarriage. Although they had no hard evidence that these miscarriages were caused by herbicides, this discovery increased their questions.

6 In the spring of 1980, the Stringhams proposed that the Lincoln County Medical Society sponsor an initiative petition to get a measure on the ballot in the November, 1980 election that would decrease herbicide spraying over watersheds and limit roadside spraying so people would not be involuntarily exposed. The medical society members attending the regular meeting in April passed a motion in favor of sponsoring the petition seven to two.

7 The Stringhams returned from vacation a few weeks later on a Saturday to find that members who had not attended the first meeting had scheduled another one for the following Monday to reconsider the earlier vote. Two independent experts from California would present information on herbicides before the new vote.

8 The doctors felt they needed their own expert to present information so they arranged for Dr. Epstein to appear via satellite on the local religious cable channel to make his own presentation and answer questions from medical society members.

9 The vote this time was 14 to 7, again in favor of society sponsorship of the initiative motion. Both Stringhams campaigned actively for the measure, which was defeated 10,000 to 6,000 in the general election that November. The harassment they suffered during the campaign, along with the needs of their three boys and Dr.

Renee Stringham's recent bout with breast cancer, has caused both Stringhams to be less active now.

In graf 10, I bring things up to date by saying that one of the doctors is still treating the same patients.

10 Dr. Chuck Stringham is still treating many of the same 20 patients that got him and his wife involved in the first place. Included among his newer patients are many women from the Five Rivers area. All have similar problems, according to Dr. Stringham: "suspicious uterine bleeding, menstrual irregularity, and abdominal pain."

But such a controversial story needs balance, so I sought out a doctor on the other side of the controversy. I let him take issue with my main sources in grafs 11, 12, and 13, in kind of an "equal time" rule.

11 Other doctors in the country take issue with the Stringhams or anyone connecting herbicides to illness. Dr. Donald Forinash has been in practice in Newport, a town nearer the heavily sprayed areas than where the Stringhams live, since 1958.

12 Dr. Forinash says he has seen "hardly any" patients complaining of herbicide-related illness during that time. "My practice doesn't include many of the hill folk," he adds. "Herbicides have a short life. They are not a permanent part of the soil. Much of the [controversy] comes from a dioxin craze. Truly dioxin is, without a doubt, one of the most potent chemicals in the world. Dioxin, at most, is only an impurity that has been pretty well eliminated. Most of the people complaining [have ailments that are] completely compatible with anxiety states—dizziness, lightheadedness, nervousness."

13 Dr. Forinash does not think there are enough data to say that herbicides cause medical problems. "Caution is advised," he continued. "But, as yet, with the exception of dioxin, there is not hard evidence that this is a real problem. If there was a great danger from herbicides, we wouldn't be wondering about it, we would know about it."

I called another more neutral physician for comment and found him to be in agreement with my main sources. (It was not a matter of picking from a wide variety of doctors; there aren't that many treating patients who got

14 Another physician is not so sure. Dr. Peter J. Cookson is a pathologist who has practiced in Newport for 10 years. Although not actively involved in the herbicide issue on one side or the other, Dr. Cookson says he began to wonder about the relationship between spraying and health two years ago when he had two cases of anencephalic infants.

sick as a result of exposure to herbicides.)

In grafs 15 and 16, I let him present his concerns. Note, too, that I again use a medical term here without explanation.

15 "In my experience, in all my years of training at the University of Pennsylvania Medical School, I had not seen any anencephalic cases," he said. "I talked to my instructors and asked when they had last seen one—among the 5,000 deliveries per year at the hospital. They hadn't seen any. They remarked, 'that is a lot to see in such a small, podunk place.'"

16 Since that time, Dr. Cookson has not seen any more cases. "But they haven't been spraying since then, either," he added.

In graf 17, I bring in the county health officer and let him give his point of view in this graf and in 18 and 19. I also add material in brackets which augment the point made in the quote. This is a good way to bring pertinent information to the attention of readers, even by intruding on a source's quote.

17 The county health officer, Dr. Ethan Wilson, thinks the public reaction to spraying has had another consequence. "At the state level, there has been a decision to minimize spraying because of the hot spots and local reaction," he said. "Things are slowing down. Companies [which are still allowed to spray] have had to be more covert in announcing their plans because of the incidents. [A helicopter used for spraying was burned two years ago, and a large piece of logging equipment was set afire in June, in two different parts of the Coast Range.] There is also much more public awareness."

18 Dr. Wilson said the recent cases in the county he is aware of resulted from known exposure that caused headache, nausea, and abdominal pain. The symptoms disappeared the next day. "I'm uneasy about the long-term effects of herbicides," he said. "We just don't have the data. It's a question of what won't show up for years."

In grafs 19 and 20, I hint at the news peg: the problems rural areas have with herbicide spraying and the health plan that was worked out as a result.

19 The county itself is also much more aware of how to handle herbicide-related problems than most rural governments. Because of a rash of problems over the past few years, the Lincoln and Benton County health officers in 1981 worked out a plan, with help from an Oregon State University scientist, to respond when people call to complain of illness and link that illness to herbicides.

20 The caller is asked for details on when and where the incident happened. If the illness has been prolonged, the health department collects blood and urine samples and sends them for analysis to the Oregon Department of Agriculture. The health department also submits examples of foliage and livestock damage to the agriculture department. Last year there was little response, according to Gail Stater, environmental health program manager for Lincoln County.

Graf 21 begins a section on why things are worse this year.

21 "This year is another story," said Ms. Stater. "The difference is the amount of spraying. It's an emotional-political-economic issue."

I use the next three grafs to expound on one incident and relate it to the larger problem of spraying.

22 This year's most celebrated incident occurred on May 11 when a Little League team practiced on a school playing field in Toledo, just east of Newport. That night and the next day 12 boys and nine parents had come down with headaches, intestinal cramps, and vomiting. The health department was asked to investigate and discovered that the school district had sprayed the field with NS 610 herbicide on May 5.

Sun Played a Role

23 In the intervening period, four other teams had played on the field with no ill effects. It had been raining intermittently until May 11, a sunny day. The sun apparently caused the bad reaction then. A delay in reporting the incident also caused a delay in making blood and urine tests. "If it's more than 48 hours, there is no chance of getting significant levels to do significant tests," said Dr. Wilson.

24 The problem has always plagued physicians trying to prove herbicide poisoning elsewhere. People wait to go to the doctor beyond the time when complete data can be obtained, thus lessening the chance to prove their illness is herbicide-related. "Beyond 24 to 48 hours, the chance of getting anything measurable is pretty negligible," said Ms. Stater.

In graf 25, I begin my summation. I leave a space between the previous graf as a signal to readers that something else is going to

25 The matter of herbicide spraying—for both defenders of the practice and opponents of it—will doubtless go on as long as there are forests and people living near them.

happen, similar to darkening a theater to indicate different scenes in a play.

The article could have ended with my summation, but I had a good quote that expanded upon what I had said. I returned to one of my doctor sources and had him conclude for me.

26 Concludes pathologist Dr. Cookson: "My opinion is the cases [of deformed babies] showed up after a year of intense spraying. They disappeared after spraying stopped. Anyone can argue that this was not caused by the spraying. I can't prove it. If they start spraying again, we'll see funny-looking babies again. If we do, I'm going to ask those guys, you spray and then you drink the water."

8

Writing about Things that Happen to You

As a writer you sometimes have at your disposal an interview subject you don't have to cajole into talking to you or travel great distances to reach: yourself. Writing about things that happen to you is a perfectly acceptable kind of article topic if it is carefully handled and you are a good writer. The subject may be fairly commonplace and mundane, as long as you write about it in a way that will be interesting to others. Usually, only two approaches work: humor, preferably of the self-deprecating kind, and sorrow. You can usually grab the attention of an editor if what you are proposing will make readers laugh or cry.

Reporting and Writing Personal Articles

Choosing a Subject of Interest to Others

The secret behind this kind of article is to pick a subject with which readers can readily identify. Finding such a story possibility isn't like any other. You can't look anything up in reference books or call an expert. Instead, you have to rely on your instincts as a writer and your skills in selecting a topic others will want to read about.

Your search for a subject will probably take one of three avenues:

- You experience something unexpectedly that, after it happens, seems like a good story idea (see Article #1 later in this chapter).
- You deliberately participate in an event in order to write about it (see Article #2).
- You conjure up something interesting out of something simple (see Article #3).

Whatever the approach, it is important to ask yourself several questions:

- Does my topic hold any interest beyond my immediate family?
- Can readers identify with it?
- Does the topic have any kind of news peg that links it to broader concerns?
- Can the topic be written about in a humorous, moving, or uplifting way?

Recalling Details

As in any kind of article, details are very important in writing this kind of piece. It is such detail that will allow readers to experience what you as a writer have experienced. Sights, sounds, smells, colors, moods, physical description—all of these particulars are crucial.

If the story is about something that happens to you unexpectedly, you need to take a lot of notes about your impressions either during or after the event. In Article #1 reprinted later in this chapter, Kevin Miller writes about his one-year battle with a serious illness that almost killed him. The writing of the article was a cathartic experience, a way to come to terms with a traumatic event in his life. Because he was so ill, he did not take notes at the time, of course. The details of his ordeal came flooding back into his mind after he decided to write an article, however.

The preparation for writing an article about an event you deliberately take part in is similar. You take copious notes of what happens to you step-by-step and the outcome. The difference comes in the fact that you are planning to write about your participation so you will be more aware of everything than if you were trying to recall details after the fact. In Article #2, free-lance writer Susan Hauser proposed to the Leisure and Arts editor at *The Wall Street Journal* that she be a judge in the Miss Oregon USA beauty contest and write about the experience. Using the humorous style she has come to specialize in for the *Journal* (she says she specializes in

Box 8.1 Suggested Markets

Articles about things that happen to you can be placed in a variety of publications:

- Sunday magazine sections of newspapers
- *The Saturday Evening Post*
- *Reader's Digest*
- *Modern Maturity*
- *Newsweek* (the "My Turn" piece in every issue)
- *Redbook*

the "weird beat, anything quirky" for that newspaper), Hauser wrote a very funny story.

Writing about something you conjure up out of a rather ordinary aspect of your life requires an entirely different approach. Instead of recording copious details, you need to be able to recognize the opportunities which abound in things you do every day. The trick is to extrapolate into a larger concern from that seemingly simple occurrence. Is there something funny or sad about taking out the garbage or doing the weekly shopping or operating a gas pump in a self-service station? In Article #3, California free-lance writer Wendell Smith interested editors at *The Saturday Evening Post* in an essay on word use which he thought of while watching the classic film, "Casablanca."

Weaving in Broader Concerns

The "broader concerns" noted in the heading refer to two important elements of this kind of article. First, your subject may have some kind of link with a larger event in the local or national news—known as a "news peg." Or, you may be writing about an event or topic a lot of people have experienced.

Either approach necessitates an awareness on your part about what is happening in the world around you. What time of year is it (do you want to get a job as a department store Santa)? Has some kind of trend emerged that people are aware of or affected by (how about a piece on spending the night in a homeless shelter or standing on the corner with a "Will Work for Food" sign)?

Keeping First Person under Control

As noted elsewhere in this book, it is best to keep yourself out of most articles as much as possible. The use of first person is often the refuge of a lazy writer. It takes more skill to avoid it than to succumb to its use.

In writing about things that happen to you, however, you have to use first person. To avoid it would be ludicrous because the key element of what you are writing about is your involvement. It is through your eyes that readers will experience vicariously what happened to you in reality. Although you should not overdo it, the use of first person is perfectly permissible in this type of article.

Three Writers Write about Themselves

Personal Experience

Kevin Miller's compelling account of his battle with a life-threatening illness almost defies analysis. It is very well written and heartfelt as only something a writer has experienced first-hand can be. Stories of personal experience such as this only come along once in a while. And, of course, due to the nature of the subject matter, this was one event Miller would just have soon skipped.

Article #1

LIFE SUPPORT

—by Kevin Miller

The power of Miller's account speaks for itself. The opening line ("The sickness arrived gently") is simple, but effective. With it, he sets the tone, defines the topic, grabs the reader's attention and keeps it. He accomplishes all of this simply by telling what happened to him and how it made him feel.

1 The sickness arrived gently.

He makes the transition by starting his story: the date, what he was doing, and why things didn't seem quite right.

2 Barely a year ago, on Sept. 4, 1991, I sat at my desk at *The Register-Guard* in Eugene and frowned at my computer screen. I was writing one more of the hundreds of newspaper stories I'd written since graduating from Oregon State in 1978, but this time my typing was sloppier than usual.

3 My fingertips tingled. I looked at my hands as if they were someone else's, then shook them from side to side. I got up and took a break, but the tingling continued.

In graf 4, where he first mentions the illness that was overtaking him, Miller uses a good analogy to describe its effects ("my body was like a building"), eliminating the need for any lengthy medical explanation.

4 I hadn't a clue that I was in danger, that a disease called Guillain-Barre Syndrome had begun to devastate my nervous system, stripping away the "myelin sheath" around the nerves. My body was like a building infested with a dangerous pest that attacked the electrical system, eating the insulation off the wiring and causing it to short out. What I was feeling in my fingertips was like the flickering of a few lights. Soon most of the building would be dark.

5 But on that day at the office I was more puzzled than worried. I'd worked on my wife's station wagon at home the previous day and had then written a long story. Maybe I'd just overdone it with my hands. I'd had the flu a couple weeks earlier, and neither my wife, Terri, nor I had been getting much sleep, mostly thanks to the two other people in our house, 4-month-old and 2-year-old daughters. I decided to go home and rest.

Graf 6 is an effective one sentence paragraph

6 That night my toes tingled, too.

He continues the narrative in grafs 7, 8, and 9 . . .

7 I woke up the next morning and discovered that it was hard to walk. As stupid as it seems in retrospect, instead of heading for the emergency room, I called and made an appointment to see a doctor that afternoon. I told the receptionist that it wasn't terribly urgent.

8 By the time I shuffled into the young internist's examining room, my face felt like it feels when the dentist uses a lot of novocaine. After a brief examination, the doctor made a tentative diagnosis and went to call a neurologist. I asked someone to get Terri, and she came in with the kids.

9 Erin, our older daughter, squirmed on my lap as the doctor returned. I needed to go to the hospital right away, he said. The neurologist would meet us there. A nurse brought a wheelchair, Terri pulled the car around and we loaded up and made the short drive to the hospital. Terri helped me into another wheelchair, then pushed me up to the reception desk so I could do the paperwork while she parked the car and returned with the kids, Erin and Maddy.

. . . discovering in graf 10 that he can't hold a pen, something any reader can sympathize with in that it is such an easy, everyday task.

10 The woman at the desk asked for my insurance card, but I couldn't pinch it hard enough to get it out of my wallet. Then she needed my signature on a form. Twice she handed me a pen, twice it slipped through my fingers and onto the floor. I was embarrassed and confused.

11 Soon I was in a bed upstairs, where the neurologist pricked my skin with pins and tested my reflexes. For a while my feet shot out when she thumped below my knees with her little rubber hammer, but soon that reflex was gone and the legs just hung there. My face was increasingly numb. The doctor stuck a needle into my back to get some spinal fluid for testing. I felt weak. My mother and stepfather and my in-laws arrived from Salem. It was hard to lift my legs. Doctors and nurses talked of moving me to intensive care.

In graf 12, the real horror of what was enveloping him takes hold and he describes it well: "The thin layer of nonchalance" was cracking and "a wave of terror rolled over me." He felt "like I was being removed from my life."

12 I needed a lot of help to get from the bed to the gurney, and then I was wheeled out of the room toward the ICU. Terri kissed me, then my mother bent down to do the same, trying to smile through the mask of tension on her face. The thin layer of nonchalance that held back my fear began to crack, then it shattered and a wave of terror rolled over me. As the gurney started down the hall and I saw the light fixtures going by above me, there was a clear, desperate sensation of being taken away from my wife, my children, the people who loved me. It felt like I was being removed from my life. Tears in my eyes, I asked Mom to help Terri with the kids.

The reporter in him returns as he begins to describe the ICU in graf 13.

13 Even in the high-tech world of a modern hospital, the ICU was startlingly full of wires, tubes, hoses, electronic gadgets and strange-looking machines with digital readouts. The noise was constant: Beeps of various tones and duration, a constant whine from the pump which circulated air through a special Gore-tex mattress on my bed, the odd hiss-click sound of the respirator. In the few times I have returned to say hello to the nurses who took care of me, I have been struck by how out of place the patients look in their rooms. Like ships in drydock for repairs, being tended quite carefully and expertly, they are clearly out of their element.

14 Any normal sense of time recedes in such a place, and the next week or so seems like one very long day in my memory. I had been injured before, and during my student days had even edited the *Barometer* for a while from a bed in the OSU infirmary, after a knee operation led to blood poisoning. But nothing in my experience compared to this. Within 36 hours of when I first felt my fingers tingling at work, Guillain-Barre turned me into a quadriplegic who needed mechanical help to breathe. A breathing tube was placed in my mouth. Intravenous lines were jabbed into my left arm and right upper chest. Wires for a heart monitor were glued to my skin. A tube was inserted to carry away urine.

In graf 15, Miller pauses in the narrative to describe the disease and its background.

15 Guillain-Barre, also called GBS or "French polio," strikes only about 15 people in a million each year. Doctors aren't sure of its cause, but they know it's not hereditary and they know it often occurs after a bout with the flu. In 15 years of newspaper work I had written and read a lot of stories about people with weird diseases, but all I knew of Guillain-Barre was that I had heard the words somewhere.

16 Soon my own neurologist, a friend who had treated me for minor problems before, was called in and took over my case. He and other doctors told me and my family that there was little they could do to halt my immune system's attack on my nervous system, although they did order a blood-cleansing process that sometimes slows the haywire immune response. They said that once the attack subsided, my body would probably begin the long process of healing itself.

Miller uses graf 17 to personalize his problem. Rather than talk about

17 In the early days in the ICU, I listened to the doctors for any nuance, any hint of my fate. Most people with Guillain-Barre eventually

regaining the use of his legs and arms, for example, he talks about walking and holding his children and putting his arms around his wife. This tells readers something about the author and what is important to him.

healed most of the way back to normal, the doctors said, but it took months and often years. A few people, they conceded, did not heal at all, and many healed mostly but were left with what the doctors called "deficits." Odds were great, they said, that I would someday walk again, hold my children, put my arms around my wife. But first the disease had to run its course, and I would have to be patient, they said.

18 Usually when doctors had told me to be patient, it was because I wanted a cast off my leg a week too early, or because a poison oak rash was slow to clear up. But there in the ICU, even while I got worse, they told me not to worry, I would probably be fine, in a year or so. Slowly it dawned on me that they were saying they were pretty sure they could keep me alive while the disease ran its course, but they were powerless over the disease itself. I trusted my neurologist and knew him to be competent, and I expected him to escalate the medical battle until he defeated my illness. But he was telling me it was the disease that was in control. I despaired.

In graf 19 Miller describes how his health continued to deteriorate and he tells readers what that meant: he could breathe only with a plastic tube in his neck.

19 The paralysis worsened until I could only move my head from side to side. I couldn't even keep my eyes closed, so they were taped shut when I slept. When it became obvious I would need the respirator for a while, a doctor cut a small hole in my neck and inserted a "trache," a small plastic tube. That meant the air going into and out of my lungs bypassed my vocal chords, so I could no longer speak.

20 It was one thing to have a breathing tube in my mouth or nose, but now my body had been altered so I breathed through a hole just below my adam's apple. It seemed like a permanent arrangement, and my terror mounted.

In graf 21, Miller talks about his problems in communicating—a tough one for a reporter used to making his living at doing just that.

21 Communication took extraordinary effort because I couldn't move except to turn my head, I couldn't speak and my face was paralyzed. One day a small sliver of paper settled near my nose as a nurse ripped open a sterile dressing. I spent the next four hours trying to get someone to understand that it was driving me nuts.

22 Sometimes I kept trying to make myself understood until someone got the message. Other times I gave up and thrashed my head from side to side, crying in frustration. Almost always my wife knew what I was saying, which reinforced my sense that we were bonded by much more than a piece of paper and a couple of rings. I saw her as my protector, and I wanted her near me constantly. Many of the nurses and therapists could understand me too, and some of the doctors, although they often seemed too busy to try.

23 Most patients are in the ICU for a few days at the most. The stays are so short that the hospital bills ICU time by the hour, not the day. I lived in the unit for more than three months, and was in the hospital for twice that long, including a brief stay in a nursing home. The six months of extreme measure taken to keep me alive and help me recover cost an average of about $2,700 a day. I was profoundly grateful for decent medical insurance, for high quality care, and for a mostly dedicated, mostly compassionate legion of people to deliver that care.

In graf 24, he discusses in vivid language how he felt as he began to recover: from "highly exaggerated sensations of pain in his brain" to "repeated episodes of psychotic terror."

24 For the first few months of my illness, despite the paralysis, my damaged nerves sent constant, highly exaggerated sensations of pain into my brain. As happens with many people who are kept alive by a respirator for week after week, I had repeated episodes of psychotic terror that I was suffocating. Drugs helped a little.

25 My paralysis often caused me to be disoriented. I would be absolutely positive that my body had levitated above the bed and was about to float down to the floor, or I would be sure one of the nurses had set a heavy object on my feet. Most of the time when I wasn't asleep or overcome by pain, I was trying to figure which of my perceptions could be trusted. I daydreamed, and sometimes thought of all the crazy, risky things I had done, especially in my college days, with nary a scratch.

26 Some of the doctors, nurses and therapists ignored my pain and distress, but many bravely faced it with me. I dreaded the ones who pretended nothing unusual was happening, but I learned the schedules of the others, and I craved the times when they would be on duty.

In graf 27 Miller notes in painful-to-read details about how one doctor treated him: he jammed a breathing tube through his nose until he caused "a starburst of pain and an audible crunching sound."

27 One of the doctors who had an almost comical difficulty dealing with reality once had to get a breathing tube through my nose and down into my airway. He encountered resistance somewhere up there between my eyes, and with no more warning than a mechanic gives a bolt that won't turn, he forced the tube through whatever was in the way. There was a starburst of pain and an audible crunching sound that made other doctors and nurses wince. But the mechanic remained impassive, and then he finally spoke to me. Instead of acknowledging that he had just done a necessary but astoundingly painful thing to my body, he noted that the ceiling lights were awfully bright. He apologized for the glare.

In graf 28 Miller, though paralyzed, is still able to expect some control over his situation by vowing that this particular doctor "will never get near me or anyone I care about again."

28 I am sure he is not a bad man, and he did get the tube where it needed to go, but he will never get near me or anyone I care about again.

29 What I wanted most from the people in the hospital was connection to reality. I wanted them to say, "You must be scared," and "I know this hurts." I wanted them to look at the pictures and cards my wife had put up around the room, to see that I was not a thing to be tended, but a husband and a father, and that relatives and friends, including several OSU classmates, cared enough to send me good wishes or prayers.

30 As the experience dragged on, I went through dangerous bouts of pneumonia and eventually developed a massive blood clot in my leg, which threatened to move into my lungs and kill me. I wondered if ever again I would pick up my children, make love to my wife, cast a fly to a rising trout. Occasionally, I heard of a death in a nearby room, or I saw a body covered in a blanket being wheeled into an elevator. In the most morbid of moments I tried to imagine what my daughters would know of me if I died and they were left with only snapshots, newspaper clippings and their mother's memories.

31 I was told to concentrate on what I wanted to do when I recovered, and I thought of standing atop a short cliff near a beach cabin where we stay, watching the waves while Terri and the girls played in the sand.

32 Tears, something I probably hadn't shed enough of before I got sick, were among my only means of expression. I cried out of pain, out of frustration, out of joy, out of gratitude. Sometimes the nurses and therapists who had become my friends cried with me. But they also joked with me and told me about their children and the houses they were trying to buy and how their love lives were a mess. Some of them broke rules to give my wife and me private time.

In grafs 33 to 36, he chillingly details how a separated respirator hose almost cost him his life.

33 In at least one case, I am pretty sure a nurse's friendship saved my life. Someone who had fiddled around with my respirator tubing had repeatedly triggered the machine's alarm, and had turned it down or off and then forgotten to reset it. A little later, the respirator hose suddenly separated from my trache tube and flopped onto the floor, leaving me with no air.

34 I couldn't wave my arms or make a sound, and my call pad, which I normally activated by hitting with my cheek, had slipped out of reach. Within about 30 seconds, I understood that unless someone happened to come into the room, I was going to pass out and maybe die.

35 One of the nurses who took care of me was a woman who was known among her peers for being highly proficient but almost too compassionate, sometimes getting to know her patients so well that she became emotionally involved. She had done so in my case, befriending my family, writing me a poem, buying me a poster of the beach when she learned that I visualized the surf to help calm myself.

36 She wasn't assigned to me that shift, and the nurse who was assigned to me was in another room with a patient. But the nurse who had let herself become my friend just happened to walk by my room, and she just happened to poke her head around the doorjamb to say hello, and she saw the blue tube dangling to the floor. She hooked me back up and sounded the alarm.

In grafs 37 to 40, he talks about his "most intimate relationship"—that with his respirator. He treats that piece of equipment like a person, an entity that saved his life.

37 Aside from the people who experienced the illness with me, my most intimate relationship in the hospital was with the respirator. The machine sat there beside the bed, just off my right shoulder, keeping me alive through the corrugated tube that snaked over to the hole in my throat. Sometimes at night I would awake to the sound of someone breathing heavily, right beside me. But it wasn't a new roommate—there were no roommates in the ICU. It was the respirator, wheezing and sighing as it pumped air into and out of my lungs.

38 The respirator, a big blue box with a small keyboard, gave me life but it also took away my body. Everything below the tube in my neck belonged to the machine, it seemed. The respirator, not me, controlled how often and how deeply I inhaled. When I felt like coughing, no sound came from me but an alarm sounded on the machine. When a doctor wanted me to take a deep breath to try to clear my lungs, he nodded to a respiratory therapist, who pressed a button on the respirator. I hated that machine for being so important. But without it my wife and daughters would be coping with the first anniversary of my death.

39 My breathing problems were the biggest threat to my life, and most of my care was aimed at getting me ready to breathe on my own if the paralysis ever left the muscles in my chest and abdomen. For about 10 weeks it appeared that that might not happen, even while other muscles came back to life, and I began to move my arms and legs. The doctors grew increasingly frustrated. One afternoon one of them checked me over, told me I was doing great and then went out and slumped onto a stool at the nurses' station. I saw him shake his head, and I clearly heard him say to a nurse, "I don't know if we're ever going to get this guy off the respirator."

40 Only days afterward there was a flicker of nerve activity in the muscles of my chest, and the doctors began talking about weaning me off the machine. I had assumed all along that if I survived to that point, breathing again would be easy. I was wrong.

41 It turns out that as natural and subconscious as healthy breathing is, it is quite easy for the body to "forget" how to do it. The first time the respiratory therapist turned the machine to a neutral setting that would let me breathe on my own, I was stunned to discover that nothing happened. I had to consciously will the muscles in my chest and abdomen to contract and release, contract and release. If I didn't, my body received no oxygen.

By graf 42, Miller is talking about his recovery and what it meant: learning how to eat, to write, and to remember to breathe.

42 Later I would discover that I had to relearn other basics, such as feeding myself and writing my name, but breathing on my own was the most important goal of my recovery. The doctors told me to inhale no more often than once every five seconds. For an hour or more at a time, I would lie there in bed, watching the second hand on a big wall clock as I willed myself to take breath after breath. It was quite mind-numbing, but I was able to do it for longer and longer periods until finally I passed the big test, which was to make it through the night.

In graf 43, he talks about the biggest event in his long road to recovery up to that point: a doctor decides to pull out the trache tube ("I had my voice back.") Even though it is early morning, he calls his wife with the good news.

43 Early that morning, the pulmonary specialist, after some lobbying from the respiratory therapist and my nurse, decided to pull the trache out. Soon the plastic tube was gone, a bandage in its place, and I had my voice back. I could neither hold nor dial the phone, but the nurse did it for me and then held the receiver to my ear while she wiped the tears from her eyes.

44 "Hello?" answered my wife's sleepy voice.

45 "Hi," I said in a weakened, slightly squeaky version of a sound we'd both wanted to hear for three months. "It's me."

He moves on to a discussion of his physical therapy and several setbacks he suffered along the way in grafs 46 and 47.

46 The next day, Dec. 14, I was out of the ICU and into a regular room, which I soon left for the hospital's rehabilitation unit. There I celebrated an alternately joyful and sorrowful Christmas with my family. Soon afterward my left leg began to swell, and an ultrasound revealed the huge blood clot. It threatened to break loose and cause a life-threatening pulmonary embolism, but that was dealt with when doctors inserted a small metal filter in the big vein below my lungs. The setback slowed my recovery enough that I spent much of January and February in a nursing home, to save the insurance company money while I got strong enough for rehabilitation.

47 The people in the nursing home took fine care of me in some of the most difficult working conditions I've seen. There, I was no longer confronted with the reality of dying young but with the equally sad reality of living long and being alone.

In graf 48 comes another big event: he learns to walk again.

48 It was in the nursing home's small, low-tech physical therapy room that I stood up for the first time. No one knew if my weakened legs would bear my weight when I pulled myself out of the wheelchair between parallel bars, and no one was more surprised than I that I could stand, bearing most of my weight on my arms. Within a minute or so I was exhausted and had to sit, but I was thrilled enough to call friends and family to report the news. The next day I was back in the hospital in rehab, where a talented team of doctors, nurses and a team of therapists focused on getting me ready to go home.

Miller uses a wonderful analogy in graf 49, likening his time in rehab to being in college ("it cost a lot of money, . . . limited time . . . [and needing it] to be ready for real life and my job").

49 Being in rehab was a little like being in college. It cost a lot of money, there was a limited time to get it done, and when it was done, I needed to be ready for real life and my job. In the physical therapy gym, where the therapists bent, twisted and cajoled me into getting stronger and more flexible, there was a desk with a computer and keyboard available to patients. During most of the breaks between sessions I would wheel myself over there and bang away on the keys, getting a little more accurate each day, slowly proving to myself that I'd be able to return to reporting.

In graf 50, he tells the amusing story of returning to work to discover the story he had been working on nine months before still in his computer and "seriously past deadline."

50 I left the rehab unit for home on March 10. Slowly, as my body repaired itself, I moved from wheelchair to walker to crutches to walking on my own. On July 7, I went back to work, opened my file area in *The Register-Guard* computer and discovered that the story I was writing on the day my fingers went numb was still there, half-finished and seriously past deadline.

In graf 51, Miller begins to wind things up. The use of "today" lets readers know where they are. He talks about how he feels, what he can now do physically, and how it felt to be in a wheelchair, especially upon returning to his college campus (grafs 52-54).

51 Today, my feet are still a little numb and partially paralyzed, and I have a slight tremor in my hands. I can barely get a size 18 fly onto a 6X tippet, which is something I used to do in near darkness, standing in the middle of a river. I walk OK but not too far, I can barely outrun 1-year-old Maddy, and 3-year-old Erin can quite literally run circles around me. If I ever recover physically enough to forget my illness, there's a permanent oval scar on my neck to remind me of it when I shave. Erin calls it my "throat owie."

52 During the time between my return home and my return to work, my family and I made increasingly ambitious trips to test my strength and provide a change of scenery. One of those trips was up the highway to Corvallis, to visit the campus. Spring term was winding down, and students were studying for finals in the MU as I wheeled myself down the big hallway beneath the flags, Erin on my lap, Terri beside me with Maddy in a backpack.

53 The building, the entire campus seemed much larger and more daunting from the seat of a wheelchair, and I found myself marveling at how difficult it would have been to negotiate the campus in a wheelchair. But I also felt the same old sense of safe familiarity I always felt on the OSU campus. It's one of the things about OSU that people often make fun of, especially people from the town where I live now.

54 But sitting here in my wheelchair, watching comfortable young people pore over texts with their feet propped on the sills of the MU Lounge's massive windows, I found myself thinking that maybe a bit of safe familiarity isn't so bad, considering the other things that can come along in life.

The real ending to the article (grafs 55 to 57) takes place on the Oregon coast, the very scene he had envisioned during the depths of his illness. As he watches his wife and

55 A few weeks after the visit to campus, we spent a weekend at a beach cabin near a small cliff above the sand. We'd stayed there only a few weeks before I got sick, and it was the beach I'd imagined seeing when I was in the ICU and needed to boost myself out of depressions.

56 I couldn't get down the uneven rock stairs

daughters play on the beach, he takes a deep breath and waves to them—two very simple actions, yet both big accomplishments after what he has been through.

from the cliff to the sand, but Terri and the kids could. As I stood there watching, the girls' voices sailed up and over me on gusts of wind. "This is real," I thought. "This is my life."

57 I took a deep breath, the kind you take when you've cried enough times about something. My wife smiled and waved. I smiled and waved back.

After the article appeared in "Oregon Life," the Sunday magazine of *The Register-Guard* in Eugene, Miller got 60 letters in the first few weeks. Most were from admirers and fellow sufferers. One came from a staff member at Walter Reed Army Hospital in Washington, DC who suggested that the article be used in a training manual for respiratory therapists.

Participation in an Event

The power of observation and humor came through in this piece by Susan Hauser. She adopts a conversational style which immediately draws readers in.

Article #2

JUDGE NOT LEST YE BE JUDGED

—by Susan G. Hauser

Hauser sets the jaunty and slightly irreverent tone she uses in many of her articles for the Leisure and Arts page of *The Wall Street Journal* in the first sentence. Her admission that she had "guilt" over her role in a beauty contest entices readers.

1 Okay, so I didn't burn my bra in the '70s. Maybe I should have. It would help assuage my guilt over the role I played in the 1991 Miss Oregon USA contest.

She quickly answers questions raised in readers' minds by explaining that she was a judge of that contest.

2 I was a judge. I was one of four women and three men who pored over every detail of 21 nubile young bodies so we could determine which of the contestants would best represent the people of Oregon.

She begins to poke fun at the whole idea by noting that contestants could be "talent-free."

3 Unlike aspirants to the Miss America title, contestants for Miss USA and Miss University are allowed to be talent-free.

But, she quotes a pageant official who says that the young women need to be good "spokespersons."

4 "But," explained Donna Lee, coordinator for the Miss Oregon USA event, tapping her head with her finger, "they have to have what it takes up here to be a spokesperson."

In grafs 5 to 10, she gives a very funny account of her interviews with contestants. For example, she notes that they all chose similar personality traits.

5 Our opportunity to hear the prospective spokesperson speak and to gauge the contents of her head came during the first segment of the judging, the personal interview.

6 We were allotted five minutes per contestant, with about a 30-second breather in between. We judges sat at tables arranged in a circle, and each girl moved from table to table, from judge to judge, to dazzle yet another with her wit and charm.

7 To aid the judges in their evaluations, the girls carried fact sheets that listed three personality traits. For the first two traits, most said compassionate and caring. The third trait was usually a toss-up between intelligent and funny.

8 I asked one of the funny contestants what was so funny and she snarled, "Whadya mean?" Okay, so maybe she should have checked intelligent. Or left the third trait blank.

With tongue in cheek, she goes on to explain that many of the young women were pursuing law degrees.

9 For their career goals, a huge proportion of the girls claimed to be pursuing law degrees, usually in conjunction with another discipline, for example, law and psychology or law and aerobics.

She thinks, however, that only one girl was honest: she wanted to be an eagle "and fly all over this great land of ours."

10 After hearing such lofty goals, I admired all the more the 1990 Miss USA contestant who stated, "I want to be an eagle and fly all over this great land of ours." At least she was honest.

In graf 11, she notes that after spending *five minutes* on their personalities, the judges would spend *two days* examining their figures, a subtle poke at the whole concept of beauty pageants.

11 The day after the personal interview marathon, the real pageant began. Now that we had devoted five minutes of our attentions to their personalities, we would spend the next two days examining their figures in various states of dress and undress.

In grafs 12 to 15, she recalls the judging process, noting funny things she observed along the way. Notice her

12 One after another, the girls were trotted out, first wearing evening gowns and high heels, then wearing swimsuits and high heels. Naturally, you'd never see a woman in high

phrasing, "the girls were trotted out," a comparison, perhaps, to a horse auction.

heels at the beach—she'd get stuck in the sand—but the ability to walk in high heels without wobbling is another mark of a good spokesperson.

13 We were required to rate the girls' appearances on a scale of 1 to 10, just as we had judged their five-minute displays of personality. The other judges, most of whom had done this sort of thing before, knew immediately that I was a neophyte when I asked what the criteria were for judging the girls' sashays down the runway.

14 I'm a quick study. It didn't take me long to figure out we were rating the contestants on—pardon the unladylike expression—T&A.

15 I'm ashamed to admit I really got into it. My eyes roamed from head to toe of every contestant as I mused, "Is this one worth a 10? Naaah. A little too fleshy there, sorry. And sweetie, you could use a bit more upstairs. But get a load of those! Whew! They get a 10 but the caboose gets a 3 . . ."

In grafs 16 and 17 she notes the reaction of the other judges to the young women and how the preoccupation with physical attributes transformed the judges.

16 After the first night of judging I noticed a transformation in the judges. The three men, who looked very distinguished in their tuxedos, began acting like fifth-graders. When we were out of the public view, they'd jab each other with their elbows and giggle.

17 As for the women, we began checking each other out. I suddenly realized that the dress I'd worn on the first night of the pageant tended to hide my, ahem, charms. I was not going to let my fellow judges be the only standouts.

Her work as a judge caused even Hauser herself to change the way she looked (grafs 18, 19, 20).

18 Before the evening of the pageant's grand finale, I kicked my Birkenstocks in the closet and dug out a pair of high heels. It was not too long ago that I considered these things instruments of torture, Now I was trying them on and thinking, "Gee, these would look great with my Speedo."

19 I rummaged through my underwear drawer and found a garment I used to be ashamed to possess—my push-up bra. Then I poured myself into a dress that exposed a great deal of my chest and thighs.

20 When I arrived at the pageant that evening, I saw that the other female judges had done the same thing. As for the men judges, they had become downright giddy. The sexuality among us was so thick you could cut it with a stiletto heel.

In graf 21 she tells us who won—and why.

21 Then we got down to work, narrowing the field of 21 contestants to 10 semifinalists, and then naming the winner. The new Miss Oregon USA, Olga Calderon, is beautiful and will be a terrific spokesperson. Besides that, she's got a great body.

In grafs 22 to 26, Hauser returns to the guilt theme she established in the first paragraph, in a clever way. She tries to feel better by going to a lecture by Gloria Steinem.

22 Once the pageant was over, I felt guilty about my wanton display, as well as the pleasure I derived from rating the physical attributes of my fellow females. To salve my conscience, I bought a ticket to hear Gloria Steinem when she spoke in Portland recently.

23 From where I sat in the back of the cavernous hall I could hardly see her. But her words about self-respect and sisterhood stirred my soul. There was hope for me. I would rise like a phoenix from my shame.

After the speech, she works her way to the front, examines the feminist leader closely . . .

24 After the standing ovation, I worked my way closer to the podium so I could see the legendary feminist. Finally, I stood just a few feet from her side.

25 Ms. Steinem wore a miniskirt that wouldn't quit. Her abdomen was flat, her hips nicely rounded, her butt firm and her figure well-proportioned. Her long, shapely legs looked like they were on a moon launch.

. . . and gives her a numerical ranking.

26 I gave her a 10.

Conjuring up a Subject

The topics of such articles are seemingly limitless. With the right combination of imagination and humor, a skilled writer can create an article from a conversation, as Wendell Smith did in the following piece from *The Saturday Evening Post*.

Article #3

Smith uses the structure of a conversation with his wife while watching the classic film "Casablanca" on television.

In graf 2, he makes the point that he will expound upon in the remainder of the piece: whether the use of "less" in one sentence uttered by a character is correct.

In grafs 3 to 15, he continues to argue the point with his wife, giving examples of why the word usage is wrong.

SCRUPLES IN THE FOG: CLEARING THE AIR ONCE AND FOR ALL ABOUT A CLASSIC ERROR OF GRAMMAR

—by Wen Smith

1 We were watching the colorized version of "Casablanca" on Ted Turner's network, taping it on the VCR. Color didn't affect the dialogue, and one of my pet peeves of usage was still there.

2 It came, as it always does, near Bogart's moment of decision when Claude Rains says to him, "Apparently you are the only one in Casablanca who has even less scruples than I."

3 "I don't see anything wrong with it," my wife said when I mentioned the mistake.

4 "Nobody can have less scruples," I said. "The word less just doesn't go with things you can count, like scruples."

5 "How about 'less calories'?"

6 "Never," I said, "It has to be 'fewer calories, fewer scruples.' Fewer goes with things you can count."

7 "Who counts scruples?" she said.

8 "Whether you count them or not, they're countable things. But less goes only with stuff you can't count, like truth."

9 "I think there are many truths," my wife said. She has a way of cutting to the heart of things, bypassing details. I tried to make my point another way.

10 "Many truths, yes, but not many truth. It's like cash." She said nothing, but I could hear her thinking and knew she was thinking you can count cash.

11 "No, you don't count cash. You count nickels and dimes and quarters. You never see one cash or two cashes."

12 "Not up close," she said.

13 "That's why you can't count it. You can have less cash, but not fewer cash."

14 "Not quite true," she said. "I couldn't have less." She is always talking about reality when I'm talking about words.

15 "There's no such thing as a number of cash," I said. "Like all uncountable things,.cash comes in amounts but not in numbers."

In graf 16, he begins his closing, by noting that the film is ending. Then, he gets into another exchange with his wife over something a character said.

16 "Casablanca" moved towards its finale. Bogart was saying to Bergman that their troubles didn't amount to a hill of beans in this crazy world.

Grafs 17 to 25 continue the back and forth.

17 "Is a hill of beans an amount of beans or a number of them?" my wife asked. I think she knew the answer, but she was testing me. She had heard somebody in the family say that I didn't know beans.

18 "It's a number," I said. "Fewer beans, not less. Beans are like scruples."

19 "What happened to the fog?" she asked. "In the black-and-white version there's lots of fog." It was true. In color, the fog in the final scene didn't show up well. The atmosphere was no longer quite right.

20 "Here's looking at you, kid," my wife said along with Bogey. But without the fog, the line had lost some of its impact. Why did Ted Turner have to go and clear everything up?

21 "There's fewer fog in color," she said, testing me again. She knows better than to say "fewer fog." You can't count fog.

22 "Less fog," I said, "not fewer."

23 "Fog or not, Ingrid is going to board that plane and leave Bogey behind. If he had less scruples, he'd beg her to stay."

24 "Fewer scruples," I said.

25 "Well, in color his scruples seem less," she said.

In graf 26 he subtly works in a line from the movie's hit song, "As Time Goes By": "the fundamental things apply." He clinches the proper usage by example: *less* fog, *fewer* moments.

26 Like the fog, the scruples did seem less, as well as fewer, in color. Color smooths the edges. In black and white, the fundamental things apply. When it was over, we agreed that "Casablanca" in color, even with less fog, has no less appeal than it has in classic black and white, and no fewer moments to remember.

He ends the simple, but clever essay by using the famous "play it again" line from the film.

27 "Play it again," she said. And we did.

9

Writing about Places

o novelist and travel book writer Paul Theroux, much of what is written about places and traveling to them is second rate:

> The literature of travel has become measly; the standard opening, that farcical nose-against-the-porthole view from the plane's tilted fuselage. The joke opening, that straining for effect, is now so familiar it is nearly impossible to parody. How does it go? "Below us lay the tropical green, the flooded plane, the patchwork quilt of farms, and as we emerged from the cloud I could see dirt roads threading their way into the hills. . . ."
>
> I have never found this sort of guesswork very convincing. When I am landing in a plane, my heart is in my mouth; I wonder—doesn't everyone?—if we are going to crash. . . .
>
> Meanwhile, what of the journey itself? Perhaps there is nothing to say. There is not much to say about most airplane journeys. Anything remarkable must be disastrous, so you define a good flight by negatives: you didn't get hijacked, you didn't crash, you didn't throw up, you weren't late, you weren't nauseated by the food. So you are grateful. . . .
>
> . . What interests me is the waking in the morning, the progress from the familiar to the slightly odd, to the rather strange, to the totally foreign, and finally to the outlandish. The journey, not the arrival, matters; the voyage, not the landing. . . .
>
> (Theroux, 1979)

Theroux made his mark as a writer of travel books with his 1975 best seller *The Great Railway Bazaar*, an account of his journey by train from London to Tokyo and back again. But he had already been writing travel articles for magazines for 10 years when that book was published. He had spent that time, in his words, "writing with both hands." Namely, he used the fees for his travel pieces to finance his fiction writing.

What set Theroux apart from most travel writers of the time was his vivid imagery and crankiness. His were not the words that read as if they were written by the publicity department of a railway or a hotel or a ministry of tourism. As "Stranger on a Train: The Pleasures of Railways" reveals later in this chapter, his are words that tell readers precisely what happens to him from the moment he leaves home. The piece, half of which was published in *The Observer* in London in 1976, the other half given as a 1981 lecture (and not reprinted here), illustrates how Paul Theroux's style changed travel writing into a kind of travel literature.

Background to Travel Writing

Before Paul Theroux, most travel pieces were a cross between advertising and publicity. Although Sunday travel sections and a few travel magazines had existed for years, most contained articles that portrayed all trips as idyllic journeys where no one lost luggage, stayed in a dirty room, or gagged on bad food.

Travel sections became popular after World War II when more and more people began to have the money to go overseas for pleasure. They were curious about exotic places and the means of conveyance to get them there. People also began to travel extensively in the United States.

Articles were usually semi-breathless, first person accounts written in a fairly pedestrian way. One aim was to create interest and excitement and give readers the feel of foreign lands. The other was to sell advertisements to hotels, resorts, airlines, travel agencies, and government tourist departments.

The trend was healthy in one important respect: it got Americans—up to then largely insular and parochial—to explore the world. But the approach was flawed in another respect: it soon became apparent that travel sections were so dependent on advertisers and travel writers so beholden to the sponsors of their free trips that neither could be objective and perform the necessary service required of good travel writing. In short, travel writers soon had the reputation of being little better than prostitutes, selling their skills to the highest bidder.

In the 1980s, this tendency in travel writing began to change. The venerable travel section of the Sunday *New York Times* had never been as bad as similar sections in lesser papers, but it started paying more attention to who paid the expenses of the travel writers submitting material. "The *Times* pays all expenses," says Susan Hauser, a Portland, Oregon free-lance writer who has just started writing for the travel section. "You cannot even go on a press junket if you pay your own expenses."

The other publication breaking new ground was *Conde Nast Traveler*, a monthly magazine published by the same company that owns *Vanity Fair* and *Vogue*. In a magazine niche where only good news and upbeat stories predominated, articles in *Traveler* began in the mid-1980s to tell a few of the problems encountered when going overseas. Its tone was irreverent, its content at times bordering on exposé. Readers loved what they found in its pages and advertisers soon followed. As a result, *Traveler* (1991 circulation 700,000) thrived.

Maintaining Ethical Standards

The taint of some travel writing in the past creates a dilemma for free-lance writers wanting to research and write about places. Travel articles constitute a good source of free-lance income. They are fairly easy to do, fun to write, and are almost like getting a paid vacation. The problem comes in the fact that few Sunday newspaper travel sections—the main market for free-lance travel articles—can afford to pay all the expenses for writers as they gather their material.

Although professional journalism organizations regularly decry the slippage of ethical standards at their professional meetings, they do not put such objections in print, at least as specifically applied to travel writers. The Code of Ethics of the Society of Professional Journalists covers the subject broadly in Part III, Ethics:

> 1. Gifts, favors, free travel, special treatment or privileges can compromise the integrity of journalists and their employees. Nothing of value should be accepted.

The American Society of Journalists and Authors Code of Ethics and Fair Practices does not mention the subject at all.

How can you avoid the inevitable ethical concerns that your travel article was bought and paid for by whatever entity (hotel, airline, city or state tourist bureau) you are writing about and whose "hospitality" you have accepted?

- *Pay your own expenses.* This is the cleanest and safest way to avoid problems with objectivity. If you sell your article later, you can declare the expenses on your taxes as a business expense.

- *Plan a trip so that you do more than one story while away.* In this way you can expect multiple fees (and possibly expenses) from several publications. You might do several travel articles from the trip or a travel article and an article on another subject while you are in the same vicinity.
- *Investigate the possibilities of doing a travel article about an area after you have been assigned to go there to do a non-travel piece.* In this way, your expenses are already being paid and you can research the other piece while you are in the area. The original magazine will probably not object as long as you are not doing the travel piece for a competitor.
- *Work for a publication that has no problem with providing free services.* Oregon free-lancer Rob Phillips writes regularly for several in-flight airline magazines and always gets free airfare to his destinations. Although he seldom does travel articles for these magazines, he could do so while gathering information for the profiles and business articles he normally researches and writes.
- *Accept the payment of all expenses as a last resort.* You should do this only if the publication you are writing for agrees that you can do so. Then, make it clear to whomever is paying the bills that you plan to write an objective story. Under no circumstances should you agree to show copy to your "sponsor."
- *Avoid junkets,* those all-expenses-paid boondoggles where no story will result and you will emerge as tainted. Such trips are usually blatant in their goal to put a whole group of writers in debt to the sponsoring organization or company. If the destination has good story possibilities, it is better to go back later on your own.
- *Be sure to check the written code of ethics* or accepted practices of all publications you work for regarding free trips or junkets before you embark on any course of action.

Writing the Travel Article

In a typical travel article, your goal is fairly simple: you go on a trip and report what happened to you. Your audience are people who are planning trips and looking for destinations. Of all the kinds of articles covered in this book, the travel article is the most consumer-oriented. The ideal travel article will help readers avoid problems you encountered. Most Americans are finicky travelers: they want everything to be as comfortable and clean as it is at home. The facts you give them will tell would-be travelers the extent to which they will have to rough it.

Box 9.1 Suggested Markets

Travel articles can be submitted to a number of varied markets:

- Sunday newspaper travel sections
- *Travel & Leisure*
- *VISTA/USA*
- *Conde Nast Traveler*
- Airline in-flight magazines

Susan Hauser, who writes travel articles for the Sunday *New York Times*, has a fairly straightforward routine in preparing her pieces: "I include factual information and my own feelings and experiences. You need to include a bit of yourself. Tell readers what you experienced, including problems."

The question of using first, second, or third person arises more in travel writing than in other kinds of magazine writing. After all, you, the writer, have experienced certain things on your trip and your main aim is to convey the results to your readers. It is natural to slip into first person—and perfectly acceptable to most travel editors. Second person is another approach to try and can involve the reader. As with all other kinds of writing, however, third person is best. Just state the facts and keep yourself out. The choice is up to the writer, of course. Whichever approach you choose, be consistent. Don't start out in third person and later switch to first or second person.

All travel articles need a strong lead stating the main premise of the article. In the articles reprinted later in this chapter, the writers told their readers very directly what they were likely to read in the paragraphs to come. In article #1, the lead does just that ["Freeport (with L.L. Bean) and Kittery—designer-outlet meccas both—put Maine on the shopping map"]. Article #2 has a wittier tone ["There are two sorts of people who like trains, and I am neither. The first is the railway buff, for whom trains are toys . . ."]

From the lead, the travel article progresses to acquaint the reader with the locale. Good transitions are necessary to take readers from spot to spot, subject to subject. As you go, you cite your observations and findings and quote the people you have met (or have called later to gain more information). One unique aspect of travel writing is that every time you mention a store or a museum or another tourist attraction, you need to give the address, phone number, and hours of operation. This will help readers who plan to visit the places described in your article.

Travel articles about cities or parks or museums or other specific destinations should include precise instructions on how to get there. The *Times* always has a boxed sidebar to accompany the article headlined "If You Go." The sidebar may tell you to "take Exit 50 off the Interstate and drive five miles before turning left," etc. This is yet another example of providing valuable consumer information.

The endings of travel articles vary widely, as in other kinds of writing. Some just end when the journey does. Others tie into the beginning in the classical cyclical approach that finishes things up more completely for readers. The choice depends on the writer and the material.

Kinds of Travel Articles

The travel section of a recent Sunday *New York Times* offers a good example of the kinds of stories travel writers can propose and, hopefully, research and write.

- *Practical advice.* A regular column called "Practical Traveler" talks about the advantages of taking a bus trip.
- *News of use to travelers.* A section called "Travel Advisory" includes news items about subjects of interest to travelers. This particular issue featured stories on the new system the State Department is using to issue travel advisories on dangerous countries around the world; the rising cost of rental fleets; a new kind of lift ticket at ski areas; the new visitor center at the NASA Space Center in Houston; and the danger of too many helicopters flying over Niagara Falls. A sidebar rates "Deals and Discounts" at various hotels and in various countries.
- *Questions and answers.* Readers write in with their travel questions and the editors answer.
- *Articles about shopping.* The Times calls this regular feature "Shoppers World" and it is strictly consumer oriented.
- *Articles about destinations.* The classic travel article gives readers an account of a trip—what you experienced and how they might experience it too. The writing is colorful and is best if it reads like you were telling someone a story as you show your slides. The consumer stuff can be put in a box at the end. The *Times* section contained several articles of this type: "Across Ireland, Leisurely," "A Night on the Town in Tokyo," "Breakfast Tradition: Seaweed at 7," and "Bargain Lodgings in Rural Japan."

- *Guide to a town, city, or state.* The *Times* always includes a feature called "What's Doing" which is little more than a rundown of things to do in a particular place. The writing is fairly pedestrian. The key to this feature is the information conveyed. The pieces are like pages from a travel guidebook.
- *Articles about things related to travel.* This particular issuė of the *Times* contains an article called "Packing by the Book" which lists items writers have packed—or had their characters pack—as they embarked on journeys. Ideas for this kind of piece might include a history of luggage or baggage tags or travel posters or a hundred other topics.

Two Travel Pieces

Two very different kinds of travel writings are exemplified in these selections. The first, from the travel section of the Sunday *New York Times* is a straight consumer information piece that takes the reader shopping in Maine. The second expounds on the joys of train travel. In this short piece, Paul Theroux illustrates why what he writes is travel *literature* rather than travel writing. Through humor and sometimes acid observation, he brings readers along with him to wherever he is going.

Article #1

TREASURES OF A MAINE PORT

—by Cynthia Hacinli

The lead sets the tone: the article is about shopping in a Maine town.

1 FREEPORT (with L.L. Bean) and Kittery—designer-outlet meccas both—put Maine on the shopping map. But for those weary of traffic and bargain-mad tourists, the Victorian maze of boutiques and galleries in Portland's Old Port are welcome relief.

Grafs 2 and 3 give readers an idea of what is there and the physical layout of the shopping area.

2 There isn't a Banana Republic or Benetton in sight. Instead, one finds an eclectic mix of wares from the ridiculous to the sublime. The neighborhood itself, a historic district circa 1870, is a pleasurable place to stroll even for those who are only window shopping.

3 Exchange and Fore Streets, the two main drags, form a T from which other streets and alleys spin off. This makes for an easily walkable five-block grid bounded by Commercial Street and the waterfront on the south, Congress on the north, Union on the west and Pearl on the east.

Graf 4 tells a bit about the town's history using good details.

4 Most of the buildings in the Old Port were put up in a flurry of construction after the Great Fire of 1866. (The spark was an Independence Day firecracker.) These brownstones, warehouses and commercial buildings have been meticulously preserved. Mansard roofs, arched windows and Italianate flourishes are everywhere, and when new sidewalks were laid after the fire, the city decided to use brick.

Beginning in graf 5, the writer starts a section on antique shops, a natural transition from the historic discussion in graf 4. For each one she visited she notes name, address, telephone number, sample contents, and prices (grafs 6 to 11).

5 Antique shops are a natural in such a setting, but contemporary goods are also creatively displayed. Two outstanding arts and crafts outposts selling works by Maine artisans, as well as those from other parts of the world, are the Nancy Margolis Gallery, 367 Fore Street (207) 775-3822, and Abacus, 44 Exchange Street, (207) 772-4880. At Nancy Margolis, form meets function with a bit of whimsy thrown in. Handmade wedding bands, Joe Spoon's brass candelabra with vine bases, a child's chair done in a frog motif and Lauren Cole's trompe l'oeil tables with handpainted bowls of beans, sliced tomatoes and other artifacts of the 90's fill this spare, elegant showroom. A mobile of papier-mâché figures in acrobatic poses is $45. An electric-blue porcelain bowl reminiscent of half a broken eggshell and overlaid with gold leaf is $130.

Throughout the article, the author's descriptions are full of vivid details that will help readers visualize the objects and their setting.

6 The more cluttered Abacus, 44 Exchange Street (207) 772-4880, feels less like a gallery and more like a shop. Objects run from a bark pencil, $7, and linen-covered notebooks by Anna Dembska, $18.50 and up, to polished bronze flatware with zigzag handles, $125 for a five-piece place setting, and a totem chair by Steven Spiro in walnut and cocobolo with an exaggerated backrest made of wavy strips of wood, $2,800.

7 The Stein Glass Gallery, 20 Milk Street, (207) 772-9072, deals in sleekly functional, decorative and sculptural pieces. Robert Wilson's three-dimensional stack of handblown clear and blue glass cubes with painted gold accents is $6,700. A 24-inch plate with colorful strings of glass woven into the center by Michael Trimpol is $300 and a slender blue vase $140.

8 At African Imports and New England Arts, 1 Union Street (207) 772-9505, tribal masks and fertility dolls—many of them antiques—from Ghana, Kenya and Nigeria share space with primitive paintings and sculptures by New England artists. Ink, wood, canvas, fabric, beads, paper, reeds and light are used in these modern works, and the results are highly original. A feather-light gourd bowl from Kenya is $7; a 19th-century Nigerian wood headdress with a carved face motif is $450. A Kenyan kikoi, or rectangle of fabric to wrap around the body, is $95.

9 Indonesian handicrafts in wood and fabric dominate at Tao Imports, 372 Fore Street, (207) 773-6884. The colorful modern shop is filled with Javanese Batiks, ceremonial puppets and gaily painted wood animals and spirits. A winged wood horse, traditionally hung over a baby's crib to ward off evil, is $56.

10 Closer to home, the Maine Potters Market, 376 Fore Street, (207)774-1633, is a cooperative of 15 Maine potters with a smattering of styles. A round terra cotta sundial by April Adams and Alan Burnham is $38. Peggy Anne Mack's majolica-style painted ceramics have impressionistic greengrocer and seafood themes. An oval casserole with a lobster motif is $75.

11 Across Moulton Street, Maxwell's Specialty Housewares is the place for New England-made ceramics and household goods such as distinctive dalmatian-spotted Bennington pottery ($4 to $40) from Vermont, and handsome reproductions of wooden Shaker boxes from Hanover, N.H. ($22 to $72), can be found at Maxwell's Specialty Housewares, 384 Fore Street, (207) 773-7977.

In graf 12 the author switches from crafts to jewelry stores by linking the latter to the former. Again, names, address, telephone number, sample items, and prices are included.

12 Many jewelry makers sign on with crafts galleries, but a few have struck out on their own. Fibula, 50 Exchange Street, (207) 761-4432, shows the old-world work of several artisans in a spare atelier featuring a Victorian fainting couch. Gold drop earrings with bronze Roman coins from A.D. 200 to 400, pink tourmaline and dark blue opal, are $950. Janic Grzyb's vermeil doughnut-shaped cufflinks are $175.

13 Up a creamy spiral staircase at 30 Exchange Street is Jeweler's Work, (207) 773-6824, a retail and wholesale showroom of eight jewelers, a couple of whom solder and drill on the premises. Edith Armstrong's ethnic flavored 18-carat vermeil earrings with cabochon garnets are $200; Elizabeth Prior's silver tube brushed-finish bangles inlaid with amethyst, citrine and peridot are around $365. Sally Webb's shiny silver rings with geometric overlays and tourmaline are $60 to $80.

14 Antique jewelry collectors will revel in the caches at Geraldine Wolf Antique Jewelry, 26 Milk Street, (207) 774-8994, and Conceits, 7 Moulton Street, (207) 761-4681. Geraldine Wolf specializes in Victorian and Art Nouveau pieces as well as exquisite sterling silver boxes and flatware. A pre-1890 gold Oriental seed pearl and diamond crescent-and-star pin from England is $625. A large sterling silver square belt buckle, circa 1910, is $39.

15 Conceits mixes new and old with avant garde designs and vintage costume jewelry from the turn of the century to 1960. A five-inch-wide Art Deco cuff in pewter is $225. Silver cross earrings from the 40's with raised designs and tiny turquoise-colored red stones are $45.

Graf 16 switches to textiles . . .

16 High-quality Victorian textiles and table linens are available at West Port Antiques, 8 Milk Street, (207) 774-6747. A plain white linen tea towel is $7; a turn-of-the-century Irish linen tablecloth and four napkins with elaborate cutwork is around $62. For quirky collectibles, try Auntie's Things, 37 Wharf Street, (207) 879-0789, where a glass cocktail shaker-style ice crusher from the 1940's is $5, floral painted English tea tins are $10 and up, and an antique Seth Thomas brass ship's clock is $245.

. . . 17 to books . . .

17 The literary-minded might take a turn around Little Nemo's World of Books, 420 Fore Street, (207) 874-2665, where stacks overflow with first editions and other vintage tomes and wooden boxes are filled with old maps and engravings, Cola-Cola ads and *New Yorker* covers. Eugene M. Fryer's travelogue "The Hill Towns of France," published in 1917 by E.P. Dutton, an apparent forerunner to Peter Mayle's

"Year in Provence," sells for $10. Allen Scott Books, 89 Exchange Street, (207) 774-2190, has cushy chairs and couches and a diverse collection of vintage, rare and used 20th-century books in a warren of smallish rooms. A standout in the strong art and design section is a handsome 1989 reissue of "Pyne's British costumes," $35, William H. Pyne's survey of British dress in the 18th century. A collector's 16-part leather limited-edition biography of Napoleon Bonaparte is $650.

. . . and 18 to vintage clothing.

18 Vintage clothing, albeit from a later period, can be found at Steamer Trunk, at 58 Exchange Street, (207) 773-3357. A white cotton lawn Victorian day dress is $75; a nifty pink beaded 50's sweater is $20.

The rest of the article talks about stores selling new items (grafs 19 to 24).

19 For new clothing and accessories, options abound. Amaryllis, 41 Exchange Street, (207) 772-4439, takes the global approach to getting dressed with clothes by Putamayo, stylish sportswear in natural fibers, one-of-a-kind dresses and quirky jewelry. A jean jacket embroidered with flowers is $94. The sophisticated men's and women's duplexes at Joseph's, 410 Fore Street, (207) 773-1274, are ideal stops for the chic garb from name designers like Lubium, Max Mara and Susie Tompkins. A dark greek silk women's blazer by Go Silk is $245. An olive double-breasted wool suit by Zigone for men is $640.

20 Carla Bella, a brand new women's clothing boutique at 469 Fore Street, (207) 772-1703, has clothing for the office and for going out on the town. A black and white houndstooth wool suit with jacket, long narrow skirt and oversized black fabric buttons is $280. Communiques, 3 Moulton Street, (207) 773-5181, is the place to find ultramodern urban wear at reasonable prices. Street Life cotton T-shirts, Twiggy-style baby doll dresses, and hobo hats are tucked in the back of what is essentially a very hip card-gift shop. A black leather belt with silver keepers and details is $36.95. Portmanteau, 18 Exchange Street, (207) 774-7276, is a good stop for classic canvas bags and rainwear. Carpetbags, duffels, briefcases and knapsacks with leather and tapestry trim are all made right here. A black canvas knapsack with Aztec trim is $35.50.

21 There are also those stores that defy pigeonholing. Covent Garden, 13 Exchange Street, (207) 775-3790, a shop in the English country mode, sells oils and potions for the bath by Caswell-Massey and Kiehl's, as well as European linens, painted Italian glass bottles and other accessories for the good life. A plush cotton terry kimono-style robe with wide peach and white stripes from France is $230.

22 Ecology House, 49 Exchange Street, (207) 775-4871, caters to the environmentally minded with items like reusable canvas lunch bags for $7.95.

23 The Whip & Spoon, 161 Commercial Street, (207) 774-4020, has everything from pickled fiddleheads to a wicked-looking Henckel knife. This kitchenware-cookbook-wine emporium is loaded with gadgets and goodies from the world over. A marble "hot stone" grill from France is $22.95; truffle, cognac, pork and chicken liver paté is $9.95 per pound. For sheer fun, the Old Port Kite Shoppe, 3 Wharf Street, (207) 871-0035, is the source for plastic kites, box kites, Japanese silk kites, twirling styrofoam kites and classic diamond-shaped numbers with Matisse-inspired patterns, from $3.50 to $150.

The article has no fancy ending. It stops as the writer completes her journey. Perhaps the writer felt there was nothing served by a fancy return to the lead. It was, of course, her choice.

A sidebar, "Dining in the Old Port," lists restaurants in the area.

24 A true sign of the times is the recently opened Condom Sense, 424 Fore Street, (207) 871-0356. The curious will find designer condoms in this upscale boutique. Some, such as the mini-condom, $3.50, the full-body condom, $17.95, are the stuff of jokes. But most, like the blue Trojan three-pack, are the real thing.

Article #2

STRANGER ON A TRAIN:
THE PLEASURES OF RAILWAYS

—by Paul Theroux

Theroux begins his article by talking about the two kinds of people who like

1 There are two sorts of people who like trains, and I am neither. The first is the railway buff, for whom trains are toys. With the mind of a

trains. He notes quickly that he doesn't fall into either category. His prose is simple and lively and establishes his theme nicely.

child and the constitution of a night-watchman, he has been elderly in that pipe-stuffing British way since he started to smoke; he enjoys running his thumb along the coachwork and jotting down engine numbers on a greasy notepad, and though he smiles bizarrely when the whistle blows, he doesn't climb aboard: he is going nowhere.

2 Put your feet up—get the bennyfit, say the second sort. Their knowledge of trains is non-technical. They like the space, the convenience; they like fuddling and fussing from carriage to carriage, juggling cheese rolls and pale ale, or just sitting, dozing, darning socks, doing the crossword and gloating out the window at the traffic jams: "Another level-crossing, Doris. Look at the silly buggers!" Barrister and criminal, publisher and printer, all crammed elbow to elbow in the compartment with *Wankers* spray-gunned on its walls. They are going to work, or home for the weekend, or to the coast for a bit of fun. They aren't travelers—in a sense nothing alien is human to them; they are non-drivers and Season Ticket-holders—they love chatting: in the area of small talk they are the world's true miniaturists. They have, each of them, a destination.

Beginning in graf 3, he discusses why he likes trains by telling about a recent journey to escape an Atlantic hurricane. In the process, he makes the travel itself the story, with few, if any, consumer elements.

3 I know I am not a railway buff, and I prefer not to travel with a destination in mind. Mine is the purest form of travel, a combination of flight and suspended animation. I enjoy getting on trains; I loathe getting off. For instance, last summer in Massachusetts my brother told me a hurricane was on its way. Even the tiredest and most mooching West Indian hurricane, when it reaches New England, causes floods, broken windows, power failures and a kind of fricassee on the television screen. I helped my brother secure his stables, bought a biography of the writer of weird tales, H. P. Lovecraft, and boarded the train for New York. In New York I caught "The Lake Shore Limited" for Chicago and en route my book proved an invaluable conversation piece, since most of my fellow passengers took the title, Lovecraft, to be that of a sex manual. I spent an afternoon in Chicago and at bedtime, instead of looking for a hotel, took "The Panama Limited" to New Orleans:

dawn in Winona, breakfast—ai-yugs and gri-yuts—in Jackson, mid-morning in the swamps of Louisiana, a vision of the Jurassic Age. My one regret, when I arrived, was that "The Southern Crescent" (New Orleans-New York) was fully booked. For a terrible minute, in the station at New Orleans, I contemplated a trip to Laredo, Texas, and "The Aztec Eagle" to Mexico City. The Laredo train was waiting. I could imagine the temptations in Mexico City: "El Mexicali" to Nogales, a sleeper on "El Jarocho" to Veracruz, or the three-day journey on Number 49, via Palenque, to Merida and thence to Guatemala, Nicaragua and who-knows-what *ferrocarril* in Costa Rica? I resisted, and walked to the French Quarter, ate five dollars' worth of oysters and a few days later was on my way back home through the deep South—perhaps Alabama? It was very dark—and the steward was moving through the Lounge Car shouting, "Last call for dinner! If you don't come now you ain't going to get no dinner, and you ain't going to hear this no more!"

A simple, one sentence paragraph allows him to change tone.

4 The hurricane had passed.

Readers discover in graf 5, however, that this was not to be about any one journey but several—all speaking to the point of Theroux's love of trains. He takes readers from Mississippi to Mandalay and explores the general topic of talking to strangers.

5 That week was pure pleasure. I had wide berths, a good book, an afternoon in Indiana and a morning in Mississippi. Durant, Mississippi, is not Mandalay, which is a pleasant surprise, because Mandalay is unremittingly dull. And I had good company. To get an Indian on "The Howrah Mail" talking you have first to answer a number of his questions: nationality, occupation, marital status, destination, birth sign, and how much you paid for your wrist watch. They are prying questions, but they license you to be similarly inquisitive. No such preliminaries are required on American railways. To get an American talking it is only necessary to be within shouting distance and wearing a smile; your slightest encouragement is enough to provoke a non-stop rehearsal of the most intimate details of your fellow traveler's life. In one sense, this is the third degree turned upside-down: instead of being tortured with questions you are tortured with replies. This sounds like criticism; I mean it as praise, for conversationally I am a masochist, and there is nothing I like better than putting my feet up, tearing open a can of beer and auditing a railway bore in full cry.

In graf 6, he continues to talk about fellow train travelers, bringing them into the minds of readers with various good phrases: baring their souls, strolling the aisles, sitting around in pajamas. He compares their freedom deftly to airline passengers strapped in chairs like "candidates for electrocution."

6 It is well-known that the train is the last word in truth drugs. All the world's airlines have failed to inspire what one choo-choo train has: the dramas of "The Orient Express" and a whole library of railway masterpieces. A rail journey is virtually the only occasion in travel on which complete strangers bare their souls, because the rail passenger—the calmest of travelers—has absolutely nothing to lose. He has more choices than anyone else in motion: unlike the air-traveler strapped in his chair like a candidate for electrocution, he can stroll, enjoy the view and sleep in privacy in a horizontal position—he can travel, as the native do, the six thousand miles from Nakhodka to Moscow, in his pajamas; unlike the person on ship-board, he can restore his eyes with landscape, eat whenever he chooses and never know the ghastly jollity of group games—and he can get off whenever he likes. He can remain anonymous, adopt a disguise, or spend the five days from Istanbul to Tehran canoodling in his couchette. The train offers the maximum of opportunity with the minimum of risk. A train journey is travel; everything else—planes especially—is transfer, your journey beginning when you arrive.

Theroux allows his anger at many modern trains to come out in graf 7. He uses the problems of British Rail to exemplify what many trains have become.

7 I am speaking of long journeys, good services, comfortable seats and berths. British Rail, in its characteristic frenzy of false economy, removes the dining car, abolishes coffee, foreshortens the train, and at the same time retains a brakeman on trains where no brakeman is needed and continues to ensure—on a simple journey from, say, Waterloo to Salisbury—that your ticket is examined no less than five times. For this thumb-twiddling and for braying, "I say that British Rail is second to none in the world!", the head of British Rail is handed a knighthood and enjoined to become part of the already grotesquely overmanned British Establishment. A long, fairly pleasant train journey is possible in Britain if one takes the sleeper to Glasgow and then, via Inverness and Wick, to Thurso, varying on the way back by heading for the Kyle of Lochalsh.

Trains in India (graf 8) are better and he says so.

8 But they order these things better in India. You can leave Jaipur at midnight and, after changing to "The Grand Trunk Express" in Delhi, not arrive in Madras for four days—which can be extended to a six-day rail gala if you go on to Rameswaram at the tip of India's nose, or a full week if you make the short crossing of the Palk Straits and take "The Talaimanner Mail" in Sri Lanka for Colombo. And it's another day on a pretty train from there to Galle.

His final graf continues the "train dropping" he does so well. He compares the good points of trains all over the world, putting readers in them—eating exotic things and looking at exotic places. He ends with one last glimpse of him starting a conversation as the train speeds by out of view.

9 "The Orient Express" used to be a four-day affair, but why stop in Istanbul when six days and three trains later you can be in Meshed, close enough to Afghanistan to hear gunfire in Herat? Turkish trains have plush bedrooms, Iranian trains serve kebabs, "The Frontier Mail" out of Peshawar dishes up curry, everyone gets a banana with his morning tea on "The Golden Arrow" to Kuala Lumpur; Thai trains have shower rooms (a huge stone jar, a dipper and a well-drained floor), Russian trains have a samovar in every coach, and ones in Sri Lanka have special compartments for you if you're a Buddhist monk. There is a telephone booth on the Amtrak "Metroliner" between New York and Washington and a pop-group on "The Coast Starlight" (Los Angeles-Seattle). "The Vostok" (Nakhodka-Khabarovsk) serves caviar; you can buy roasted sparrows and grasshoppers on most Burmese railway platforms, and everyone in the dining car of "The Izmir Express" (Ankara-Izmir) is presented with a loaf of bread: tear off a hunk, attack your portion of stewed eggplant, *Imam Bayildi* ("The Imam Fainted"), and either examine the greenery of Anatolia or sip one of their dusty but gamin white wines and say to the lady at the next table, "I can't help admiring your hat—"

References

Theroux, Paul. 1979. *The Old Patagonian Express*. Boston: Houghton Mifflin, pp. 4–5.

Theroux, Paul. 1985. *Sunrise With Seamonsters*. Boston: Houghton Mifflin, pp. 126–129.

10

Writing about How to Do Something

The original credo for *Popular Mechanics*, first published on January 11, 1902, still holds for free-lancers who write "how-to" pieces. Any subject covered in his magazine, declared founding editor Henry Haven Windsor, would be "written so you can understand it." Windsor made his magazine the first to present mechanical and scientific material using a popular approach, in language that was written with simplicity and clarity.

The magazine has thrived in the years since (1991 circulation 1.6 million) and dominates a small but lucrative market that also includes *Better Homes & Gardens Do-It-Yourself* (1991 circulation 450,000); *The Family Handyman Magazine* (1.3 million), *Home Mechanix* (1.2 million), and *Workbench* (910,000). In addition to these traditional markets, "how-to-do-it" articles also appear in a number of specialized magazines, whether they be on how to clean a sleeping bag (*Outside*), tie a fishing fly (*Field and Stream*) or repair a ski binding (*Skiing*).

The Secret of Success

The market is small because there are relatively few publications within it. Perhaps more important to free-lance writers is another

Box 10.1 Suggested Markets

There are a number of markets for the "how-to-do-it" article:

- *Popular Mechanics*
- *The Family Handyman*
- *Home Mechanix*
- *Workbench*
- Specialized magazines of all types (from fishing to skiing)

aspect of this small market: not everyone can do this kind of article. Thus, if you have the knack, you will probably thrive because the truly superior writers in this niche are hard to find. "There aren't as many writers pitching ideas to us as you'd think," says Frank Vizard, electronics and photography editor at *Popular Mechanics*. "Maybe they are put off by the technical aspects of what we want."

Writers will do well in this market if they learn how to take a technical subject and explain it in a simple way, often using a step-by-step approach. To accomplish this task, they can get valuable experience (and help augment their incomes) by writing for trade publications, which follow a similar concept. How-to-do-it magazines also resemble trade publications in the narrow kinds of advertising they solicit and include. As a result, readers buy both kinds of magazines for their ads as well as the editorial material.

A look at the November 1992 issue of *Popular Mechanics* reveals the kind of articles its editors are seeking. The cover story is about "The Art of Crafting Fine Furniture." Indeed, the cover also notes that this is a "Special Woodworking Issue." A closer look at the contents reveals that the issue contains six short pieces on how to build six different kinds of furniture—from a mahogany clock to a folding card table. Other articles featured on the cover are a comparative look at minivans, how to paint your car, and how to winterize your boat. The issue contains articles under major section headings about automobiles, boating, home improvement, aviation, science/technology, and electronics. The issue also has a piece commemorating the 90th anniversary of the magazine: an article on how America's war machines have kept its military on the cutting edge.

The secret to successfully writing a how-to article involves three elements: choosing the proper subject, properly explaining how to do it (whatever "it" is), and keeping the writing simple.

Choosing the Proper Subject

Before you spend hours racking your brain for *the* perfect subject, read the magazine thoroughly. Vizard says that free-lance writers frequently make the mistake of submitting ideas that reveal immediately that they are not familiar with the magazine and what a typical issue contains. He thinks they should also know what articles have run over the previous year so they don't duplicate them. "A lot of writers don't look very deeply into the magazine," he says.

It's also important to pick a subject not covered on a regular basis in the particular magazine. Vizard notes that many free-lancers submit ideas on topics that a staff editor covers: "If a guy pitches me on a subject I know well, I'll write the article."

Developing a specialty (or specialties) can help ensure that your ideas don't end up as someone else's article. In order to acquire and maintain a background in that subject, you'll need to subscribe to technical publications and gather background information from technical specialists you keep in touch with regularly. This reading and these contacts will provide you material on the latest developments in a given field as well as story ideas.

Explaining How to Do It, Whatever "It" Is

The process of explaining to someone how to accomplish a task is best done in a step-by-step way. You can achieve your goal best if you reduce the process to the bare essentials. For example, imagine what you would say to a 5-year-old child if he or she asked, "What are you doing?"

You should never write about how to do something unless you have done it yourself—more than once. Your reputation—and that of the magazine accepting your work—will suffer great harm if readers try to follow your instructions and fail. It is perfectly acceptable if they fail because of their own inabilities to accomplish the task. They should not fail, however, because you did a poor job of explaining the process to them. Just as a food writer will lose credibility if readers discover a flaw in a recipe, a how-to-do-it writer will suffer the same fate if his or her own formulas don't make sense or contain errors.

As with any piece, the "how-to-do-it" article begins with a lead to set the scene. In this paragraph, you lay out the task at hand in a narrative or news-oriented manner.

> Outside, the cold gray skies are punctuated by drifting flurries that gradually settle to the ground and form a thickening blanket

> of snow. Inside, you reach for another log to toss on the hearth, and then put your Topsiders up by the fire. . . .

This nicely written narrative lead sets the scene and allows readers to visualize themselves resting snugly by the warm fire. The transition comes in the first sentence of the next paragraph:

> Winterizing maintenance is a fact of life for boaters, and it's not confined to those living in the northern half of the country. . . .

The paragraph goes on to expand upon this idea, then ends with the setup to get readers into what they are looking for:

> Here's how to make sure that when you put your boat to bed it doesn't wake up with a cracked block, shorted wiring or heavy corrosion.

What follows are unnumbered sections telling readers what to do to winterize their boats. The headlines instruct in a step-by-step fashion: "start with the hull," "next comes the engine," "don't forget the trailer."

The article—as well as almost every other one in *Popular Mechanics*—includes easy-to-understand drawings depicting various steps in the process. As a free-lance writer of articles of this kind, you can improve your chances for success with editors if you include your ideas for illustrating your proposed article. Become familiar with what the magazine uses in the way of charts and other graphics and make your suggestions accordingly.

Keeping the Writing Simple

Although the readers of how-to-do-it pieces are not stupid, they are people who do not readily know the information being conveyed to them. If they did, they would not be buying these magazines and reading these kinds of articles. Thus, the writing levels need to be basic and simple, or, as the late author Truman Capote put it, "clear as a country creek."

This is no time to show off your prowess as a computer hacker, a carpentry wiz, or an overall technical wonk. Your readers will not be impressed. What *will* impress them, however, is clear, readable narrative based on your direct attempts to accomplish something and your interviews with experts who are skilled in doing so too.

The best way to write the how-to-do-it story is to move quickly into second person. Even if you don't usually write in that voice, addressing the readers as "you" will rapidly draw them into your story and establish a connection.

Box 10.2 Writing for Trade Publications

At its most rudimentary, writing for trade publications closely resembles the "how-to-do-it" writing described in this chapter. Readers of trade publications are looking for guidance on how to conduct their trade and/or profession, much as readers of *Popular Mechanics* are trying to learn how to build a clothes tree or a bird house. They are also eager to find out about new products.

The difference comes in level of sophistication and basic approach. In most trade magazines, you do not cover your material in a step-by-step manner. You do, however, imply such a numbered list.

- Here is how a surgeon perfected a new technique or how a patient reacted to a drug.
- This is how a civil engineer built a bridge—or why another bridge fell down.
- This is how this business succeeded—or why it failed.

In all cases, readers of the trade article can draw conclusions and put lessons learned to work in their own fields.

There are a number of advantages to free-lance writers who work with trade publications:

- Sheer numbers mean expanded markets. The 4,452 trade magazines and newspapers published annually in the United States greatly enhance your prospects of getting into print.
- Multiple markets grow out of one company. Many trade publications are owned by companies putting out a number of individual titles. This means that once you have an "in" with an editor at one magazine, it might be possible to parlay that contact into work for another editor at another magazine owned by the same company. For example, Crane Communications publishes everything from *Advertising Age* to *Automotive News* to *Plastics News* to *Modern Healthcare*. Although one writer can't possibly have the expertise to write for all of these diverse publications, it might be possible to work for similar ones. Thus, it might be possible to use your expertise in, for example, the automotive field and sell ideas to *Crane's Automotive News* or *AutoWeek*, or in another subject area, *Plastics News*, *Rubber & Plastics News*, and *Tire Business*, all of them owned by Crane.
- Experience can be gained in working for trade publications. You can get valuable experience and clips for your portfolio by working for these magazines and newspapers.
- Editors are not as demanding. Given the difficulty of finding good writers who can handle technical material, trade editors are more easily satisfied than their counterparts on consumer magazines once they find a writer they like. They aren't as apt to shop around constantly for someone more trendy.

- Pay is steady. Fees from trade writing are not as high as with consumer magazines, but you may make more money in the long run simply because you will be working more regularly. Also, you may be able to get fees from several publications in the same company, something that is more rare in consumer magazines.
- Writing can be easier. Because you are writing for readers who know the technical field your article is covering, you don't have to explain as much as you do with an article for a consumer magazine where general readers don't understand every specialized field. Thus, you can get by with using technical terms in a trade article and not explain them. You still have to have a thorough understanding of the subject and have good sources you trust. Moreover, you should never fall into the jargon of your technical sources. Trade writing shouldn't be turgid and boring.

It is relatively easy to get into trade publication writing:

- Develop an expertise in several fields for which there are trade magazines or newspapers. The easiest choices are those allied to your areas of expertise as a free-lance consumer magazine writer. For example, there are hundreds of medical trade publications for a medical and health writer, and an equal number of publications serving various businesses that a business writer might examine.
- Do background reading and research in the fields you choose.
- Develop a group of experts to call on for basic guidance, story tips, and help when you don't understand a subject you are reporting.
- Research all the available publications in the fields you select as possible markets. Write for sample copies and examine them for kinds of articles, writing style, overall formats.
- Prepare and submit query letters as you would for any consumer magazine.
- Look for connections between a trade magazine subject you are preparing and a future query to a consumer magazine. Most editors look to the trades to hear about developments before they become general knowledge. Your idea may speed that process.

As noted in Chapter 4, trade publications have been around for over 100 years. They are an important part of journalism although one that is often ignored. Indeed, the approach many consumer specialized publications take is right out of the trades: here's how to do something and if you follow what someone else did, you, too, can be a success. The magazine business was saved in the 1960s and 1970s—and thrives today—because of the trend to specialty publications copied from trade magazines and newspapers.

As a free-lance writer, you will open up vast markets—and potential income—if you look to the trades.

This is exemplified in the article on winterizing boats:

- "... if you don't prepare for it, [emphasis added] you run the risk..."
- "Before you decommission your engine..."
- "Be sure you understand..."

A good variation of second person is a kind of implied second person or implied you. In this approach, you talk to the reader without always using "you":

- "Closely inspect the exterior hull..."
- "Next, look for blisters or bulges..."
- "Change the oil filter..."

Your writing will be enhanced if you jot down ideas, phrases, and technical terms as you carry out the process. Initially, your thoughts will be fragmentary and disjointed, but you will at least have achieved the beginnings of an outline of how to proceed.

Other great aids will be a Roget's Thesaurus (in dictionary form) and a technical reference book pertaining to whatever field you are writing about. The latter will keep you accurate technically; the former will keep you from repeating words endlessly. Repetition of words may be satisfactory for emphasis in some kind of writing but will bore readers much of the time. You shouldn't follow this advice to the point of absurdity, however, by using too many arcane words.

The New Product Article

Another type of article presents a market for the writer of more traditional "how-to-do-it" pieces: the "how-it-works" article. Such an article details new products and their performance. Frank Vizard of *Popular Mechanics* explains: "While a magazine like ours does and will continue to have its fair share of how-to-do-it articles, I think it's also our role to offer how-it-works type articles. The world is increasingly being filled with new technology. Not only do people need to be conversant with new technology, they also have to be able to manipulate it to their best advantage. People can't go around blindly pushing buttons—all they do is waste time and they don't get the most out of the technology. When it comes to technology, it's our job to explain to people what it is, how it works, and how it is used."

Such articles usually give readers information about new products, often grouping more than one in a single article and comparing their features and performance. As a result, they act as a kind of testing service for readers because they detail good and bad features as well as price. In this approach they resemble articles in trade publications.

The writer of a new product, how-it-works article must be knowledgeable about the equipment being reviewed. She or he must also arrange to test it. Usually, manufacturers will be willing to allow you to use their new product because mention of it in an article will help promote it. They are even willing to take the chance that you won't like it and will say so in print. You must resist any pressure from those who loan you the equipment, however, because any such influence will ruin the objective nature of your article and call into question your ethics.

Your reporting for this kind of article consists of using the product and taking careful notes to record what happens. You should detail specifications and prices. You also need to find a theme with which to tie everything in the article together.

Article #1

SPEAKERS OF THE HOUSE

Heard but hardly seen, the latest three-piece loudspeaker systems deliver big sound from small packages

—by Frank Vizard

Frank Vizard, electronics and photography editor at *Popular Mechanics*, practices what he preaches in this article written on a free-lance basis for *Video Review*. He sets the tone in his first paragraph: to enjoy home video one needs to add external speakers. But there are problems in doing so: the speakers are too large and detract from the decor of a room.

1 Enjoying home video to the max generally means adding external speakers that enhance soundtrack quality and complement the action on the screen. But speakers sometimes constitute a problem—especially in Dolby Surround or Pro Logic installations. In many situations they're too large or too numerous for the available space. And from an aesthetic standpoint, big boxes contribute little to a room's decor.

In graf 2, he brings readers in by addressing them as "you" and resorts to some plays on words ("speakers seen and not heard" and "lend an ear") to make a transition to his subject. The article will be about

2 If you're among those who believe that speakers should be heard and not seen, you ought to lend an ear to a new class of speakers that offers big sound from small boxes that are virtually invisible.

what he calls "big sound from small boxes."

How can this seemingly remarkable thing be accomplished? He explains in grafs 3 to 6, using terms like "woofer" that his expert readers will understand without explanation.

3 Describing these speakers as a disappearing act is an accurate representation, because concealment is part of their purpose. Instead of following the traditional approach, whereby two boxes handle all the bass, midrange and treble notes, sound reproduction chores are divided among *three* speakers. Let's explain this paradox.

4 Bass notes, which usually require a large woofer in a large enclosure for accurate reproduction, are generated instead by a module about the size of an overnight bag. Midrange and treble notes are handled by two speakers that are light enough for wall mounting and small enough for concealment among houseplants or bric-a-brac.

5 The beauty of this approach becomes apparent once you understand that deep bass notes are omnidirectional in nature—meaning they don't seem to emanate from any particular location. Consequently, you can place the subwoofer module anywhere—and place it out of sight behind or beneath a chair, couch or other furniture.

6 What you're left with is a pair of "satellite" speakers that produce the upper frequencies of the musical spectrum, and provide the stereo image and directionality. These speakers vary in size from "minis" as small as milk containers up to a still-compact size commonly referred to as "bookshelf" speakers. Thanks to the subwoofer module, the sound you'll hear has the deep, solid bass not normally available from small, shelf-mount speakers.

He continues the theme in graf 7 by calling the subjects of his article "stealth."

7 Within this "stealth" class of small three-piece systems there are varying methodologies at work. As a rule, the more discreet systems employ satellite speakers with sturdy but lightweight plastic housings. Other companies marry the subwoofer module to traditional-looking bookshelf speakers, which are generally larger and offer less placement flexibility.

8 Different tacks are taken regarding the subwoofer modules as well. Many of the subwoofer modules can be described as bass-reflex speakers. Identified by a small port or vent in the side of the cabinet, bass-reflex speakers can deliver louder bass on less amplifier power than totally sealed enclosures of the same size. On the downside, a poorly constructed bass-reflex speaker can sound "boomy"—something you should evaluate in a listening test before you buy.

In graf 9, he begins to discuss specific systems, commenting on quality and characteristics ("tight, accurate bass" and "suspension speakers are not very 'efficient' ").

9 Not every subwoofer module is a bass-reflex speaker. Both the Cambridge SoundWorks Ensemble and the Polk Audio RM 3000, for example, utilize what's called the acoustic suspension principle, where the woofer is housed in a sealed enclosure. This design yields tight, accurate bass even though relatively small woofers are used. The drawback is that more amplifier power is needed to drive acoustic-suspension speakers to the same volume level as bass-reflex speakers. In audio lingo, acoustic suspension speakers are not very "efficient."

He continues this process in grafs 10 through 17 by comparing other systems.

10 Cambridge SoundWorks uses two slim subwoofer modules for bass reproduction, in what might be interpreted as a way to equal or surpass the output of a signal by a single bass-reflex speaker. Cambridge asserts that using two modules prevents low-frequency cancellation, which can occur when two stereo channels are combined into a single subwoofer. Two slim subwoofer modules also provide more placement flexibility, according to Cambridge. But you'll have to look for two hideaway spots instead of one.

11 Polk Audio takes a more elaborate approach that's reflected in the high price of its RM 3000. Two 6 1/2-inch woofers operate as acoustic-suspension speakers, but fire into a chamber housing a 10-inch woofer. This larger woofer, through which all the sound passes, acts as a "passive radiator" to filter out unwanted upper-bass frequencies that might impart a sense of directionality to the listener.

12 Bass directionality is not a sin in and of itself, but it does restrict placement of the sub-woofer modules to a location near the satellite speakers in order to maintain a focused stereo image. The lower the "crossover point" between the subwoofer and the satellite speakers, the less likely it is that the subwoofer will produce sound with directional characteristics. The accompanying chart shows the crossover frequency—measured in a scale from 20 to 20,000 Hertz—at which the subwoofer and satellite speakers split sonic responsibilities.

13 Manufacturers encourage you to experiment with the placement of the subwoofer modules. Bass response usually improves when the woofer fires off a reflective surface such as a wall or floor. With subwoofer modules like the Altec Lansing System 3, though, a reflective surface is already attached in the form of a panel opposite each woofer. This negates the need for a reflective surface nearby, and makes the System 3 much more flexible to arrange.

14 Bang & Olufsen, meanwhile, takes a more decorative approach with its Cona subwoofer. The circular Cona fires downward, using the floor as a reflective surface. Its circular shape, though, means the Cona can't hide—except in plain sight, as a plant stand perhaps.

15 Another stealth system of note is the Pattern, from Atlantic Technology. Although speakers usually rely on a separate receiver or amplifier for power, the Pattern has a 15-watt amp for each satellite and a 30-watt amp for the subwoofer, all built into the subwoofer module. The Pattern also has three inputs for connecting a variety of audio and video sound sources.

16 The Pattern plays much bigger than its power specifications would suggest. If there is a product flaw, it's the lack of a remote control in the package for power, volume and source selection. Atlantic Technology is working on a more elaborate home-theater version of the Pattern, which will include extra satellite speakers and a Dolby Pro Logic decoder.

17 The Pattern is also noteworthy in that the two stacked cubes that comprise each satellite can be rotated 360° relative to each other. The satellite speakers in the Bose AM-5 system, in the company's Acoustimass line, are similar in that they rotate as well. Given this twist-and-shout flexibility, some sound from the satellite speakers can be aimed directly at the listener and the rest bounced off the walls and ceilings for a more enveloping effect.

He begins to sum up in graf 18, talking about advantages of all the systems detailed thus far.

18 If the Bose, Atlantic Technology, Altec Lansing, Cambridge and similarly made satellites are wall-mounted with their supplied brackets, a speaker system becomes virtually invisible. Stealth systems that use larger bookshelf speakers for their satellites are still viable, but are less flexible in satellite placement.

The article ends in graf 19 by calling the speakers "strong but hardly silent partners"—another good play on words.

19 Traditional bookshelf speakers, though compact, imply that deep, full bass is an option and not a necessity. That's like asking a guitar player to strum with the bottom string missing. Now that bookshelf speakers have found a strong but hardly silent partner in the hideaway subwoofer, the full range of sound can be heard again—discreetly.

The article includes photos of all systems covered and a chart listing manufacturers, model numbers, dimensions, and prices. All a reader needs to do is to go to a store and place an order. (A chart is a particularly effective sidebar in an article like this because it adds information that does not fit easily into the body of the article.)

11

Writing the Long Article

In magazine parlance, "long" article usually means "cover" article, that is; the most important article and the one that is depicted on the cover with a photograph or illustration. The magazine cover story is the equivalent of the front page of a newspaper or the first item on a network television news program.

What "Cover Length" Means

"The cover story is the hallmark of a magazine," says Bill Ingram, editor-in-chief of both *Medical Tribune* and *Medical World News*. "The success or failure of this or any magazine depends on the cover story. The cover story is the big adventure, the thing that shapes the whole magazine. It is the opening act, the style setter, the big attraction, the great white way."

In the never ending quest for the designation "hot book"—the magazines advertising agencies steer clients to because readers are talking about them—the choice of cover subject is very important. It is no accident that sales racks for magazines have been moved from the rear of most supermarkets to checkout counters. Publishers aim for that last crack at a customer's wallet and the impulsive choice to grab an issue and put it on the turntable next to the milk, bread, and canned goods.

The result of such last minute buying decisions can bring in millions more in revenues. Indeed, a few magazines depend on newsstand sales exclusively for their revenues. *People*, for example, came into being in 1974 determined not to rely on paid circulation. A more recent Time Warner publication, *Entertainment Weekly*, also relies primarily on newsstand sales.

The selection of the topic to which the cover photo and accompanying article should be devoted is of crucial importance. How can editors be sure of their choices, especially with so much at stake? "What we think we know is that young sells better than old, pretty sells better than ugly, sports figures don't do very well, TV sells better than music, music does better than movies, and anything does better than politics," former *People* managing editor Richard Stolley said as the policy of relying on newsstand sales began to pay off in the late 1970s.

At the other end of the sales spectrum is *Time*, which gets 90 percent of its sales from paid circulation. Here the choice of cover subject is made with other factors in mind (newsworthiness, topicality, agenda and trend setting). Yet, publishers and ad agencies still watch newsstand sales figures carefully as a kind of weekly vote on how good the covers are.

Occasionally, a cover photo can gain prominence for a magazine and an editor, no matter what the article says. This happened in 1991 when Tina Brown, editor of *Vanity Fair*, chose a photo of a nude and pregnant Demi Moore for a cover. The interest and outrage created by the cover suddenly made *Vanity Fair* a "hot book." Brown herself was rewarded later by being named editor of another Conde Nast magazine, *The New Yorker*.

Picking a Subject in Need of Long Treatment

Most of the time, free-lance writers remain above the fray when it comes to deciding which articles to feature on the cover. They may hope for the prominence such a selection brings, but they rarely have anything to say in the matter.

Writers can influence the amount of space to be devoted to their articles by what they put in their original query letters. By suggesting word length and paying attention to topic, free-lancers can at least get the attention of editors and start the editorial thought process that might ultimately result in cover placement.

In querying editors about subjects worthy of 3,000 to 5,000 word treatment, writers should keep several factors in mind. First, the subject should be broad enough and interesting enough to attract reader interest. Also, there should be enough material available about the subject—either through interviews or research or both—to

Box 11.1 Suggested Markets

Long articles can be sold to a variety of publications:

- *Atlantic*
- *Harper's*
- *Smithsonian*
- *New York Times Magazine* (or any Sunday newspaper magazine)
- Public relations magazines

complete the article. In addition, the subject should lend itself to the "special" treatment long and/or cover articles get: good photographs and illustrations, informative graphs and charts, breaking up copy into several sidebars—all for better reader comprehension.

Organizing, Reporting, and Writing the Long Article

After you have gotten the idea, gathered enough material to prepare a query, queried an editor, and gotten the nod to write the article, you will need to put more effort than usual into reporting and writing when the article you are doing is a long one. Its length and possible placement on the magazine's cover make it special and you will have to live up to the faith the editor has placed in you.

Organizing

Your organization of the long article will be enhanced if you think of it in terms of individual tasks to be accomplished.

- Sit down and think through the things you have to do to complete your task, writing down the goal of the article and who the magazine's readers are.
- Make a list of who you have to interview, jotting down their telephone numbers and addresses beside their names so you won't have to look them up later.
- Make a list of questions you want to ask your sources.
- Make a list of non-interview resources you hope to gather (government documents, printed materials, books, articles, letters) and where they are located.
- Make interview appointments, write letters requesting the documents, or go to a library to get the other references you will need.

Reporting

From your list of tasks to be accomplished you can determine the most efficient course of action for your actual reporting.

- Conduct the interviews.
- Prepare your notes for use by going over them soon after the interview to fill in information you observed but did not write down, and to decipher your handwriting before you forget what it says.
- Listen to and transcribe your tapes of the interview.
- Read the other reference material, highlighting with a marking pen information you may want to include.

Writing

For some free-lancers the interviewing and researching are the most interesting aspects of the job and they approach the actual writing of the article with some hesitation. For others, just the opposite is true. In either case, it is helpful to keep a few things in mind.

- Don't be intimidated by the sheer volume of material you have to deal with.
- Work out a theme for the article and begin following that theme in your lead paragraph.
- Try outlining the article by labeling its main sections and the various sub-elements to be included in each section.
- Outlining does not work for everyone, however. You can substitute a less formal organizing technique: once you have your theme in mind and have read through your interviews and other material, just start writing.
- As you proceed through the material you have gathered, mark off the various segments—a quote here, an excerpt there—as you use it, so you won't inadvertently include it more than once.

(For more about magazine article writing in general, see chapter 18.)

Anatomy of Two Long Articles

Oregon free-lancer Rob Phillips got the idea for an article on the perils of success by reading a piece in *Newsweek* about a man in New Hampshire at the height of his career who suddenly committed suicide.

"I clipped it," he recalls, "and started looking at *Newsweek*'s sources. I almost always go to people and interview them in person but it occurred to me that I couldn't do that in this case, because it would mean observing a clinical relationship between a psychologist and a patient. I knew I wouldn't have that access. I won't travel, I decided, I'll call them. For an investment of about $45 in phone calls, I'd have my story."

By this time, he had decided upon his approach: the main theme would be the perils behind success; namely, people who achieve success, then panic that they won't ever do anything more in life. He pitched the idea to the editor of one of his steadier free-lance outlets, *World Traveler*, the in-flight magazine of Northwest Airlines. After some delay, Phillips got the commission to do the story. He also sold a rewritten version of it to another magazine, giving it the theme of "encore anxiety," something coined by one of his sources.

To prepare for his interviews—which he did not do before getting the magazine's agreement to publish—he checked three or four books out of the library and read them, so "I would not be embarrassed by my questions." He made his calls ("lots of listening and taping") and was soon ready to write.

"I write for me," says Phillips. "A lead has got to be good to keep my attention. I try to write a story so that early on, readers feel comfortable. I use short sentences, short words, and make sure the anecdotes are plentiful. Unless you use lots of anecdotes, your article will read like a term paper.

"If I can get readers through the first page, I don't feel the same compulsion to use short sentences and uncomplicated words. I can be more didactic. By then, the reader has some investment in the story."

Phillips both tapes his interviews and takes notes. He prepares a complete transcript only of key interviews. The others he listens to again in order to improve his notes.

"I visualize the whole story and lay it out in my mind," he continues. "I used to follow the trail wherever the peanuts went. Now I'm comfortable with thinking through the whole article. If I'm lucky, I know the end before I begin the story. Sometimes I have two endings. I used to tie the end with the beginning. Now, I'm less likely to do that. I don't write in first person, but I think we stand too far off by always using third person. I don't back away from second person."

Phillips likes the longer article.

"You can take time to explore a subject rather than merely stating it," he says. "You give readers a better grasp of it. You can put one foot ahead of the next. In the short article, you don't have time to explain things. You don't have room for many flashbacks."

Such an article has its drawbacks, however.

"Sometimes I have to stretch my material but try to avoid letting readers know I'm stretching. I want to hold readers without getting them bogged down."

Article #1

A NEW LOOK AT SUCCESS

—by Rob Phillips

The writer draws his readers in by using second person ("you're," "you"). He puts the reader into a setting where people are likely to encounter other people—an airplane.

1 The next time you're on an airplane, look at the people you're with. Chances are whoever you look at first will not be harboring any particular fear of success nor any particular fear of failure—well, failure maybe, but certainly not success. Who would fear success if it brought money, power and prestige?

He draws them in even more by encouraging them to glance around the cabin at fellow passengers ("That woman over there").

2 That woman over there. Let's call her Jane (the name is invented, but she's real). Jane is in the newspaper business. She works at one of her dad's newspapers. Her colleagues say she is competent, but arrogant and abrasive. They're worried about the day she'll replace her father as editor in chief. Now that her father's health is failing, she's worried, too.

("That man. . . .") "Remember," says Phillips, "the reader is always there."

3 That man in front of you, let's call him Robert. He is a recognized scholar. At 34, he was named chairman of his department. Over the last five years he has demonstrated "consummate skill in handling a wide variety of difficult budget, personnel and academic matters." Those were the words used by the search committee when it unanimously recommended him for appointment as Dean of the College of Humanities. The president agreed and offered Robert the job. Robert accepted. But now he can't shake the feeling that he's not good enough to be a dean. He feels like an imposter. He thinks his success up to now has been mostly a matter of luck.

Phillips has given his "characters" fictitious names to protect their privacy, yet they and the situations they represent are real. It is better to use this device—as long as you

4 Stuart, the man across the aisle, was his club's racquetball champion last year. He lost this year in the final match, maybe because he partied too much the night before.

tell your readers you are doing so—than the more old-fashioned and overly dramatic initials (as in, "we'll call her J.S.")

In graf 5, he pulls together the people he has just introduced and tells readers what they have in common and why readers should be interested. They all suffer from "encore anxiety."

5 For different reasons, Jane, Robert and Stuart are dealing with the same problem. It is what Boston-area psychologist, author and consultant Dr. Steven Berglas calls "encore anxiety," a paralyzing fear that they won't be able to repeat a prior success.

He uses grafs 6 through 9 to expand upon each case in greater detail.

6 Jane, the editor-apparent, is the right age. Encore anxiety shows up in a person's late 30's or early 40's, Berglas says. And she has the right background: She is the boss's daughter. Anyone whose career has been boosted by family connection, knows what Berglas means by the "noncontingent success"—success not strictly the product of one's own effort. A person who starts in the middle of the ladder has to move more than a rung or two to be considered successful. No wonder Jane is anxious. No wonder she's arrogant and abrasive. She is demonstrating "Wizard of Oz" behavior, Berglas says. "If you scare them off, they won't know how scared you are."

7 Robert's fears about his inadequacy as a dean may be traced to his childhood. Freudians would see Oedipus lurking in the shadows, interpreting Robert's achievements as department chairman as a symbolic victory over his father for the affection of his mother. Having won the battle, Robert immediately treats his victory as a fluke to avoid retribution from his father.

8 A less complicated explanation might note that, as a child, Robert was never quite good enough to meet his parents' expectations. Three A's and a B on his report card would immediately draw attention to the B. The bar was continually being raised for Robert. No wonder he's anxious now about an "encore." No wonder he fears being exposed as incompetent. Each time he succeeded as a youth, he was told he wasn't quite good enough.

9 And Stuart, the former racquetball champion. He handled his encore by getting loaded the night before. It insulated him against the possible embarrassment of defeat. Intentionally or not, his self-handicapping behavior created doubt about why he failed in the championship match. Had he not partied all night, he might have won. On the other hand, had he not feared the loss of his title, he might not have partied all night.

In graf 10, he returns to a discussion of encore anxiety itself and how people with it can be helped.

10 Encore anxiety is not fatal, and people do learn to cope with it, sometimes with expert help. So suppose Jane and Robert and Stuart master their anxieties and go on to success. Jane becomes a good editor, even mellows a bit. Robert is every bit as good a dean as a chairman. Stuart turns his racquetball skills to tennis and is on his way to the top. All three are successful in their own right. Now what?

In grafs 11 through 14, he tells readers what books and popular magazines say about the malady and success in general.

11 There are four hundred and seventy-eight books in print in the English language with the word "success" in the title. Forty more are due by August. They explain how you, too, can become successful.

12 The first book ever published on success was Benjamin Franklin's, "Poor Richard's Almanac." It said that character values—honesty, persistence, hard-work, frugality—were the secret of success. Horatio Alger confirmed the point two centuries later. Success then came to be defined as personal magnetism (Dale Carnegie) and mind power (Norman Vincent Peale, Napoleon Hill). More recently, and more cynically, success has been described in terms of games and one-upmanship, as in lunching for power and dressing for success.

13 Now a handful of writers are busy defining success once more. Swimming against a tide of popular optimism are those who warn of the "downside" of success. Magazine articles and books have surfaced with titles like "The Strange Agony of Success," (*New York Times*), "The Perils of Success," (*Forbes*), "Overstressed by Success," (*Newsweek*), "Feelings to Watch Out For When on the Brink of Love or Success," (*Cosmopolitan*), "The Emotional

Fallout of Success" (*Douglas LaBier*).

14 Their collective message is not as depressing as their titles. In fact, if you read to the end you discover there's a redeeming new way to look at success.

The short, sweet sentence provides an effective transition.

15 First, the downside.

Beginning in graf 16, Phillips discusses the drawbacks to success, devoting a paragraph to each one.

16 Successful people can count on losing their privacy, the experts say. Former tennis star Arthur Ashe bitterly complain[ed] about the so-called "public's right to know" that he [was] HIV-positive. Basketball star Larry Bird tells a reporter he can't go to a shopping mall without drawing a crowd of people seeking an autograph. Movie star Michelle Pfeiffer says she has become "public property," telling Barbara Walters on ABC-TV of the time an ambulance was summoned to her home to assist a friend who had gotten sick. "Before they left for the hospital," Pfeiffer said, "one of the attendants asked for my autograph."

Being used by others (17) is one drawback.

17 Successful people also say they've become wary about social contacts, never being sure if people seek them out for who they are or what they've become. As Lady Astor once put it: "The penalty of success is to be bored by the people who used to snub you."

Losing their knack for success (18) is another. He uses good quotes to make his points.

18 Others worry that they're going to lose whatever made them successful in the first place. The winner of the Baldrige award for exemplary business management one year nearly loses the whole company the next year because its executives are preoccupied by telling themselves and others how they did it. "Success can't be blueprinted," says Charles Garfield, author of *Second to None*. "There are too many factors outside conscious control, and conditions constantly change."

19 Edsun de Castro says he was forced out of the chairmanship of Data General three years ago when he was unable to persuade his company to develop new products to regain the industry lead. "I couldn't convince the organization to act as aggressively as it should have," he tells *Forbes* magazine writer Esther Dyson. "Companies and people tend to stick to what they think made them a success," Dyson concludes, "not to what really made them successful, the act of coming up with a better idea."

20 Some successful people feel let down after accomplishing a major goal. Having put Neil Armstrong on the moon to make his "giant step for mankind," the team that put him there immediately felt as if it had taken one giant step backward, Garfield wrote in an earlier book, *Peak Performers*. "Since we had known how it felt to soar, business-as-usual was a crash landing."

21 Boredom is another fallout of success. Having demonstrated that he could do the job over the past eight years, the president of a West Coast university says he has the antidote for the boredom borne of success. His notion of the "ideal job," he says, would be that of an internal administrator who moves from one troubled campus to another, staying only long enough to put things back in shape and then move on. "There's enough similarity among campuses to be able to do it," he says. "and enough challenge to make it interesting."

In the previous examples, Phillips uses material he has researched and gotten from other publications or from conversations with friends and acquaintances. In graf 22, he brings in quotes from one of his telephone interviews.

He continues this in grafs 23 through 27.

22 Perhaps 20 percent of all successful men, says psychologist Steven Berglas, "turn to adultery, adventure-seeking, aloneness, or alcohol and drug abuse." Like Stuart, the erstwhile racquetball champion, some are prone to self-handicapping behavior—"victims of a virus," Berglas says, "that lies dormant unless it's given the right environment to flourish."

23 Dr. Kathleen V. Shea, a Chicago-area psychologist, says success actually diminishes the perception of self-worth among many of her clients who work in sales and marketing. They tell her they feel successful only if they "make club" (the million-dollar club), or manage to meet constantly rising sales quotas.

24 But when they burn out, they're in trouble, Shea says. "They seem to feel they are what they do," meaning their success as human beings seems to be measured only in terms of their success in sales.

25 Other successful people battle guilt, Oedipal or otherwise. "Graduate students accepted at Harvard sometimes feel they have no business here," says Dr. Harry Levinson, a Harvard Medical School faculty member and founder of the Levinson Institute of Belmont, Mass. "They feel they have fooled somebody to get here. They feel they are acting only 'as if' they were entitled to be here."

26 Other successful people battle feelings of self-betrayal. Members of the International Women's Media Foundation were asked recently if they would pursue the same career if they could start over again. Ninety percent said yes. But 75 percent agreed that "women who have successful careers end up sacrificing too much of their family and personal life."

27 "After finishing interviews for a research project some years ago," says psychologist Douglas LaBier, "the people I was interviewing would often say to me, 'You know, the real problem is that I hate my life. I like the perks but my life is too thin, too boring and I don't know what to do.' Over half of adults are unhappy with their lives," LaBier says.

28 LaBier, a Washington, D.C. therapist and author of *Modern Madness*, says success has made some people feel "empty and detached." Physical symptoms include gastrointestinal upset, high blood pressure, fatigue, headaches, and sleep disturbances. Emotional symptoms include chronic indecisiveness, anxiety, clinical depression, rage, and in some cases, self-destruction.

In graf 29, he tells the story that interested him in this subject in the first place: of a successful businessman who killed himself because he feared he was letting others down.

29 New Hampshire businessman Rick Chollet was one of them, even though he seemed to have it all. He was happily married, had a thriving business, was loved by colleagues and employees. A year ago he wrote a note which said he had found the "torture of living" too much to bear. He locked the garage door, climbed in his BMW and turned on the engine. "People put him on such a pedestal," his wife said later. "He constantly feared letting them down."

Having taken readers to rock bottom, Phillips begins in grafs 30 and 31 to go back up the hill to a section

30 Finally, many successful people turn to conspicuous consumption of "things," as if trying to prove the cliche that in the end the one with the most toys wins.

of how to conquer encore anxiety. He proceeds to list various factors, using good quotes and examples.

31 Did poet Emily Dickinson have it right when she wrote, "Success may be counted sweetest/by those who ne'er succeed"? Would it be better to cultivate failure than success?

32 Hardly, these experts say. The trick is to re-define what constitutes success.

33 Some cite Freud, who said the "hallmarks" of mental health are the ability to love and the ability to work. Others quote Aristotle, who said the crucial element of a successful life is balance. Or they spot a recent quote from actress-wife-mother Mariel Hemingway, who said: "One minute you're the hottest thing going, the next they don't know who you are. That's why I thank God I have a real life"—clear evidence of what psychoanalysts call a "healthy, differentiated ego."

As he did when discussing the drawbacks of success, Phillips devotes one paragraph to each tactic for overcoming encore anxiety.

34 Former president Jimmy Carter devotes a portion of his retirement to building homes for Habitat for Humanity. Microsoft billionaire Bill Gates tells a reporter: "I'm not motivated by money. . . . What's it got to do with anything?" America's largely-unappreciated homerun king: "It's something I don't think about any more. My life doesn't revolve around baseball. I'm a happy man. Hank Aaron is at peace."

35 An upwardly mobile executive declines a company transfer. A sales executive argues for elimination of bonuses. A young medical doctor cuts his practice (and his income) to four days a week to make more time for his family. A successful businessman wears a beeper at the office so his wife and children can reach him whenever they want.

36 Charles Garfield tells of a successful entrepreneur, a founder of his company, who derives more satisfaction from volunteer service than from his work. He restructures his life to give more time to his church. And his partners think he's "a little crazy," Garfield says. "One thought it was a plot to go off and leave them with the business. Another said he understood, and wished he had made similar decision when he was young."

37 Steven Berglas tells his seminar audiences that all executives should be "sentenced" to do some kind of community service. "Go and be a part of a community," he told a *Time* magazine interviewer. "Be an Indian, not a chief. Lose your identity in a group. The healthiest people have that kind of commitment."

38 The recent decline of the economy has forced people to reassess how they view success, adds Douglas LaBier. It has helped them discover that real success combines achievement with fulfillment—"the New Normalcy," LaBier calls it.

Beginning in graf 39, Phillips very adroitly brings readers back to the lead and subsequent paragraphs: they are once again glancing around at their fellow passengers in that airliner in the sky.

39 That man who just walked down the aisle of your airplane. Maybe he was recently the owner of a million dollar company. Maybe he had been drinking too much and spending too many nights in strange beds. Maybe he had been feeling bored by success.

40 A Boston psychotherapist had such a client not long ago. The man told his family and his staff that he was going to sell his business, take some time off, then look for another business. He assured the therapist he'd be "all right." He simply needed a new challenge.

He uses the remaining five paragraphs to expound on the man's story and draw lessons from it for readers.

41 The man sold his company. For the first time in years he had time for things he had only stolen time for before: travel, recreation, reflection, relationships. He was miserable.

42 Even the new business opportunities didn't look right. Each time, the market or the product or the fabrication process or his own gut said no. He always knew there was an element of luck with his first business but he couldn't be sure it would be there this time around. Besides, the old management team had split up. The market had gotten more complex. The competition was way out front. Conditions had changed—and so had he. Maybe, he told himself, maybe I've lost my nerve.

43 A year after he sold the company he was in therapy. It took a year and a half, but with the therapist's help, he learned to cope with the anxiety of whether he could repeat his first success.

44 Last spring the man was on an airplane flying to a distant city to close a deal with his new company.

45 His first question to his therapist was, "What if I fail?" Perhaps his next question should be: "What if I succeed?"

Sometimes, an idea for an article can be triggered by seeing something which then jibes with something else in a writer's memory. This happened to Jack Fincher, a former *Life* magazine staff member and free-lance contributor to *Reader's Digest*, *Smithsonian*, and other magazines. While watching a Public Broadcasting System series on the 1918 flu epidemic, Fincher recalled the experiences of his own family with death from that disease.

"I had always been able to interest them in somewhat obscure subjects of interest to me," he recalls. His hunch was right and he quickly got the approval from *Smithsonian* editors to proceed. He was able to gather the material for the article largely through library research of books and U.S. government health records. He augmented that by conducting interviews with survivors and experts.

Article #2

AMERICA'S DEADLY RENDEZVOUS WITH THE "SPANISH LADY"

In 1918, while the war in Europe still raged, we found ourselves fighting a killer flu for which there was no cure.

—by Jack Fincher

His lead is simple, dramatic and effective. The personal account of a fight between brothers at first seems an unlikely way to begin the article . . .

1 The brothers stood in the cooling dust of an East Texas autumn, hitting each other as hard as they could. Murlin, two years younger at 16, had struck first. Wright was their widowed father's favorite, and Murlin was sick of it. Yet with their little brother, Neal, looking on, it seemed somehow fitting that Wright should strike the last blow, battering Murlin, dazed and bloody, to the ground.

. . . but he explains it nicely in the second graf: the fight caused one brother to run away and join the army, where he caught the flu and died.

2 Wright, dreading what their stern sheriff father might do to punish him, did what many a young man has done to escape an unhappy household. He ran off and joined the Army. A few days later word reached home from the camp in Dallas: come at once, your son is gravely ill. His father found him lying unconscious on the cold stone floor of a makeshift military hospital, its exhausted staff too overworked by the influenza raging round them to notice. Wright died on October 18, 1918.

In graf 3, Fincher reveals the family connection and extrapolates out from one family's story to the world at large ("one small, sad design in the vast tapestry of a fatally infectious disease as common to the fabric of American family life then as it is rare today").

3 Murlin was so guilt-stricken at his brother's death that he never talked about it. I know, Murlin was my father. Only after he died did my cousin tell me the story. At that, it was but one small, sad design in the vast tapestry of a fatally infectious disease as common to the fabric of American family life then as it is rare today. Times were so different then. Grown-ups and children were so quickly subtracted from the world by so many diseases that we no longer have to fear. My grandmother, for instance, died before Wright. She sewed her tubercular sister's burial shroud and then died of the disease herself. Her youngest son was born tubercular. He died before his mother.

By graf 4, he takes his readers to the real subject of his article, the influenza epidemic worldwide.

4 For millions of people fortunate enough to have escaped the horrors of World War I, the plague struck as the fighting neared its end and displaced war as the tragic centerpiece of everyday life. It was known as the Spanish flu and it spread worldwide. In just under a year, starting in the spring of 1918, it killed more than 22 million people, at least twice as many as died in the "war to end all wars." Some estimates, including people who died of complications, go as high as 30 million.

In grafs 5 and 6, he continues the background to the onset of the flu, using more statistics and a quote from a magazine and a nurse.

5 In America, with curiously little fanfare, the flu brought to death a half-million souls, five times as many Americans as died in combat in France. How we tried to cope with the flu and its side effects became what historian Alfred Crosby calls the "greatest failure of medical science" ever.

6 "Never before," an article in *Science* magazine stated in 1919, had there been, "a catastrophe at once so sudden, so devastating and so universal." Describing 1918 here at home, a nurse from Milwaukee said that it was the "year men cried."

From here, Fincher takes readers into the heart of his subject. In graf 7, he builds interest by discussing the beginning of the epidemic.

7 The first mild wave of the epidemic began in March 1918 when a mess cook with chills and fever reported for sick call at Fort Riley, Kansas. Pvt. Albert Gitchell said his head and muscles ached and his throat felt sore. By

Grafs 8 and 9 continue the background.

week's end there were 522 such hospital admissions at the fort. Despite the quickening effect of fever, vital signs including heartbeat were slowed by a profound systemic depression. Doctors were puzzled. Disturbing, too, the illness seemed to hit hardest among robust people in their 20's and 30's, a period when resistance is normally high.

8 Yet nobody seemed terribly worried at first, not even when a dozen other overcrowded camps were struck. Military authorities and the government were still concentrating on how to get enough fresh troops to France, where Gen. John J. (Black Jack) Pershing was planning the first American offensive, one that everyone hoped would end the war. Besides, flu had been around since Hippocrates first noted a probably Athenian epidemic in 412 B.C. Centuries later, the Italians christened it influenza di freddo, "influence of the cold." Still later it came to be believed that some "vicious quantity" or sudden shift in the atmosphere mysteriously communicated the disease to whole areas. Fort Riley was a famous cavalry post, and right before the outbreak, it had experienced just such an atmospheric change when gale-force winds shrouded the camp with a noxious pall of prairie dust and stifling smoke from burning horse manure.

9 But exactly what was communicated nobody knew. In fact, though flu shots are of some preventive help today, there is still no known cure for most of influenza's many forms. In 1892, Germany's Richard Pfeiffer thought he'd found the answer in throat cultures of flu patients in Berlin: a blood-nourished bacillus—a rod-shaped bacterium—one-sixteenth the size of a red corpuscle. Other medical researchers weren't so sure. They suspected the existence of invisible microorganisms—viruses (*Smithsonian*, November 1987). But nobody had really pursued this early lead. Why should they have? Flu ranked a distant tenth among the world's causes of death and aroused little concern compared with dread diseases like diphtheria. By and large, too, its initial symptoms in 1918 produced a relatively mild and apparently temporary condition of the kind that used to inspire the old medical school quip, "Quite a godsend! Everybody ill, nobody dying."

10 People were used to death in 1918, not only at the distant fighting front but in crowded training camps. The 46 deaths that followed at Fort Riley were simply attributed to the complications of pneumonia, and the Army quickly went back to training two million men under crowded conditions and shipping them across the North Atlantic. Often they were packed into airless freighter hulls, floating test tubes for breeding virulent, improved mutations of an infection whose only constant, epidemiologists would learn to their dismay, was change. By the summer of 1918, when the latest batch of U.S. troops landed in France, plenty of flu got off with them.

Tension mounts in graf 11 ("By fall, vomiting, dizziness, labored breathing and profuse sweating . . .") as he gets into an account of various "horror stories" around the world (grafs 12 and 13) and in the U.S. (graf 14).

11 By fall, vomiting, dizziness, labored breathing and profuse sweating were added to the previously mild symptoms. Sometimes purple blisters appeared on oxygen-starved skin. Projectile nosebleeds from pulmonary hemorrhages occurred, too. Victims often went into paroxysms of coughing, spitting out pints of yellow-green pus. Flu victims began dying in larger and larger numbers, some violently, within a few days, their lungs, so doctors said, occasionally resembling "melted red currant jelly."

12 From France this second wave of flu spread west to England and south to Spain where it killed eight million Spaniards, which is how it came to be known as Spanish flu, and even, ungallantly, "Spanish Lady." It was called Blitz Katarrh when it struck eastward into the ragged ranks of the Kaiser's army in Germany, and as Konrad Adenauer, then Mayor of Cologne, put it, leaving thousands "too exhausted to hate." On it swept to Russia, China and Japan; down to South Africa and across to India (where 12 million people died of it) and soon to South America. The Spanish Lady's speed beggared belief.

13 The disease had already begun to produce far-flung horror stories. As Richard Collier writes in *The Plague of the Spanish Lady*, one man in Rio de Janeiro asked another where the streetcar stopped, thanked him politely and fell over dead. On a Capetown tram, seven riders, including the conductor and driver, collapsed and died within one three-mile stretch. And in the goldfields south of Johannesburg, Collier reports, an engine operator was hoisting a steel cage full of miners to the surface from deep underground when suddenly a shower of incandescent light detonated in his brain. He reached for the brake lever and froze, his hand rendered powerless to act. The cage kept going, banged against the lift's overhead frame, tore loose and fell back into the shaft, plunging 24 miners to their deaths. Flu exonerated him.

In graf 14 he inserts a sentence about the World Series to provide contrast as well as historical reference point.

14 Among Americans the disease was primarily confined to the Army for several months. On September 3, 1918, a civilian case was documented in Boston. A week later, as Babe Ruth and the Red Sox beat Chicago in the World Series, three men dropped dead on the sidewalks of nearby Quincy. From Maine to the Gulf, from Florida to the Puget Sound, fed by the mass movements of uniformed men and by their contact with civilians, cases began popping up first by hundreds, then by thousands. Statistics pyramided to roughly 10,000 domestic deaths in September. Up to 90 recruits a day were now dying at Camp Stevens, Massachusetts, and Dr. William Henry Welch, the nation's most renowned pathologist, was called in to perform autopsies on bodies "blue as huckleberries." Afterward, shaken, he admitted a truth that the medical establishment hates to share with the public: "This must be some new kind of infection."

Beginning in graf 15, he compares public health agencies then and now (16) and goes on to write about the primitive health conditions then in existence (grafs 17 to 24).

15 For the government and American medical authorities, it was crucial not only to find a cure and a preventative but to insure against possible public panic. Then, as it would now, the main official responsibility lay with the Surgeon General of the United States, Rupert Blue, a quietly competent 26-year career veteran, who had fought bubonic plague in San Francisco and yellow fever in New Orleans.

16 Today, the Public Health Service (PHS) is a far cry from what it was in 1918. Devastating infectious diseases like diphtheria, scarlet fever and smallpox have now all but been eliminated. The PHS now commands a yearly budget of $13 billion, a uniformed corps of 4,500 "shock troops" spread over all 50 states, and some 42,000 Civil Service doctors, scientists, technicians and administrators, not to mention such research installations as the National Institute of Allergy and Infectious Diseases, and the Centers for Disease Control in Atlanta, which have become so prominent lately in the struggle to control and cure AIDS. In 1918 Blue had only a relative handful of doctors and researchers to help him, and a yearly budget—even then regarded as a pittance—of less than $3 million.

17 Flu was not then a reportable disease anywhere in the United States, and many states did not even bother to file death statistics with the federal government—or to keep them at all. Because it was viewed as a common and usually mild disease, it was unlikely that Blue would have had the authority to impose a quarantine or to prevent ships carrying influenza cases from docking. The federal government was far less powerful and pervasive than it is today. Blue's office lacked not only funds but the necessary medical data to do much. He finally decided that it would be impractical to attempt a massive quarantine, a decision that, in retrospect, was probably wise.

18 And sanitary practices in those days were primitive. Restaurants scraped uneaten meat from their customers' plates back into soup stock, then stored it in grimy, germ-ridden ice-boxes. In apartment buildings without plumbing, many tenants simply heaved their sewage into any nearby alley. In city slums and most rural areas, children slept several to a bed.

19 Because of the war, which was America's first priority, more than one third of the nation's 140,000 doctors were in military service and every day more were called up. Trained nurses were even scarcer. Some communities had neither. On October 11, Congress unanimously voted $1 million to cope with influenza; however, a bill to establish a PHS reserve corps was passed too late to do much, if any, good.

Desperately, Blue set about recruiting physicians for the Volunteer Medical Service Corps, a backup organization for the PHS.

20 Eventually he also called upon the states to ban large gatherings. Contrary to political cartoons of the day (and even the *Journal of the American Medical Association*), Blue confirmed Doctor Welch's diagnosis. The bug was not your garden-variety influenza This was some kind of relentless new killer.

Good transitions move the story along effortlessly.

21 Alas, other dangerous infections were in the air—fatuity, folly, finger pointing and wishful thinking. Cities as diverse as Santa Fe, San Francisco, Philadelphia and Seattle bragged that they need not worry—the flu would be kept at bay by their ideal climates. People were presented with a welter of official commentary and patronizing reassurance, much of it nonsense. A community doctor in Arizona, perhaps trying to keep the lid on panic, reported 50 fresh cases as follows: "all mild, four deaths." Mild? An 8 percent death rate?

22 The New York City Health Commissioner, Royal Copeland, seemed hell-bent on single-handedly jawboning the epidemic into remission by blaming it on unsanitary Europeans. "You haven't heard of our doughboys getting it, have you?" he asked in airy disregard both of the evidence and the fact that existing rules of censorship forbade any such news from being published. "You bet you haven't, and you won't. No need for our people to worry." Copeland was not the only one who opposed Blue's flu alarms. In Missouri, one official even dismissed the flu as "Hun propaganda." Partly to avoid panic, mainly because it was overshadowed by the war, some newspapers tended to downplay the epidemic, just as the country would at first downplay the spread of AIDS.

23 In general, Blue's plea for enforced limitations on public gatherings to prevent spread of the disease fell upon ears deafened by the din of martial music. Thirteen million young men—ideal fodder for infection—were still jamming public buildings to register for the draft. In late September, a national subscription to finance the war effort got under way from coast to coast with mammoth rallies, parades and canvasses. In Philadelphia 200,000 marched; in San Francisco, 150,000. Did no one but the Surgeon General reckon the danger? Chicago did. After a rainy procession, tens of thousands were told to go home, shuck their wet clothes and take a purgative. Evangelist Billy Sunday joined the patriotic rush and dismissed the whole affair as a German ploy: "There's nothing short of hell they haven't stooped to do since the war began. Darn their hides!"

24 It wasn't long before the nation's thin, blue line of surrogate health officers started fining public spitters as well as handkerchiefless sneezers and coughers, and issuing calls for mandatory face masks. Sales and production of masks exploded. Workers wore them in offices and in factories, and in some cities you couldn't climb on a bus or a trolley without one. But there was plenty of heated argument and plenty of backsliding from people who didn't believe masks helped and didn't like being told what to do.

Graf 25 breaks the account of tragedy with some lighter anecdotes (Fincher calls them "oddities") and graf 26 gives more statistics.

25 And, as so often happened with the flu, tragedy was marked by comic oddities. A pair of newlyweds in San Francisco left an indelible impression on a young doctor friend by telling him they'd worn therapeutic masks and nothing else—when they made love. In Tucson, Judge L. C. Cowan fined a window washer for removing his mask to blow the panes dry. Widely worn, masks probably were marginally helpful in the general way of hygiene and as a discouragement to intimacy.

26 As flu hopscotched around the country, the death toll mounted: from 2,899 in August, to 10,481 in September to 196,876 in October; in the last four months of 1918, well over 300,000 died. Both sexes and all races were hit. Surprisingly, a general exodus failed to occur; the poor couldn't afford to run, and because the disease seemed quixotic, the rich never knew where to go to avoid it.

In graf 27, Fincher is ready to answer the question, "why?" He continues to

27 Historians still ask themselves how more than a half-million Americans could die in hardly more than ten months, in the most

expand upon this in grafs 28 and 29.

lethal internal convulsion since the Civil War (498,000 soldiers dead in four years), without laying a comparable mark on the country's psyche. But the astonishing truth is that during the epidemic few people were in a position to see the big picture, and not one of the few was actively in charge overall, though the resulting chaos, assessed in retrospect, would result in an expanded Public Health Service with an excelled reporting system. Moreover, only one man, President Woodrow Wilson, possessed the means to mobilize national consciousness. But except when the flu threatened to disrupt troop movements or hamper vital arms production, Wilson was far too busy prosecuting the "war to end all wars" to bother with a silent foe that ebbed and surged like wildfire, burning itself out here, moving on there. And where it concerned soldiers this foe was often protected by the cloak of official censorship.

28 Not that any of that would have mattered in the end. For nothing helped, really. Cause and cure—transmission and prevention—all remained mysteries. Transmission? Almost surely airborne by human breath, but what a Pandora's box of potentially ill winds that was. Phone booths were padlocked and streets sprinkled; cashiers were equipped with finger bowls of disinfectant. Public places from dance halls, pool rooms and movie houses to libraries, schools and ice cream parlors, even red-light districts, were buttoned up. Churches and saloons were shut tight, too, though not without spirited resistance.

29 But controlling possible contagion on such a scale was virtually impossible. One sanitation officer counted 199 individual chances for exposure in any citizen's average day. Victor Vaughan, Acting Surgeon General of the Army, thought that ten daily contacts was more realistic, but even that number, if carried to a logical conclusion, could multiply to millions of infections a week.

30 At a West Coast Navy base, guards were ordered to shoot to kill anyone attempting to enter or leave without official permission. Drinking fountains were sanitized hourly by blowtorch, telephones drenched in alcohol.

Draftees were given "close order drill," keeping a 20-foot interval. Yet such Herculean efforts were mocked by inexplicable immunities. Waterbury, Connecticut, suffered 753 deaths in one month alone. Milford, 20 miles away, escaped completely. In Montana, people were baffled by the relative lack of flu among butchers, Methodists and underground miners.

Beginning in graf 31, he uses one word transitions ("Prevention?" "Cure?" "Cause?") to carry readers along.

31 Prevention? There were plenty of vaccines. Illinois alone tried 18 different kinds without success. Across the land, doctors rushed to create prophylactic solutions. Certain he had located the best, the mayor of Boston ordered his secretary to carry a batch to San Francisco via the 20th Century Limited, a crack express train. Seventeen thousand Bay Area hopefuls lined up for doses despite widespread assertions that such "soups" offered nothing more than a sore arm. One wit claimed the popularity of the shots was simply a result of the spinach ethic—being so unpleasant, they must be good for you.

32 Cure? Today we know there was none, so understandably in 1918 the medical profession was baffled. Naturally, good old American home medicine bulged with all sorts of cures, from tiny doses of strychnine and kerosene to red-pepper sandwiches and something called Bulgarian blood tea. Nostrums ranged from the bizarre to the superstitious. As a preventative, people variously sprinkled sulfur in their shoes, wore vinegar packs on their stomachs, tied slices of cucumber to their ankles or carried a potato in each pocket. According to one belief, if you placed a shotgun under the bed the fine steel in it would draw out fever. In New Orleans, people bought voodoo charms and chanted. "Sour, sour, vinegar V, keep the sickness off of me." One Volunteer Medical Corps general championed "breathing through the nose, chewing food well, and avoiding tight clothes, shoes and gloves." One mother in Portland, Oregon, buried her 4-year-old girl from head to toe in raw, sliced onions. An appalled Chicago physician summed it all up as "poly-pharmacy run riot."

33 Cause? In some areas Pfeiffer's bacillus was detected almost daily in influenza victims, in other places it was absent altogether. Intrepid military volunteers were injected with 13 different strains of flu bacillus, had their throats swabbed with pulmonary secretions from the sick and allowed the inside of their noses to be painted with a broth of pure bacillus. Nothing happened. Indeed, in New York an entire family of six was stricken, each member found to be infected with a different bacterium. It was chillingly ineluctable—as in the ditty recited on playgrounds everywhere:

I had a little bird
And its name was Enza.
I opened the window
And in-flew-Enza.

In graf 34, Fincher begins a section on the tragic consequences of the flu epidemic. The number and variety of stories he reveals is a testament to his research.

34 The tragic stories accumulated. Years later in San Francisco, Henry Burt, a secretary, would recall a frightful bridge game: "We played until long after midnight. When we left, we were all apparently well. By 8 o'clock in the morning I was too ill to get out of bed, and the friend at whose house we played was dead." A stricken Congressman and his bride, clinically gowned and masked, were married at his hospital bedside; seven hours later he succumbed.

35 "Hunt up your wood workers and cabinet-makers and set them making coffins," one health department was morbidly advised. "Then take your street laborers and set them to digging graves." Devastated Pennsylvania had learned the wisdom of that country saying through grim experience. In one week a total of 5,000 people died in Pittsburgh and Philadelphia. So overwhelmed was the latter city that 528 bodies piled up in a single day awaiting burial. More lay beside the gutters or in rooming houses.

36 As fear spread, laws and law enforcement in some cities grew savage. In Chicago, charges of murder were demanded against landlords whose sick tenants died after their heat was turned off for non-payment of rent. In New York City, 500 people were arrested for violating "Spitless Sunday": doctors were fined for failing to report new flu cases.

37 Violence and vigilantism flourished. Strangers from notoriously infected states who got off the train in some New Mexico towns were told to move on. A Montana rancher intercepted a doctor on the road and forced him at gunpoint to treat his family. In *Memories of a Catholic Girlhood*, Mary McCarthy tells how her father drew a pistol on a conductor who was trying to shunt his ailing family off the train bearing them to relatives in Minneapolis. San Francisco's authoritarian, chief public health officer, who was a stickler for masks, was sent a bomb containing black gunpowder, buckshot and broken glass. Frontier justice may have reached some sort of zeal when Prescott, Arizona, made it a jailable offense to shake hands, adopting the proposal from an obscure Italian Fascist newspaper publisher named Benito Mussolini.

38 By mid-autumn, public services were crippled everywhere. Some shipyards working on war contracts reported that their employees were ill. In Pennsylvania and Kentucky, officials demanded that the Army send medical help to coal-mining towns to sustain the vital war effort.

39 For every 1 who died in the United States, an estimated 50 had the disease. Some took advantage of the pandemonium to steal or to seek oblivion in drink for weeks on end, but for the most part, as A. A. Hochling wrote, "There were two principal categories of people: those afflicted with the disease and those who endeavored to save them."

40 All that could really be done it turned out, was to keep the patient quiet, warm, fed and medicated against other life-threatening communications, but even that put a terrible burden on the people who were well, though sick, still able to get about. Everywhere the call went out for anyone with two hands and a willingness to work. Helping their prostrate relatives small children cooked, kept house, cared for and cleaned up after the sick. Some, like those of their elders unable to face the plague, wandered the streets in a daze. Minneapolis police set up a special search for parents of a hundred homeless youngsters found alone and hiding. In Chicago, a laborer crazed by the illness of his wife and four children screamed, "I'll cure them my own way" and cut their throats. Families called the authorities to report the terminally ill, then quickly fled their homes in terror.

41 With churches closed, people prayed elsewhere, sometimes using crude outdoor altars as they did in Maine where a priest set up a table and a cross in a garage doorway, and worshipers knelt in the snow. Some deeply believed that the plague had been visited on the world as Divine punishment for human sinfulness. Acting Army Surgeon General Vaughan gave voice to a different, but statistically chilling, thought: "If the epidemic continues its mathematical rate of acceleration," he announced, "civilization could easily [disappear] from the face of the Earth."

42 Stretched to the breaking point and worked to exhaustion, doctors and nurses labored on. They pumped railroad handcars to reach isolated cases, made their rounds by horse and newfangled airplane. Not only did they treat whole families, they assembled and handed out food and blankets; they milked cows, cooked, built fires, heated water, and bathed and dressed the helpless. They grabbed meals from the family stew pot and fell asleep on the nearest couch. Or dozed upright in their buggies, warmed by heated bricks wrapped in newspapers as their horses were given free rein.

43 And gradually a kind of dogged selflessness, sometimes amounting to heroism, became commonplace. Businesses, hotels, fraternity houses, private clubs, even the exclusive Vanderbilt farm in Rhode Island donated their premises for emergency hospitals. Private automobiles and taxicabs, as well as the limousines of society matrons, chauffeured medics and served as ambulances. Off-duty police and firemen drove ambulances and carried stretchers. Department stores distributed relief supplies and opened phone banks so people could make emergency calls.

Volunteers canvassed house-to-house searching for those too weak to cry out for help.

In graf 44, Fincher notes the first glimmers of hope for an end to the scourge ("the long day's night began to fade").

44 Fitfully, the long day's night began to fade. People who had the disease and survived, either by chance or because of care that prevented pneumonia, the most common and most deadly complication, seemed to be immune from further episodes. Like a storm, the Spanish flu eventually blew itself out. On November 7, a false Armistice sent a million people streaming into the streets of Philadelphia to kiss and hug and dance in defiance of every public health tenet. When the real Armistice was signed four days later there was no holding back a war-weary nation. Factory whistles blew, church bells and fire bells rang, and in Chicago 16,000 police could not keep the joyous crowds from jamming together. A third wave of flu—harsher than the first yet milder than the second—was still to come by year's end. But as far as the people were concerned, the real crisis had passed. Psychologically, at least, the end of the war had upstaged it.

Using the device of a space (as in the change of scene in a play), Fincher sums up beginning in graf 45. He recapitulates the statistics (46, 47, and 48) and ties the killer disease of 1918 with the killer disease of today, AIDS (49).

45 Despite panic, foolishness and even some blatant cowardice, historians tend to give the population full marks under fire: "To an amazing extent, enthusiasm was successfully substituted for preparation and efficiency," Alfred Crosby observes.

46 More than 25 million Americans were infected, perhaps a billion beings worldwide. Direct U.S. economic losses have been put at $3 billion, but an insurance industry expert calculated the influenza epidemic as an "actuarial nightmare," which would ultimately cost the United States alone ten million years in productive lives cut off in their prime. "Nothing else," writes Crosby, "no infection, no war, no famine—has ever killed so many in as short a period."

47 And yet, he adds, the influenza epidemic "has never inspired awe, not in 1918 and not since." There were isolated literary masterpieces like Katherine Anne Porter's short novel *Pale Horse, Pale Rider*, but many of the best-selling college history books in the United States fail to mention it and one understates the deaths by half.

48 As for the mysterious Spanish flu virus, it seemed to vanish from the planet as if it had never been. Since then there have been plenty of milder ones of course. Today we know that influenza viruses have a genius for assigning new forms when an old one has run its course. The World Health Organization isolates each new flu strain, analyzes it and, if antibodies prove low in global population samples, annually modifies the effective, existing vaccine to combat what might otherwise become another universal antigen. It is tedious work, and even now there are no guarantees for the cure. The existence of antibiotics, however, would probably minimize the number of deaths from complications such as pneumonia, which killed many of the victims in 1918.

49 As evolutionary biologist Stephen Jay Gould recently told an AIDS-lecture audience: "We've had a couple of generations of great fortune: since the . . . flu epidemic of 1918, there has not been a [lethal] pandemic disease that struck the human population. If you look through human history, a pandemic is everyday biology. With our usual hubris we felt that we'd learned through technological advances to be free of it forever. But we're not."

Fincher ends his article very simply by taking readers back to the uncle they were introduced to in the lead.

50 Rest in peace, Uncle Wright.

12
Writing Reviews

It is impossible for a free-lance writer to earn a living exclusively by writing reviews. People who review various creative works as their sole source of income are usually full-time employees of newspapers and magazines, not free-lance writers. There are several reasons for this limited market. For one, reviews are essays and good essays are precise and to the point: an average of 750 to 1,000 words. No publication will pay as much for a review of that length as it will for a 3,000 word article. Second, reviews are made up of opinion, telling whether a reviewer liked a work well enough to recommend it to others. While the process takes time—reading a book or seeing a film, play, or television show—it does not involve nearly as much effort as researching, reporting, and writing a 3,000 to 5,000 word article.

Another factor is that reviews have limited reader interest. Except for specialized publications, few readers want to peruse more than one or two reviews in a given issue of their favorite periodical. Reviews cover specific creative works and not all readers are interested in knowing about every new offering. A film buff may not be interested in a new television sitcom; a restaurant goer may not care about a new biography or novel. Moreover, editors cannot justify publishing as many reviews per issue—if they publish them at all—as they do conventional articles. As a result, they will not assign them to even a free-lance writer they use regularly with the same frequency they do articles.

Nevertheless, free-lance writers should not ignore review writing entirely. Such essays are challenging—because of the need for clarity, succinctness, and well-reasoned opinion—and fun to do. You will also be rewarded with free books and movie and play tickets, along with a modest fee of probably $100 to $200, except for major publications which pay more. There is also a certain prestige associated with reviewing that you can use to good advantage. By including reviews in your portfolio, you may attract other work.

The writing of reviews is quite different from other magazine writing discussed in this book for several reasons:

- *Opinion is everything.* Unlike the articles noted in previous chapters, reviews need to contain a lot of your opinions or they aren't reviews. Readers are looking to you for guidance on whether they should buy the book or the movie ticket, or waste their time on a new TV show. Your opinion should be *informed* opinion, however. You need to develop more than a passing interest in a genre. This means you should be well read or knowledgeable about film techniques, for example, or how food should be cooked and seasoned to be considered good.
- *Interviewing is not necessary.* You base your opinion on your own experience, not by talking to sources as you would to prepare other articles.
- *Information counts too.* Along with your thoughts about whether a creative work is good or bad should come details about plot, story, or facts. A good review weaves such detail into the opinion, both to support the subjective comments and to teach readers something about the work.

If you are interested in writing reviews, it is probably wiser to start with local or regional publications than national ones. You can use local clips later to sell reviews to periodicals with a broader reach. The process begins with a written query or a phone call to an editor. If no one is reviewing regularly or at all, chances are good that the editor will give you a try. Even small newspapers like to include book, film, and play reviews as an alternative to a steady diet of often bad news.

From here, you can branch out. One way to do reviews regularly is to set up your own syndicate: talk a number of papers in your area into running your reviews once or twice a week and paying you $50 per submission. Or, work out an arrangement with a real feature syndicate or news service to sell your reviews to various outlets. The ultimate kind of reviewing is that done for national magazines and newspapers. You will have the best luck if you approach editors for whom you are already working. Will they let you write reviews? All they can say is no.

The process of writing the reviews themselves begins with your reading or viewing of whatever work you are considering. If it is a book, you need to take notes and mark passages as you go. If it is a visual medium, you should also take notes on factual information (character and actor names, director, studio, network) and write down critical observations as they occur to you.

This done, you should look over your notes—and the work itself, if possible—and begin to write. There are four main approaches to reviewing:

- *Reportorial*. This is a descriptive method in which the reviewer describes the book, film, TV show, or play as a reporter would, expressing an opinion only slightly. This style is used for reviews in most major publications.
- *Classical*. In this method, the reviewer considers the work in relation to the standards established by tradition in the field. Scholarly journals follow this style.
- *Panoramic*. Reviewers following this method use historical perspective to consider the new creative work against those of the past in the same category. A few national magazines (*The New Yorker*) follow this approach.
- *Impressionistic*. In this method, reviewers consider the work and write about it as it affects them as human beings. This approach works best in art and music reviews and, possibly, restaurant reviews.

Most reviews for consumer publications today follow a reportorial approach: telling readers what happened and whether you liked what you read or saw. Reviews written for more academic or specialized markets usually use one of the other three styles.

A review begins with a first paragraph in which you state your theme or give an excerpt or plot summary to attract reader interest. From here, you proceed by continuing to give your opinions backed up by excerpts and examples. You need also to include consumer information (price, publisher, theater, TV channel, restaurant location, etc.). A review shouldn't just stop, it should end by being tied to the lead paragraph in a circular fashion or by leaving readers with a provocative idea.

One final word about reviewing in general: you needn't worry about getting into legal trouble for expressing your opinions. Reviewers—along with editorial writers and sports writers—are protected under the doctrine of fair comment and criticism. Under this rule, courts protect writers who comment on and criticize the work of others, as long as that comment is restricted to their work,

Box 12.1 Types of Reviews Compared

Medium	Influence	Style	Payment	Perks and Privileges
Book	Except for prominent placement in key Sunday book review section, probably nil.	Reportorial, Opinion essay	Free book, smallish fee from publications	An avalanche of books from publishers
Movie	Except in large cities where a good review can influence attendance, probably nil.	Reportorial, Panoramic in discussing past films of director, actors	Free tickets, smallish fee	Special screenings, press kits loaded with background material.
Play	Life or death with *New York Times*. Otherwise, minor influence on attendance.	Reportorial, Panoramic, Classical	Free tickets, smallish fee	Admittance to dress rehearsal, opening night; playbill; published versions of play
Television	At times might influence networks to change undesirable trends, save low rated shows; otherwise nil.	Reportorial, Feature, Investigative	Smallish fee	Special screening, press kits, loaded with background material.
Restaurant	Can bring diners to undiscovered cafe, keep them away from a place serving bad food.	Reportorial	Smallish fee, price of meal reimbursed	Big expense account (you need a strong stomach, as well as the metabolism to remain slim)

is factual, is free of malice, and does not get overly personal.

Five kinds of reviews will be covered in detail in this chapter: book, both fiction and nonfiction; film; theater; television, both fictional and news/documentary; and restaurant. These are genres of most interest to readers of popular publications, hence their inclusion here. Other kinds of reviewing—like music, dance, or art—are not covered because they require special education and training beyond the capabilities of most free-lance writers. It isn't enough to say you like a concert or a painting, you owe it to your readers to base your opinions on a greater depth of knowledge.

In any kind of review you write, always remember that it is more fun to be critical, even slashing, in what you write than it is to give a work nothing but praise. Don't criticize just for the sake of criticism; but on the other hand, don't gush over everything—especially inferior work.

Book Reviewing

The dominant medium for reviewing new books in the United States is *The New York Times Book Review*, published each week as a section of the Sunday edition of that newspaper. The *Review*, first published in 1896, is important for several reasons. It is published in New York, the publishing center of the country. Publishers place most of their advertising budgets in the *Review*, so it has many pages, both for the ads and the reviews. It attracts prestigious reviewers. Placement of a review on the front cover often assures good sales or even a spot on the best seller list. Any review at all, even a negative one, will boost sales just because the *Review*'s editors have selected the book out of the literally thousands it receives for consideration annually.

The *Review* sometimes generates controversy for its choice of reviewers, for example, picking someone who is known to dislike an author or his or her work (deliberately inviting an unfavorable review), or conversely, to be a friend or business associate of an author (deliberately inviting a favorable review). Reviewers are selected for their expertise in the subject of the book and identified at the bottom of the page so readers can make their own judgment about fairness.

Beyond the individual reviews it publishes, *The New York Times Book Review* exercises its greatest influence through the best seller list appearing in each issue. The rankings, based on computer-processed sales figures from 3,080 bookstores and wholesalers serving 28,000 other retail outlets, have a big impact on book sales nationally.

Box 12.2 Unconventional Free-Lance Writing

There are several kinds of unconventional and nontraditional writing a free-lancer might successfully pursue. Although similar to reviews in the expression of opinion, these genres are somewhat different:

- *Columns.* Most feature syndicates are constantly looking for new column ideas. With the market as flooded as it is, however, the approach must be truly unique to attract attention. From humor to politics to any number of specific topics in between, the choice is up to you. The approach has got to be one that can be sustained over a long period of time. You must also ask yourself if you have the staying power to send in one, two, or three 500- to 750-word columns each week. Successful columns are distributed by feature syndicates which sign up a number of subscriber publications (usually daily newspapers) and pay you a set fee based on the number you have attracted. (The names and addresses of feature syndicates are listed in *Writer's Market.*)
- *Essays.* The writing of essays seems today to be something from a bygone era. For many publications, essays have gone the way of weekly installments of serials (a la *Saturday Evening Post*). A small market does exist for personal essays, however, primarily in the Op-Ed pages of newspapers, academic literary reviews, and political opinion journals. The topics can range from politics to the more personal views a writer has towards life to humor.
- *Fillers.* Fillers, the small, often humorous, asides magazines and newspapers used to use to fill up space when articles fell short, are almost as archaic as essays. They usually involve newspaper headlines and stories with a double meaning or funny things that happen to you or that you hear about. This is a tough market because humor is often in the funny-bone of the beholder and not funny to others. It is also hard to write something with the proper cadence so that the buildup and punch line come out correctly. Both *The New Yorker* and *Reader's Digest* accept this kind of short piece, along with many smaller publications. The competition for space in these two national magazines is fairly stiff, however.

You won't get rich by attempting to place any or all of these unconventional kinds of writing but, as in all free-lancing, what have you got to lose? At worst, the editors you contact will say no. But perhaps, on occasion, they will say yes.

The dominance of the *Review* means that few other newspapers even have separate book sections. Two notable ones appear in the *Los Angeles Times* and the *Washington Post* but neither have the impact of the *Review*. Part of the reason is tradition and part is their puny size: because publisher advertising is much less, they cannot run as many pages.

The most other newspapers can do is a page or two of book reviews, again because of the absence of publisher advertising. *Time* and *Newsweek* used to run more reviews than they do now. They restrict them mostly because of space limitations. Many specialized magazines publish reviews of books about certain subjects, whether that subject be politics or sports or science or whatever.

Two trade magazines are very influential with their readers: *Library Journal* (for libraries) and *Publisher's Weekly* (for bookstore owners).

Except for the news magazines, all book review sections or pages use free-lance writers to review books.

Fiction

In reviewing works of fiction, you should give an overview of the plot, without revealing surprises. You need to tell the type of novel you are reviewing—popular, historical, mystery, psychological, science fiction, children's, horror—and indicate the locale of the story.

You should introduce the main characters and indicate whether they are believable. Do you—and will readers—care about them? Does what they say make sense? The use of excerpts will help you make your points, either straight narrative or dialogue.

How is the writing? How well does the story move? Is it plotted well? Is it interesting? If the book is based on real events, does it contain errors? How does it compare to other books by the author?

And, finally, a review needs to answer the big question: Should the reader buy this book? You don't always have to say so outright, but should at least imply the answer through the comments you make.

Book reviews should include the title of the book, author's name, publisher, number of pages, and price. The latter serves as valuable information for consumers because book ads rarely include price any more. This data can be listed at the beginning of the review or in the body, depending on the style of the publication buying your review.

To write the following review of a novel, the editors of *The New York Times Book Review* chose another novelist. This is a common practice, apparently because of the feeling that someone who has written fiction would be familiar with plotting, characterization, and dialogue.

Fiction Review

This reviewer does not mince words: he likes what he has read ("powerful new novel"). He goes on to give a short summation of the plot by asking several questions.

He makes his transition by using the names of two key characters and continues to summarize the plot.

In the next three paragraphs (3, 4, 5) he lets direct excerpts move his review along.

BEFORE AND AFTER
by Rosellen Brown
354 pp. New York:
Farrar, Straus & Giroux. $21.

—by Michael Dorris

1 Rosellen Brown's powerful new novel, *Before and After*, addresses, more than anything else, the cherished concept of personal independence. To what extent is a family free of the community in which it dwells? How closely is each of us tied to the fate of those we love? Do any of the traditional means by which we attempt to define ourselves—education, good name, success, political integrity—insure our protection when a chance event intrudes?

2 Ben and Carolyn Reiser, the people at the center of *Before and After*, certainly seem safer than most. Ben is a sculptor of ascending reputation, while Carolyn is a capable pediatrician; their children, Jacob and Judith, are bright, attractive teenagers, occasionally baffling to their parents but for the most part a source of pride and satisfaction. Tucked into their interesting rural New Hampshire house, the Reisers are friendly toward their Yankee neighbors, keeping their urban sophistication subtle, turned down. Long-term and year-round residents, they're rooted by choice if not by birth, just slightly, self-consciously pleased with the accommodations they've made. Ben, especially.

3 "Then the bell rang.

4 "It rang into the ordinary noises of our day. It rasped so harshly that when I tried to go back to it, or just before, it sounded like the gong they ring at boxing matches, urgent, a rip through space and time, promising cruelty and pain.

5 "I've heard about stories, how they're really just a finely strung architecture of *the way things were* and *the way things turned out*, held together—or divided, would be better—by the most terrible word, the word that lifts the roof off, lands the ax blow, curdles the milk. The blood. All the world's change, its doom, its fatality, is in it: *Then* . . ."

He resumes his own summations in graf 6 . . .

6 Like an avalanche, crushing facts thud into Ben and Carolyn's comfortable existence: a girl, a not especially remarkable or particularly nice girl, has been brutally murdered. She was last seen with Jacob—apparently they had secretly been a couple for some time—and now the Reisers' beloved son, the boy with eyes "the color of new jeans," is nowhere to be found.

. . . and 7.

7 That first day, after the local policeman departs, Ben finds damning evidence in Jacob's car and instantly, instinctively, out of primal loyalty, makes a shocking choice from which there is no easy retreat. The deeds of one family member implicate another, who implicates still another, and on and on in a rapidly escalating chain reaction.

In graf 8, the reviewer tells readers about the author's previous works and the strengths of this story ("deftly, artfully").

8 Ms. Brown, whose previous novels include *Tender Mercies* and *Civil Wars,* is tenacious in her examination of each major character. Deftly, artfully, she strips away the delicate shelter of conventional relationships—husband and wife, parent and child—and reveals a dangerous arena where virtual strangers, each with his or her own priorities and set of understandings, vie in mortal contention for the choice of values that will predominate and prevail: integrity or survival, love or self-respect. The lines of demarcation blur, altering with the ebb and flow of circumstance, of subjective interpretation.

The reviewer expands on the overview of the story in grafs 9, 10, and 11, noting at times how good it is: a "read-until-dawn page turner."

9 *Before and After* is all about broken rules and skewed allegiances, about being cornered and having no weapons save the familiar tools salvaged from a prior life. A bucolic town, once friendly and folksy, closes ranks against outsiders who have contaminated its "sweet once-upon-a-time." Predictability is replaced by chaos as the jarring revelations of secrets accumulate. Balance is replaced by a world that tilts wildly, utterly destabilized by acts as mundane as taking a picture postcard out of the mailbox or catching a matinee at the local movie theater.

10 As the intricate plot develops—and this novel, for all its philosophical provocation and literary merit, is also an unabashed, read-until-dawn page turner—Ms. Brown shifts the focus of her interest from husband to wife, daughter to son, and back again. Characters emerge sharply, their latent personality traits heightened by the test of crisis. Ben assumes the mantle of an almost Old Testament paternity while Carolyn, the scientist, strives to maintain a clinical analysis of the situation. Jacob, in one of the book's most emotional scenes, wrenchingly communicates the wider context of the crime, and Judith, staggered by the collapse she witnesses in every direction, retreats into herself.

11 Of her brother, whom she has always held in awe, she eventually decides: "He deserved to kill himself. At least, if he did that he could prove his honest sorrow. Otherwise—he was doubly guilty if he lived, and her father was worse. She saw the smile, slightly mischievous, slightly menacing, altogether unfamiliar, that he'd shown while he spun out their foolproof lie. Whenever Snappy caught a bird or a squirrel or even a little lizard, she made a strange sound in her throat, a plea, almost. It was odd, excited and frightened at the same time. A quaking noise. That was what he'd looked like, in some funny way. She had no words for it; she had no name, right now, for her father."

12 Carolyn, appealing for some sign of recognition, even empathy, from the dead girl's mother, is equally at a loss:

He resumes using direct excerpts in graf 13 to let them move his review along and interest readers.

13 " 'We're—we're probably going to lose our son,' she said quietly, and hot tears gathered in the corners of her eyes. Could she really dare to instruct this woman in their shared tragedy? 'I've spent a thousand hours not sleeping, thinking about Martha. I just want you to know. It won't change things, but if you could—'

14 " 'What?' Mrs. Taverner spoke her first words harshly, 'If I could *what*?'

"Carolyn shrugged. 'I don't know.' She reached out for the frame of the stall door and held it gratefully. 'If you could think of us as—'What? 'Human? As parents—a family, I mean, who's also—so—helpless?' "

He sums up the lessons of the book in the last paragraph.

15 In the end, of course, the Reisers' road doesn't come to a melodramatic end; Rosellen Brown is too original and truthful a writer to depend on easy solutions. Instead, imperfect American justice is meted out (and captured on videotape), and people "with congruent wounds" find a measure of comfort in one another, then move toward the acceptance of their enduring scars. The path smooths, breaks back into a dappled light, but its destination is no longer clear. Nor, for those involved even on the periphery of this domestic disaster, will it ever be completely so again.

Nonfiction

With nonfiction books, you need to tell the kind of book you are reviewing: current affairs, biography, autobiography, history, travel, reference, business, self-help, or whatever. You must give the background of the author to indicate his or her ability to handle the material. Is that material accurate or does the book contain errors?

How good is the writing? Even though the book is factual, it still should move along well enough to interest readers and not get unnecessarily bogged down.

If photos or illustrations are used, how good are they? Do they add to the quality of the book or detract from it?

Even though you must tell readers how you liked the book, it is also important to include several paragraphs on what the book is about, interspersed with excerpts to back up your points.

Sometimes, you may want to write your review as an essay in which you put forth your opinion on the subject and review the book—or one or two others on the same subject—almost secondarily.

As with fiction, nonfiction reviews should include title, author, publisher, number of pages, and price.

This review of a political autobiography, which appeared in *The New York Times Book Review*, was written by a *Times* White House correspondent.

Nonfiction Review

NOFZIGER
By Lyn Nofziger
370 pp. Washington:
Regnery Gateway. $21.95.

—by Maureen Dowd

She states her theme in the first paragraph: the vendettas and alliances of Washington insiders.

1 For a long time, I've wanted to take a black Magic Marker and draw a genealogical chart. Modeled on those family trees found in the beginning of romance novels spanning three generations, my chart would trace the trellis of vendettas and alliances that connect Washington officials, spouses, strategists and consultants.

She ties that theme to the book under review which she notes in graf 2. Her summation is brief, but compelling (a "tangle of Republican debts and double-crosses").

2 Unless you are a political junkie, you may not have much interest in Lyn Nofziger's autobiography, *Nofziger*, but his tales are invaluable for illuminating the tangle of Republican debts and double-crosses.

She describes the author in graf 3 . . .

3 A conservative tough guy who worked for Richard Nixon and Ronald Reagan, the author offers blunt and salty opinions from his years as journalist, press secretary and lobbyist. Many readers will remember Mr. Nofziger as the reassuring spokesman, in the frightening hours after the assassination attempt on Mr. Reagan, who jotted down and conveyed the wounded President's quips.

. . . and his writing style in graf 4.

4 His prose style is rambling, repetitive and cheerfully retro. At one point he disdainfully describes John Sears, Mr. Reagan's 1976 campaign manager, as "the kind of person who ordered chicken instead of steak for his main dinner course." He complains about a secretary who became a "women's libber" and recalls that he was "crying like a girl" when Gerald Ford triumphed over Mr. Reagan at the 1976 Republican National Convention.

She calls the author "irreverent" in graf 5 . . .

5 More irreverent about power and perks than most Washington insiders, he still looks at things from a parochial angle. Here is his description of the time he persuaded Mr. Reagan, then Governor of California, to try to warm up his image by coming east to make a speech on welfare:

. . . and authenticates that comment with an excerpt (6).

6 "I picked the wrong date—April 5, 1968. . . . When the Reagans arrived in Washington . . . I met them at the plane with the bad news. 'We're going to have to go through with this,' I told them. 'But we're not going to get any publicity. Somebody has shot Martin Luther King.' "

She sums up the book ("no airbrushed memoir") and the author in graf 7, relying, no doubt, on her experience as a White House correspondent to provide personal details.

7 This is no airbrushed memoir. He describes Mr. Reagan as "a jewel" but "no genius." Perhaps Mr. Nofziger's setbacks—a stroke, a conviction on charges of ethical violations that cost him most of his lobbying business and $1.8 million in legal fees before it was overturned by a Federal appeals court, and the loss of a daughter to cancer—left him feeling that life is too short and too mean to mince words. Not that the scruffy, pun-loving Mickey Mouse tie-wearing politico ever did much of that anyway.

She ends the review with a very effective 10-paragraph series of pointed and funny excerpts that reveal more about the book than would further comments by her.

8 Herewith, a sampling of Lyn Nofziger's insights about the Republican family tree.

9 On James A. Baker 3d: "His best buddy is himself, James A. Baker 3d. The President runs a poor second, as he may eventually discover. . . . One of his hobbies is wild turkey hunting. It has inspired my definition of fratricide: Jim Baker bagging a turkey."

10 On Mr. Reagan's opinion of George Bush as a possible Vice President: "Ever since the New Hampshire campaign, during which Bush had handled himself badly in a row over who should participate in a debate, Reagan had thought him a wimp.

11 On Mr. Reagan's opinion after Mr. Bush became Vice President: "Bush, he decided, was not after all a wimp."

12 On Mr. Reagan running for Governor in 1966: "He . . . got away with denying that, in referring to efforts to preserve California's famed and endangered redwood forests, he ever said, 'A tree is a tree. How many more do you have to look at?' My secretary, Judith Kernoff, had it on tape, but that was something we didn't tell him or anyone else, so he was free to do one of the things he has always done best—convince himself that the truth is what he wants it to be."

13 On Mr. Reagan's tenure as governor: "There were no women in the highest part of the hierarchy. Just men, a couple of whom, it turned out, not only were men but appeared to like men. It isn't that we were deliberately sexist, just that we were naturally sexist. . . . While on the general subject, there also were no blacks, Jews or Mexicans in that uppermost echelon."

14 On why Mr. Reagan had no women officials in his White House inner circle: "There never had been, and Reagan probably figured, if he bothered to figure at all, that that's the way it was supposed to be."

15 On Nancy Reagan: "One thing about Nancy, you can tell when she's angry with you. You either get hollered at or get the silent treatment. To the best of my recollection Nancy was really angry with me only four times, including when she tried to get me fired in 1967–68, which was the second time. The first was during the 1966 campaign. I noticed she hadn't been speaking to me for a few days and I didn't know why. So I asked the candidate, 'Is Nancy mad at me?' 'Well,' he said, 'she didn't like the remark you made about her perfume. You hurt her feelings.' Oops! The lady had been wearing a gardenia perfume, which I can't stand, and I'd—kiddingly, I thought—made a remark about dime store perfume."

16 On Richard Nixon's advice after the assassination attempt on President Reagan: "'Don't let him make any major decision until he is entirely well,' Mr. Nixon advised. 'You don't make good decisions when you're sick. I was recovering from pneumonia when I made the decision not to burn the tapes.'"

17 On President Bush: "Reagan's handpicked successor, George Bush, has dashed whatever hope many of us had that he would carry on the Reagan legacy. . . . Meanwhile, back at the ranch, as the sun sets over the Pacific, it is plain that Ronald Reagan doesn't know it, doesn't believe it, or no longer cares."

Movie Reviewing

What is arguably the most popular form of nonhome entertainment, the movie has been the subject of critical attention since the 1930s when *The New York Times* began to publish reviews regularly. Before this time, publishers gave the stars of silent films and early talking pictures "fan magazine" treatment rather than attempting any serious discussion of quality.

Beginning with its expansion after the death of longtime publisher Adolph Ochs in 1935, the Sunday *New York Times* has given motion pictures lengthy treatment in a special arts section in the years since. The section publishes reviews and features about actors and directors; reviews appear in the daily paper too.

Time magazine also started publishing movie reviews during the same period. An early reviewer at *Time* was James Agee, who went on to become a novelist. His influential reviews in that magazine in the late 1940s were among the first to be so well written that the observations they made about film were almost secondary to the essays themselves.

Equally memorable in recent years has been Pauline Kael, longtime movie critic at *The New Yorker*. Her usually very long reviews used the panoramic method of comparing the film under consideration to similar works in the past, reflecting her great knowledge of motion pictures as the one-time manager of a theater in Berkeley, California. As Movie Review #1 indicates, she could often be utterly scathing in her comments.

The main points to consider in reviewing a movie are the story line (without revealing surprise endings) and the acting abilities of the people playing the characters. How good is the writing, as indicated by the dialogue, believability of the characters, and originality of the story? How good is the direction? Film, after all, is a director's medium so it is to the director that a reviewer looks to cast blame (or praise) for what is up there on the big screen. Equally essential are the sets, costumes, and camera work. If special effects are important—as they increasingly are in modern movies—how good are they?

In your review, you should tell something of the plot and use the names of the characters (followed by the names of actors playing them, in parentheses). Then, you need to express your opinion about the movie as a whole and answer the big question for readers: is it worth the $7 to $10 they will have to pay to see it?

The use of other information varies with the style of the publication. Some list director, writer, and studio before the review begins, others do not note such things except in passing.

The first review reprinted here shows Pauline Kael at her best.

She is funny in her ridicule of the movie and its cast. Kael tells the story and compares it to other past adaptations. She also gives a good plot summary and ends with a final slashing comment. As with all of Kael's reviews, this one is a clever combination of insight and wit—a combination that defies analysis. Thus, readers are invited to simply sit back and enjoy.

Movie Review #1 "MADAME X"

—by Pauline Kael

1 There has been much praise of the originality of William Dozier, producer of the new "Batman" television series, in insisting that the performers keep straight faces; but really Ross Hunter pioneered in this field. In his latest production, "Madame X," there is little danger of the performers' breaking up, because they are so masked and taped they couldn't laugh if they wanted to. Anyway, I doubt if those connected with this movie will have much to laugh about for a while, though audiences may.

2 "Madame X" has one of the "classic" (which, in Hollywood, means perennial) pop-movie themes: a woman is forced to abandon her baby and, years later, having committed a murder, is defended by . . . her very own son, who does not know that . . . she is his very own mother. It jerked tears in silent-movie houses in 1916 and again when Pauline Frederick played the role in 1920; and in 1929, with the great Ruth Chatterton, directed by Lionel Barrymore, it was one of the most celebrated of the early talkie courtroom dramas. In 1937, Gladys George gave it the benefit of her superb technique and her gin-and-tears voice that seemed to have found new lower octaves at the bottom of a glass. These were actresses who knew how to carry a load. And they could get into a broken-down old vehicle and get some mileage out of it.

3 Lana Turner hasn't the power or the technique.[1] She's not Madame X, she's Brand X; she's not an actress, she's a commodity. And instead of attempting to update the story so it might make some sense to modern audiences, the Hunter production just buries it under layers of other commodities. The idea is you're supposed to go see it for the gowns, the furs, the jewels and the furnishings, and the sumptuous "production values." That would make sense if, for example, you were going to see Capucine in some breathtaking clothes (that may not be movie art, but it's another kind of art and, in its own way, satisfying). But Miss Turner does not wear clothes well: she wears them as expensively dressed, aging women without much style wear them. Which is not a treat to the eye or the imagination. Her "lavish wardrobe" and the "lush surroundings" are merely gross, and the production values consist of atrocious color and pathetically obvious camera setups.

4 At the opening of the film, a matronly-looking woman and a man of indefinite age get out of a car in front of a mansion, and we realize they

[1] In her alcoholic sequence she projects a lewd, grinning depravity that is the most interesting thing about her, but she does not use it as an actress.

are supposed to be young newlyweds. She seems to be wearing a Lana Turner mask, but before we have time to react, they are greeted by what seems to be a young girl, waiting at the door of the house to welcome them. The groom calls out, "Hello, Mother," and then the youthful apparition comes close, as we see, with horror, that she is wearing a Constance Bennett mask. There were gasps in the audience.

5 Upper-class mother Bennett and bride Turner are supposed to be a social world apart, but they are alike as two frozen peas in a pod. The dialogue came out of cold storage, too: "Oh, Clay, I don't share your life—I only exist in a cubbyhole of it." The bride and groom are named Holly and Clay. Holly greets Clay with lines like "Oh, Clay, it's so good to have you home." And he musters up the energy to respond, "I'm so happy to be here." Holly is lonely when he's away: "I guess I needed to feel needed." She doesn't really even want to go to that dinner party that leads to her ruin, and she wouldn't have except that the hostess says, "You'll throw my seating off."

6 The average age of the cast must be at least fifty. As Turner is supposed to be a ravishing young beauty, the production is designed like a cocoon to protect her. There isn't a young actress in the cast, not even among the bit players. This Madame X isn't about mother love; it's about mummy love.

7 It isn't even imitation of life; it's just imitation of movies. This movie is in love with the glamour of old movies. It turns Holly (short for Hollywood?) into a Flying Dutchman, just to get her into more clothes, more decor. To compensate for all those swell clothes, she keeps suffering: not one moment of fun in twenty years. The dialogue begins to comment on the movie itself: "You couldn't cope." "She's worn out in spirit as well as in body. She can't endure much more." "Life has long ceased to have meaning for me."

8 How can we react to experiences like this film? At the screening where I saw it, some of the same people who were laughing at it also cried in the sad places. Later, I heard that the company was looking for the "instigators" of the laughter: in true paranoid Hollywood style, they can account for it only by a conspiracy.

9 "Madame X" presents, in an intensified form, a common problem of movie interpretation. Children sometimes interpret movies in terms of what they actually see on the screen, and the adults with them often try to explain what they are supposed to see, so that the children will be able to follow the plot. We would be in the midst of some gigantic confusions if the themes and story lines of all those movies with pouting marshmallows like Lana Turner or iron maidens like Joan Crawford were to be interpreted at the level of what we actually see. No Hollywood plot can really encompass that many layers of ambiguity. And so we try to separate out the intentional from the unintentional, what we are supposed to see from what we see. In general, the wider the gap, the less connection the movie has with art or talent or any form of honesty.

10 The conventions of the period protect us, to some degree, from seeing what we're not supposed to. It is this lack of protection when we see old movies on television that often makes them seem so absurd: what audiences of the movie's period were willing to ignore is now nakedly exposed.

11 "Madame X" is so excruciating not only because the actors and actresses do not embody what they're supposed to, but because the movie depends on the conventions of the MGM style of the forties. It is spiritually dedicated to the worst of old Hollywood—the Hollys and the Clays. How small an aspiration—to want to make a glossy forties' women's picture—too piddling even to be called decadent; but the clock can't be turned back, even to that. File your regrets at the nearest five-and-dime.

In the second movie review reprinted here, a regular *New York Times* film reviewer uses first person to tell readers what she thinks, beginning in the first paragraph.

Movie Review #2

REDFORD LANDS THE BIG ONE

—by Caryn James

The review starts off by praising both the director (Robert Redford) and the ostensible subject (fly fishing). The reviewer likes them both as displayed in "A River Runs Through It." She calls it "one of the most ambitious, accomplished films of the year," high praise from any critic.

1 Here are two things I never thought I'd say: I like a movie about fly fishing, and Robert Redford has directed one of the most ambitious, accomplished films of the year. "A River Runs Through It," Mr. Redford's beautiful and deeply felt new movie, puts him in an entirely new category as a film maker.

In graf 2 she compares this movie to Redford's other directorial efforts.

2 The earlier films he directed, "Ordinary People" (1980) and "The Milagro Beanfield War" (1988), were competent but never hinted that there was a genuine artistic vision behind them. Now they seem like apprentice work for "A River Runs Through It," a film whose subtlety and grace disguise the fact that this is an artistically risky project.

She summarizes the plot in graf 3 . . .

3 Mr. Redford had to succeed big or not at all, because the story sounds sugary enough to make your teeth ache. Early in this century, two brothers and their Presbyterian-minister father learn about love, understanding and how fishing the Big Blackfoot River of Montana brings you closer to God. The word boring is bound to crop up about a film that tries to prove that fly fishing is next to godliness. And though the photography is exquisite—the powerful, sun-kissed river is surrounded by lush green hills—pretty pictures only take you so far.

. . . warning readers not to "fall asleep" if it sounds too corny (4). She then explains the contradictions inherent in the story.

4 But don't fall asleep yet. Like Norman Maclean's autobiographical story, on which it is based, the film is filled with thorny contradictions. Mr. Redford depicts the emotions of people unable to express the depth of their feelings. He creates an unsentimental film about a past that is ripe for cheap nostalgia. And one of his main characters is a man who is never meant to be understood at all. Anyone who expects this film to be simple-minded and simple-hearted is coming from the wrong direction.

She continues the telling of the plot in graf 5.

5 Though Mr. Redford does not appear in the movie, his voice is heard throughout as that of the unseen narrator, Norman Maclean, an old man looking back at his life. The story begins in 1910, when Norman and his younger brother, Paul are boys. This is a family in which their fond but stern father (Tom Skerritt) insists that everyone sit at the table until Paul finishes his oatmeal; the small boy stares at the congealing mess in his bowl for hours.

She returns to the subject of fly fishing in graf 6, assuring readers not to worry about overly long fishing scenes.

6 But the minister is also an expert fly fisherman who teaches his sons to be reverent about the miracles of the natural world. "In our family there was no clear line between religion and fly fishing," Mr. Redford says, his narration perfectly balancing the wit and sincerity of the opening line from Norman Maclean's 1976 novella. Throughout the film, the fishing scenes—don't worry, they are not long or about bait—create the sense that each man is at one with nature but is quite separate from the other people in this family where emotions are rarely expressed.

7 As a young man, Norman (Craig Sheffer) is the studious, dark-haired one, who returns home after years at Dartmouth to find that the golden-haired Paul (Brad Pitt) has become a reporter. Mr. Pitt looks astonishingly like the young Robert Redford, with the same mischievous grin and crinkly smile. The resemblance probably has less to do with the director's ego than with Mr. Pitt's charismatic presence and ability to project Paul's glamorous aura so powerfully.

8 Paul is equally blessed and tortured. He is distant from his family but has an evident deep love for them; he is charming and bright but also a hard drinker, a gambler, a brawler. He is at peace only when fishing, in the place where he discovered a profound affection for nature.

She gives her first slightly negative comment in graf 9 (a key plot line is not explained adequately).

9 For too long in the film, Paul seems an alluring but underwritten character, whose demons are never explained or explored. Only at the end does it become clear that he is meant to be a beautiful mystery. Paul is an enigma to viewers because Norman—and it is his story to tell, after all—cannot understand him any better than we can. Finally, their father preaches a sermon that sums up the meaning of the film: "It is those we love and should know who elude us. But we can still love them. We can love completely without complete understanding."

10 It would have helped if the narration had hinted at this mystery sooner. There are lines in the book ("It is a shame I do not understand him.") that would have accomplished that easily enough. Such foreshadowing on screen risks becoming too blunt; as it is, the film errs on the side of subtlety.

She lets readers know in graf 11, however, that this is a minor flaw.

11 Still, this flaw doesn't overwhelm what is lively and heartfelt about the film. It doesn't upset the lovely balance Mr. Redford achieves in rendering his characters' contradictions.

She compares this Redford film with his others to say that he has "learned well."

12 He has learned well from his earlier works. "Ordinary People" was supposedly about repressed emotions. In fact, the story of an unemotional family's delayed reaction to a young man's death had characters emoting all over the place. The farmers in "The Milagro Beanfield War" felt a spiritual connection to nature, but that kinship seemed abstract, proclaimed instead of dramatized. But "A River

Runs Through It'' makes the Macleans' unexpressed emotions and religious affinity with the natural world moving and believable.

She ends her review (graf 13) with the "lyrical, elegiac end" of the film itself. Her last line again praises the director who, she thinks, has "grown up."

13 By the time the film arrives at its lyrical, elegiac end, it has earned all the feeling that comes pouring out. Mr. Redford's narration is straightforward and calm, allowing the poetry of Norman Maclean's written words to carry the emotion: "Eventually, all things merge into one, and a river runs through it." At last the Sundance Kid has grown up.

Theater Reviewing

Although the writing of play reviews goes back to Aristotle (384–322 B.C.), the power and prestige of theater critics is a modern phenomenon. Longtime *New York Times* theater critic Brooks Atkinson, for example, is the first and only such reviewer to have a Broadway theater named after him. He established the predominance of whoever occupies the *Times* theater critic's chair, although none of his predecessors or successors have been so honored. Indeed, the *Times* critic, Frank Rich, is more reviled than beloved.

The source of this strong opinion rests with the power of the *Times* theater critic to make or break a show. A favorable review will cause people, quite literally, to line up at the box office the next morning to buy tickets. An unfavorable review may cause a show to be closed immediately, even though millions of dollars may have been invested in its production. This power exists in reviewers at other New York newspapers and national magazines, but not to such a great extent.

On a more local level, a favorable or unfavorable review may influence attendance during the run of a play, but won't cause producers to close a show the next morning or extend its run.

The theater reviewer is essentially a reporter, acting as the eyes and ears of the would-be patrons. As the critic sits in the darkened theater examining the program (often called a "playbill") for pertinent details about the show and jotting down impressions in the dark, he or she is trying to fathom whether the play is good enough to be recommended to others.

Reviewing a play is a lot like reviewing a film: you give a synopsis of the play and tell who the characters are, along with their real names (in parentheses). An important difference exists with plays, however: they are performed live. No unusual camera angles or special effects can make up for bad acting or a bad script. Thus, you as a critic must look for other elements: how well do the actors project their lines? How well does the story move along? How are the sets, the costumes, the lighting, and the acoustics of the theater?

The review should also include information about the playwright, other works of that playwright (if any exist), and whether the play marks any kind of change. The director and producer are important too. The name of the theater and the planned run of the play (possibly with box office phone number) should also be indicated.

As a part-time reviewer, you will probably be dealing with local productions most of the time. In doing this, you may at times encounter some of the same hostility found in restaurant reviewing. An unfavorable review will bring threats of advertising cancellation. You may also encounter anger from actors and their families. If you have reviewed the performance honestly and fairly, you have to hope your editor will support your article.

In any production, local or professional, you owe it to your readers to judge the production in terms of the sophistication of the players. In a high school production, you have a right to expect that the lines have been learned, that actors don't bump into the furniture, and that the play is within the range of the players—that is, it isn't too difficult or too simplistic. For college level productions you have the right to expect all of this plus a sense of well-prepared characterization (the actors have done their homework), a strong sense of clarity and focus, and good technical elements (lights, costumes, sets, sound).

Professional theater should reveal a very strong sense of characterization and a mastery of all of the elements of style a director and a cast are expected to produce. For a director, this means attention to a play's look, interpretation, acting, and consistency. For actors, it means making the characters believable.

In this tightly written review of a Broadway play, *New Yorker* critic Edith Oliver smoothly weaves details of actors, playwright, set designer, lighting expert, and director into a description of plot and overall production quality.

Theater Review

CHEZ ROSENSWEIG

—by Edith Oliver

In a very long lead paragraph, Oliver begins assuring fans of the

1 Admirers of Wendy Wasserstein (fan club may be more like it) will be relieved to know that she is as romantic as ever, and that her

playwright that they will like her new work. She then paints a picture of the scene for readers by describing the setting, main characters, and story line.

head is in the right place, too, while her tongue remains safely in her cheek. I use the word "romantic" because her new play, "The Sisters Rosensweig," at the Mitzi Newhouse, is more in tune with her "Isn't It Romantic," of some years ago, than the recent "Heidi Chronicles." "The Sisters Rosensweig" takes place in the elegant London sitting room of Sara Goode, nee Rosensweig, a twice-divorced American Jew who is the European director of the Hong Kong and Shanghai Bank. (It's interesting to note that the small stage of the Mitzi can, under the right auspices, seem as spacious and lavish as any in town; in this instance, the auspices are John Lee Beatty's, and the exquisite lighting is by Pat Collins.) The occasion that launches the action is the celebration of Sara's fifty-fourth birthday, and her two younger—but not much younger—sisters are coming to her house to celebrate. They are Pfeni, a free-lance travel writer, and Gorgeous, a wife and mother who is about to embark on a personal-advice TV program but at the moment is shepherding a group of Jewish ladies on a pilgrimage to the Crown Jewels. (She bears a more than incidental resemblance, by the way, to Dr. Ruth.) We begin with Pfeni's arrival: Sara asks her to "talk to" her rebellious daughter, who plans to leave for Lithuania with her left-wing working-class boyfriend as soon as the party is over. Then Pfeni's beau, a bright bi-sexual director, brimming with high spirits and bitchy anecdotes, arrives; he, in turn, has invited an associate of his from America. The associate is a hearty, noisy Jewish manufacturer of fake fur who, once established as a guest, refuses to budge, determined to crash this family occasion. He is also determined to woo and win Sara, who, although her career is moving successfully along, feels she has come to a personal stop.

In graf 2 she intersperses elements of the story line with her observations: the play is funny, the mood warm.

2 The funny incidents and the funny lines fly by, so quickly that one is almost unaware that a story is being told, and the laughter is all but continuous until Pfeni's beau confesses that he misses men ("So do I," she says), and their inevitable breakup leaves her disheartened. By the end of the play, Sara, having secretly crept up to bed with the brash visiting American—"How was it?" asks each of her sisters the morning after—realizes that many emotional possibilities are still open. Nothing is over—not even life with daughter. Pfeni pulls herself together, and cheerfully lights out for foreign parts, ready to resume her career; and dear Gorgeous, having been presented with a pink outfit from Chanel by her grateful ladies, decides to cash it in and go home to that TV program and her husband and children. The mood is warm and gemutlich but never foolish. Jean Kerr once described a kind of play that gave her a pain as "an Irish aren't-we-adorable?" "The Sisters Rosensweig" is not a Jewish "aren't-we-adorable?" There isn't a sentimental key in Wendy Wasserstein's typewriter.

In an unusual reversal of standard form, she does not mention individual performances or use real actors' names until the third and final paragraph. She calls them, in turn, "superb," "irresistible," "inspired."

3 The performance, under the direction of Daniel Sullivan, is superb. Jane Alexander is remarkable as Sara Goode; Frances McDormand and Madeline Kahn are Pfeni and Gorgeous. Robert Klein, a one-man explosion of sex and mirth, is the visiting American furrier; John Vickery is a blithe spirit if ever there was one; Patrick Fitzgerald is almost irresistible as the boyfriend, his words lightly tinged with brogue; Rex Robbins is an upper-class diplomat invited for the festivities; and Julie Dretzin, making her theater debut, is Sara's daughter. (Welcome!) The casting is fine throughout and, in the case of Miss Alexander, inspired. Who would have thought the lady to have had so much comedy in her?

Television Reviewing

"For all its influence on American life, broadcasting has received only intermittent study as a cultural and social force. . . . This is probably a principal reason why so much broadcasting is as bad as it is."

The late Jack Gould, longtime television and radio critic for *The New York Times*, was discussing the medium he spent a career examining. He made the comment in the 1950s, then seemed to set out to disprove it. Over the next 25 years, Gould would become the most persistent and consistent reviewer of TV and radio and, because he had the backing of a great newspaper, was able to influence all of broadcasting. His power rested less with "killing" a bad show (no network could afford to cancel a show immediately because of a bad review), than with commenting upon trends—like too much violence or rigged quiz shows—and, eventually, influencing networks to reverse them.

As it had with movie and theater reviewing, the *Times* became the first major national publication to examine television critically. As that medium came to dominate the lives of Americans, other dailies as well as weekly and monthly magazines followed suit.

Typically, a publication will begin the new television season in the fall by running a series of stories on upcoming programs. As the season progresses, the focus shifts to miniseries, made-for-TV-movies, documentaries, and other special programs. At times, a reviewer might look at any trends that emerge or write about individuals appearing in series or specials. If changes occur on a program—even a long-running one—it might merit a second look.

Series and Specials

Reviews of continuing series appear when the program debuts, and thereafter only if it makes news or is canceled. (Once in a great while, a campaign waged by TV reviewers and viewers can save a program from extinction, as happened in the 1980s with "Cagney and Lacy" on CBS.)

In writing a TV review, you should give a brief review of the show's main premise, then tell how well it works. Is the story line believable? Are the characters people anyone cares about? How good is the dialogue? How well does the story move? Does it hold your interest? You should give a sample plot of one or two episodes you have seen. You need to discuss the characters and give the actors' names. Most important of all, you should give your readers your opinion about whether they should watch the show or switch channels.

In the case of one-shot programs or miniseries, you should cover the same points as above, with an additional aspect: How good is the production? If done in the studio, how realistic are the sets and the costumes. If filmed outside, is the location well selected? What is the quality of the photography? Reviewers and viewers expect more from something the networks call "special." If the program is an adaptation of a work from another medium (a play or a book, for example), you should compare it to the original. If it is an original work, you should evaluate the writing. In both instances, dialogue, plot, and pace are important.

Name of director and writers should be included in any kind of TV review, along with network, day and time the program will be shown.

Series Review

In this *New Yorker* review of a television situation comedy, James Wolcott takes a second look at a long-running series and tries to explain its popularity. He begins by giving the background of the "star," Roseanne Arnold, including direct quotes to make key points. It also sets the theme of exhibitionism.

ROSEANNE HITS HOME

—by James Wolcott

1 When Roseanne Barr (as she was then known) began as a standup comic, her voice was somewhere between a squawk and a quack—a squack. She sounded like a grievance committee doing a duck call. Standing on the stage of the "Tonight Show," she didn't have the fingertip polish of a Jerry Seinfeld or a Billy Crystal. She was stubby, squat. She giggled, averted her eyes from the camera, repeated herself. Even when she stood with her arms locked, like an Eskimo getting her picture taken, she seemed to shift around inside. In describing her glamorous life as an American housewife ("I prefer the title 'domestic goddess' "), Barr was cranky but cute, a butch Erma Bombeck. Her sheepish blush, her aw-shucks amateurism, softened the bite of her material. But there was willpower to burn packed in that bucket of pudge. A Jew raised in Mormon country, Barr intended to move from the wrong side of the tracks and set herself smack in the middle. Little did we know she intended to hold us hostage to her exhibitionism forever.

The second graf continues to discuss Arnold, making the point that, for all her own personal excesses, her show is good.

2 Ever since Roseanne launched her own sitcom, her life has been one big unpopularity contest. Her outrages have been tried in the kangaroo court of the supermarket tabloids. The tattoos, the poundage, an ugly divorce, the marriage to the comedian Tom Arnold, their mud bath together for Annie Leibovitz's camera, the rendition of "The Star-Spangled Banner" and crotch grab that earned her a stern "tsk" from President Bush, the charges and countercharges of child abuse within her family, the annual mowing down of producers, writers, and crew members on her show, the feud with Arsenio Hall (whom she called a triangle head), "mooning" incidents, more tattoos—it's been a regular barbecue. But some performers feed off flak. All that outside frenzy makes them focus close-range. Now in its fifth season, "Roseanne" (Tuesdays, ABC) has never been more centered, more apt. Even though it's the No. 1 show in the country, it has inspired few copycats. Like Ring Lardner's fiction, its offhand humor is harder than it looks. It seems like a simple recording of reality until you realize how much is surfacing.

Graf 3 discusses the locale and story line and introduces main characters. It notes, too, a key change in the general plot line.

3 A darkened snapshot of suburbia, "Roseanne" is set in the heartland—Illinois. The go-go giddiness of the parents' generation—hippies on Harleys, saddling the wind—has slowed into grubworm subsistence. Last season, Roseanne's younger daughter, Darlene (Sara Gilbert), went into such a protracted funk about her sucky life that she turned into mold. This season, gangrene has claimed the whole family. Roseanne's husband, Dan (John Goodman), had to cough up his bike shop to creditors. Cutbacks cost Roseanne her job at the mall. Her older daughter, Becky (Lecy Goranson), eloped with some loser and will probably be home leeching before long. What keeps them going is their gift for getting each other's goat. That's the American way. Where most sitcoms sound metallic, sarcasms springing like mousetraps in the characters' mouths, the scripts for "Roseanne" never stiffen into strips of type. They enjoy a loose, lazy fit, as if they'd been dug out of the hamper. The wisecracks have the broken-in feel of family lore. The cast has developed such a sure delivery and shorthand rapport that they barely bother to move their lips. They think aloud to each other in a clear mumble.

He uses graf 4 to praise the cast as a whole, calling it "unbeatable," and describes the unique attributes that each brings to the show.

4 It's an unbeatable cast. A generous force with sensitive feelers, John Goodman has gained so much weight this season he's in danger of becoming all gut. (It was bad enough when he rounded the bases in "The Babe.") But there's been no comparable sag in his performance. As Roseanne's sister Jackie, still searching for Mr. Right, Laurie Metcalf uses the feed-bag drop of her face to convey rising expectancy and dashed hopes meeting at different speeds. (Her eyes express hurt before the sag hits her cheeks.) Roseanne herself has shed the shell she had when the series started, no longer crouching behind the kitchen table as if wearing an umpire's chest protector. Her voice is lower now, dunked in coffee. Never a ray of sunshine, she has learned to satirize her own caustic vibe. One of the funniest episodes of the last couple of seasons featured the family quaking in fear as the calendar reaches the red-letter date of her . . . P.M.S. It was shot like a horror spoof, her mood stalking the house like a monster—the hormone that ate its young. The show used P.M.S. as a metaphor to mimic and mock the power Roseanne Arnold has, as star and co-executive producer, to make everyone's life on the set miserable.

In the fifth graf the reviewer returns to Arnold and what he calls her "impacted anger."

5 Yet it's more than a matter of her being the boss. There's an impacted anger in her, an ache with no off switch. At first guess, men seem to be the source of that anger. "Roseanne" has been called a feminist payback series, because of its belittling of Dan's beer-drinking buddies, whose idea of a good time is a burp contest. (One of the ape-men was played by an amusingly shifty Tom Arnold, who always acted as if he had something running down his leg.) But these stunted boys are nothing but noise, nuisances rather than nightmares.

He notes the possible secret of the show's success: its maternal orientation.

6 The real rue on "Roseanne" is directed at the maternal line. "Roseanne" is a show about daughters warped and maligned by their mothers. Trying to squeeze through the door is Shelley Winters as Roseanne's grandmother, so punch-drunk she seems unsure of her own identity. She blinks fast, as if shuffling faces of former acquaintances in her mind, hoping to make a match. Her soul hides in a dense fog of flesh: every time she visits, it's the return of the Blob. At least, she's somewhat jolly. Far scarier is Roseanne's mother, played by Estelle Parsons, whose cracked voice creaks like a rocking chair as she sits in judgment. When her visits are announced, the whole family weaves like a gospel choir afflicted with woe. One of those control freaks with X-ray ability to find fault, Parsons' Mom masks her carping as constructive criticism, using that classic cop-out, "I'm only trying to *help*, dear."

In the final long graf, he sums up the premise and returns again to Arnold's anger and the exhibitionism discussions he featured in the lead.

7 It's enough to make one snap. What with such a passive-aggressive pair of role models, it's a miracle Roseanne isn't eating with one hand and drinking with the other as her car hurls off a cliff. No one would begrudge her a primal scream. And the dysfunctional fallout doesn't stop with her. Roseanne's own sourness has seeped into the system, affecting her daughters. Darlene is chronically dour, Becky a runaway bride. But at least they engage in open hostilities instead of relying on inflections. What's refreshing about "Roseanne" is the honest sadistic chuckle Roseanne has as she finds new ways to embarrass her brats. (Like that sweet-sixteen party she threw for Darlene last week. "You really ought to do something special for her," said Jackie, to which Roseanne replied, "You mean passing her big head through my loins wasn't enough?") She bugs them. They bug her back. Humor is what keeps them from killing each other. But laughter is only a temporary release of tension. Given the pressures of the show's weekly grind, we probably shouldn't begrudge Roseanne Arnold her excesses. On camera, she's in control. Off camera, her exhibitionism may be what keeps her from imploding.

News and Documentary

News and documentary programs resemble one another in that they both deal with facts. News is broadcast "live" while it is happening or soon thereafter. Magazine shows like "60 Minutes," "48 Hours," "20/20," "Primetime," and "Dateline NBC," are produced in advance but are still based on true events. To attract viewers, however, many deal with their material in a villain/hero, suspenseful-ending, finding-the-drama-in-everyday-life manner.

A documentary, on the other hand, is usually produced well after the event it portrays has taken place. To interest viewers, however, a documentary film maker needs good production values in camera work and lighting, a good narrator, an interesting and well-written script, good photography, and a compelling subject. The drama, heroes, and villains present in fictional programs may also be evident in a documentary, though not so overtly characterized. The inclusion of background facts on the subject is necessary to acquaint readers with what the documentary is about.

Documentary reviews should concentrate on the accuracy of the facts and the quality of the presentation, including interviews, photography, and use of archival film footage. The quality of the script is important too. Does it make the subject interesting and believable? Should viewers watch this program?

Because of low ratings, the networks have all but abandoned the one-hour documentaries they produced in their heyday. Now, most are shown on Public Broadcasting, especially in such weekly series as "Frontline" and "Nova."

As with fictional television, the network or station, day, and time of the program should be included in this kind of review.

News Review

TELEVISION: KNOCK OFF NEWS

—by Robert Goldberg

In this review, regular *Wall Street Journal* TV critic Robert Goldberg takes a look at a new NBC news program. The writer states his theme in the first paragraph: NBC has been "desperately" trying to come up with a news magazine show that works.

1 For the past 2 1/2 decades, NBC News has been desperately trying to invent a news magazine show that works. In all, it's gone through 17 of them, exhausting just about every day of the week: "First Tuesday," "Prime Time Saturday," "Summer Sunday," and then some: "Yesterday, Today, and Tomorrow."

He compares NBC's situation with that of ABC and CBS, both of which have successful programs. He ends the graf (2) with a question . . .

2 Over so many years, it must have been especially galling for NBC executives to see CBS and ABC raking in the big bucks, first with "60 Minutes" and "20/20," then with "48 Hours" and "Primetime Live." Why can't we do this? they must have been asking themselves. Why can't we create a program without a day of the week in the title? Why can't we come up with a news magazine that someone will watch?

. . . which he answers in graf 3, doing an about-face from the gloomy lead.

3 The short answer is, they can—and they have. Amid an overwhelming barrage of hype, "Dateline NBC" (Tuesdays, 10 p.m. EDT) was launched two weeks ago, and viewers seem to be tuning in. And there's no reason they shouldn't. "Dateline NBC" is the perfect knockoff.

Graf 4 mentions the anchors and explains the premise of the program.

4 Featuring two attractive, youngish hosts—Stone Phillips and the resurrected Jane Pauley, "Dateline NBC" offers all the requisite elements of a television news magazine: a little investigative reporting, a little human interest, a trend or two, and perhaps a profile thrown in. If that sounds suspiciously like "60 Minutes" or "20/20," both Mr. Phillips and executive producer Jeff Diamond come from "20/20," senior producer David Rummel is from "60 Minutes," and the show itself is even touted as "a combination of '20/20' and '60 Minutes.' " These folks aren't worried about being imitative. They revel in it.

In graf 5, he talks about the show's investigative reporting team—an element of its success.

5 If short on originality, the program nonetheless covers its bases smoothly and professionally. It is blessed with one of the best investigative teams on TV, the duo known as "Batman and Robin"—reporter Brian Ross and producer Ira Silverman.

In grafs 6 through 11, the review gives a rundown on the first program, commenting on the quality of each segment ("good, old-fashioned investigative feature," "tug at the heart," "a fairly interesting story.")

6 In the first show, Mr. Ross presented a segment on a Washington fund-raiser who bilked little old ladies in Iowa out of their hard-earned savings, appealing to them for money as the "chairman" of various conservative organizations. Actually, we're told, "he was the chairman of nothing except the fancy-sounding cons he dreamed up." Complete with surveillance-style video and ambush interview techniques, this is a good old-fashioned investigative feature.

7 "Dateline NBC" seems especially at home with the soft and fuzzy pieces. A segment on two kids with Down's syndrome is a real three-hanky affair. Ms. Pauley tells us the story of Jason and Mitchell and their parents, "pioneers who dared to ask, 'What if?' " Through early intervention and hard work, the boys learned to read, to get ahead. In fact, Mitchell just graduated from high school. This is the best kind of tear-jerker, one that doesn't even pretend to be anything else. It has a happy ending and a good moral, that hardships can sometimes be surmounted and that "people with disabilities are individuals."

8 More disturbing are the stories that tug at the heart under the guise of news. There's the feature about "a nationwide drug problem," which turns out to be doctors who misread labels and give their clients the wrong medicine by mistake. The piece trots out a series of tragic gaffes. It's as sad as can be. But is it news?

9 Then there's the segment about "killer weather." Hundreds of Americans die in storms and tornadoes each year, and, apparently, the government's weather warning system is antiquated. Reporter Michele Gillen talks to the grieving widow of a man who dies in the howling winds of a violent storm. "In your heart," she asks, "who's responsible for your husband's death?" The widow sighs, "the administration of that Weather Service."

10 And finally, there's the piece that led off last week's show, an investigation into a Pennsylvania company that kept selling supplies to Iraq even when it became clear that war in the Gulf was imminent. A fairly interesting story, made more interesting by a congressman's vague but ominous accusations of "very high officials greasing the path" in Washington. But the segment never went further. Instead, it was built around brokenhearted moms and dads of Scud victims weeping at a memorial service as a soldier plays taps.

11 This is the brand of story, or non-story—longer on hand-wringing and finger-pointing than fact—that "Dateline NBC" seems to be making its own. Each starts with a nugget of information, then goes way over the top with it. And each builds to a sniffling woman who delivers a line like, "When I want to talk to my son, I go to his grave" or "My kids are growing up without a dad."

He begins (graf 12) to bring the review to a close with a characterization of the hosts (she is "warm and cuddly . . . but certainly no reporter").

12 It's the kids-without-dads school of news. Fittingly, it's presented by two pseudo-journalists on a glitzy set sitting behind what looks like a baby grand piano. There's the tenderhearted Ms. Pauley, a warm and cuddly host but certainly no reporter, and the somewhat harder-nosed Mr. Phillips, who seems to have gone to Anchorman Academy to perfect his earnest glances and dramatic enunciations.

In graf 13, he notes that he thinks this show "will last" and tells why.

13 Despite all the above, it's my bet that this 18th try will last. There are talented people involved, and they're working with a format that's a proven winner. Most importantly, NBC has finally promised the long-range support necessary to get a news magazine off the ground. It's a matter of economics for the network: News magazines are currently so popular they deliver the same number of viewers as drama or comedy, and cost only half as much.

He ends with a back-handed compliment: the show will make it, but the staff will "just have to make it good."

14 So for the folks at "Dateline NBC," the future looks like this: Their show will be a success. Now they just have to make it good.

Restaurant Reviewing

Restaurant reviewing, one of the newest forms of criticism, began in the mid-1960s in magazines like *New York* as another kind of reader service. The idea caught on with big city newspapers as a means to attract trendy and affluent readers who eat out a lot.

Not surprisingly, restaurant owners like reviews when they are favorable. Indeed, a rave review in a widely distributed magazine or newspaper can bring a line of people waiting to get in the door, quite literally, the next night. These owners are less pleased when a review is critical. For this reason, magazines and especially newspapers in smaller markets often avoid publishing restaurant reviews because they fear owners' wrath—and resultant ad cancellations.

To be done correctly, a restaurant review should be totally unbiased. A reviewer's identity should remain a secret, lest owners and head waiters recognize a name and improve service and food quality. Gael Greene, longtime restaurant critic for *New York* magazine, is never photographed full face. Her photos always show her in a large, broad-brimmed black hat with her head bent slightly away from the camera.

Of all the kinds of reviews outlined in this chapter, restaurant reviewing should combine both the reportorial and impressionistic methods: what happened the minute you stepped inside the door, how the service proceeded from there, and how the food tasted.

When it is carried off well, the restaurant review is fun to write. It should include: the name, location and operating hours of the restaurant, plus credit cards accepted (as part of the consumer service angle of this kind of review); the circumstances of the evening (how fast you were seated, how the service was, how you liked the decor); other special factors important to readers (whether the place has a new owner, or a new chef, or is totally new itself); and most important of all, the quality and presentation of the food.

Indeed, the bulk of your review should focus on the food, from appetizer to main course to dessert (with special names noted and prices put in parentheses). You need to talk about taste and seasoning, and quality of cooking. To do this, don't be afraid to add hefty portions of adjectives. If possible, you should take several people with you so you can sample what they order (with their permission, of course) or at least ask them to describe what they are eating. This gives you a broader range of dishes to discuss in your review.

Of all the different kinds of reviewing, restaurant reviews lend themselves best to first person. After all, you are reporting what happened to you. Such reviews can be written just as nicely in third person, however.

GO CHIC AND YE SHALL FIND

—by The Insatiable Critic/Gael Greene

1 When you rush to judgment on a winged stallion, it sometimes pays to mosey back to the scene on a turtle. Just because **Baraonda** came into feverish being as a safe house for the chronically chic didn't mean the kitchen couldn't one day find its soul. Still, I never imagined the perfection of tonight's miraculously al dente spaghettini with lobster, most of it pulled from the shell, moist and tender with caramelized garlic and bits of tomato and parsley. Or the lusty pleasure of orecchiette with broccoli di rape and bits of savory sausage.

In this review, *New York* magazine restaurant critic Gael Greene decides to return to an establishment (highlighted in boldface) she had not altogether liked before. She gives readers a few hints of what she had said before in paragraph 1 ("rush to judgment," "a safe house for the chronically chic"). By the third sentence, however, it is clear that she has changed her mind ("I never imagined the perfection of tonight's miraculously al dente spaghettini with lobster"). Note her food descriptions ("moist and tender," "lusty pleasure").

In graf 2, she notes that the restaurant has been in business two months and gives an idea of the atmosphere and size ("constricted cubby").

2 Two months into the fray, under a tidal surge of Europods and pals of *il padrone*, Enrico Proietti (*Ciao, bella*, kiss-kiss), not to mention mesmerized neighbors, tables are impossible to snare in this constricted cubby. Indeed, three hunky stags have been persuaded to chow down at a miniscule table for two with the lure that their corner is reserved for a party . . . "all women."

She continues to discuss the size by describing how small the place seemed on the night she was there because of the presence of guests at a bridal shower. She also talks about the waiters and how they are dressed ("bared midriffs, quadriceps").

3 Is it madness or macho, surrendering a third of your postage-stamp-size territory into a bridal shower? Well, *baraonda* means "crazy fun," so now the house's leggy SWAT team, the Loreleis with bared midriffs, quadriceps, and shoulders toting coats and tending bar, moves among the nubile bridesmaids. The bride has climbed onto a chair. Our waiter, Enrico's brother Alberto, the John Belushi of Second Avenue, pretends to pull a microphone down from the ceiling and broadcasts the play-by-play into a cork. A jigsaw master has angled the tables for the ultimate sardining. "It's just till spring," says Enrico, a grown-up cherub, smiling sweetly as he eyes the sidewalk in winter drear, dreaming of tables that will tumble outside come balmy nights. Navigating nonexistent aisles, waiters suck in their stomachs, whirl, and collide.

In graf 4, she goes on to explain that the owner has improved things since her previous visit ("I might have guessed that the perfectionist Enrico . . . would coach the kitchen out of the mud"). She then gets into a description of a typical meal from start to finish ("garlicky bruschetta," "cookies and bits of cake"). She also notes the range of dishes and the prices. She scolds the owner for not

4 I might have guessed that the perfectionist Enrico, a skilled home cook himself, would coach the kitchen out of the mud. The spirit that plotted the walls, the playful sketches and murals, the silly but appealing splotched woodwork of the entrance, the welcoming bowl of tomatoes on the sideboard, also searched out the first-rate country bread and decided that a meal should begin with garlicky bruschetta (yellow tomato, red pepper, or mushroom) and end with cookies and bits of cake, both on the house. And this largess is not a gesture to soften the blow of inflated prices. That remarkable lobster pasta may be just $16 (depending on the market; others range from $12 to $14, with half-orders at $6), and entrees are $20 or less (though the never-too-thin crowd stays that

telling callers that he does not take credit cards ("it's rude").

way by sharing pasta and salad and drinking red wine). New to the wine list, a Dolcetta d'Alba Coppo '91 at $23—how about more labels at that tariff or less? And it's rude not to warn us about the cash-only policy when we call to book.

Graf 5 is the heart of the review as far as food aficionados are concerned: it describes some of the food and how it tastes ("grilled baby squid with hot pepper and lemon," "light gnocchi with slivers of artichoke, garlic and parsley"). In Greene's party (she usually takes guests so she can taste more dishes without calling attention to herself as a critic), only one meal is bad.

5 From the kitchen: grilled baby squid with hot pepper and lemon. A special of smoked bocconcini with red peppers. Sprightly *tricolore* salad. And light gnocchi with slivers of artichoke, garlic, and parsley, a pasta that's almost a salad. Alberto fetches one regular his favorite penne with fresh tomato, "very spicy" (not on the menu). From a quartet of carpacci (beef warm or cold, tuna, and salmon with turbot), we try half-cooked beef under a melt of Fontina perfumed with truffle oil. Of all our entrees, only the Milanese veal chop with its fashionable salad topping is a flop, listless and bland. And does anyone like spinach salad in a glop of creamy cheese dressing? We send it back to be more lightly dressed, and it's still a sloggy mess, though the roasted goat cheese that accompanies it is fine.

In graf 6 she goes on to dessert, with mixed results (the espresso sauce on the white chocolate mousse is "stirring," but the homemade gelati is "overwhipped").

6 The host is full of ideas for dessert, too, hoping you won't be able to resist a semi-freddo of zabaglione with orange sauce, or chocolate-pudding cake in the Piedmont style with caramel sauce and amaretto cookies, or the lemony creme brulee with strawberries. The cloying sweetness of white chocolate mousse is cut by a stirring espresso sauce. Too bad all the homemade gelati are overwhipped, but blood-orange sorbetto, even though icy, strikes a rousing citric note.

Her return for brunch on another day is less pleasant. The door is locked, the room is chilly and the kitchen "totally spaced out." The whole thing is "a foggy notion" and even the music is wrong. The food is served in the wrong order and everything has too much salt. She predicts, however, that the owner will

7 Brunch is still a foggy notion when we arrive to find the door locked at noon on Sunday, the room chilly, and the kitchen totally spaced out. It takes some persuading to get the waiter to trade "crazy party" music for fragile-morning pop. Seems it's the first day on the job for the lunch-time chef, and the bruschetta arrives after antipasti, the focaccia only as it emerges tardily from the oven. There's too much salt here, not enough there, marring the artichoke-and-fennel salad with oranges and the sauteed artichoke with Parmesan and mache (no sign

"master daytime" as he has the night.

of the advertised pistachios). And there's no taste of mushroom at all in a vapid risotto. But a lush toss of shrimp, radicchio, and parsley over tagliolini in tomato cream almost makes up for the strikeouts, as does sliced sirloin with rosemary and olive oil for just $15. Having watched Proietti bring his fun house this far, I predict he'll master daytime, too.

In graf 8, she asks the question on readers' minds: "is it worth the struggle to get a table?" If you like "noise and crowded quarters . . . absolutely," she concludes. If not, wait for the spring and sit at a sidewalk table.

8 Is it worth the struggle to get a table? If manic capers and noise and crowded quarters tickle your happy bone, absolutely. Or wait for the first spring breeze and lease a sidewalk seat.

The review ends with the obligatory paragraph on name, address, phone number, hours, and the fact that the restaurant does not accept credit cards—all important consumer information.

9 *Baraonda, 1439 Second Avenue, at 75th Street (288–8555). Lunch, Monday through Saturday noon to 3 p.m.; brunch, Sundays noon to 4 p.m.; dinner, Monday through Saturday 5:30 p.m. to 1 a.m., Sundays till midnight. No credit cards.*

PART III

Before Pen Strikes Paper (or Cursor Strikes Screen)

> There is a certain philosophy I buy into. I believe every person has one good story in them.
>
> —Sally Lee, Senior editor, *Redbook*

13

Researching and Becoming an Expert

To be successful against the horde of competing free-lance writers, you must develop some kind of specialty that sets you apart. This might be in one or two fields like medicine or business or politics, where you set out to excel against all comers. Or, if you live in a small city or in the country, you might want to become an expert in your state or region—to be the writer that every magazine editor calls when they want an article on the Pacific Northwest or New Mexico or wherever.

The experiences of two writers make this point.

Hilda Regier has been a successful free-lance medical writer for 13 years in New York, a city with more free-lance writers per square mile than any other in the country. She has always been a medical writer and editor, working in staff positions on such publications as *Medical World News* and as the editor of *Legal Aspects of Medical Practice* before turning to free-lancing full time in 1980. She thinks it is a good idea to specialize or she wouldn't have stuck so long in medical journalism. Yet, given the highly technical journals she writes for now, she has had to become even more specialized, to learn, in effect, a specialization within a specialization.

From more general medical writing for *Medical World News* to writing about medicine and the law for *Legal Aspects*, she now spends much of her time writing about laparoscopic surgery, a new technique to remove gall bladders. "One of the joys of journalism is learning new things," she says. "Given time to research, almost anyone can attack any subject. When it comes to medicine, it helps to have a background like mine." So thoroughly has she immersed herself in this one area that doctors now call her with story ideas and sometimes questions. She expects to make $25,000 to $30,000 this year.

Jack Fincher, on the other hand, did not specialize in any one subject in the 20 years he free-lanced from a base in Ashland, Oregon, a small town near the California border. Before he quit to write screenplays, Fincher worked successfully for some of the biggest magazines in the country, primarily *Reader's Digest* and *Smithsonian*. He accomplished this by positioning himself as *the* free-lance writer to call in his region. "You have to be a hired gun, ready and willing to write about anything," he says. "I'm interested in anything and everything. If they assign me and pay me money, I'll write about my garden—what plants are in it, what dynamic process is going on to make them grow."

Fincher was lucky. Because of the many connections he made while on the staff of *Life* magazine from 1964 to 1970, editors called him or knew who he was when he called them. "There was definitely an 'old boy' network on *Life*," he continues. "When people heard I was free-lancing, they called me. One thing led to another. Soon, I was writing for 10 magazines. I've been told that my living in Oregon was an advantage. I could easily go to San Francisco or Los Angeles. I relied on trust and personal connections. In New York you can go to lunch with an editor, but you might be one of five other guys hustling the same idea."

When he got established, Fincher was able to concentrate on *Reader's Digest* and *Smithsonian*, both of which offered him contracts agreeing to publish his work. "I did hearts and flowers for the *Digest* and could indulge the intellectual side of me at *Smithsonian*, writing about subjects like popular history and sociology that interested me." In his biggest year, Fincher made slightly less than $40,000.

Becoming an Expert

Choosing Your Subject Matter

Your choice of subject matter as a free-lance writer will probably come fairly naturally. To find out, ask yourself several questions:

- What am I interested in?

- What do I have a background in?
- What am I good at writing about?
- Does the region I live in have enough marketable story ideas to interest the editors and publications at which I plan to aim?

Developing a Specialty or Two

After you decide what topics to concentrate on—and, for reasons of financial security, you should choose more than one—there are a few basic steps to take next.

Gather general knowledge

Read several basic textbooks on your subjects or take a basic course at a local university or community college. Sometimes the general knowledge you are seeking will not come from a book but from publications put out by an organization you plan to write about, like the court system or stock market. For example, most local court houses publish an informational booklet to give to people serving on jury duty. The New York stock market (and elsewhere) publishes a guide to operations intended for the general public. Although you will need to delve a lot deeper to ultimately develop your specialty, such publications are a good place to start.

Build on your own knowledge

Once you have gained some general knowledge about the fields you plan to focus on in your writing, you should build on that knowledge by attending regional or national conferences or meetings at your own expense. Even if you don't initially get a story idea from the meeting, you will hear important topics discussed, be able to pick up handouts, technical papers, and sometimes free books, and meet important figures who may later become sources. Also, if you do something as a hobby or an avocation, make it part of your pitch to editors. Oregon free-lance writer Rob Phillips, a longtime private pilot, has as one of the mainstays of his writing *Flight Training* magazine, for just this reason.

Put together your own reference files

As you learn more about your chosen topics, establish files of newspaper, magazine, and journal clippings for use as reference in future articles and queries. The process works well if you get into the habit of saving pertinent items and filing them by subject, people, or organization. Remember to date newspaper clippings (so you'll know later how current the information is), but don't bother to mount them on paper, unless they are so small they will be

Box 13.1 A Free-Lance Writer's Basic Reference Library

A reference library is an invaluable aid to a free-lance writer. For an initial expenditure of $100, you can set yourself up for years and only have to buy updated versions of several books every few years.

- *A good unabridged dictionary*. Either the latest edition of the *Random House Dictionary of the English Language* or *Webster's* are two good choices. While you may not want to haul it out for every spelling check because of its cumbersomeness, an unabridged dictionary is invaluable for more difficult definitions and word usage and even biographical and geographical entries.
- *A paperback version of the unabridged dictionary*. This is what you should keep handy for checking spelling and meaning in a hurry. It should be dog-eared from use.
- *The latest edition of the world almanac*. These are published annually by several publishers. Although you may go blind from reading the small type, this is the perfect (and most inexpensive) way to find out obscure facts you may want to sprinkle into your articles, whether that be the world's longest river or who won the Academy Award for screenwriting in 1968.
- *A good atlas*. Paperback atlases are available but their small size and bad binding makes it hard sometimes to read the maps. If possible it is best to treat yourself to a hardbound version. *National Geographic*'s is the best, but is expensive. *Rand McNally* and *Hammond* publish slightly less expensive editions.
- *A thesaurus*. A thesaurus lists synonyms to use in place of words you may be using all the time. The original *Roget's Thesaurus* is hard to use because it isn't in alphabetical order. The version in dictionary form is easier to navigate.
- *Bartlett's Familiar Quotations*. This standard is only available in hardback, but is worth a one-time expenditure. It offers a good way to add mood- or theme-setting quotes to your articles.
- *A guide of guide to grammar and usage*. There are old standards like *Elements of Style* by William Strunk and E. B. White and *Fowler's Modern English Usage* or newer works. You need some place to turn for help with such questions as the difference between "effect" and "affect."
- *State reference or fact books*. Many states or cities publish almanac-like books of facts and statistics annually which are useful and usually available at a small cost.
- *Local or organizational telephone books*. You can find out a lot about a city by reading a phone book, not to mention the chance it offers to get names and addresses. Companies and other organizations also publish internal phone books that give telephone numbers and exact job titles for people you may be interviewing. These internal phone

books are not always available to the public but a writer can usually get a copy if persistent. They are invaluable resources. After all, the Watergate story was really broken when *Washington Post* reporters Bob Woodward and Carl Bernstein got a copy of the highly restricted phone book of the Committee to Re-elect the President and started calling sources at their normally unlisted home numbers.

- *Reference books in your subject areas*. Whether you are a medical writer needing a medical dictionary or a political writer wanting facts and figures about a state senate campaign, there is a valuable reference book for you. (In the case of medicine it's *Dorland's Illustrated Medical Dictionary*; in politics it's *The Almanac of American Politics*). Hundreds more references and annual yearbooks put out by specialized publications are also available. It all depends on what your needs are.

crumpled and lost. Magazine and journal articles are printed on stiffer paper, so you won't have to do anything more than staple them together. They will probably already be dated. One caution: Keep up with this task because a stack of newspapers and magazines you accumulate over six months will become too daunting. Making this system work means you have to think of this specialty area—at least subconsciously—every time you pick up something to read.

Keep up with the technical

There are many technical journals that will help you keep informed on technical issues and advancements. Such journals aren't always available, however, because circulation is limited and subscription costs are high. If your public library does not buy the journals you need, you might make an arrangement with the local college or nearby medical school or research lab to gain access to its publications. Explaining who you are and your purpose may give you the chance to read the journals you are interested in or at least scan them and make copies of pertinent articles.

Cultivate good sources

Working a specialty field as a free-lance writer is like working a beat as a newspaper reporter: a lot depends on the sources you cultivate. In free-lance writing a good source can provide both story ideas and useful background information. It is great to be able to call up one of your experts and ask for an explanation when you become stumped and can't find the answer in any standard reference. You can repay these experts by taking them out to lunch or dinner.

Another "payback" may be simply your use of their name in your article. For story ideas, experts can be best used by simply calling them periodically and asking them what is new.

Use the resources of the magazines you work for

Although you won't be accorded all the rights and privileges of a staff writer, it is possible to get help from the publications you write for on a regular basis. This means access to their private libraries and reference books, their suggestions for sources to call, and even use of any computer databases they might subscribe to. After all, it is to their advantage to help you do the best article possible. Sally Lee, senior editor at *Redbook*, does everything she can to help the free-lance writers she assigns to articles. "I collect material here for them, articles and books, and then I messenger or Fed Ex it to them," she says. "I show a continuing interest in their progress." Although few editors are that nurturing, many are ready to help if you ask them.

Lessons in Free-Lancing: Researching

A chance, almost offhand mention of a possible story idea in a letter to a magazine editor led me into one of the most interesting assignments of my career and into a field I tried to expand upon in a book.

The magazine was the slick quarterly, *EXXON USA*, that used to be published for an external audience by Exxon, the large petroleum company. The editor was Downs Matthews. The subject was bowhead whales and other marine mammals of the Arctic.

I had interviewed Matthews for a chapter on company magazines in a book I wrote on public relations. In thanking him for his help, I mentioned that I had recently moved to the Oregon coast, not far from the Oregon State University Marine Science Center, and wondered if he would be interested in my doing an article on the whale research going on at that facility. As with most Americans, I had always been in love with whales, and figured such an article might interest the readers of his environmentally conscious magazine. (This, by the way, was long before the oil spill of the *Exxon Valdez* besmirched that company's environmental image probably forever.)

He replied fairly rapidly that he was not interested in whale research in Oregon but asked if I would be interested in going to the Canadian Arctic and Alaska to do an article on bowhead whale research in those areas.

I was, of course, thrilled at the prospect of going to such an exotic land to write about such an exotic creature. I had been to Alaska twice before but never the Arctic or Canada. Adding to my enthusiasm was the fact that this would be a summer trip.

I answered his note by return mail, agreeing to do the story and sketching my own background in writing about science in general and marine mammals in particular.

Twelve days later I got the assignment.

"Very well, let's plan to turn out an article on the marine mammals of the Beaufort Sea," wrote Matthews in the first sentence of a two-page letter outlining both what he wanted and the sources I should contact to get my information. He included their telephone numbers and addresses. He also provided valuable background information on bowhead whales, seals, and walruses. He ended the letter by telling me the required word length, my deadline, and the fee I would be paid.

"The purpose of this article, then, is to take an unvarnished look at these marine mammals and report what is known about them," he wrote in summation.

Matthews also attached a half-page synopsis of what the article should contain: a description of the animals, what is known about them, and details of research to learn more. The purpose of the story was to report that oil development could be conducted without risk to marine mammals.

As time went on, he sent a lot of other background material on the subject, which I filed away for possible use in my article and in preparing my questions.

The key source who Matthews asked me to contact "first of all" was Mark Fraker, a zoologist working for an environmental consulting firm in British Columbia who was conducting bowhead research in the Canadian part of the Beaufort Sea each summer. I called Fraker and flew up to his office near Victoria, B.C. for a preliminary, fact-finding interview in June.

Fraker was one of those sources writers dream about: quotable, friendly, not too technical, and a veritable fount of information on others I should contact, not only to learn about bowhead whales but about the other marine mammals I would be discussing in my article. He also gave me a number of scientific papers on bowheads and marine mammals written by him and others.

He agreed to let me accompany him for several days in mid-August when he would be heading a team of scientists and technicians operating out of the tiny village of Tuktoyaktuk, Northwest Territories, Canada, on the Beaufort Sea. The group would be counting the elusive whales as they migrated to and from their summer feeding grounds from their winter range in the Bering

Sea. It would also be carrying out some acoustical studies to determine if the offshore oil rigs in the Canadian Beaufort harmed them in any way. (At that time, there were no such rigs in the U.S. waters.)

As summer began, I was well into organizing what would be a major trip. I called sources in Alaska recommended to me by Fraker, Matthews, and others. I accepted an offer from Matthews to stay at the Esso camp in Tuktoyaktuk, given the scant supply of hotels in that small place. Matthews made all of the housing arrangements at the camp.

All of my expenses would be paid, as were my preliminary expenses. I kept track of all telephone calls and all of the costs incurred on my one day preliminary trip to see Fraker at his Victoria headquarters.

I made my own arrangements and, due to schedule conflicts by several sources, set the trip for August 17–27. This meant a change in delivery date to September 15 from August 1, which Matthews readily agreed to.

I read the background material and prepared the questions for what was sure to be a fascinating trip and, I hoped, a good article. In chapter 16, I'll discuss my questions and my interviews.

—Ron Lovell

Lessons from This Lesson in Free-Lancing

1. You never know when or where an assignment will come from.
2. Sometimes, suggesting one idea can lead to another if the timing is right and luck is with you.
3. A good editor can help immeasurably by providing source names and useful background information.
4. Background research material is important, but a writer has to have in-person (or telephone) interviews and observe things on-site to have a truly complete and interesting article.

14

Cultivating Editors and Marketing Yourself

Establishing a good relationship with an editor or two is the key ingredient to your success as a free-lance writer. Editors decide which queries to read and approve, which writers to reward with assignments. You can't get anywhere without editors.

Cultivating Editors

How to Begin

Your knowledge of the markets at which you are aiming with your query letters is the most important thing you have to offer an editor who does not know you. Once you have decided which subjects to specialize in, you need to figure out which magazines cover those fields. There are several ways to proceed.

Consult Writer's Market

This book, brought out each year, lists magazines by category, indicating editorial concept, kinds of articles preferred, word length, payment, whether the publication accepts free-lance material, address, phone number, and editor names. Editors frequently play a kind of musical chairs so chances are the person listed in even the latest edition of *Writer's Market* will not be in the same job. The same company puts out the monthly *Writer's Digest*, which contains some updated information such as editor changes. You can also call the magazine for the correct name or look at a recent issue. By perusing the information about the magazines in the categories listed in *Writer's Market*, you also can get an idea of where you want to send your query letters (see chapter 15).

Visit a library

A trip to the public library or a university library to look over magazines can give you a feel for what they contain, what they might be looking for, what average word length is, and the general impression the magazine imparts through its editorial content and advertising pages. Magazines have their own personalities and, as a potential writer, you need to decide whether that personality meshes with your own. Oregon free-lance writer Rob Phillips spends one day a week in the library. "What I do is not systematic," he says. "I look at the cover, see what's inside." Adds Jack Fincher, "Editors always say, 'Analyze our magazine.' You've got to immerse yourself, to marinate yourself in several issues of the magazine, figure out why they might want this kind of story. It's trial and error but it [the analysis] eliminates a lot of wasted motion. If you don't read the magazine, you run the risk of sending in something they would never use. Your ideas tip off that you have read their magazine."

Send for sample copies of magazines

Phillips does this frequently. "I read my junk mail," he says. "If I get an offer to receive a free copy of a new magazine, I send back the card. So, it costs me 29 cents to see a magazine and I usually wind up getting several issues."

Write for a copy of writer's guidelines

These guidelines, which many magazines prepare and send out, are expanded versions of a listing in *Writer's Market* (see Box 14.1). Reading about the exact needs of the publication gives you a better idea of what to submit and how to submit. Guidelines also include specific names and titles that are often outdated in *Writer's Market*.

How to Proceed

Once you are familiar with the magazines in your areas of interest, the next step is to decide on several ideas that seem appropriate

Box 14.1 Sample Guidelines

GUIDELINES

Thank you for your interest in writing for The Nation.

We are a journal of left/liberal political opinion -- 125 years old this year -- covering national and international affairs. We publish weekly except during the summer when we move to a bi-weekly schedule.

We are looking both for reporting and for fresh analysis. On the domestic front, we are particularly interested in civil liberties; civil rights; labor, economic, environmental and feminist issues and the role and future of the Democratic Party. Because we have readers all over the country, it's important that stories with a local focus have real national significance. In our foreign affairs coverage we prefer pieces on international political, economic and social developments.

As the magazine which published Ralph Nader's first piece (and there is a long list of Nation "firsts"), we are interested in publishing new (sometimes young) writers.

While detailed queries (a page or two) are preferred, we're happy to consider finished pieces on timely issues. We ask that you double-space and that you include a SASE with unsolicited manuscripts.

We run full-length pieces of 1500 to 2000 words and (signed) editorials of 500 to 750 words. Calvin Trillin has made us famous for paying in the high two or very low three-figures -- that is, from $75 for an editorial to $150-225 for a full-length piece. Deadlines are 10 days before the magazine goes to print for stories, 4 days for editorials. The magazine goes to print on Thursdays.

Queries and submissions on books and the arts should be addressed to our literary editor, Elsa Dixler, at the same address.

Let us hear from you.

The Editors
Summer, 1992

and gather enough material to write a query letter. "Pick a magazine you like, read what they're doing, and see if you have an idea that fits," says Fincher. (Query letters will be covered in depth in chapter 15.) At this point, the thing to remember about writing query letters is to include enough information to interest and entice an editor without investing a lot of your time and money. The old cliché "time is money" could have been written about free-lance writers because it is so applicable. It is foolish to research an article, write it, and submit it without querying first. You won't get very far as a free-lance writer if you continue to do that because you will waste too much time.

What to Expect

National magazines receive thousands of queries from free-lance writers each year. The statistics for three very different magazines are staggering: *Smithsonian Magazine*—12,000 to 14,000 a year; *Redbook*—"thousands"; *National Review*—over 5,000. On large magazines a senior editor or articles editor is usually responsible for handling all queries. Normally, this editor has a number of assistants to screen and give a first reading to all query letters. Depending on the topic, the way the query is written, and whether it is addressed to a specific person or "to the editor," the query letter will be passed along to the senior editor for consideration. A badly written query that is not on a topic within the magazine's area of interest will be rejected. A query that is addressed "Dear Editor" with no specific name will probably be thrown away without further reading. On a smaller magazine, one person reads every query and decides which should be rejected or pursued.

Magazines get an equal number of unsolicited manuscripts. These go into what is usually called a "slush" pile and are read and considered in the same manner as queries. Unless an article really grabs the attention of an editor, however, it runs a greater risk of being discarded or rejected than does a query. For one thing, it takes longer to read an article. For another, it may anger the editor, especially if guidelines or the *Writer's Market* blurb say "no unsolicited manuscripts accepted" or some such wording. It is far better to query first, even if your manuscript is complete.

When an editor likes your idea, you will probably get a letter offering to publish it, along with suggestions about the approach or the need for more information. You will also be given a deadline, specified work length, and a proposed fee. Fees vary widely from magazine to magazine. Some pay by the word in the final edited article. Others pay by manuscript page of what you submit, while still others pay a flat fee for the article based on length and importance (for example, a cover story will bring more money than an article, while an article will bring more than a news brief).

Some magazines will ask you to sign a formal contract as part of the process of agreeing to publish your article. Contracts may be worded simply and directly, or be so complicated that you feel the need for legal counsel. A standard contract assigns to the magazine first serial rights which allows one time publication, retaining all other rights for you. You must also usually affirm that what you have written is original and that you have not signed away the rights to any other publication. Contracts also specify the fee to be paid.

Sometimes, a magazine asks you to sign a "work for hire" agreement which is a slightly different contract under whose provisions the magazine is considered the writer for copyright purposes and owns the copyright. This technique has been condemned by the American Society of Journalists and Authors but is still used on occasion.

Cultivation Begins

After you have submitted a query, wait a week or two and then call to inquire about its status. "When you've sent a query to an article editor, pick up the phone and call," says Jack Fincher. "What have you got to lose? Don't be discouraged. Call again." A telephone call is better than a follow-up letter because it is just as likely to be buried as the original query. A call will show your interest and, in some cases, daring. It is intimidating to call a New York editorial office and get through the gauntlet of secretaries most magazines set up to protect their editors. You may not connect even half the time, but if you do, you have started a dialogue that, when combined with a good query and, later, a well written article, may lead to a good relationship.

Cultivation Continues

The real cultivation of editors starts after your first query has been accepted and you have gotten your first assignment to write for a magazine. Most editors want you to succeed with their publication because your success will make them look good. But they are extremely busy people so you need to take careful steps to keep them happy:

- *Call periodically*. It is wise to keep in touch with editors you are working with to inquire about the status of a query or to try out an idea or just to say hello. This can turn a business relationship into a friendship.

- *Respect their time.* "I recognize that when they have their head in their work, a phone call is an interruption," says Rob Phillips. "I regularly have four-minute conversations with editors."
- *Visit them in person whenever possible.* "Anytime I'm in New York, I have lunch with editors I work with," says Fincher. "I'd drop in and say, 'I'm here, let's have lunch. If not, let's have coffee.' You need some way to get your foot in the door. The most important thing is to have the personal contact. Sooner or later, they'll read what you write. Once you have an assignment, you have a basis on which to proceed. You have to be persistent. The squeaky wheel gets the grease."
- *Be a professional at all times.* Stick to the word limit you've agreed to in advance and never miss a deadline. It is also advisable to use the approach you proposed in your query and not alter it drastically. The editor bought a particular idea; don't give him or her another one, at least without discussing it first. Sometimes an editor might modify your original idea, however. "Editors like to tinker with ideas and ask you to change something," says Phillips. "When this happens, you negotiate and say, 'I hadn't thought about that angle.' I always submit to an editor when an editor's voice has an edge to it."
- *Look at editing changes with an open mind.* When your article is finished and you have submitted it for final editing, you need to make up your mind in advance not to fight every minor change in your writing. It is an editor's job to edit and you have to expect a certain amount of alterations to your copy—style, grammar, and changes in the lead are the most common. In some respects, you should welcome the help of another professional, given the fact that free-lance writers often work in such a vacuum, without the opportunity to show their work to other writers or editors for suggestions. The problem comes when you encounter a compulsive editor who makes the story into one he or she has written. That kind of encounter is one to be dreaded. If you wind up with that kind of editor, you either have to submit to the changes (after trying to negotiate away at least some of them), or have a big argument that may result in your not writing for the magazine again. Another alternative is to ask that your name be removed from the article. You'll still get paid but might have made your point without totally severing your ties to that editor or magazine. Rob Phillips, for one, never argues with an editor in terms of editing. "I grit my teeth and keep quiet. There is rarely something so grievous that I complain. I decided a long time ago that I was not going to get hung up on my prose."

The relationships you establish with editors are very important.

Even the most solid standing can end overnight if an editor leaves. A new editor might have another group of other writers he or she is used to working with and you will be out. You will then have to start over with that magazine or abandon it altogether and search for greener pastures (see Box 14.2).

Marketing Yourself

Although your ideas and writing ability will make you attractive to editors, there are several other, more subtle, factors that will indicate your seriousness in pursuing free-lancing, either on a full-time or part-time basis. They involve establishing an office, buying proper equipment and investing in stationary and business cards. These actions on your part will signal—to yourself and others—that you are serious about free-lance writing.

The Importance of "Place"

Some writers brag about their ability to write in any setting, whether sitting at the kitchen table with children romping around them or in the back seat of an old Chevy parked by a mountain stream. They are probably lying, or at best, stretching the truth more than a bit.

It is vitally important in free-lancing to have your own version of Ernest Hemingway's "clean, well-lighted place." You need a refuge from the rest of the household that is quiet, comfortable, and has room for all the paraphernalia of your work. The room need not be large, but it should be yours. Such an office is important even if you live alone.

"When I started free-lancing full-time, I had part of the house renovated as an office, a room across the breezeway from the house," says Jack Fincher. "The room already had a bathroom and kitchenette. I added a 16-foot desk to hold a typewriter and computer, with pigeon holes and a sorting table. I wanted to demonstrate to the Internal Revenue Service that this was a legitimate office."

Rob Phillips converted a bedroom into his office. He took the doors off of a closet and installed bookshelves, and had a desk custom built to hold a computer, the keyboard, printer, and files.

New York free-lance writer Hilda Regier converted the dining room of the old brownstone she owns in the Chelsea section into her office. This 14 x 21 foot, high-ceilinged room contains all the usual: chair, desk, filing cabinets, and a library table to hold

Box 14.2 When Editors Leave or the Format Changes

All the careful cultivation of editors at various magazines will not help you if the editor you work with leaves or gets fired. A new editor might bring in a group of free-lance writers he or she is used to working with and not be interested in working with the magazine's current stable of writers.

This is precisely what happened at the *New Yorker* in the fall of 1992, when Tina Brown took over as editor. She had been given a mandate to change the venerable magazine and apparently felt she could accomplish this goal only by jettisoning many of the writers who had been with the magazine for years. The old relationships and contracts these writers had worked out with the *New Yorker* were ended quickly and they were looking for new outlets for their work.

Any free-lance writer can face a similar fate. A nice, cozy relationship with an editor which has resulted in a listing for you in the staff box as a contributing editor may end abruptly when your name disappears and your ideas are rejected. In this case, you have no choice but to start over and attempt to establish a new relationship with the new editor. Sometimes, this means following new guidelines for what ideas are acceptable and getting used to an entirely new format.

At other times, a magazine's format changes even though the editors remain the same. In such cases, owners dictate changes in format to boost circulation and advertising sales or editors decide the magazine needs a new look. Whatever the cause, the changes may mean that what was once acceptable no longer is. And you, as a free-lance writer trying to sell ideas, will have to adjust. Such changes may also mean that you make less money.

In 1990, *Medical Tribune*, a weekly newspaper for doctors that uses work from many free-lance writers, changed its format to accommodate a new design. In the past, these writers could submit six- to eight-page articles (approximately 1,500 to 2,000 words) and be paid $50 a manuscript page. Most of what they sent in would be published. Under the new format, stories were limited to an average length of 300 words; 500 words for page 1 or very important subjects. This meant that writers had to work harder to write more stories to make the same amount of money as before, theoretically five times as hard. Each story means a separate query or telephone conversation with an editor, separate interviews, and separate lead and article writing. In short, to remain a valuable asset to *Medical Tribune*, free-lance writers had to work harder for less money.

In the troubled economic times of the early 1990s, editor and format changes were common and writers have had to adjust to both situations frequently.

background material. She added a large antique breakfront with shelves for books above and storage space for paper below.

Equipment to Buy

Furniture

You need a large desk at a height that feels comfortable. You may put your computer on the desk or prefer to buy another table to hold it and the accompanying printer and keyboard. It is a good idea to have another space for spreading out materials you are working on. You need a comfortable chair at a height that goes with your desk. Whether wooden or upholstered it should fit your back and support your body adequately for the long hours you will likely be sitting in it.

An office needs a lamp or lamps in all the principal work areas, the desk and computer table, especially. Replicas of old banker's lamps are popular now and so are gooseneck movable lamps such as drafters use over their drawing boards. Whatever model you choose, a lamp should shine directly on your work space.

Other furniture depends on your needs. A bookcase for reference books is a good idea, but not essential. Filing cabinets for source material, old interview notes and copies of stories after you have submitted them will help you keep organized. It might also be wise to have a storage cabinet for paper and other supplies.

Computers

Whole books are available about choosing the right computer so a section of this chapter can hardly do the subject justice. Suffice it to say that to succeed in free-lance writing today, you will have to buy a computer. Not only will you need it to increase your speed and efficiency, but most editors will require you to submit your articles on disk along with hard copy. You may choose an off-the-shelf standard or laptop model or, like Rob Phillips, hire a computer consultant to put together a custom-made system with various manufacturer's components to fit your special needs. You definitely want a good word processing program and might want to add the capacity to keep your business records on computer as well. In selecting a word processing program, pick one that is compatible with the systems used by your principal magazine customers.

Printers

The old—and cheap—dot matrix printer may not suffice as editors get more and more demanding and require letter quality print. A laser printer is probably the ultimate in variety and quality but may be out of your price range. It's best to see a computer consultant or talk to the people in your computer store.

Fax machines

This relatively new device has rapidly become a phenomenon in businesses of all kinds. The ability to accept original documents on paper, scan the documents with electronic sensors, and then transmit them over distance and spit out copies or facsimiles in companion machines is truly revolutionary. If you are in free-lancing for the long haul and have the money to spend, it might be wise to buy your own. Prices range from $300 to several thousand. With a fax, you can submit late copy or revisions to editors and receive edited copy and reference material from them in return. If you buy a fax, select one with only the basic features you need. If you don't think you'll be using one all that often, you may want to make a deal with the copy/fax store around the corner to accept your incomings. You can, of course, send your outgoings for a fee, usually about $1 a page.

Modem

A modem is a device that links your telephone to your computer and allows you to transmit data over telephone lines. You probably don't need both a fax machine and a modem. And, with either one, you still will probably need to mail the computer disk containing your article to the editor so it won't have to be re-keyed.

Telephone answering machine

If you are on the telephone a lot or away on research and reporting trips frequently, it is probably a good idea to buy your own telephone answering machine. Because some of the inexpensive models malfunction frequently, it is wise to buy one of a little better quality to avoid problems. Also, prepare a business-like message to record for your callers. Garbled, overly cute, or poorly worded messages create a bad impression. And, change your messages frequently to reflect where you are. If you are going to be gone for two weeks, say so, and the date of your return and don't leave the standard "I'll return your call as soon as possible." Another advantage of this equipment is the fact that it enables you to avoid being interrupted when you are working. If you screen your calls in this way, however, be sure to pick up the receiver if an editor is on the line.

Letterheads and Business Cards

When you begin as a free-lance writer, you'll want to look as professional as possible. Later, your work will speak for itself; but in the beginning, it is important to display some semblance of your seriousness by investing in your own letterhead and business cards. For $100 you can look like you mean business.

Letterhead

You should settle on an eye-catching, contemporary design that gives your name, address, telephone number, and fax number if you have one. You may also want to include a line about what you do. I prefer to use "magazine writer, book author" on companion memo pads that match the letterhead in type style (see Box 14.3), but not on the paper used for letters. I use stationery for formal correspondence, and the memo paper for billing magazines and to jot off quick notes. Rob Phillips uses "free-lance journalist" on his letterhead. Hilda Regier creates her own letterhead on her computer. Jack Fincher has never needed a letterhead.

Business cards

Even if you do not invest in your own letterhead, you must have your own business cards clearly identifying you as a free-lance writer or journalist. Some sources are suspicious of talking to people who are not staff members of publications. A business card will reassure them. The cards should contain your name, address, telephone number, fax number if you have one, and the identification line (free-lance writer, etc.). If you have a letterhead too, the type on the card should match it (see Box 14.4). When identifying yourself to a source, you should never lie about your free-lance status and imply that you are a regular employee. Simply say, "I am so and so on assignment for such and such." If you are doing the story on speculation with no firm commitment from a magazine, say you are a free-lance writer and hope for the best. A few publications realize the sometimes precarious status of free-lancers and issue press cards to regular contributors (see Box 14.4). This satisfies the overly suspicious or those who think that all who write for a living are issued some kind of press card from a giant tribunal in the sky. (It also might bring you across police lines or out of tight places on occasion.)

Setting Yourself up as a Business

You can declare your free-lance writing as a business, certainly if it is your only means of financial support, but even if it is on a part-

Box 14.3 Sample Stationery

RON LOVELL

Magazine Writer, Book Author

P.O. Box 400, Gleneden Beach, Oregon 97388, 503-764-3254

time basis only. In order to satisfy the IRS that you aren't merely pursuing an enjoyable hobby, however, you have to be able to prove that you are a serious writer and get paid money to write.

Keep careful records

Maintain records on your computer or in a more old-fashioned ledger. Keep track of every expense associated with your writing: supplies, postage, telephone, fax transmissions fees, copying fees, equipment purchases or rentals, depreciation of equipment, travel, books, research, subscriptions. This means recording it and keeping

Box 14.4 Sample Business Card and Press Card

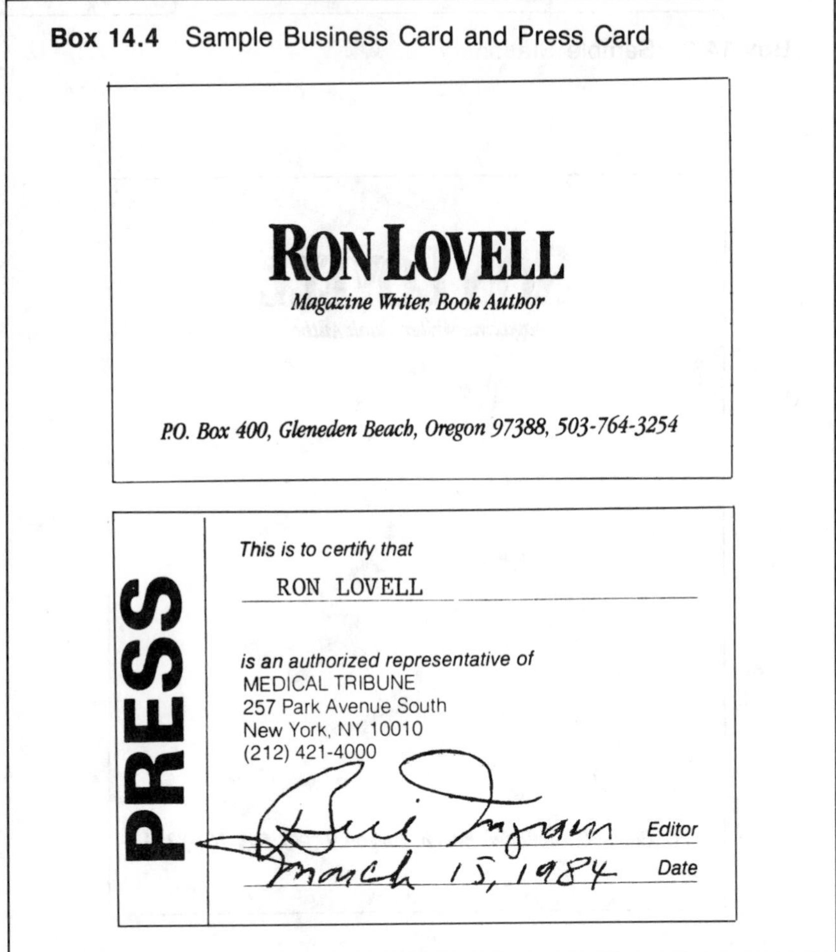

receipts. You also need to keep track of all your free-lance writing income. All your publishers will send you Form 1099 early in the year before taxes are due. While you don't send these in with your tax return, the publishers do send copies to the IRS and they can easily be cross-checked with your income totals. Also, remember that no taxes are withheld from your payments. It is your responsibility to pay them, probably quarterly on your estimated income.

RON LOVELL
Magazine Writer, Book Author
P.O. Box 400, Gleneden Beach, Oregon 97388, 503-764-3254
PRESS
This is to certify that
RON LOVELL
is an authorized representative of
MEDICAL TRIBUNE
257 Park Avenue South
New York, NY 10010
(212) 421-4000
Editor
March 15, 1984
Date

Keep your office separate

Another reason to have a separate room as your office is the ability to declare what is called "home in office." In this way, you can take expenses for the portion of the upkeep on that room devoted to your office as deductions on your income taxes: light, heat, major repairs. This can be tricky so consult a tax preparer before submitting this deduction the first time. The IRS also has available booklets which explain it.

In a January 1993 decision, the U.S. Supreme Court made it harder for people who do some, but not all, of their work at home to deduct their home-in-office expenses. The high court said the availability of the home-in-office deduction rested on two considerations: 1) the relative importance of the activities performed at each location, and 2) the time spent at each place. Many tax experts said that this did not apply to even part-time free-lance writers if they did their work in their office at home. It seemed aimed more at doctors, for example, who saw occasional patients at home and did billing from there, but did most of their work elsewhere.

Other Considerations

One of the worst aspects of your free-lance status is the absence of any benefits. Young or old, you need to think about such matters and act accordingly. You should set up your own Individual Retirement Account or similar private pension plan. You should purchase your own health insurance. Occasionally, such insurance is available to members of local or regional writing groups. In this way, a "pool" of members lowers the risk and attracts an interested company. Your premiums will probably be lower than if you pay as an individual, but make sure the coverage meets your needs. If you leave another job where you are covered by health insurance, see if you can convert that policy to one you pay for yourself.

15

The Art of the Query

Your success as a free-lance writer will often depend on how well you write query letters. Just as a good résumé and cover letter may help you get a job, a good query letter may help you get your idea accepted and your article published. In a query letter to an editor you outline your ideas for an article you want to write and list your credentials for doing it. You have just a few seconds to evoke interest and save your letter from being either ignored, rejected outright, or tossed into the waste basket.

Queries are as different as the writers writing them and the magazines being targeted.

"The type of query varies with the magazine," says Jack Fincher, former *Life* correspondent and free-lance writer for *Reader's Digest* and *Smithsonian*. "Some—like the *Reader's Digest*—want you to dramatize your story in the way it would appear. *Smithsonian* wants a straightforward elucidation of the facts, though even they like to be intrigued, titillated, and provoked by the proposal. I write queries as I write the piece itself—a straightforward elucidation of the facts. It's hard to say what magazines want. It varies and changes with the magazine—a one-page, straight up front letter filled with facts, or a one-page outline, or a chatty letter. You always need a news peg about why you are doing the story now or at all and why you should write it instead of someone else. You include your résumé and photocopies of some of your past stories, no more than half a dozen to illustrate the kind of story you write."

New York medical free-lance writer Hilda Regier says she "tries to be provocative in the first graf. I also send along something I've done to show my style."

Oregon free-lance writer Rob Phillips says he writes query letters in a kind of formula fashion. "I begin with the lead of the story and put in a hook to intrigue the editor. I realize that editors are very busy and won't have much time to read my letter. I give a deadline I can meet and the length I propose. I include a gentle urging to respond, as in 'If this is something of interest to you, I'd look forward to hearing from you.' I avoid saying that this is a dandy idea. I let the editor make that decision. Editors know best what they want. I include a list of recent publications attached to the letter. I keep it short. Editors don't want pen pals."

Writers who develop a long standing professional relationship with an editor are seldom asked to submit formal query letters. They know what the editors want and what the publication will be likely to run so well that a simple one or two line note ("How about a story on such and such?") will suffice, as will a phone call. Consequently, their editors know how they write and the kind of copy they will very likely deliver.

Susan Hauser is in that position with the "Arts and Leisure" editor of *The Wall Street Journal*, for whom she has free-lanced for seven years. "From my first piece on the big sale of T-shirts at the Harvard Co-op, my editor has liked almost everything I suggest. I do anything quirky—the weird beat. They've mostly been light news features, more recently participatory things like the 'Dial-a-Sailor' program at the Portland Rose Festival and following the horses at the Rose Festival parade as a 'pooper scooper.' I've been a judge at a beauty contest and played the tambourine for the 'One More Time Marching Band' at Disneyland and the Tournament of Roses Parade in Pasadena. In fact, I've done this so much that one of my children once bragged, 'My mom can be in any parade she wants.' " Hauser says she avoids queries by staying in touch with her editor and knowing precisely what he wants.

Bill McKibben is also in the enviable position of not needing to submit a query letter in the conventional manner. As a former *New Yorker* staff member and author of two successful books, *The End of Nature* and *The Age of Missing Information*, McKibben is often sought out by magazine editors to do articles. "I write magazine pieces as a kind of decompression between books," he says. "I tend not to write an article cold. I'll call up an editor and say what I'm thinking about. The editor will say, 'Fax your idea to me.' I tend not to work with people I haven't established a relationship with." McKibben writes regularly for *The New York Review of Books*,

Outside, and *Conde Nast Traveler* and contributes occasionally to *Rolling Stone*, *Natural History*, and several book review sections.

How to Write a Query Letter

Unless you have such a good relationship with an editor that you can send a few lines of explanation or chat briefly on the telephone, you are going to have to write a query letter. The query need not be a task to dread. Writing a successful query letter is a challenge. Writing a query is also a good way to organize your thoughts in a way that will help you write the final article, once you get approval to do it.

Your task begins before you ever sit down to write your actual query letter. You must study the magazine you are aiming at to make sure your idea will fit, in the process figuring out the name of the person to whom your letter should be addressed. You must also do enough research and possibly even some reporting on the topic so you will be able to write about it authoritatively in your letter. The trick lies in not spending too much time on a topic you may not be able to sell and thus be compensated for. You can probably get enough information in a phone call or two and through library research. Something has obviously intrigued you and you must convey that kind of interest and excitement to the editor you are contacting.

The Address and Salutation

The letter begins with the name of the editor, his or her title, the magazine name, and address. You've got to do the necessary research to know precisely who to write to, even if it means making a quick phone call to the magazine to find out. A letter addressed to "Dear Editor" will probably be thrown away immediately, no matter how good the article idea.

The First Paragraph

You must grab the attention of the editor in the first paragraph of your letter. You can do so by making the writing dramatic, the sentences filled with lots of facts. You might even write this paragraph like a lead. Indeed, you might even use the lead for the article you will write if you get the assignment.

Box 15.1 Writing the Cover Letter

A cover letter, as the name implies, is sent with the final article after you have completed it. In this sense, "cover" has two meanings: it goes on top of the first page of the article, and it conveys or covers some information the editor receiving it needs to know.

Essentially, cover letters are important as re-reminders of your article and yourself. Editors are busy people, as has been noted repeatedly in these pages. Even though they have agreed to run articles and established deadlines and even fees, many weeks and articles and writers have intervened.

A cover letter is a simple reminder of earlier promises, both yours to submit a certain article by a certain deadline; the editor's to accept and publish it and pay you.

A good cover letter should be short. After the salutation, it should get right down to business:

> As you agreed in your letter of January 15, I am submitting a XXX word article on such and such.
>
> (Next should come any extenuating circumstances you have encountered.)
>
> I wasn't able to interview so and so [or] the photos I hoped to arrange were not possible [or whatever].
>
> (Be sure to describe how you have made up for this.)
>
> I did secure an interview with her chief of staff, however, which should serve as a good substitute [or whatever].
>
> (End with a pledge to do as much as necessary to help get the article in print and express the hope to see galleys for first checking.)
>
> Please let me know if I can provide more information or help. I'll look forward to seeing galleys sometime soon.
>
> (If you have source material to submit, mention that too.)
>
> Under separate cover [or] I am also including copies of Dr. Smith's latest article [or] the complete transcripts of the trial [or whatever] for your information and use.
>
> (Then, just sign off, perhaps with a subtle plea for future work.)
>
> Thanks for this assignment. I'm looking forward to working with you in the near future.

A final reminder: you should not veer drastically—if at all—from whatever was agreed to in the editor's response to your query or the contract you signed. This goes for deadline, word length, and thrust of the article. The deadline was set for a reason and it is highly unprofessional to miss it. Word length is equally important. Coming in short will leave a hole, coming in long will require editing. Both practices are bad and reveal your lack of professionalism. Learn to sacrifice your wonderful prose in the interests of future work. Sometimes, there may be a good reason to change your approach due to things you encounter in your reporting and writing. That is permissible—unless it is very major—but you need to keep your editor informed about what you are doing so there are no surprises.

The Second Paragraph

You make your transition to the second paragraph in a way which captures interest by telling why you have written the letter. It is best to get right to the point: "My reason for writing to you is . . ." or "With this letter, I hope to interest you in . . ." You must throw in other peripheral information that bears on your main purpose: observations about the importance of the subject, similar articles and why your idea is better, or the fact that nothing has been done before.

The Third Paragraph

You tell the editor a bit about yourself and your credentials for doing the article you are proposing. If you are including a résumé or list of publications, the mention of yourself need not be extensive, perhaps only a reference to the attached material. You might also note past work you have done for the magazine and perhaps people known to the editor who could vouch for you.

The Signoff

The last paragraph probably need be only a sentence or two. In it, you restate the obvious: you hope this idea interests them and hope to hear from them about it soon.

A word about length: unless a magazine specifies otherwise in *Writer's Market* or their own guidelines, keep your query letters to a page or page and a half maximum. The people you are contacting are extremely busy and are probably only reading your letter because of the scant hope that it may contain something new and interesting. If you go on and on over several pages before getting to the point, they won't stick with your letter. Get to the point fast and hook them right from the start. Remember, too, that editors judge writers not only by their articles but by the letters written to get approval for those articles. Be succinct and germane and let your own style shine through in that first paragraph.

A word about grammar, spelling, etc.: It goes without saying—although it will be said anyway—that your letter must be flawless in grammar, spelling, and presentation. Typos are no excuse, nor is the fact that the "Spell Check" feature on your computer didn't catch the error. Edit your letters carefully. Also, in talking about presentation, invest in an attractive, personal letterhead—one that invites viewing and reading. A query letter is a representative of you. You would not show up for a job interview in jeans, a T-shirt, or uncombed hair, so don't send an editor the query-letter equivalent.

Anatomy of a Successful Query

Several years ago, I submitted a query letter to the editor of *The Quill*, the monthly magazine of the Society of Professional Journalists. I am analyzing it here because it resulted in the approval to write an article and because it contains all the elements of a good query.

As a reader of *The Quill*, I could easily discover who the editor was and the address. I also knew that he had just taken over his post, a fact I hinted at later.

My first paragraph did not turn out to be the lead of my eventual article but I wrote it as if it were. In it, I tried to convey the facts and the drama of a situation many Oregonians had lived with for several years: the establishment of a commune by followers of an Indian guru on a ranch in Eastern Oregon and the efforts of one reporter on *The Oregonian* to expose it. I gained my facts from newspaper clippings and my own interest in the subject over the years it had been in the news. Without so stating, I knew the magazine ran this kind of behind the scenes look at how a big story was covered. I also thought its audience of professionals, journalism educators, and

Mr. Mike Moore, Editor
The Quill
53 West Jackson Blvd., Suite 731
Chicago, Illinois 60604

Dear Mr. Moore:

1 For over four years the followers of the Indian guru Bhagwan Shree Rajneesh have alternately fascinated and horrified Oregonians from their commune in the high desert of Eastern Oregon, Rajneeshpuram. Now, after the Bhagwan has gone into voluntary "exile" in his native India and his top lieutenants have fled prosecution in the state, the commune is breaking up. One of the persons most responsible for bringing the real story of Rajneesh and his followers into the open is Les Zaitz, a reporter for *The Oregonian*. It was Zaitz's 20-part series on the sect that helped topple the group most responsible for such illegal activities as poisoning state and county officials, other commune members, and threatening others; fire bombing buildings; conducting illegal wiretapping of the commune; and even trying to spread food poisoning through salad bars to a whole town. Zaitz's work last summer and since the story intensified this fall has won him the enmity of the Rajneeshees. In fact, he was among nine Oregonians targeted for death last year.

students would be interested in reading about it.

In my second graf, I made the transition directly: "My reason for writing to you now is . . ." I went on to note why I thought the proposed article would be of interest to readers. I said that Zaitz had agreed to talk to me even though he had declined to speak with the writer of an article on cults for the *Columbia Journalism Review*, a competitor of *The Quill*.

2 My reason for writing to you now is to propose that I do an article for *The Quill* on how Zaitz covered this story. Sects and cults are a common thing now so his methods and observations would be of interest to your readers. He had agreed to talk to me if I get the nod from you. (He and two co-workers refused to be interviewed by the *Columbia Journalism Review* for "The 'Cult Beat' " in its current issue.) With his editor's permission, he thinks the sect is less likely to sue than they once were.

Next, I added some background material to heighten the editor's interest: a newspaper clipping about the cult's planned murder of Zaitz. I also added my résumé. Normally, I describe my background right in the letter, but I was getting concerned about length, so I decided to attach a résumé which included a brief list of recent publications. I also had had an earlier connection with the magazine under a previous editor and had even been listed in its staff box as a contributing editor for a year or so. I mentioned this connection in passing to strengthen my credentials with an editor who did not know me.

I closed this graf by stating the obvious: I want to work for the magazine again and hope this article will be my vehicle for doing so.

3 For your information, I am enclosing a story about Zaitz's planned murder as well as my own résumé for your information. As you can see, I have written for *The Quill* before and was a member of the publications committee during my service on the board three years ago. I would like to begin doing pieces for the magazine again and hope you will agree that this is a good suggestion.

My closing paragraph was short. I wished him luck as

4 Good luck to you as editor. I'll hope to hear from you soon.

editor (unnecessarily gratuitous and ingratiating, perhaps) and said I hoped to hear from him soon (obvious but needed to be said in closing).

Sincerely yours,

Ron Lovell

In his reply 11 days later, Mike Moore at first seemed intrigued then kind of backed away from any firm commitment.

Dear Mr. Lovell:

1 An interview with Zaitz might be intriguing, depending on exactly what you have in mind and what he has to say.

He asked me a number of questions to ask of my main source (these later became key parts of my own interviews and guided the approach I took in the article).

2 I'd be interested in knowing *how* Zaitz developed the story—how he got his leads, how he followed them up, what sorts of blind alleys he traveled down, what sorts of roadblocks he encountered, what sorts of misinformation (or "disinformation," as the CIA likes to call it) he was given either by members of the cult or by government officials. In short, I'm looking for a how-we-did-it piece that a reporter, editor or news director could relate to and find helpful in some practical ways. (Such a story, by the way, should also refer to mistakes Zaitz made. Everybody makes mistakes, and the rest of us can benefit by reading about them. And it makes the story more human and therefore more readable.)

He gave me guidance about what he wanted included and left out: nothing on the philosophy of the guru, concentrate on the reporting.

3 I don't have much interest in substantive details regarding the philosophy and actions of the cult. That material should be included only insofar as some of it is necessary to provide context for describing problems encountered in the reporting.

4 I fear I'm going too long here. Based on your query, we're on the same wavelength. Nevertheless, it's sometimes useful to get such things down on paper.

He continued by asking several other questions, including one about libel due to the controversial nature of the subject.

5 A couple of concerns: Was Zaitz *the* key reporter in uncovering the details of the commune—not only at his paper, but in general? By its mere presence in the magazine, our story will inevitably suggest that he *was* the key reporter. That's fine with me, so long as we can back it up.

6 And, too, I'm concerned about possible libel. At least for the first draft, I'll leave the legal judgments to you and Zaitz. But at some point, I may have some questions regarding possibly libelous material.

Although the letter had begun with a tone that suggested he would need more information before committing himself to publishing my proposed article, he wound up by agreeing to run it and even telling me the fee. (That amount was later raised to $750 because the article wound up being a cover story. Other events pushed its appearance to May.)

7 We would use the piece in our March issue. The deadline for that is mid-January. Are there any problems with that?

8 We'll pay $500. Okay?

Let me know soon how you expect things to proceed.

Best,

Mike Moore
Editor of *The Quill*

Anatomy of an Unsuccessful Query

"Of the 1,000 query letters we get each year, 900 of them are unsuitable," says Sally Lee, senior editor at *Redbook*. "Because there are so many bad queries, competent proposals really shine."

#1 Electrolysis Idea

Sally Lee: "The removal of unwanted facial hair is a valid beauty topic for a woman's magazine. The problem with this query is that it proposes an inappropriate length (2,000 words) on a very narrow subject and offers few fresh insights into the subject. Apart from the issue of AIDS contamination, the article would be just a primer on a familiar subject.

"If we ran an article on electrolysis, we'd include it as part of a larger article on

After many years of struggling with unwanted facial hair (and trying every available method of temporary removal), I finally got up my nerve to try electrolysis. The lack of detailed information available about the procedure combined with my surprisingly pleasant experience prompted this query. I propose writing a 2,000 word article for *Redbook* which would answer your readers' questions on the subject of permanent hair removal, such as:

- How does electrolysis work?
- How did I find a reputable electrologist?
- How does a salon visit differ from a clinic?
- Will it hurt?
- How much does it cost?

new measures to remove facial hair or the dangers of doing so or the potential scams in electrolysis. We'd look for a fresh angle.

"Also the writer never gives me any indication that she is qualified to write this article with any authority. The fact that she suffers from unwanted facial hair is important, but she seems to have little medical or beauty background and her list of potential sources for 'expert' opinions does not reassure me that she will present the last word on electrolysis."

- What are the chances of catching AIDS from the needles?
- How long does it take?
- Are there any side effects?

Some professionals in the business of electro-epilation consider it a cosmetic procedure, while others view is as an invasion of the body that should be performed only by a medical professional. My interviewees for the article would include:

- A registered nurse training in dermatology who runs a private clinic.
- An electrologist who works out of a beauty salon.
- A woman who has experienced electrolysis both at a clinic and at a salon.
- A dermatologist who will discuss risks and possible side effects.

Since electrolysis is more risky and more expensive than other methods of hair removal, it warrants more in-depth coverage than it has received. I believe this article would be informative and interesting to your readers. If you agree, I can be reached Monday through Friday, from eight to five, at (---) ------- I also have enclosed a self-addressed stamped envelope.

Sincerely,

#2 Maple Syrup Idea

Sally Lee: "She has not targeted this query. She is wasting her time and wasting our time. The lead sentence is boring, ungrammatical, and generally a very bad start. Right off, I saw that 'writing' and 'years' were misspelled. The writer makes no attempt to make the subject interesting.

"Maybe the article could be refocussed for a regional magazine, a gourmet

I would like to write for your magazine an article on maple syrup, looking especially at the grades of syrup that are created during the sugaring season (late February until early April) and how they are used. A number of sugarhouses in New England offer pancake and waffle breakfasts during this six-week period as a way of allowing visitors to sample the different types of syrup (light, medium and dark) as well as other uses of syrup (sugar-on-snow), maple milk and some others).

The article I have in mind would discuss how maple trees are tapped, how the sap is turned into syrup, the differences between the grades, how inventive people use the syrup as well as

magazine, or a travel magazine. An article detailing a fall tour of maple syrup sugar houses in Vermont, for example, would be quite appealing."

what distinguishes real syrup from commercial Aunt Jemima stuff.

I have writting [sic] for a variety of magazines over the yeras, [sic] including *Connoisseur*, *Better Homes and Gardens* and *Art & Antiques*.

Let me know what you think.

Very truly yours,

#3 Automatic Teller Machine Idea

Sally Lee: "This is not a bad query, but it's too narrow. For a national magazine, a new type of crime, but ATM should be part of a larger focus on something like new crimes of the 90's women should watch out for.

"The way a national magazine like ours is divvied up, there is only so much space. Our magazine has to touch the most readers with its articles. Something like this needs to be part of a roundup. You couldn't write more than 300 to 400 words on this as a new domestic form of armed robbery.

"One thing that marks this writer as an amateur is her inclusion of prizes she has won. This is like having a star on your head that reads, 'Amateur.' Don't say anything about this, include your clips instead."

Last week, an *L.A. Times* report revealed that there are as many as six ATM (Automatic Teller Machine) robberies in the country every day. As ATM usage increases due to the convenience and ease with which people can access their money, the number of ATM-related crimes also rises. In New York City, one of the hardest hit regions, a tough new ATM-safety law was recently adopted. In Los Angeles, similar ordinances have been proposed, but strong opposition is expected from the banking community.

As women are more frequently the target of these crimes, I believe that the young mothers who read *Redbook* would benefit from an article on ATM safety. The article I propose will include true stories from victims of ATM crimes and advice from bank personnel and law enforcement officers on what hazards to avoid and what to do if you are confronted while using your ATM card. City Councilman Joel Wachs, who proposed ATM safety ordinances for Los Angeles, will also be quoted.

My writing credits include three books in the entertainment industry and magazine articles for *Women's Circle*, *Children's Digest*, *Sunshine Magazine* and *The Palmetto Press*. I was recently awarded third prize in a 1992 Florida State Writing Competition. I am enclosing a sample of my writing.

Senator Charles M. Calderon of California, author of a bill currently pending in the legislature which would increase the penalty for

ATM crimes, calls ATM robberies "the crime of the 90's." We all need to be aware of the dangers and know how to avoid being the next victim of this epidemic crime.

Sincerely,

Concludes Lee on the subject of query letters: "A lot of people make queries too narrow like these, others make them too broad, such as wanting to write an article on men/women relationships; you want to knock them on the head and shout, 'Focus, focus.' All of these queries missed the mark for a lot of different reasons. It's hard to say, for example, that the maple syrup one is a bad idea. The right article for the right magazine could be an award winning idea. There is no such things as a bad idea, only a wrong approach, a wrong target."

All of these writers got a form rejection letter from *Redbook*. All queries are read by one of Lee's assistants ("It's good training for them," she says). "You can't start a query—or an article, for that matter—slowly and hit your stride by page 3. The assistant won't get to page 3. Make sure you work on your lead."

One final caution: Lee responds to all query letters, even those without a SASE (self addressed stamped envelope) included. However, she warns, "some magazines throw away all queries and unsolicited manuscripts without a SASE *without even reading them*."

16

The Art of the Interview

All writers have the secret dream of asking such penetrating, pertinent questions that those they are interviewing will be stunned and electrified. That kind of effect is not possible every time you sit across from a source whose help you need in completing an article, but it does help not to take interviewing lightly.

The interview is a crucial part of free-lance writing (or holding any job in journalism, for that matter), and it has been for more than 130 years (see Box 16.1). Along with the ability to type, the ability to ask questions of strangers in a face-to-face or telephone interview is a skill you need to master.

Reporters and writers use all kinds of techniques to interview. These run the gamut from the confrontational, why-did-you-steal-the-money approach of "60 Minutes" to the kinder, gentler, technique of morning television feature programs. What works for one writer does not necessarily work for another. It is best not to reach too far in selecting your approach. If you aren't a blunt, tough-talking person, don't attempt that method when you are trying to get someone to answer questions. On the other hand, if you are not by nature a "schmoozer" and loaded with charm, don't try to fake it.

Not that having an "approach" is really necessary. Your technique will emerge as you gain more experience and it is best not to force it. What is more important is to prepare for each interview carefully so that it will yield what you are after: good quotes and information you need for your article.

Box 16.1 Horace Greeley Launches Celebrity Journalism

In 1859, Horace Greeley, editor of the *New York Tribune*, interviewed Mormon leader Brigham Young for two hours in Salt Lake City. The results made history: the first instance where a person's answers to a reporter's questions were printed in a question-and-answer format and in direct quotes. The informal interview—not tied to a specific event—was thus launched as an ideal way to find out details of the lives of famous people. In effect, the celebrity journalism industry, so successful today, had been launched.

Although somewhat stilted when read today, the Greeley/Young interview is interesting nevertheless:

TWO HOURS WITH BRIGHAM YOUNG
Salt Lake City, Utah, July 13, 1859.

My friend Dr. Bernhisel, Mormon Church, took me this afternoon, to meet Brigham Young, President of the Mormon Church, who had expressed a willingness to receive me at 2:00 P.M. After some unimportant conversation on general topics, I stated that I had come in quest of fuller knowledge respecting the doctrines and polity of the Mormon Church and would like to ask some questions bearing directly on these, if there was no objection. President Young avowed his willingness to respond to all pertinent inquiries. The conversation proceeded substantially as follows:

[Early questions deal with church doctrine]

H.G.: What is the position of your church with respect to slavery?

B.Y.: We consider it of divine institution and not to be abolished until the curse pronounced on Him shall have been removed from his descendants.

H.G.: Are any slaves now held in this territory?

B.Y.: There are.

H.G.: Do your territorial laws uphold slavery?

B.Y.: Those laws are printed—you can read for yourself. . . .

[More answers dealing largely with church doctrine]

H.G.: Can you give any national explanation of the aversion and hatred with which your people are generally regarded by those among whom they have lived and with whom they have been brought directly into contact?

B.Y.: No other explanation than is afforded by the crucifixion of Christ and the kindred treatment of God's ministers, prophets, and saints in all ages.

H.G.: How general is polygamy among you?

B.Y.: I could not say. Some of those present have each but one wife; others have more; each determines what is his individual duty.

H.G.: What is the largest number of wives belonging to any one man?

B.Y.: I have 15; I know no one who has more; but some of those sealed to me are old ladies whom I regard rather as mothers than wives, but whom I have taken to cherish and support.

[The interview continued with further discussion of having more than one wife.]

—*New York Tribune*, August 20, 1859

Preparing for the Interview

Research and Question Preparation

Getting ready for the interview begins as soon as you have gotten an assignment or had your idea accepted by an editor. You need to find out as much as possible about the person and the subject. You can go to the library and look up pertinent book and periodical references from which you can photocopy what you need. If you have kept files on your areas of specialty, you may have clips to consult. The person to be interviewed might send you background material or his or her public relations person might do so as well. Your editor might also have sent you useful information. From whatever source, you then proceed to use this material in working out your questions.

Some writers find it best to write out all questions in advance, least controversial first, tough questions last to allow rapport to build. Others like to jot down only broad subject areas and then phrase them at the time, depending on circumstances of the interview itself. It is a good idea to group questions by subject so your interviewee is not forced to jump back and forth in thought processes.

Setting up an Appointment

Arranging an appointment with an interview subject may not be as easy as it sounds, especially if you are a free-lance writer. If you are a staff member of a prestigious magazine or newspaper, mere mention of that affiliation will usually be enough to open all doors.

Saying you are "Ron Lovell, free-lance writer" may not. You should never lie about your status, but it is perfectly fine to say you are "on assignment" for such and such a magazine or, "I am a free-lance writer working regularly for such and such." If you are doing the article on speculation, you must say so—and hope for the best.

Beyond that, your best approach to setting up an interview is to go through the person's public relations office. In the absence of such an office, your only choice is to try a secretary or other assistant. Often, one of the main duties of such an employee is to protect and defend the boss from all interruptions. Here, persistence, extreme politeness, and out-and-out "sweet talk" will be necessary. When all else fails, call the potential interviewee's home or go there—or the office—and wait until you have an opportunity to ask your subject for an interview. In any case, be sure to tell the person why you want to interview him or her and explain his or her part in your final article.

Selecting a Site

An office is the best place to conduct an interview, especially if the person you are talking to cuts off phone calls and other interruptions. The person is thus on home ground surrounded by familiar things and feels more at ease and in control of the situation. At times, you might want to conduct an interview over lunch or dinner. Although this can be a pleasant experience and might relax the interviewee, it can be hard for the writer, trying to balance pencil and note pad with knife and fork. Notes can often wind up with salad dressing stains and coffee cup rings on them.

For a profile, you should conduct at least one interview in the person's home to get a feeling for how that subject lives and also to get the chance to talk to family members. Here, questioning skills may be less important than the writer's powers of observation.

In any kind of story, no matter how broad the subject and how many people need to be contacted, it is best to talk to people one-on-one. Never try to interview more than one person at the same time because it is hard to tell who is talking and generally quite confusing. A business executive may insist that a public relations person be present. If so, you should make it clear that that person should not speak until spoken to and you have every right to object if the PR person constantly interrupts and cautions the source not to answer. The good ones will only be there to help and will otherwise keep quiet.

The Interview

Be Punctual

Once an appointment has been made, you have no excuse for being late. An out-of-breath arrival by a writer mumbling apologies and explanations gets the interview off to a bad and defensive start. It will quickly undermine your ability to establish careful control of the interview and to get the material you need to write the article.

It is better to be kept waiting by the source than to be late yourself. That way, the interviewee will begin by apologizing to you and thus, be a bit on the defensive. While you wait, you can look around the outer office for clues to the person you are about to meet and even ask the secretary a question or two.

Asking Questions

The interview will probably begin more smoothly with a little small talk—the weather, some personal fact you know about the person because of your earlier observation and research ("I notice you sail" or "I went to UCLA too"). Don't overdo it, however. A busy person may resent the wasting of time. You will have to judge the situation for yourself and cut off the personal patter accordingly. Do be sure to thank your subject up-front for making time for the interview.

Get right to your questions after these preliminaries, restating the subject of your article. Ask your questions and record the answers as the interview proceeds. You should phrase your questions in an easily understood manner and not include your own opinions and biases. You should also avoid asking leading questions with predetermined answers ("Don't you think this is true?") or questions that can be answered with a single yes or no. A particularly laconic and taciturn interviewee will stifle an interview if asked these kinds of questions. You will have gone through all your questions in ten minutes and have only a half page of unusable notes to show for it.

People develop different styles. Some interviewers prefer to act somewhat uninformed and let the subject lead them toward greater knowledge ("I don't know much, please bear with me"). With some people—both interviewer and interviewee—the direct approach may be best ("Why did you do this?" or "What did you do?")

If a person refuses to answer a question or be drawn out on a subject, leave it for the time being and come back to it later. Some questions may never be answered, but a person will usually not grant an interview unless he or she plans to say at least something about the most likely topics of the interview. At times you may have to persevere at the end of the interview and try to get a reply by saying, "You haven't answered my question." If a second or third try fails, give up that line of questioning. During the interview, don't underestimate the value of silence. You can sometimes get a person to answer simply by waiting him or her out. Few people can sit for very long in absolute silence, especially if a question has been directed to them. Try not to be the one who "gives in" and talks.

To keep control of the interview, you may have to bring your interviewee back to the subject at hand. By accident or intention, people sometimes talk about things that have nothing to do with what you came to discuss. If this happens, just restate the original question and get the person back on track.

As you ask your questions and record the answers, pay attention to your interviewee's body language. Is he nervous or relaxed, fidgeting in a chair or playing with paper clips or a pen or pacing the room? Does she make eye contact when answering? (It goes without saying that you will look all your interviewees right in the eye when asking your questions and, as much as possible, when listening to answers.)

Handling Difficult People

At times, because of the topic or the person being interviewed, a writer will know in advance that the exchange is going to be a difficult one. Some prefer to wade in with full force, no holds barred, matching obnoxiousness with obnoxiousness. At other times, an interview might turn hostile and confrontational unexpectedly. When it does, it is best to change the subject and try to move things back to more civil ground. The chance for hostility is the best reason to save tough questions until last. You can sometimes restart a stalled interview by simply asking, "Why?" (The peculiar horrors of interviewing scientists, doctors, and engineers is covered in Box 16.2.)

Following up on New Information

Occasionally, writers will pick up something during an interview that they will recognize immediately as more important than the original subject. When this happens, you should seize the opportunity to question the source without revealing that what he or she has said is of extreme interest. In these instances, it is best to go on with the interview and return later to the new subject. This

Box 16.2 Interviewing Scientists, Doctors, and Engineers

Writers working for trade and technical publications will often encounter the challenging experience of having to interview scientists, doctors, engineers, and other technical professionals who: 1) use complicated and unfamiliar terms frequently, and 2) act in an arrogant and suspicious manner some of the time.

The complicated subject matter can be dealt with by careful preparation for the interview. Read everything you can about the technical subject under discussion and anything you can get that was written by the person. This will help you frame your questions. In the interview itself, stop your source for an explanation anytime you don't understand something said, unless it is so rudimentary that you will be embarrassed.

The arrogance and suspicion are harder to counter. Part of the suspicion comes from the structure of science and medicine where scientists and doctors are not rewarded for talking to reporters and writers. Instead, they succeed by working for years in laboratories, then publishing their results—after they have been checked by their peers—in prestigious journals. If they get too "popular" their peers will look down upon them. A writer can only argue about the value of public knowledge of a scientist's work to assure future funding.

Another reason for the suspicion may be a scientist's or doctor's past encounter with a reporter who misquoted and misused technical material. You can only argue that you are careful and plead to be given the chance to prove it.

The arrogance of the overly smart is harder to deal with. The only answer may be out-and-out flattery.

way, you will avoid rattling the source so much that he or she decides too much has been revealed and refuses to talk. On the other hand, don't be like many White House reporters at televised presidential news conferences who get so caught up in their own questions that they let new information slide by.

Going "off the Record"

Only experienced interviewees will use the device of placing an interview "off the record," that is, making it unavailable for publication and restricting its use to background information. Many of the people using the phrase really mean "not for attribution": they do not want their name identified with the story. The best approach on controversial interviews is to work out some ground rules in advance. In this way, some information can perhaps be unattributed and the rest usable and attributed to the source. Be sure to mark such things carefully in your notes so you can tell the difference later.

If a source tells you something in strict confidence and you agree on the spot not ever to use it, you are ethically bound by that agreement and it is best to put down your pen and turn off your tape recorder. This puts the person at ease and removes any temptation you might have later to use the restricted material. It is not acceptable, however, for a person to make the whole interview "off the record" or "not for attribution" during or after the interview. If this happens, try to talk the person out of such a drastic step. After all, if the source did not want to be interviewed for publication, why did he or she agree to talk to you in the first place? If push comes to shove and the person is adamant, you might do well to find other sources on the same subject who will talk to you on the record. But that course should only be a last resort. You must use all your powers of persuasion to convince your interviewees to go "on the record."

Ending an Interview

Almost any interview is an imposition on someone's time. Everyone is busy, as are you, so be gracious and grateful for whatever time you can get. It is wise to be conscious of staying within whatever time constraints have been agreed to in advance. It is wonderful to get an hour to talk because a lot can be said in that amount of time. When more than one interview might be necessary—say, at home and at the office—keep each session to an hour, unless the source wants to go beyond. A busy person may agree only to a half hour and you probably are not in any position to argue. Generally, if things are going well, people will keep talking and you'll get your extra time. If your source seems willing, however, keep on asking questions. Don't get so hung up on the time, however, that you constantly look at your watch. This will look to your source like you are impatient to end the interview when just the reverse is true! It is best to keep time by another clock in the room or by glancing slyly at your source's watch.

When it is time to go, make sure you have followed up on all loose ends in your notes—marked by large *X*'s to trigger your memory. If you don't understand something now, you certainly won't understand it when you start writing, so ask your follow-up questions. Then ask one final question: "Anything else?" This rather open-ended remark allows your sources to say anything on their minds and can sometimes bring forth a flood of new information.

And, most of all, don't be afraid to ask what, on the face of it, might seem like a dumb question. That may bring the most interesting response of all.

Be sure to thank your source and leave an opening to call back to clarify points if necessary. It is best not to agree to show copy unless your employer requires it; many public relations magazines do, consumer magazines do not. A useful substitute to the delays and loss of spontaneity that showing copy brings about is to call back to read quotes or other portions of your article to the source for the correction of errors only.

Taking and Recording Notes

Taking notes of what sources tell you in interviews is one of the most difficult parts of journalism. You ask your questions, sources start to speak, you write down what they are saying while they have, in the meantime, gone on to another topic which you are desperately trying to remember. It can be a maddening experience, especially when your source talks very fast. Of course, everyone pauses for breath now and again and this will enable you to catch up. You can also catch up on your note-taking when an interviewee goes off on a tangent, nodding profusely as if the extraneous is really pertinent. Don't ever ask a source to slow down. You don't want to call attention to your note-taking.

It is always a good idea to have your notebook and pen or pencil in plain sight from the moment you enter a room. If you think you can calm a source by chatting for a while without pen and paper and then pull it out later with a flourish, you are wrong. A person may panic at the sudden appearance of your note-taking materials to a greater extent than if they are visible at the start of the interview.

It is never a good idea *not* to take notes of any kind, turning yourself into some kind of human tape recorder who must rush from the interview to the rest room or your car and try to reconstruct what has just been said. The potential for error is great and you will have nothing to back you up later if your source says he or she was misquoted. Even Truman Capote, who took no notes during hundreds of interviews for his epic account of multiple murders in Kansas, *In Cold Blood*, was criticized later for this technique and many of his sources said they had not said what he said they said. Without notes, you have nothing to refute such claims.

To be a successful writer, you must teach yourself to be a fast and accurate note taker. It is not necessary to learn shorthand in the way many reporters in England are taught, but it is wise to develop your own kind of shorthand—abbreviations that mean something to you ("&" for and, "w/o" for without, no "a" or "the").

At the top of the first page, it is a good idea to write the name of the source and the date, as well as the page number, lest the sheets get out of order. It will help organize your article later if you number the answers corresponding to the numbers of your questions.

To Tape or Not to Tape

The question of whether to use a tape recorder in interviews is as old as the development of the machine itself. It is comforting to know that everything said in the interview is being recorded. With the interview on tape, there is no question about accuracy or whether or not a statement was made. It will make you feel more secure to know you have a taped record of everything that was said. On the other hand, it is a real pain to sit through that interview again and again in order to transcribe it. And, if you are on deadline, it may be impossible.

If you tape only, you may run the risk of a malfunctioning machine, a blank or garbled tape, and no usable material from your interview. This is one of the most empty feelings a writer can have and a true disaster: no notes, no tape, no story. A good compromise is to do both: take good notes and tape the interview too. That way you can clear up discrepancies in your notes—or make up for your bad handwriting—by listening to what was said on the tape.

If you use a tape recorder, buy a good one that will not break down. Try it out in advance for sound level so you can simply set it down on a table in front of your source without a great deal of fussing and yelling of "testing, testing," into the microphone.

Tape recorders, for all their value, are often disruptive. It is a rare source who does not keep glancing nervously at the recorder and is not self-conscious at its presence. At times, it seems like some people view the recorder as an eavesdropper, even though it is probably to their benefit to have it there. If an interviewee objects to the use of a recorder, turn it off and forget it. If you insist on it, your source may get more nervous or even hostile. Never try to conceal your use of a tape recorder. That is not only unethical, it is illegal. Once in a great while, a source may insist on using his or her own tape recorder too, to have a record of what has been said. You, of course, will have to agree.

Telephone Interviews

The telephone can be one of your most useful tools. As a free-lancer on a limited budget, you can't always travel to your interviews. The next best thing is a telephone interview, which can always be taped via a plug connecting your recorder to your phone. Whether you tell the person you have called that you are taping the conversation depends on laws in your state. Most states allow calls to be taped if one person involved in the conversation is aware of it. That person can be you. Most of the time, you'll probably want to mention that you are taping the call to improve accuracy.

It is truly amazing what people will tell a perfect stranger over the telephone. Much of this has to do with how you start and whether your voice seems friendly and unthreatening. Even if you do most of your interviews without written questions, it is a good idea to prepare a script before you conduct telephone interviews. You need to tell the person who answers your call quite quickly: who you are, why you are calling, how he or she fits into your planned article, and get off the first good question. That question should interest them and allow them immediately to see why you have called them. You don't want their first reaction to be, "Who is this guy? I'm too busy to put up with this interruption." Before you begin your questioning, you should probably ask if this is a good time to talk and, if it isn't, make an appointment to call when it is more appropriate. Remember, a telephone call is always an interruption.

Tone of voice and telephone manner help build confidence too. If it helps to smile when you talk, do it! Speak slowly and clearly and never show anger at how rudely you might be treated. Telephone interviewing can definitely be enhanced by "buttering-up" and schmoozing.

When given the choice of interviewing someone face-to-face or over the telephone, chose the former. Your article will be better served if you talk in person.

After the Interview

There is nothing more difficult for a writer to encounter than "cold" notes, a record of a past interview that has been allowed to sit around for a long time, so that you can't read your handwriting or remember details you didn't record at the time. Even if you aren't going to write your article immediately, you should review your notes as soon as possible after the interview and fill in things you abbreviated or only noted in passing. You might also add things you did not write down at the time of the interview: how a person acted and looked, details of the room. If you can, this is also an ideal time to listen to the tape as you follow your notes, again filling in things you left out.

Some magazines will want to get all your source material in preparing your article, including your interviews. If this is a requirement, you will have to provide a transcript of the tape, not the tape itself. In such instances, you might best preserve your sanity by hiring a professional typist with the proper equipment (a headset to listen and a foot pedal to stop and start the tape) and the patience to do this rather tedious work. Sometimes, the magazine will pay for this service.

There is no better tool for a writer than the interview. Short of observing something yourself—a rare occurrence for most people in journalism who hear about most events after the fact from people who were there—the interview is the only tool. Even with careful preparation, good questions, and a working tape recorder, however, some interviews go badly from the start. Either you or the interviewee is having a bad day, the chemistry between you is wrong, you make them angry—there are many things that can go wrong. When it does, don't despair. Retreat with your notes and live to fight—or interview—another day.

Lessons in Free-Lancing: Interviewing

Interviews for the article on marine mammals of the Arctic (reproduced in chapter 18), were easy to prepare for since the editor of the magazine had given me many more source names than I would need.

My first step was to figure out the general thrust of the article and who I would need to see to get the information to complete my assignment. I planned two trips: to the Canadian Arctic to observe the scientists doing their work; to Alaska beforehand, to find out what the state and federal governments were doing to protect marine mammals from harm and, secondarily, to handle the increasingly political aspects of the story.

I called ahead and had no trouble setting up interviews in either locale. In Alaska, I talked to scientists at the University of Alaska Arctic Environmental Information and Data Center in Anchorage for an overall look at the problem of protecting whales and other marine mammals from humans. At this stage, I was an almost blank slate. I knew very little about the subject and I proceeded with one question, "Will you tell me what you know?" They could and did, with me asking clarifying questions as we went along. I also got a number of very valuable reports from the group on their studies of the bowhead whale and Eskimo hunting and subsistence practices. My several hours with these people was time well spent. I would repay their generosity by quoting them accurately by name and listing the name of their organization, a factor that might possibly help in future funding efforts.

I next journeyed to Fairbanks, site of the office of an Alaska Department of Fish and Game scientist who gave me material on all the non-whale marine mammals of the region—seals and walrus. I asked him simple questions too: what is the status of these creatures; how will they be affected by oil exploration. I also picked up as much background material as I could carry: official reports, scientific articles, newspaper clippings. I did not refuse anything because I did not know then what I might need later.

This leg of my journey over, I returned to Seattle, the best way to proceed to Canada. I flew from there to Edmonton, spent the night, and then made my way to the site of the research—the tiny native village of Tuktoyaktuk on the Beaufort Sea. Exxon had arranged for me to stay in its oil workers' camp—really a series of mobile homes linked by passageways and set across the bay from the town on the hard tundra.

Because it was August, weather was not a problem. But I did have trouble getting around, especially across the bay to the actual town out of which the scientists were operating. One day, I went by supply boat; another by company helicopter; a third by Zodiak, a small rubber raft that goes like fury.

Once I got to the scientists, my reporting was easy. I "hung out" and asked questions when I could. I was fortunate to get to go on one flight to observe whales.

My biggest stroke of luck came on my last day. The lead scientist—and my main source—had convened a meeting of all sponsors of his work, government and private. In a small house on the edge of the furthermost point of North America as a long summer Arctic day drew to an end, I was able to listen while the scientists told where they were in their research and showed slides of their aerial observations. I just sat in the corner and listened and took notes. It was a reporter's dream.

When I left on the company supply plane the next morning, I had what I needed for a thorough article, as well as the memories and experience of working in this remote area. Now I had to put my experiences and the information into an article that was accurate, meaningful and readable.

—Ron Lovell

Lessons from this Lesson in Free-Lancing

1. Sometimes, a story that is planned carefully can work out almost effortlessly, with little more on the writer's part than showing up and listening and taking good notes.
2. In such cases, you may need to abandon old practices and wing it, as I did on this story. I knew in my mind what I needed to find out but I didn't really need to ask many questions. (My usual practice is to write out many questions in advance. That wasn't necessary here because my sources gave me what I needed after I asked them to tell me what they were doing, the problems encountered, and how factors like oil exploration were affecting the mammal they specialized in.)
3. Good sources are worth their weight in gold. The success of your story rests with the sources you select to interview (as well as your skill in writing the final article).
4. Selecting your sources may be like playing Russian roulette. Luck plays a big role and, even with careful selection, you still wind up with duds from time to time. (Fortunately, on this story, I had some of the best sources of my career.)
5. Don't be afraid to admit that you don't know much about the subject. By all means, do your homework, but don't be reluctant to approach your subject and your sources in a "blank slate" kind of way.

PART IV

Writing Magazine Articles

> Writing is very easy. All you do is sit in front of a typewriter keyboard until little drops of blood appear on your forehead.
>
> —Red Smith

17

From Humble Beginnings Do Mighty Articles Grow

Ask 10 free-lance writers how they begin their articles and you will probably get 10 different answers. There is no magic formula for starting a magazine article. It is something most writers dread because it is difficult. After the usually enjoyable period of interviewing and research—and possibly travel—to gather the material for your article, it is tough to confront the blank screen of your computer or empty paper in your typewriter. You sit and wait for the right words to form and the cursor seems to be mocking you as it blinks and blinks.

The Lead as a Springboard

The first or lead paragraph is the most important thing you will write because it sets the tone for what is to follow. It is the lead that brings readers in and entices them to move on and complete your article. You won't be able to capture the attention of readers if you don't have an interesting lead.

The process of lead writing is never easy. Even experienced writers sometimes have trouble deciding how to begin. Most writing begins with thinking about what you are going to say and how, at least preliminarily, you are going to organize your material. In these ruminations, you may get an idea or two about a good lead. At other times, a good lead may come to you back in the information gathering stage or when you are taking a shower. If it does, write it down and save it for future use.

On the other hand, a lead may still be eluding you long after you are ready to begin writing. If this occurs, don't despair. It happens to all writers. You can usually get beyond this temporary writer's block by starting to type your notes or beginning to write and organizing material into paragraphs you will probably eventually use in your article. Another way to break the dreaded writer's block is to think of your lead as a letter and write "Dear Mother" at the top. After you have fashioned a coherent telling of your story, you can remove the salutation. This kind of thing will usually get you moving and, before long, a lead will come into your head and onto the page, as if by magic. Come to think of it, writing itself sometimes seems at least partially magical or inexplicable.

Kinds of Leads

Once you are ready to begin your article, there are a number of different kinds of leads you can choose.

Narrative

The narrative lead is the most compelling kind of lead because it interests the reader with vivid language and colorful description. It tells a good story as if a narrator were speaking.

> The desert sun beating against the aluminum skin of the Swissair DC-8 pushed temperatures inside the aircraft to as high as 105°, the only wind outside stirred up a dust storm. And the smell from clogged toilets permeated the stale air inside the plane. Mothers strained in this suffocating atmosphere to amuse children lest they cry and their captors take them away.

The aim of this lead was to give readers the feel for being held hostage in an airliner in the Jordanian desert by Palestinian guerrillas.

> New York City's Bowery: the original Skid Row. Abandon all hope ye who land here. Dead drunk on cheap wine, crawling with vermin, the derelicts in this strip of flophouses and bottle-littered streets are setups for exposure, communicable disease, cirrhosis. You wouldn't expect these victims of broken dreams, failed marriages, and blasted careers to go see a doctor. Now,

> in a pioneering effort, volunteer teams from the Manhattan Bowery Project lead derelicts to a five-day detoxification program in a 50-bed facility atop the decaying Shelter Care Center for men on the edge of the Bowery.

This lead attempts to bring readers into the Bowery and allow them to visualize what life is like there.

Descriptive

The descriptive lead, as the name implies, describes something for readers, and sets the scene for them. The words of this lead bring the readers into a room as if they had witnessed what is being described. It differs from the narrative lead only in that it is less panoramic and encompassing in scope. Also, what is described has usually been observed by the writer.

> The Eskimo couple had been drinking all night and now it was morning. The one-room tar-paper shack on the edge of Nome contained no conveniences. While the younger of nine children played languidly, the older ones sat about looking sullen. The Bureau of Indian Affairs official tried to converse with the couple, but their answers were unintelligible.

The lead attempts to bring the reader into the Eskimo shack and see the sad scene.

> The bearded man was obviously tired. He walked across the hall toward a group of union officers. "What do I have to do to get a grocery order?" he asked. The officers directed him to a nearby table.

The lead gives the hint of strain and worry being felt by a man involved in a five-month strike at a Utah copper mine.

Summary

The summary lead is the lead favored most often by the writers of news stories. As its name implies, this lead summarizes the facts of the story, using the long-established formula of the five W's and H: who, what, when, where, why, and how. If your article has a news orientation, this kind of lead may work.

> After 23 years, Britain's National Health Service is under such strong fire that major modifications seem inevitable. At a time when the U.S. is moving toward some kind of nationalized care, its very principle—achieving improved services at lower cost—seems to be in jeopardy in the country famed for making it work.

The lead introduces an article on the problem of Britain's National Health Service by juxtaposing it against possible plans for a U.S. system.

> As Ranger 7 sped to its target on the moon to take some historic lunar pictures, its progress was followed and controlled by equipment in a new four-story command center built to handle deep-space probes. While the headlines were being written, the men and women at the $14.6 million Space Flight Operation Facility at the Jet Propulsion Laboratory in Pasadena, California were getting ready for their next job: two eight-month-long Mariner probes to Mars.

The lead uses the news peg of a mission to interest readers in an article about the new command center that controls such flights.

Delayed

The delayed lead puts off mentioning exactly what is going on in the story. It attempts to entice the reader to continue by hinting at what is to come. Writers using this lead must be sure to "pay off" or explain the lead fairly quickly lest readers get confused and abandon the article altogether.

> The passenger list for the chartered PanAm flying boat "Dixie Clipper" was headed by a "Mr. Jones." It was only when the pilot noticed that "Jones" was to be accompanied by Harry Hopkins, Admiral William D. Leahy, and six others that he realized who passenger number one really was. "Mr. President," he told him, "I'm glad to have you aboard, sir."

The transition quickly identified "Jones" as Franklin D. Roosevelt.

> For Holcomb, Kansas (population 281), fame arrived with what some residents now call "that book." Truman Capote's *In Cold Blood* relates, in meticulous detail, the 1959 murder of the village's most prominent family: Herbert Clutter, his wife, son, and daughter. The book was published in 1966 and 350,000 hard cover copies and 2 million paperbacks have been sold thus far. Since then, Holcomb hasn't been able to get away from it all. And now the Clutter tale is about to be told again.

The transition explained that a director was beginning to film the movie version of the book in the tiny town.

Quotation

This lead begins with a quotation from one of your sources. If the quote is good, the lead will be good. If not, just the reverse will be true and your lead—and possibly your article—may fall flat. To be effective, the quote you select should set the tone for the article with its dramatic effect or its ability to sum up concisely what is to come. As with the delayed lead, the quotation lead needs to be explained quickly so readers will grasp the concept and continue reading.

> "It's a hell of a lot of work. That's all I know."

This quote sets the tone nicely for an article about how power was being restored to the Watts area of Los Angeles after the riots there.

> "When I entered prison, the first thing the old-timers told me was 'For God's sake, don't get sick here.' After a while, I understood what they meant. I thought, 'If I get sick I'm going to die.' "

This quote by a prison inmate nicely set the tone for an article on prison medicine.

Another way to effectively use quotes is to refer to your copy of *Bartlett's Quotations* and select a quote by a famous person that encapsulates what you are going to write about. If the selection is a good one, you needn't use any transitional device to get readers into the story. They will know and immediately realize the appropriateness of the quotations.

For example, to introduce an article on the legal rights of teenage patients:

> "Children should be seen and not heard."
>
> —Anonymous

Or, to set the tone for an article on people who cheat on their taxes:

> "In this world nothing is certain but death and taxes."
>
> —Benjamin Franklin

Ironic or Startling Statement

In this kind of lead, you literally trap readers into going beyond your lead by forcing them to find out what you are talking about. As with delayed leads, however, you must explain what you are talking about fairly quickly lest you lose the reader forever.

> This is a story about two people and herbicides.

> It's a drug with a cult of its own, not freaks or thrill-seekers, but people who have used it medically or known those helped by it.

> From the start, the marriage was something out of a fast-selling-novel-turned-tear-jerking motion picture: Rich society girl marries handsome medical student from poor background and

> helps him become famous plastic surgeon. The fictional version always had a happy ending. The real thing decidedly did not. The woman was dead and her husband was accused of the murder.

In all of these instances, readers are bound to wonder what will come next and, as a result, will probably read on.

Other kinds of leads abound, but often are a prelude to trite writing. In any kind of writing, the writer aims for quality and should always stretch to reach it. The leads explained thus far in this chapter will bring out the best in those who use them.

The choice of what lead to use is up to you as the writer. You have made a series of choices throughout the entire process. You have picked a topic and picked the sources to interview and research. You have selected a proper market.

Now will come the next big decision: how to begin. As this chapter illustrates, there are many choices. Your decision may be determined by the material, the style followed by the magazine you are writing for, or even your mood when you sit down to write.

But your choices won't end here. As the next chapter reveals, the beginning paragraph is just that: a jumping-off point. You must still decide what material to include, how to arrange it, how to transition out of the lead, and how to end well.

18

The Heart of the Matter

There comes a time in any journalistic endeavor when you have to call a halt to your research and interviewing, pull together what you've got, and start to write. Some people prefer the preliminary fact-gathering and put off doing something with the material as long as possible. Others love the writing process most of all and can't wait to get started.

Whichever predilection fits you, you will need to come up with an approach that gets you started—and finished in enough time to meet your deadline.

Getting Started

As chapter 17 noted, writing the lead paragraph is usually the first step. Whichever kind of lead you select, the mere process of putting something down on paper will usually serve as a kind of launching point for the rest of your article.

Because most magazine articles are reasonably long—2,000 to 4,000 words on average—and cover a subject in more depth than a single source newspaper story, you will have collected a sizeable mound of material by the time you are ready to write. Along with your interview notes you may have clippings from other publications, articles or technical papers your sources have written, and other printed material ranging from books to government documents. It can be fairly intimidating—if you let it.

The best way to avoid feeling overwhelmed is to stack the material on your desk and organize it. First, go through your interview notes and make sure they are understandable. Then, go through the reference material and highlight with a colored marker the material you think you will use. Discard everything you won't need, or at least put it to one side in case you might want some of it later. Now the pile of raw data won't look quite so intimidating.

Preparing an Outline

One way to proceed at this point is to prepare an outline of your article as it seems to be shaping up. From lead paragraph to big finish, along with all paragraphs in between, you outline major sections with Roman numerals, subsections with capital letters, and other parts with numbers and small letters, just like you learned in junior high school. This allows you to think on paper by using a kind of shorthand and by putting down in terse form the major points of your article.

An outline has another advantage: it removes some of the anxiety you may feel about writing your article. If you can whip through an outline in a half hour or so, writing the final article may not seem as gigantic a task.

"Winging It" Without an Outline

Another way to go is to plunge into the writing without preparing a formal outline. In this approach, you work out a theme and a rough order of priorities for the facts in your head. You have gone through the interview and reference material beforehand so you know what is there. You have probably reached some conclusions and a point of view by this time as well. Once you have decided upon your lead, start writing, pouring over your material as you go until you've reached the end.

Some writers prefer this method (including yours truly). It is less cumbersome and time consuming. It also makes your writing more spontaneous. It is important to proceed through the entire article quickly without pausing to smooth out rough spots. Just get it down on paper or on your screen. Then, you can go back to edit and fine-tune the material.

Devices to Move the Story Along

As you get into the actual writing of your article, there are several devices that will keep things moving.

Transitions

A transition is a word or phrase that will get you (and the reader) from one paragraph to the next. The most important transition needs to be made from the lead to the second paragraph. A fairly simple way to do this is to pick up a word or phrase from the lead and repeat it.

Lead: On the surface, there is little of medical interest about Howard Hughes except the recently reported decline in his own health. The reclusive billionaire spends thousands each year waging a reverse public relations campaign to keep news of his personal life and enterprises out of the media. This effort, plus his own inaccessibility, holds authoritative information to a minimum and the man and his works open to wild speculation.

Transition: That speculation extends even to Hughes' philanthropic works, for below the surface, there is much medical interest in the man. Buried in the complex organizational charts of his $2 billion empire is the Howard Hughes Medical Institute in Miami. . . .

The transition is made by re-using the word "speculation."

Another good transitional device is to characterize what you have explained in the lead in a phrase or a sentence. This works especially well with dramatic narrative leads, like the example from Chapter 17.

Lead: The desert sun beating against the aluminum skin of the Swissair DC-8 pushed temperatures inside the aircraft to as high as 105°, the only wind outside stirred up a dust storm. And the smell from clogged toilets permeated the stale air inside the plane. Mothers strained in this suffocating atmosphere to amuse children lest they cry and their captors take them away.

Transition: The situation on that baked-clay, dry lake landing strip in the Jordanian desert, where three hijacked jetliners and hundreds of passengers were held for a week by Palestinian guerrillas, was patently miserable. But to one of the two American doctors involved, it never became as critical as it might have. [Article goes on with quotes from that doctor.]

The transition is achieved by characterizing what was described in the lead as "the situation."

Names can also be good ways to bring the reader from the lead to the second paragraph.

Lead: The passenger list for the chartered PanAm flying boat "Dixie Clipper" was headed by a "Mr. Jones." It was only when the pilot noticed that "Jones" was to be accompanied by Harry Hopkins, Admiral William D. Leahy, and six others that he realized who passenger number one really was. "Mr. President," he told him, "I'm glad to have you aboard, sir."

Transition: Franklin D. Roosevelt was traveling from Miami to Casablanca to meet Winston Churchill in January and, in the process, becoming the first president to fly while in office. . . .

The transition is achieved by the name "Franklin D. Roosevelt."

A slight variation on the use of a name is to characterize someone who has been quoted in the lead.

Lead: "It's a hell of a lot of work. That's all I know."

Transition: A foreman of a Los Angeles Department of Water and Power utility crew was commenting on the task before him. He was standing on the curb as a new power pole was brought down the street for placement in the riot-damaged Watts area. The pole itself—and such equipment as wire and fuses—had been destroyed by fires arsonists set at 329 buildings eventually destroyed in the riot.

The transition is achieved by use of the speaker's title: "a foreman."

You can use similar transition devices throughout your article to get readers from one paragraph to the next: words, characterizations, people's names.

When you are making a major change of focus or subject, it might be easier to insert subheads than try for the perfect transition. A better device is the use of the doublespace. Here, like the change of scene in a play, the extra space indicates to your readers that you want them to pause a bit before moving on. Such space is especially useful as you end your article, particularly if you are summing up what you have said before.

Bullet Marks and Boldface Phrases

In a long and complicated article, it is sometimes useful to organize some of your material with bullet marks (•). Their use, along with boldfaced phrases immediately following, avoid a stretch for complicated transitions. They also help you organize and include material that is slightly extraneous to the main point, but nevertheless important to readers.

For example, in a profile of a country doctor, the article has begun with a vignette from his life, changed to the situation for such doctors nationally, then returned to the doctor introduced in the lead. After following him around on a typical day and into the night, the article switched to his views on various parts of his job:

> For the new doctors who are interested, he has not tried to gloss over the drawbacks to general practice in a town the size of Brush:
>
> - **Paperwork.** "It's come down to where the filling out of forms is encroaching on everything else. . . ."
> - **Distance.** "All the lab work is done in Denver and this means a great deal of slowness because of the U.S. mail. . . ."
> - **Familiarity.** "I know so much about some of the people in this town, it makes it difficult. . . ."
> - **Lack of time.** "There is never any time when you don't have something that needs to be done. . . ."
> - **Effect on family.** "The kids grow up taking the responsibility of answering the telephone seriously. They know not to be surprised or disappointed because of something that happens to me. . . ."

[The article goes on to list four other areas.]

Behind each bullet and boldface phrase, the paragraphs are entirely in quotes. Without the use of this device, it would have been difficult to include this kind of material because the bulk of the article was structured around the doctor's daily routine.

Present Tense

Unless the magazines you are working for prohibit it, the use of present tense really moves any story along nicely. This means, principally, that your attribution is written as if the quote was just uttered: "says," "notes," "continues," "concludes." This means that all verbs you use to describe what you are writing about are in the present tense unless they happened in the past, say more than six months ago.

If you have done a lot of newspaper writing, where past tense is required except in an occasional feature story, you may find it hard to make the switch. Try it and you will soon see writing that is more smooth, less clunky and convoluted, and more of a pleasure to read.

Keeping Track of What You Use

In a long article, where you are dealing with a great deal of material, it is important to keep track of things as you move along. You wouldn't want to use a fact or a quote in more than one place, but you might do so because of the sheer volume of material you are including and the speed with which you may have to work to meet your deadline.

A simple way to avoid confusion and inadvertent re-use is to mark all material when you use it, most conveniently by bracketing it off to the side with a colored pen or pencil. Don't cross it out because you might want to read the original again and do not want to obscure it with carelessly drawn lines. When you are completely finished with interview notes from one source or printed material, place an *X* on the first page and set it aside.

Writing for General Magazines

You will have success writing for most general magazines if you convey your material in crisp, clear sentences that are easy for the average reader to understand. It is probably a good idea to keep one idea to a sentence, or at most, two ideas to a sentence. It is best to explain complicated terms or concepts when you first introduce them, either by setting them off with a dash or in parentheses.

It might be helpful if you think of the subject you are writing about in the same way you would explain it verbally to a friend. Don't leave any questions unanswered. Above all, make it as interesting and compelling as possible. Try to imbue the article with all the enthusiasm you have for the subject. If you have lost some of that enthusiasm, it will become evident.

Rewriting

Once your first draft is complete, leave it for a while—an hour, a day, a week, deadline permitting—and do something else. When you re-read it, you will see it with new eyes and won't be as close to it as when you first completed it. When you read it, you should look for grammar and spelling errors and, more importantly, places you can tighten the writing. Are there extraneous words and phrases you can cut out? Is everything as clear as it should be or can you rewrite some sentences to make them more understandable? Are all complicated terms explained? Does your lead really catch the attention of readers and establish a theme? Does the copy flow well via good transitions and have a logical progression from one paragraph to the next? Does the article end well—or does it just end? It is better to tie up loose ends and bring your reader to closure with a good feeling or with a stirring, dramatic passage. One of the simplest techniques to end an article is to link the end to the beginning. In this way, you have brought your reader full circle.

Nothing has been said in this chapter about style. The omission was deliberate. It is important for writers to find their own styles. What works for one will fail for another. And, you may find that you select one style early in your career and switch to another (or another) later on. Your search will end when you are comfortable with the way you are writing—and what you have written. (Box 18.1 explores one of the most controversial and compelling magazine writing styles ever developed, the New Journalism.)

Box 18.1 The New Journalism

> ". . . in the early 1960's a curious new notion, just hot enough to inflame the ego, had begun to intrude into the tiny confines of the feature statusphere. It was in the nature of a discovery. This discovery, modest at first, humble, in fact, deferential, you might say, was that it might be possible to write journalism that would read like a novel."
>
> —Tom Wolfe

Writing fact as if it were fiction is the main characteristic of the New Journalism, a writing technique that came into use by magazine writers like Tom Wolfe and book authors like Truman Capote. This approach uses detailed description and narrative and applies the techniques of fiction to nonfiction writing.

Wolfe was a pioneer in his use of this approach in articles for *New York* and *Esquire*. Capote used it successfully in his book-length account of multiple murders in Kansas, *In Cold Blood*. Many other magazine journalists have adopted this style, which is interesting to read. Readers feel they are actual witnesses to the events described, so vivid is the dialogue and detail.

In "Radical Chic & Mau-Mauing the Flak Catchers," for example, a 1970 account in *New York* magazine of a reception composer Leonard Bernstein held to raise money for Black Panther party members, Wolfe brought readers with him to the event:

> Mmmmmmmmmmmmmmmm. These are nice. Little Roquefort cheese morsels rolled in crushed nuts. Very tasty. Very subtle. It's the way the dry sackiness of the nuts tiptoes up against the dour savor of the cheese that is so nice, so subtle. Wonder what the Black Panthers eat here on the hors d'oeuvre trail? Do the Panthers like little Roquefort cheese morsels rolled in crushed nuts this way, and asparagus tips in mayonnaise dabs, and meatballs petits au Coq Hardi, all of which are at this very moment being offered to them on gadrooned silver platters by maids in black uniforms with hand-ironed white aprons. . . .

Entertaining, delightful, a pleasure to read, but is this really journalism in its truest sense? The question occurs to some readers and other writers.

Is it really possible to get such detail and quotes without, as a novelist would, resorting to fabrication? What people are thinking, how they talk, how they look, what their houses contain—including brand names. Is it really possible for a reporter to acquire all of this information by the usual powers of observation and questioning?

Practitioners say it is and Wolfe and others have made a good living at it for 30 years. The old techniques of New Journalism have been taken one step further into a genre called Literary Journalism where writers employ New Journalism techniques but do so in a less flamboyant manner.

Detractors say it is impossible to gain so much detail by using the usual reporting techniques and point to instances of fabricated quotes and composite characters based on real people. Newspaper editors are among the naysayers and have never seemed as comfortable with this style as their magazine counterparts. Even magazines don't run as many articles written in this style as they once did.

New Journalism produced some of the finest magazine writing ever. If you use it, your reporting and writing abilities will be taxed to the fullest. Don't try it, however, unless you are skillful enough to pull if off.

Lessons in Free-Lancing: Writing

Here is the original article on bowhead whales and other marine mammals of the Arctic (discussed in chapters 13 and 16) as I originally submitted it to EXXON USA. I have added some comments in the margin explaining why I wrote it the way I did.

MARINE MAMMALS OF BEAUFORT SEA

—by Ron Lovell

For me, the journey of the bowhead whales from their winter feeding grounds in the Bering Sea to their summer home in the Beaufort Sea was dramatic and interesting. I also decided that it could serve as a useful framework on which to construct my article. So, as I often do, I

1 *April. The Bering Strait.*

The bowhead whales have been gathering for several weeks waiting for the ice pack to break up. The leads in the ice that open will form the natural corridor through which the whales will migrate through the Chukchi Sea and into the Beaufort Sea, their summer feeding area. Instinct tells them to form for the journey as they have for centuries, perhaps as long ago as the time just after Alaska and Siberia were

began my piece with a section that dramatized the journey and included a discussion of the perils the whale would encounter along the way. As a clue to the reader that this section was special, I planned to have it set in italic type. I had gained the facts for this section in my reporting.

linked by a solid land bridge. Ahead on the oceanic trek lie possible perils, old and new. From their small villages along the northern coast of Alaska, Eskimo hunters are ready to kill the whales for food and sustenance in much the same way they have done for over 2,000 years. Farther along, in the Canadian portion of the Beaufort, oil companies are exploring offshore using equipment and techniques with the potential for disturbing the ancient migration of the bowheads, named for the strongly bowed upper jaw and distinctly shaped head that is their most distinctive physical characteristic.

As they swim, occasionally mating and feeding on tiny marine plankton as they go, the bowheads are oblivious to the controversy they have caused on land.

My actual lead states a conclusion I made from my reporting: the bowhead is a political whale. That said, I went on to explain why in the rest of the lead.

2 The bowhead is one of the most politicized of all whales. Their plight is under constant discussion and study by various agencies of the U.S. government, by the Eskimos, and by oil companies working in the region like Exxon. The reason for the concern is the status of the bowhead as an endangered species. Since June 1977, the International Whaling Commission (IWC) has banned the hunt for the whale, allowing an exemption only for the Eskimos, who have quotas each year. In the 1981–1983 period, for example, they are allowed to land 45 bowhead whales.

By this graf, I am ready to indicate why this is nothing new. It has been going on since the days of the Yankee whalers—beginning in 1840.

3 The bowhead's precarious grasp on survival today is the consequence of years of wholesale slaughter. Beginning in 1840, the whaling ships of New England rounded the tip of South America in search of more leviathans to kill. They gradually worked their way north and in 1843 took their first bowheads off the Kamchatka Peninsula in the Bering Sea.

In grafs 4, 5, 6, and 7, I expand on this historical killing, giving some statistics to show how many bowheads had been wiped out over the long years.

4 All whales were valuable but the bowhead was particularly prized. Even a moderate sized creature had 100 barrels of oil in its blubber (one barrel equal to about 31 gallons) and yielded 1,500 lbs. of baleen—bone-like plates in the mouth used to filter food in place of teeth. The oil lighted homes and the baleen was turned in to chair springs, buggy whips, skirt hoops, and corset stays.

5 The Yankee whalers sailed through the Bering Strait into the Arctic Sea in 1848. By 1852 over 200 ships were operating in the area, despite the danger from the ice that choked the waters, easily trapping the vessels and crushing their wooden hulls. By 1889 the whalers had followed the bowheads to their summer feeding ground off the MacKenzie River delta in Canadian territory.

6 The killing of the bowheads continued into the 20th Century from ships and shore-based stations employing Eskimos who abandoned their subsistence hunting and learned to use newer technology like the darting gun and the shoulder gun. These weapons fired small bombs whose detonation in the whale's body increased recovery rates over the traditional—and sometimes ineffective—harpoon.

7 By 1915, the commercial hunt for bowhead whales ended due to the discovery of spring steel as a replacement for baleen and because of the development of other kinds of oil. The damage to the bowhead had been done, however. An analysis of historical whaling records done by John Bockstoce of the New Bedford Whaling Museum determined that between 19,142 and 21,448 bowhead whales were killed by all vessels between 1848 and 1915. There are believed to be about 2,300 bowheads living today.

Graf 8 talks about a modern cause for controversy with international implications: the annual subsistence hunt by Eskimos, which the environmental community deplores and whaling nations use as an excuse to resume their own whaling.

8 The Eskimos resumed their subsistence hunting after the commercial exploitation ended. The bowhead has been fully protected by the IWC since 1947. In 1972, the scientific committee of the IWC expressed concern about the lack of data on the Arctic bowhead and the effect of the Eskimo hunt on population size. The National Marine Fisheries Service began to gather information on the scope of the Eskimo hunt and on basic harvest data and to obtain biological samples from landed whales in 1973. In 1976 this effort was expanded in order to determine the distribution, migratory patterns, and ways to assess abundance of the bowhead population.

In grafs 9, 10, and 11 I add another ingredient to this complicated story: the discovery of oil and the question of how offshore drilling will affect the whale migration.

9 The discovery of oil in the north slope area of Alaska and off the shores of the Canadian Northwest Territories in the late 1960's and early 1970's brought a new dimension to the bowhead problem. Would the introduction of ships, aircraft, and drilling equipment affect the migration pattern and, ultimately, the welfare of the creatures?

10 This was the concern about the Canadian exploration which began offshore almost immediately. In Alaskan waters, the oil activity was not the immediate worry. Only now is limited seismic probing for oil getting started. The oil that flows through the trans-Alaska pipeline is found on land. The Eskimo hunt provides the problem in Alaska. Angered by the IWC quota on what they consider a sacred part of their culture—the taking of bowhead whales—the Eskimos now fear that heightened oil exploration offshore will drive the bowheads farther out to sea beyond their reach.

11 A 1978 report by the Outer Continental Shelf Environmental Assessment Program of the National Oceanic and Atmospheric Administration, set the stage for federal involvement with its look at protecting the Alaskan environment while developing needed oil and gas reserves. The federal agency with the responsibility for monitoring endangered species like the bowhead whale, the Bureau of Land Management (BLM), got involved that same year. Because it has much of its experience dealing with terrestrial problems, that agency went outside to find organizations with the expertise needed to study bowhead whales and the possible effect of oil exploration on them.

By graf 12, I am closing in on what was the main point of the story: the scientific studies going on in the Canadian Beaufort Sea which I had observed and would report on in this article.

12 The focal point for the work would be in the Canadian Beaufort Sea, where the bowheads had been going for centuries and where oil companies had been working offshore since 1972. "We thought it was incumbent on us to look into questions of acoustics and disturbance, like displacement of whales and visible changes in behavior because of oil related activity," says Jerry Imm, the BLM environmental studies field coordinator in Alaska. "One of the things we are doing is to determine certain types of effects. A condition of an oil lease could be special stipulations in the permit process that would not allow operations to take place during migration."

In graf 13, I worked my way to my main source, Mark Fraker, the marine mammal biologist who was heading the field work and who I had interviewed earlier to get background.

13 The firm that won the bid to conduct the research was LGL Ecological Research Associates of Sidney, British Columbia. The scientist in charge is Mark Fraker, a marine mammal biologist. Fraker and a group of scientists and technicians, including Bernd Wursig of the Center for Coastal Marine Studies at the University of California, Santa Cruz, and Roger Payne of the New York Zoological Society, began their study of the bowheads last summer. It continued this year.

In grafs 14 and 15 I lay the groundwork for an explanation of their work.

14 Operating out of the tiny native village of Tuktoyaktuk, the group has attempted to do what no one has done before: study a giant creature—up to a length of 65 feet and average weight a ton a foot—which by its very nature eludes study of any kind, let alone that required by exacting scientists. Bowheads are most always in motion and sometimes dive for as long as 20 minutes. Where last year the group saw literally hundreds of whales, they have this year numbered in tens, for reasons unknown.

15 "This is really stepping out on the cutting edge of science," says Imm, along on a flight with Fraker to look for bowheads. "It has never been done before in terms of method and technique."

In graf 16, I begin a section about how these scientists actually attempt to count whales. In many ways this was the easiest part to report and write. Because a technician gave up his seat on the small four passenger plane, I was there too and merely had to tell what I saw.

16 Flying in a small plane at an altitude of not less than 2,000 feet, Fraker, Wursig, and two others, plus a pilot, go out daily to attempt the impossible. Another team conducts sound experiments by boat while a third group observes from a shore station.

From graf 17 to 23, much of what I wrote was actual dialogue, which I jotted down as I bumped along in the

17 "When we see them we drop dye markers," says Fraker. "Then we circle, sometimes for an hour or two." Everyone on the plane is wearing a headset and a microphone and these are

plane high over the churning waters of the Beaufort. I saw far fewer whales than the scientists did and they looked to me like white logs. It was fun and exciting and very interesting and I tried to convey those feelings in what I wrote. In order not to "Disneyfy" the mammals, the scientists never assign them endearing names. Rather than "Flipper" or "Shamoo," it's "Forward" and "White Spot."

attached to a tape recorder so that every remark is preserved for later transcription and analysis. Randy Wells, a graduate student at Santa Cruz, takes notes on the comments and Peter Tyack, a Rockefeller University graduate student, videotapes the whales. Fraker and Wursig use binoculars as they discuss specific behavior of the whales and their overall pattern of movement.

18 "Slaps tail on surface. Slaps it again and turns," says Fraker.

19 " 'White Spot' is approached," says Wursig, giving one whale an identifying name.

20 " 'Forward' is flipper flapping," adds Fraker. " 'Forward' just lies at the surface and blows."

21 As the plane circles over the vast sea, time passes quickly. Sometimes, bad luck intervenes.

22 "One day," recalls Wursig, "we found two whales and a calf and could have stayed for hours. After 50 minutes the fog rolled in. But we're slogging along."

23 Fraker and Wursig have made general observations on behavior but have little with which to compare it because there is such a small amount of information on bowheads. "It's all guessing," says Wursig. Adds Fraker: "We must establish what normal behavior patterns are before we can assess normal reactions."

By grafs 24 and 25, I felt I needed to pull back a bit and give readers a broader view of the story, by discussing other aspects of the research, such as sound studies.

24 The Fraker group has taken two approaches in its study of bowheads and oil related activity. Last summer it looked at the whales in the presence of on-going activity like ship movement and man-made drilling islands. This summer it tried to measure the effects of bringing disturbances to the whales by playing tapes of boat motors and other loud noises and recording the results on sonobuoys. Will the noises just disturb them or be so distracting that they will be adversely affected and change their migratory routes and put off feeding? Findings are still preliminary as the scientists evaluate their data.

25 "Whales apparently are more affected by boats than stationary drifting islands," says Fraker. "The mere physical presence of islands does not appear to cause them concern." Are whales likely to be affected by such changes in the environment? "Of course," says Fraker. "You accept there will be effects—perhaps positive, perhaps negative, some small, some large. We don't know. That is what we are trying to find out."

In graf 26, I gave Exxon and its Canadian affiliate, Esso Resources, credit for their funding of this research. This was being written, after all, for the public relations magazine of the Exxon Corporation and there had to be some kind of hook or peg to tie the story to the company or it would not have appeared in the publication. I must hasten to add that I was never told what to write or even how to slant what I saw. I reported what I observed. Although the first draft was checked by everyone from corporate attorneys to every source I interviewed (a real pain to me as a journalist and a time consuming process as well), nothing that was changed was changed to make Exxon look good.

26 This work and that funded by other oil companies, the Eskimos, and the state of Alaska, will go on, aided whenever possible by Exxon and its Canadian affiliate, Esso Resources, which cooperates in the research effort by doing such things as limiting its operations when whales are around and instructing its helicopter pilots not to fly so low over the water that it disturbs the whales.

By graf 27, I am ready to begin my finish. I quote a source who I felt had a broader view of the research.

27 "As Arctic biologists, some of the basic questions we don't know," says Larry S. Underwood, a research analyst in animal biology at the University of Alaska Arctic Environmental Information and Data Center. "Our understanding of some things is good but questions like why the bowheads are even in the Beaufort, or whether they will avoid it because of oil activities there or because food supplies are elsewhere, we don't know."

I continue to do so in grafs 28 and 29 and felt the quotes made a nice end.

28 At this stage, Underwood and other scientists at the University of Alaska Arctic Center say they do not see any evidence of change in the distribution and abundance of any marine mammal as a result of oil exploration.

29 "The effects are subtle," concludes Underwood, "and a long time in coming. We are in a development phase and things might change when the intensity (of offshore exploration) increases. We can do both, not upset the environment and get the oil out. We've got to do both. We can't afford not to. The great challenge is to do both."

But my article was not yet over. I wanted to follow my "tie the end with the beginning" rule and also to use the device I had started with: the journey of the bowheads as a parable for everything else. Again using italic type, I brought the great whales back through the Bering Strait and to their winter grounds. The drama of their lives seemed a fitting way to end.

30 *Far to the north, the bowheads have continued their ceaseless journey. Turning west in late August and September, they swim past the Eskimo villages where the fall hunt reduces their number. They retrace their path of spring and go into the Chukchi and through the Bering Strait.*

November. The Bering Sea. The bowheads have returned to spend another winter in ice free waters, there to remain until some ancient call commands them once again to gather at the melting ice pack.

Sidebar

To me, the most interesting part of the story here was the bowhead and its problems. Therefore, I made it the subject of my main article. I had been assigned to include information on other marine mammals of the region and the effects of possible oil drilling on them, however. I decided the best way to do this was to break out this portion as a sidebar and, after a short introductory paragraph, cover each mammal in sections divided by the bulleted and boldface name of the mammal

MARINE MAMMALS

1 Because of its unique status as an endangered species, its mystique as a largely unknown marine mammal, and the politicization of the Eskimo hunt, the bowhead whale has gotten a great deal of attention recently. A number of other marine mammals live in the Beaufort Sea area, however, and they are faring reasonably well, even with the influx of men and machines associated with oil exploration.

2 • **Beluga whales**. Also called white whales, these creatures are smaller than the bowhead (15 feet long, a weight of one ton). They migrate annually from their wintering area in the Bering Sea to the southwest Beaufort Sea in May and June. They move through leads in the ice and reach the MacKenzie River delta in late June and early July. Some leave almost immediately, but the majority spends the summer in

and a paragraph or two on each.

As should be done with sidebars, I wrote this one to stand alone. I also saw no need to do a fancy lead or a dramatic ending.

the delta and nearby Amundsen Gulf before moving westward again in August and September. An estimated 4,000 to 6,000 belugas arrive in the area and between 600 and 700 calves are born here. The hunting of belugas is an important summer activity for local natives. The whales provide winter food supplies and are as much a part of the culture as the bowheads are to Alaskan Eskimos. The annual kill amounts to about 225 belugas.

3 Esso Resources has supported studies of beluga whales since 1972. Island construction, exploratory drilling, and related activities have had no detectable effect on whale distribution or pattern of use of the MacKenzie River estuary, according to a study by Mark Fraker and his wife, Pam, another LGL scientist. Minor interference with whale hunting may have resulted from occasional barge traffic from an island in the area and from aircraft use of the landing strip on that island. Other scientists report some response to drilling operations. "They give ships a wide berth," says S.V. Cuccarese of the University of Alaska Arctic Environmental Information and Data Center. "They travel in herds and may take a day to regroup after passing a vessel. The suspended air bubbles caused by the prop wash obscures their view."

4 As with the bowheads, little is known about the belugas. Observation of them continues annually.

5 • **Ringed seals**. Ringed seals live in the fast ice zone. They spend much of the winter months feeding under the ice. Pregnant females establish lairs under the snow in March and April. Pups spend their first four to eight weeks in these lairs. This location makes ringed seals vulnerable to oil exploration activity because it takes place during the winter in much the same area as their habitat.

6 Their way of living also makes it difficult to study ringed seals. John Burns, a scientist with the Alaska Department of Fish and Game, is trying. Burns is approaching the problem in several ways. He and several colleagues are flying over areas of seismic oil exploration in a systematic way and recording changes in ringed seal behavior compared to an area where seismic work is not going on. The work has been slow and difficult. Some disruption of seals has been found. "Displacement can be tolerated up to the time pupping commences," says Burns. "Pups are born in snow dens and are sedentary after that." The cutoff point for seismic work is March 20 each year, although companies that have not completed their activities may apply to the United States Geological Survey for permits to go beyond.

7 This year, Burns has been designing a more elaborate program funded by the BLM. It will include the use of hydrophones to listen to the seals and the use of dogs trained to search out and locate the breathing holes crucial to the seals resting far below with their pups in the snow dens. This will enable him to know more reliably the extent to which oil activity displaces the seals. The dogs go on duty next year.

8 "Any intrusion of human activity into pristine regions is going to result in change," says Burns. "Whether it is positive or negative is the question."

9 • Bearded seals. This seal is highly distributed and highly mobile. From birth, bearded seals live on the pack ice and this allows them to escape disturbance, according to Burns. Population numbers in the winter are the lowest. The majority of the population lives not in the Beaufort but on the drifting ice of the Chukchi and Bering Seas.

10 • Walrus. The current population of the walrus in the Arctic is estimated at 250,000, according to joint American and Russian surveys. This number, considered by some experts to be larger than its environment can effectively support, is up greatly from the era of commercial hunting which began in 1860. By the early 1950's amounts had dwindled to from 40,000 to 50,000. The creature has been alternately managed by the State of Alaska and the federal government since 1959. It is a protected species. All hunting is done by natives. Average kills before a 1979 moratorium were 10,000 a year. The federal government and the Eskimo Walrus Commission are currently working out a suitable management plan.

11 Walrus do not inhabit the Beaufort so effects of oil exploration are not known. John Burns sees a potential impact on them—perhaps favorable, perhaps unfavorable—should large offshore production facilities be erected in their habitat in the Bering and Chukchi Seas.

Lessons from This Lesson in Free-Lancing

1. Let your material dictate your approach. I liked the bowhead saga best so allowed it to guide my article. Using research and personal observation, I hung most of my story on that whale's past, present, and possible future.
2. Don't be afraid to use gimmicks to attract readers. The italicized beginning and end were that kind of thing but I think they added to the story.
3. Let your sources help you tell the story whenever possible. After the sections of background, I switched to the scientists in the plane and let readers eavesdrop on them as they worked.
4. When you have done enough research to feel well-grounded in the subject of your article, don't be afraid to express an opinion here and there. My reference several times to the bowhead whale being politicized is an example of that. No one actually told me that in a usable quote. I drew that conclusion myself. You can't editorialize in this way, however, if the magazine you are working for does not permit such a style.
5. Don't rely on interviews only. Fall back on research material and weave it in whenever it helps move the story. I did so here in the historical background and, in various places, with official report results.

19

Submitting Your Article

Your article is complete. You have researched, reported, and written it within the agreed upon number of words. You have stuck to the approach outlined in your original query letter or in the assignment given to you by your editor. Now it is time to submit what you have taken such pains to prepare.

Manuscript Submission

Format

There is an accepted format you should adhere to in preparing your final article, whether you use a computer or a typewriter. According to *Writer's Market*, the upper left corner should contain your name, address, phone number and Social Security number (which publishers need for tax purposes later in the year; you might as well give it to them up front). The upper right corner should note the approximate word count of the manuscript, the rights you are offering for sale (see Box 19.1), and your copyright notice (not always necessary to include as the box explains). You should center the title of your article in capital letters about one-third of the way down the page, and your byline a double-spaced line below that. Next, go down two more double-spaces, indent for the paragraph five spaces, and begin your article. All articles should be double-

Box 19.1 A Writer's Rights

You may not be asked to sign any agreement dealing with rights to your article. Some magazines routinely prepare a contract for everything, others do not. Read whatever is presented to you before signing it. If nothing is mentioned, it is safe to assume that you are agreeing to sell one-time rights to your work. Period. Anything else would need to be specified in writing.

There are various kinds of rights:

- *First Serial Rights.* One time publication in a magazine or newspaper; all other rights belong to you; the most commonly used of the "rights."
- *First North American Serial Rights.* One time publication in both the U.S. and Canada.
- *One-Time Rights.* The buyer has no guarantee to be the first to publish the work.
- *Second Serial Rights.* The right to print an article after it has already appeared in another publication.
- *All Rights.* The writer gives up all claim to sell the article elsewhere.

A number of other rights may come into discussion, but usually not for an article: foreign serial rights, syndication rights, subsidiary rights, dramatic, television and movie rights.

As a writer, you do have a certain amount of protection for your work, unless you sign away any or all rights to it. Under the copyright law of 1976 (which went into effect in 1978), your writing is automatically copyrighted the minute you put one word on paper and signify your authorship with the word "Copyright" or the copyright symbol, the year and your name. That is sufficient protection in most instances and you usually won't even have to do that; the protection is understood. You won't be able to sue for infringement of your copyright unless you formally register with the copyright office, however. If you sign a work-for-hire agreement with a magazine, the magazine owns the copyright.

spaced throughout and paragraphs indented five spaces. *Writer's Market* recommends margins of one and one-fourth inches on all sides of each page. Don't number the first page. On all other pages, include your last name in the upper left corner, a dash or slash, and the page number. Resume your article two double-spaced lines below that. At the end of the last page, type "End" or cross-hatch marks (###) or "-30-," an old newspaper term meaning "the end."

If you use a computer, it will automatically conform to the predetermined format. Thus, you won't have to worry about an uneven number of lines per page, or trying to fit in one last line and having the paper move—leaving you with a ragged mess. Never staple the pages together. Use a paper clip.

Typewriter Versus Computer

Most writers have long since joined the computer revolution and purchased their own machines, at least with the capacity for simple word processing if not the fancier options. Computers have a couple of advantages over typewriters. First, they are much more efficient for editing drafts—all inserts and deletions are automatically incorporated. Second, as you key your article you will create a permanent record on disk from which you can make additional copies. (If you mail in your disk, be sure to keep a backup disk.)

Some magazines will require you to submit a computer disk along with the manuscript (or "hard copy"). They may also require that you use a certain computer program or one compatible with their system. This avoids the necessity of their re-keying the article once it has been received. A magazine's listing in *Writer's Market* or guidelines available from the publication will often specify these requirements.

In addition to the computer program, you must also be careful in the printer you use. Some magazines will not accept material printed on the older, dot matrix printers because the quality is poor. Newer, laser printers produce clean, crisp copy but are very expensive. You need to reach a compromise that is acceptable to your publishers and your pocketbook.

SASE

"SASE"—self-addressed, stamped envelope—appears in most *Writer's Market* listings or in guidelines prepared by individual magazines. This means that you should send along with the manuscript, an envelope addressed to yourself with proper postage affixed to allow the magazine to return the manuscript to you. The same holds true for query letters.

At the risk of bringing on ridicule and castigation, the author would add a slight modification to this rule. If you are sending in an *unsolicited* manuscript, include SASE by all means. It may assure a faster response—or any response. If your idea has been accepted and/or you are working on assignment, however, the inclusion of a SASE seems unnecessary. The editor will be contacting you about the article by telephone and possibly sending a galley proof of the final article for you to check. In both cases, the expense should be borne by the magazine, not you. Also, it seems somewhat defeatist to expect the article to be returned and include the means to do so.

Submitting Collateral Material

In addition to your article, you may need to submit other material to aid the editors in their work. Newsmagazines call this material a "file." Essentially it includes everything you have collected in the course of your research and writing: booklets, brochures, reports, documents, letters, clippings from other publications. In some cases, it might also include transcripts of your interviews or the actual tapes. Preparing this package can be more tedious and time consuming than writing the article itself. Susan Hauser, a former correspondent for *People* magazine, regularly had to type up all her interviews and submit them with her article over the telephone via a modem to the magazine's New York headquarters. The reason newsmagazines and some others require this is because they are essentially staff written enterprises. Thus, even though a byline may appear at the end or beginning of an article, the editors rewrite everything to achieve a kind of homogeneity. These editors also can check facts and add material from the file. A few magazines—*The New Yorker* and *Time* are the best known—have large fact-checking departments whose members use your material and other reference books to check literally everything you have written. These demon checkers put colored dots over every fact they've certified. Few magazines can afford such a system, however.

In scientific and technical publications, there is a more important reason to include source material. All writers working in science, medicine, and technology should ask their sources for supporting material at the time of the interview. Typically, this consists of articles they have written for science or medical journals or those written by colleagues. It might also include copies of official reports to funding agencies, or speeches, or even clippings from other publications. Their inclusion by you will help editors verify the information, statistics, and even word spellings you have used in your article.

Most of the time, magazine editors will want you to mail your article, the disk, and source material. Occasionally, if they are on deadline, they might want you to send the article via fax machine or modem, and follow up later with a disk and source material.

You have a variety of ways to submit your material. The most common is the U.S. Postal Service. First class, "Priority Mail" is the minimum you should choose; anything cheaper is too slow. If deadlines are tight you might want to avail yourself of the various express services offered by the postal service or other parcel companies. Though more expensive, they usually offer a guaranteed delivery date.

What Happens Next

It is natural to wonder how your editor liked what you wrote. Good editors will send a short note indicating they have received the material and will get back to you soon. Many will not communicate at all.

You can call after a week or two, but don't expect to find out much. Magazines are busy places. Articles are frequently put off from issue to issue as new material comes in that takes precedence. Given the work load, an editor might put your article aside and not even look at it until the process of putting it in the magazine begins. If you don't get a satisfactory answer the first time, you can try again in another week or so. You will have to gauge the intensity of your persistence by the relationship you have with your editor. Don't make him or her angry, but don't be ignored either.

Once in a while, a free-lancer will submit an article that is not acceptable to the magazine's editors. Sometimes it is because the writer has not delivered what was promised. Sometimes it is because the magazine's needs have changed or the editor with whom the writer worked has left. This frustrating experience is only marginally offset by payment of a *kill fee*, typically 10 to 25 percent of the rate the writer was promised in advance for the article.

After your article has been submitted, you will get paid in one of two ways: "on acceptance," or "upon publication." Payment once an editor has accepted your article and is satisfied with it is preferable, of course. You get your fee fairly quickly and can go on to other matters. Unfortunately, many magazines are following a payment upon publication policy. You will not get paid until your article is actually published in the magazine, no matter how long that takes.

When this happens, you have several ways to proceed. After a reasonable amount of time—say one to two months—you can contact the magazine by letter or telephone and ask for a reconsideration. If this fails, you may want to join and use the resources of a local or national writers organization. Such groups have grievance committees which will contact the magazine for you and try to get your fee. They also have the power to notify their members that certain editors and publications are slow to pay and difficult to deal with. In time, such a designation can make it hard for magazines to get free-lance writers to work for them.

Dealing With Rejection

Some magazines do not let writers down easily as they reject their ideas (submitted in query letters) or articles, both unsolicited or assigned. These publications will send a form letter which declines the article and mentions something about "not meeting our editorial needs at this time." They probably also mean "or any time in the future." Such form rejection letters are rude, maddening, and exceedingly unhelpful to the writer.

The best kind of rejection letter (if there is such a thing) is one in which the editor declines the idea or manuscript but gives a reason for doing so with encouragement to rewrite or submit other work. These are not all that rare but do require a dedicated and caring editor—someone willing to wade through all the material a magazine gets annually. In this case, you should view the kind letdown as the start of a possible new professional relationship, a loophole to drive a truck through. If the rejection letter suggests that a rewrite might sell, do it immediately. If it invites future submissions, do so as soon as possible.

If one letter of rejection sends you into deep depression, you had probably better consider another line of work. Having your ideas and articles turned down is part of the business of being a free-lance writer. You have to get used to it.

There are many reasons to reject an article and the quality (or lack thereof) of the writing and reporting is only one of them. The best thing for you to do is to go beyond the rejection by one magazine (and probably one junior level editor) and rewrite or resubmit the article to another publication as quickly as possible.

Multiple Submissions

A decision you will need to make early on in your preparation of an article is whether you plan to submit it to several different publications. This is perfectly permissible under the unspoken rules that govern the magazine business. Under normal circumstances, however, you will probably prepare your query and your article with one market in mind. Then, if it doesn't sell, you can submit it to another magazine. (When you do this, make sure you have made any adjustments necessary to target the article to the new market. Very few magazines are exactly alike.)

Submitting your article to multiple publishers is a good way to augment your income as a free-lancer. You need to make sure not only that the magazines are noncompeting, but that you have paid careful attention to individual requirements of each magazine. What you are doing is repackaging the basic material on a given subject to best fit the needs of each magazine. Let's say the subject is whale research. You start with a series of interviews to examine the efforts to conduct research on whales. Your basic article may run in *Discover Magazine*, which wants an overview on how scientists are trying to save whales. You then take some of the same material and do an article on the lonely job of a marine mammalogist as he or she spends months on a remote coastal promontory counting whales. You sell this piece to *The New York Times Magazine*. Finally, you sell a personal essay on the politics of whaling and saving whales to *The New Republic*.

Ancillary Items

At times, a writer can enhance the salability of an article—or improve the editorial "package" when it is submitted—by adding a few extra features: breaking the material into a main article and a sidebar or two, suggesting ideas for charts, and taking and submitting photographs.

Sidebars

In writing longer articles, it is sometimes useful to break up the main article by breaking out one or two smaller subjects into separate, shorter articles. These articles are called *sidebars* and they can be a very helpful tool for you, both in handling a great deal of material and in showing an editor that you have the sophistication to package the material you are submitting.

Some magazine formats preclude any sidebars. For example, *The New Yorker* has never run one. Others, such as the newsmagazines, Sunday supplements, and most specialized magazines use them all the time. The biggest reason for their use is the short attention span of readers who are far too accustomed to television's tendency to feed them information in small bites.

This book uses sidebars in a typical way. Here they are called boxes and attempt to highlight a point mentioned in passing in the chapter itself. Sidebars are always set off in a box and are often screened or printed in another color. They are something like photographs in that they add to the overall article and the reader's comprehension of its subject.

In selecting what to highlight in sidebars, make sure you don't select a subject that should be your main story. The easiest way to make your choices for sidebar treatment is to see what material seems to stop the flow of the main article as you are writing. Rather than fool with subheads or awkward transitions, lift that material out into one or two sidebars. In writing these sidebars, make sure they stand alone. Don't assume that a reader will look at the main article first. You can refer to the sidebars in the article ("see box" or "see sidebar") and the main article in the sidebars (as in "see cover story").

Charts

The inclusion of a section on charts is not meant to suggest that all free-lance writers should take courses and become graphic designers on the side. It does mean that you can sometimes help an editor convey the meaning of your article to readers by suggesting ideas for charts or other graphic elements at the time you submit your material. Some editors may resent such intrusion into what they consider their domain so you had better feel them out first. If they are receptive, you can send a list of ideas for ways to dress up statistics to be highlighted in your article (missile, tank, or soldier icons to indicate weapons buildups in the Middle East; rows of elephants to show the effect of ivory poaching in East Africa).

The author once proposed a cover illustration idea for *Medical World News* that was accepted by the editors and designed by the art director. The subject of the article was the terrible problems of emergency rooms. Its conclusion was that all the obstacles to gaining good, quality care made it a kind of "game" for sick people. Using the headline "The Great Emergency Game," the author wrote the copy for a board game in which a "player" went forward and back depending on the roll of the dice. Squares were marked with such inscriptions as "overcrowded facilities, delay 10 hours," "stop, fill out 10 pages of forms for admittance," "stop, staff shortages, return in 2 weeks," and "DOA, game is over for you."

Photographs

Photographs are important to any editorial package. Whether black and white or color, photos enhance a reader's comprehension of the article by showing people or things you are writing about. They also enhance the layout of a page, especially with the good reproduction many magazines strive for and usually achieve.

Most national magazines do not want a writer to have anything to do with the photos for his or her article. Editors have the resources to hire professional photographers to either accompany you when you do your interviews or go at a time before or after. In this case, your role is restricted to talking to the photographer or photo editor about the approach you will take in your article and who you will be interviewing. After that, you step back and do your part of the job—which is to research and write the article.

At other times, you may help an editor secure stock photos of things not possible for a photographer to shoot, by supplying names of agencies or individuals you have learned have such photos. The same holds true for historical photos which you may come across in your research.

There may be times, however, when you will enhance your chances of selling an article with your ability to take photographs as well. Travel articles come to mind; if you are writing about a trip you took, you could include photos too. You are not trying to become a professional free-lance photographer—only increasing the salability of your article. In so doing, you are saving the magazine the cost of hiring a free-lance photographer and you are increasing the money you will make because most magazines pay from $25 to $50 or more for each photo used. Before embarking on a photo shoot, however, make sure your editor wants you to do so.

Once this fact is known, you can learn to take good photos by following a few basic principles.

Buying equipment

The first thing you need to do is purchase a good 35mm camera. Basic, nonmotor drive models are available from Nikon, Canon, Olympus, Minolta and others for as little $300. (You can pay as high as $2,000 or more for cameras from the same companies with motor drive and sophisticated computerized autometering and autofocus capabilities. These features give you an automatic film advance mechanism.) According to Randy Wood, assistant picture editor at the *Chicago Tribune*, and a longtime newspaper and free-lance photographer, you also need a variety of lenses: a 50mm normal perspective lens for basic intermediate shots usually comes with the camera, a 35mm wide angle lens, and a 105mm lens for portraits. The extra lenses will add about $800 to your cost. A zoom lens may be an alternative to carrying more than one lens. For example, a 35mm–105mm zoom will run about $400.

Taking photos

"You should avoid staged photos," says Wood. "People want to see people in their natural element. Get up close to them. Look for details that say something about a subject, something about your story."

- *People photos*—"The most common mistake people make is not getting close enough," continues Wood, "showing the person as only a tiny fraction of the frame. If you are taking a photo of a person, focus on them, not the sky or the background. For example, take a wheat farmer at sunset—dark sky, mountains, wheat field, beautiful. I'd stand three to four feet away and, with a 24mm wide angle lens, get the farmer prominently with the background as a framing device. Use a fill flash to compensate for the darkness."
- *Travel photos*—For photos to go with travel articles, Wood suggests you take a range of photos, three at a minimum: "An overall scene setter of let's say a town, an intermediate shot of one street scene, and then a detail shot, like an informal portrait of a person on that street. Don't overload your editor with repetitive images."
- *Newsletter photos*—For such shots as someone handing someone a check or the winner of the bowling tournament, Wood tries to get the subject out doing whatever it is the story is being written about. "I ask the bowling champ to go to the bowling alley and if someone is, let's say, giving a check to help a disabled child, I'd photograph them with the child," he says. "If someone is getting a check, it represents something tangible. I try to take the photo of what they did to merit a story."
- *Mug shots*—"If I have to do a photo of a company president or board chairman and can't find anything visual, I try to portray that person's personality," he says. "If all else fails, you can shoot the person in the board room at the end of the table, using the table or wall decorations to compose a pleasing photo." Wood also takes a more conventional, head and shoulders mug shot to give the editor some choice. In any photos of people, watch out for closed eyes.

Wood uses several tricks in taking photos of people. "To put people at ease, I talk to them," he says. "It's good to have someone else there to talk to them while you work. Sometimes I talk to people first without a camera to loosen them up. I spend a fair amount of time and shoot a lot of film. I get them to talking so they are not aware of the camera."

For any photo, one element is very important. "Keep images as simple as possible," continues Wood. "Keep subjects in the foreground." It is also best to avoid distracting backgrounds and to make sure that, by accident, you won't have tree limbs growing out of people's heads, for example.

Lighting presents a particular problem for new photographers, according to Wood. Although lighting can be an elaborate aspect of taking photos, the simple use of a fill flash can solve many problems. This means that you should sometimes use a flash even for shots taken outdoors in sunlight, especially if the subject is backlit. This avoids shadows around eyes, for example, or allows shots when it is getting dark. He recommends consulting with employees at a photo store or reading the camera's operating manual for more detail.

Remember, before you take your first shot, you need to find out if the magazine you are writing for would also be interested in your photos. That accomplished, you need to know if the editor wants color or black and white shots. Then, you need to ask whether you should send raw film, contact sheets (roughly developed film showing all the frames you've taken), or finished 8x10 prints (transparencies if color is involved). If you send contact sheets, you will have to identify each frame for the editor. A print needs to be accompanied by a complete caption. To save his reputation, Wood almost never sends in raw film. "I get the film processed, do a quick edit, and throw away the bad ones," he says.

For Wood, being both reporter and photographer is difficult—at least at the same time. "It is hard to do both: to take good shots while you are getting good quotes," he says. "I'll be talking and see a good photo possibility out of the corner of my eye. It's all a bit disorienting. It's best to schedule photos at a different time than the interview." Concludes Wood: "Be prepared to use a lot of film and take a lot of time."

PART V

Keeping the (Proverbial) Wolf from the Door

The lamb . . . began to follow the wolf in sheep's clothing.

—from *The Wolf in Sheep's Clothing*
by Aesop

20

Other Writing to Pay the Bills

Beyond the magazine and newspaper writing covered so far in this book are a number of other ways to augment your income as you wait for a reply to your last query letter. In all these instances, you will be earning money as a writer, albeit a very non-traditional one. Best of all, you can continue to work primarily as a magazine free-lance writer while exploring the different kinds of writing explained in this chapter: public relations, computer, and book writing.

Indeed, if you are successful in securing commitments to do these alternate assignments, you can count on a regular source of income for doing fairly routine and repetitive work or work that, once done, brings in income over a longer period of time than the one-time fee paid to magazine writers. With the uncertainty that is inherent in free-lancing, these benefits cannot be overemphasized.

Public Relations Writing

Public relations has become one of the most all-encompassing phrases of our time—used to describe activities from selling real estate to seeking publicity for a local club in a weekly newspaper. To some, it is nothing more than "free" advertising; that is, stories printed in publications or broadcast over television or radio that extol the virtues of a product or idea in the same unobjective manner as in a paid advertisement. To others, primarily those working in what has become a large and influential part of business and government, public relations is a means to communicate the activities and ideas of an organization to inform the public and influence its opinion.

Public relations, according to *The Random House Dictionary of the English Language*, comprises "actions of a corporation, store, government, individual, etc. in promoting good will between itself and the public, the community, employees, customers." Public relations accomplishes its goals through use of a variety of tools. It is through preparation of these tools—news releases, brochures and booklets, newsletters, magazines, annual reports, videos—that free-lancers enter this world of image building and subjective communication.

These goals require a writer to leave certain assumptions and modus operandi at the door of the PR office. Public relations is not objective journalism. You are being paid only to tell your client's side of the story. Period. You can still perform your work in an ethical and honorable fashion, but it won't be the same as researching and writing an article for a consumer magazine. If that bothers you, you had better stay away from public relations writing. At the very least, you should work only for clients you believe in and avoid those whose goals you abhor. You should never do PR work just for the money.

Public relations work is accomplished in the United States by internal public relations departments of large companies; by agencies working for a number of clients; and by a combination of both. As a free-lancer, you need to cultivate people at both agencies and internal PR departments who are in a position to hire you to do various projects. They will do so for a variety of reasons. They may be short-handed and need help from time to time. They may be on a tight deadline and need something to be done fast. They may want a fresh viewpoint or like the way you write.

If you are interested in this kind of free-lance writing, you must start by building a portfolio of work to show prospective customers. Just as you list published articles in a query letter to a magazine editor, you need to assemble a representative sample of your PR work in a portfolio. Then, when you meet with a public relations staffer to pitch your services, you can run through the portfolio and show what you have done and, implicitly, what you can do for this new prospective client.

A good way to gain experience in public relations writing is to volunteer your services with a club or public service organization or even a political candidate. It is bad form, however, to volunteer to do such work for a company or agency. It will appear as though you are too desperate.

When you have succeeded in getting PR practitioners to hire you on a regular basis, you will be paid in several ways. You may be paid a certain amount for the project ($1,000 to do a brochure, $5,000 to write and edit one issue of a magazine). Or, you may be paid an hourly rate for your time. Or, best of all, you may be put on a monthly or quarterly retainer to do one thing regularly (for example, $500 a month to do a newsletter). This is "best of all" because you can rely on that amount every month for a routine assignment while you continue to pursue magazine writing.

If you are successful at public relations writing—and the chances are good that you will be, given the greater need and number of potential clients—you may have to turn down work, lest it overshadow your real love, magazine writing. After all, there are only so many hours in a given day.

News Releases

Sophisticated public relations techniques come and go, but the news release remains the most used way to reach the public. A news release is, as the name implies, a "release" of "news"—at least, news as it is defined by the organization—to the public through the media. Through a release, a PR person conveys the client's side of the story to the media directly without the filtering process that happens when reporters attend press conferences or when they interview company sources directly and present the story. Not only does the organization control the information that is released, but it avoids any errors or miscommunications that may result from telling the story to a reporter first.

The news release avoids such problems because it presents the client's point of view, with all names spelled correctly and financial figures given accurately. The big problem with releases, however, is getting them into print. News organizations receive thousands of releases every day and must choose carefully the few they run. In fact, the better news organizations almost never print a release verbatim. They will, instead, use the release as a source for a story, making telephone calls for more information and writing their own version.

Despite the odds against the use of news releases, clients and PR practitioners continue to rely on them. The chances of their use increases greatly if releases are about something that is truly newsworthy and are written accurately and free of the exaggerations and superlatives too often associated with public relations.

Writing a news release is not all that different from writing a magazine article. Its subject is more narrow and its length is much less (one to two pages maximum). The process begins with your assignment to write the release. News releases fall into several subject categories: an event, a personnel change, a new product, financial results, a statement by an official of the organization issuing the release.

Once you know what you have to do, you need to conduct interviews with people in the organization who are knowledgeable about the subject. You may then augment this detail with printed research material. Writing begins with a lead, most often of the news-oriented variety (who, what, when, where, why, and how). You should stick strictly to the facts and never cross the line into advocacy or the editorial "we." If someone is sending a message to readers, put what they've said in a quote. Avoid superlatives and never call something you are writing about the "first," the "only," or the "best." Because editors and readers may not know who your client is, it is a good idea to include a boilerplate paragraph in every release which says something like, "Such and such company is a multimillion dollar manufacturer of widgets based in Providence, Rhode Island."

Sometimes, a PR writer will be asked to write a more magazine-like story for use in one publication. This happens a lot in trade magazines. In this case, the byline will probably not be yours but the company president's instead. This is called "ghost" writing. Such articles are longer than the typical release and are often about a technical subject.

Another variation on the standard print release is a release written for broadcast stations. Here, the news is the same as the print version, but it is written in broadcast style and is usually shorter. In recent years, many large companies and PR agencies have started to prepare "filmed" releases—one or two minute compilations of film footage and script sent to television stations with the hope that they will put them on the air unchanged. They often do in smaller markets. The absence of narration allows a station to let its own anchor person read over the film and thus pretend it has prepared the segment itself.

The Anatomy of a News Release

This news release from the News Bureau at Oregon State University was issued to publicize the appearance of a former president of Costa Rica to give an annual campus lecture.

FORMER NOBEL PRIZE WINNER ARIAS TO DELIVER OSU PAULING LECTURE

The lead uses a straight news style to tell readers the who, what, where and when.

1 CORVALLIS—Oscar Arias Sanchez, former president of Costa Rica and winner of the 1987 Nobel Peace Prize, will deliver a free public lecture at Oregon State University (OSU) on Wednesday, October 28.

In graf 2, the writer expands on the lead (using "Arias' speech" as the transition) by giving the full name of the lectureship and title of the talk.

2 Arias' speech will be OSU's 11th Annual Ava Helen Pauling Lecture for World Peace. His talk is entitled, "Opportunities for Peace: Crafting the First Demilitarized Zone in the World."

Unusual for a news story, the release waits until graf 3 to give time and precise location.

3 It will begin at 8 P.M. in Austin Auditorium of OSU's LaSells Stewart Center, 26th Street and Western Boulevard.

Grafs 4, 5, 6, and 7 give readers biographical background on the speaker, to help them decide whether or not they want to attend.

4 Arias, 51, received his Nobel Prize for drafting a visionary peace plan for Central America and orchestrating the Guatemala Accord. The 1986 accord—which includes the leaders of Guatemala, El Salvador, Honduras and Nicaragua—paved the way for a ceasefire between the Contras and Sandinistas.

5 The awarding of the Nobel Peace Prize brought Arias worldwide individual recognition, but he has said he coveted the prize only for the attention it would bring to Latin America.

6 Today Costa Rica is viewed as perhaps the most stable and progressive Latin American nation. Its people are covered by a national health plan, education is viewed as the country's most important national project, and the Costa Rican military was abolished in 1948 so national resources could be focused elsewhere.

7 "We had to choose between rifles and bread, machine guns and secondary roads, tanks and schools and hospitals," Arias told *Omni* magazine in a 1988 interview. "You know what our choice was."

Graf 8 gives background on the lecture itself, who it was named for and her biography.

8 The OSU peace lectureship was established in 1982 to honor the late Ava Helen Pauling, an OSU graduate and wife of Linus Pauling, OSU alumnus and the only individual to win two unshared Nobel prizes. For more than 40 years Mrs. Pauling carried out her public work by serving in the Women's International League for Peace and Freedom, the American Civil Liberties Union, and Women Strike for Peace. She also lectured frequently on peace and human rights until her death in 1981.

The release ends with a list of previous speakers in the series. Since the people are very prestigious, their inclusion will attract the attention of readers and authenticate their decision to attend. This, after all, is the purpose of the release.

9 Previous lecturers in the series have included Linus Pauling, 1982; Paul Warnke, arms limitation negotiator, 1983; Helen C. Caldicott, founder of Physicians for Social Responsibility, 1984; George W. Ball, diplomat, 1985; John Kenneth Galbraith, economist, 1986; Adolfo Perez Esquivel, 1980 Nobel Peace Prize winner, 1987; Johan Galtung, Norwegian peace expert, 1988; Mark O. Hatfield, U.S. senator, 1989; Mairead Corrigan Maguire, co-winner of the 1976 Nobel Peace Prize, 1990; and Petra Kelly, co-founder of the West German Green Party, 1991.

Brochures and Booklets

PR practitioners use brochures and booklets as another tool to get their message across. The difference between the two lies in their format rather than their content. A brochure is a multipanel publication that is folded. (It is also called a pamphlet or a flyer.) A booklet is a multi-page publication that is stapled together rather than folded. The choice of one over the other is usually based on the amount of material that needs to be conveyed.

Conveying that material to a specific public or the general public is the primary purpose of a brochure or booklet. Companies and other organizations use both kinds of publications for a variety of reasons: to explain a new program, process, or product; to describe a new building, plant, or laboratory; to ask for contributions; to build image; and to provide useful information. These publications are reasonably inexpensive, relatively fast to produce, and can create a good impression with readers if carefully prepared.

The first step to writing brochure copy is to meet with the customer to determine the purpose of the publication and its audience. A graphic designer will probably be present as well. This person will be as important to you as the client because a designer has the power to enhance your words with design, type selection, and choice of photographs and/or illustrations. The three of you will need to decide at an early date the style of the publication, whether it will be a brochure or a booklet. Once this has been agreed upon, you will need to gather the material you will use for the text. This will probably be done by consulting company materials and conducting short interviews with people possessing the facts you need. Yours will be a search for facts, however, not good quotes. A brochure is not a news release, although it may be sent to people on the same mailing list.

The writing should begin with a theme. The best themes for brochures are those that can be condensed in a cover headline. You build from that headline to a lead paragraph and then weave in the information you have obtained. It is a good idea to break up the copy with subheads. It is also very important to end each segment at the bottom of a panel. Don't let designers continue the copy from panel to panel because readers might be confused if they start reading at a point other than the cover. If this happens, your message may fail.

It is also a good idea to return readers to the first panel or headline in your ending, much as you try to do in your magazine articles. This brings things full circle and ties up all loose ends. An additional element needs to be included: a call to action ("for more information, write . . .") or ("let us send you . . .") and a name, address, and telephone number. In some cases, a return blank might be used for readers to fill out.

The Anatomy of a Brochure

This recruiting brochure for the Oregon State University College of Liberal Arts is a typical use of that kind of publication. Its audience is high school students contemplating the choice of a college or university and the parents and counselors who help them make that decision. The brochure contains 12 panels of information College officials hope will attract new students. The copy is broken up with color photographs of campus scenes, including, for political purposes, an equal number of men and women and several minorities. The reverse side (not reprinted here) lists all majors and uses a paragraph to explain each.

The cover states the theme: "The College of Liberal Arts, the Heart of a Great University." This is the third brochure in six years published by the College. Each has had a theme that was modified over time. First came "Oregon State's Best Kept Secret." This accentuated the idea that OSU, as a professional and technical school, also had a good liberal arts program but that fact was not known by many people. Next came "The Secret is Out" which took the "secret" idea one step further. The new slogan comes from the thought that Oregon State would not be a real university without its College of Liberal Arts.

THE COLLEGE OF LIBERAL ARTS
The Heart of a Great University
—Oregon State University

The "heart" idea forms the basis for the lead sentence and the second one. The paragraph goes on to list the many values of a liberal arts degree. Note that students are addressed informally as "you".

1 At the heart of every true university is a strong program in the liberal arts and sciences. Oregon State University is no exception. At OSU, the College of Liberal Arts offers a range of courses in the arts, the humanities, and the social sciences. Such courses provide you as a student with a solid foundation for your career. They also give you a better understanding of yourself and of today's world, how it got to be the way it is, and how you can have an effect on its future. In liberal arts courses you also learn how to think critically, how to write and speak, how to appreciate great art and literature, and how governments and economic systems work.

Graf 2 starts to "brag" about the College: largest in enrollment, many majors, etc.

2 Students across the country are entering liberal arts programs in great numbers. This is especially true at Oregon State where the College of Liberal Arts became the largest undergraduate college in 1989 as more and more people recognized that OSU is an excellent place to study the liberal arts. By taking advantage of CLA offerings at Oregon State, you can get a solid liberal arts education and still take courses in OSU's professional colleges. You might major in a foreign language or psychology or music or art or English, for example, at the same time you study home economics, biology, engineering, forestry, or business. That range of opportunities is not available at any other Oregon university.

Graf 3 concentrates on the College's dedication to teaching. It concludes by talking about the kinds of degrees available.

3 The College of Liberal Arts is dedicated to teaching. CLA students have the advantages of studying at a major university while receiving the attention often available only at smaller colleges. It is not unusual for first- and second-year courses to be taught by senior faculty members, rather than teaching assistants. Students in the College have access to knowledgeable professors active in their fields.

Many faculty members are also student advisers. Oregon State's College of Liberal Arts offers a varied and exciting range of bachelor's degree programs in 12 departments, two interdisciplinary programs, five certificate programs, and four graduate programs. There are many opportunities to study abroad through programs in Europe, Asia, and Central and South America.

In graf 4, the brochure details facts about the College, with each fact set off by a boldface bullet mark.

4 For the first time in the history of OSU, more students are majoring in College of Liberal Arts programs than those of any other college. • The College has new graduate programs in Scientific and Technical Communication, Applied Anthropology, and Economics. • Our faculty members direct plays, write books and articles, create paintings, compose music, dig for archaeological relics, and conduct a vast amount of research in many areas. • Our faculty members regularly win honors and awards for their teaching and research. They have received their share of Fulbright grants and stipends from the National Endowment for the Humanities, National Endowment for the Arts, and the Oregon Committee for the Humanities. • Our graduates have done everything from winning Oscars (for special effects in motion pictures), to designing sculptures, to running museums, to taking photographs around the world for *National Geographic* magazine, to teaching high school and college, to serving in the U.S. Congress and the Oregon Legislature, to holding responsible positions in government agencies and private companies.

By graf 5, the copy turns to the value of training available in the College as a way to cope with life. It also lists the various departments.

5 Training in a specialized field and knowledge that will help you cope with life are what we offer in abundance through Oregon State University's College of Liberal Arts. You can choose a major in Anthropology, Art, Economics, English, Foreign Languages and Literatures, History, Music, Philosophy, Political Science, Psychology, Sociology, Speech Communication, American Studies, or Liberal Studies. Our departmental majors and programs are detailed on the other side of this brochure.

Graf 6 is the windup, noting that the choice is up to the reader but, again, extolling the virtues of the College compared to other institutions.	**6** In the end, of course, a lot is up to you. The college experience is what you make it. But we have more to help you make the most of your life than many other educational institutions.
The "big finish" and tie-in to the cover and lead paragraph comes in graf 7. It returns to the "heart" idea and invites readers to become a part of the College.	**7** Join us at the heart of a great University.
Graf 8 is really not a graf. Instead, it is the call-to-action, ability-to-respond section that all good brochures (and sales literature) have. It enables readers to write for more information.	**8** For more information, write or call: Dean, College of Liberal Arts Oregon State University Social Science Hall 207 Corvallis, Oregon 97331-6202 Phone: (503) 737-2511

Newsletters

Newsletters are more journalistic than any of the public relations tools discussed so far. They contain stories and photos of interest to readers and come out on a regular basis (weekly or monthly in a typical company or organization). They are usually inexpensive to produce and are often eight to 12 pages in a 8 1/2 x 11 inch format. A graphic designer might work on every issue. More often, however, a designer sets up a format and the writer follows that format (perhaps using Pagemaker or other computer programs).

There are two important purposes for an internal newsletter: it allows management to announce and explain policies and it features employees and their activities on and off the job. The first purpose is fulfilled by devoting the cover story to such policies (preferably written in a news style without exaggeration). The second comes from mentioning as many people as possible and printing their names in boldface type.

If you are chosen to produce a newsletter on a regular basis, you need to set up a strong relationship with someone in a position of authority at the company. This person will give you ideas and steer you away from areas which are contrary to company policy. You will also need to set up a means to get routine information (births, deaths, company bowling team results, etc.). A good way to get this information is to have employees fill out a questionnaire for each issue. You can consult these as you write each issue and compile short items. If you decide to write a longer story, the sheet will give you enough information to frame questions for a formal interview.

Although the purpose of a newsletter is to build morale and internal image, the tone of the writing should be factual and not "cheerleading." People will get excited and be grateful when they see their names and activities in print; you don't need to generate false enthusiasm by hyping and exaggerating everything.

As already noted, producing a newsletter on a regular basis can be lucrative. It is more remunerative than either news release or brochure writing.

Magazines

A company or nonprofit organization usually starts publishing its own magazine in order to reach external publics and to build a good image with them. If newsletters are fairly simple and inexpensive to produce, magazines need to be more elaborate and, thus, more expensive. Given the competition from consumer magazines, books, and television—all of them well-produced—an external magazine will fail unless it looks as good.

The prestige which accompanies an external public relations magazine makes it a highly-prized assignment. Thus, a company's regular employees or an outside PR agency will probably vie for the job. As a result, it is highly unlikely that a free-lance writer will be asked to publish such a magazine.

Unlikely, perhaps, but not impossible. If you should land such an assignment, follow the procedures for doing a newsletter: meet with the sponsoring company for information goals, audience, and budget; meet with a designer to work out the physical look of the magazine; decide what kind of articles and other departmental features will best serve the readers; research and write the articles; work out printing details; pull everything together by the agreed upon deadline.

The kinds of articles you choose should be ones that will interest readers while also presenting information that, in a subtle way, enhances the image of the sponsoring company or organization. To be effective, articles should have the tone of a consumer magazine, with facts first and narrow hyperbole eliminated. No one will read an article that exaggerates the importance of the company. Straight facts assembled in well-written articles will best accomplish the task.

Annual Reports

Once a year, publicly held companies are required to prepare a report of the year's events for their stockholders. The requirements dictate that certain information be included and it always is—near the back. For the past 20 to 25 years, however, many large corporations have used the annual report to discuss company philosophy, products, and employees, and have sent it to a large external audience beyond their stockholders.

In some companies, the annual report has become like an external magazine, containing articles on various aspects of the company and produced on heavy paper with good graphic design. Beyond fulfilling the financial requirements of the Securities and Exchange Commission, some companies have long used the annual report as the right vehicle to display their uniqueness and brag about their accomplishments. Some large corporations spend $100,000 to $250,000 on their annual reports.

Because of its importance, the annual report is seldom given to a free-lance writer to prepare. Instead, that assignment goes to the internal public relations department or to one of many financial public relations agencies who are familiar with SEC regulations and requirements.

What a free-lance writer might get asked to do is the material in the front of the report, the nonfinancial, image-building writing that the non-stockholding public will find interesting. "A Day in the Life of the Company" or "50 Employees Who Changed the World" or a hundred other ideas might serve as likely themes. A free-lance writer could do this reporting and writing easily.

Though corporate America is required to produce annual reports, nonprofit organizations and government agencies have adopted the idea too, even though many are not compelled to do so. An annual summation of the year's work is a good way to build image and remind both the public and the media of an organization's existence.

There is a good chance for free-lance assignments from such nonprofit groups and agencies. Without the need for intricate financial information, the process resembles a combination of magazine and brochure writing. Writers need to work out an appropriate theme with the officials in charge and then conduct interviews to get the necessary material. Good design is important too, although an overly lavish annual report by a nonprofit organization will be counterproductive to image-building.

Other kinds of free-lance opportunities for public relations writing abound. Companies often call on outside writers to prepare speeches for their executives. There are also opportunities to produce videos.

Sometimes a free-lancer is hired to stage a one-shot event, like a press conference or a dinner.

Technical and Computer Writing

Another way for free-lance writers to supplement their incomes is to do technical and computer writing. Although it takes special skills to accomplish, this kind of writing can be rewarding, both professionally and financially.

Technical writing became widespread just after World War II when both the federal government and big companies saw the need to document procedures and policies and to prepare detailed descriptions of equipment part by part and total systems. By the 1950s and 1960s, government agencies and companies working for government agencies hired large numbers of technical writers. Many were given full-time jobs, but a lot of them were brought in on a free-lance basis. At this same time, companies discovered the need for writers to prepare technical documentation and procedures manuals for their non-military, consumer products. By the 1970s, this need had extended to technical sales materials to explain increasingly complex products to potential customers.

In the 1980s and early 1990s, technical writing has, for all intents and purposes, become almost exclusively computer writing. As the personal computer has come to dominate nearly all businesses in the United States, the demand for writers to explain how these machines work and how they can be applied to various tasks has increased tremendously. And, to a greater extent than in the earlier growth period for technical writers, many of these writers are hired on a free-lance basis.

One of them is Mollie Mondoux, who has worked for Tektronix and other computer companies as a free-lance writer for six years.

Kinds of Writing

''As a computer writer, you do two kinds of writing, hardware and software,'' says Mondoux. ''Hardware writing usually involves user manuals—how to load paper in a printer or hook up various components in a step-by-step way. Software writing, on the other hand, details what happens on the screen after you turn the computer on. It is more technical because a lot of what you are writing about is not visible. Users play around and move things and see results on the screen but not what happened in the computer to make that take place.''

The process of gathering information is quite different for hardware and software computer writing. "For hardware manuals you compile the information you need by observing how the machine works and interviewing engineers," says Mondoux. "In software writing, you need to interview engineers to find out how a program works and then you must try it out yourself. This gives you a feeling for how it works and what goes on to make it work."

As with science writing or any kind of specialized writing, the free-lance computer writer cannot be frightened by technical jargon and difficult concepts. It is vitally important to feel comfortable with computers and have experience in using them.

Getting Started

Mondoux suggests several ways to break into computer writing:

- Networking with other computer writers and people in a position to hire free-lance computer writers. "You meet such people by joining organizations like the Society for Technical Communication and attending meetings of local chapters," she says. "This allows you to find out what kind of free-lance work is available, where it is, who the contact people are. Contacts are everything. One job leads to another."
- Technical writing courses give you added background and abilities to handle computer free-lance assignments. You might also meet people in the position to hire computer writers. You can also list the course on your résumé. Many community colleges also offer courses in computer hardware and software, which are helpful to the beginner.
- Volunteering to do simple computer writing projects free of charge. "I volunteered to do an assembly manual for a computer and the company hired me and I had work for three and a half years," says Mondoux. She also finds that it is better to work for large companies, because they have many departments and she has gotten a job in one department after being recommended by someone in another area happy with her work.

Positives and Negatives

Being a free-lance computer writer has a number of positive aspects:

- *High pay.* Most companies hiring free-lance computer writers pay in a range of $35 to $45 per hour. This averages out to $10,000 to $12,000 for a complicated manual at one end of the spectrum or $4,000 to $6,000 for a less complicated job.

- *Contracts.* Everything is worked out in advance in a contract between the company and the writer. A typical contract specifies that a certain project will be done by a writer for a time period "not to exceed" such and such at a rate of so much per hour by a certain deadline. In this way, you will know in advance what you are going to make. You learn to estimate the time it will take to do the job based on your past experiences and by talking to other writers. The fee may also be determined by the amount of time a company is willing to allow for a job and the hourly rate. When you know a job is available, you bid on it by offering to do it for a certain price.
- *Formats.* The format of many computer writing jobs is predetermined by company policy. This means that you have a framework to follow as you work and eliminates the need to develop a new layout.
- *Freedom.* As with any kind of free-lance writing, computer and other technical writing offers you the freedom to work at your own pace and for whomever you want to work.

There are negative aspects as well:

- *Tight deadlines.* "Everyone is always in a rush to get new products out," says Mondoux, "and each new product needs a manual or other publication to go with it. They never call an outsider in until they've realized they aren't going to be able to get it done by their own in-house writers." An example of a typical, tight schedule is two months to prepare a 150-page manual to go to the printer.
- *No expenses.* You never get paid any expenses, whether you travel to the company for consultations and interviews or make long-distance telephone calls. You can get periodic infusions of money by submitting a bill each time you reach a certain milestone, like completing so many pages (this may not be an option with some companies).
- *Purchasing your own equipment.* "You need to stay up-to-date on both hardware and software," says Mondoux, who has had to buy a new IBM PC and portable MacIntosh and hundreds of dollars of new software just to complete her free-lance assignments. "Computer equipment depreciates very rapidly," she adds.
- *Working with engineers.* "Not only do you have to be able to handle technical material, but you have to get used to working with engineers and not be intimidated by them," she says. "They don't always suffer 'fools' well. They can get very annoyed."
- *Going long periods between jobs.* "You might go a year between free-lance assignments," continues Mondoux. This is hard both

financially and psychologically. That is why the ability of a writer to do other kinds of nontechnical work is important: it helps pay the bills. (Conversely, for mainstream free-lance writers, the ability to do computer writing helps stave off famine between magazine assignments!)

Concludes Mondoux: "The ideal computer writer is someone who is not afraid of accepting a challenge and dealing with the unknown. It's a scary feeling not to understand what you are trying to write about. But after you begin to ferret out information and, by your level of ignorance put yourself in the place of the user of the equipment, it gets easier."

Book Writing

A more natural fit than public relations writing or computer/technical writing is to become the author of a book. Quite often, the appearance of a well-written article on a controversial topic will attract the attention of a book publisher. In an ideal world, you simply expand your article with more interviews and research, collect a healthy advance, and sit back and write the book.

As with most things in life, the ideal often fails to materialize. Writing a book on an interesting topic is only half the battle. Even though all your friends tell you they'll buy a copy and extol the virtues of the idea, the book will need to sell more than 50 to 100 copies.

The economics of book publishing work against the unknown author. As more and more publishers have been acquired by large conglomerates, the decisions about what to publish have fallen into fewer and fewer hands. And, these "hands" have increasingly come to rely on a few big name authors writing best sellers. These authors command large advances and, consequently, dry up the pool of money available for new writers.

In addition, it is difficult to get anyone at a trade publisher to look at your book proposal unless that idea is submitted by an agent. As an aspiring book author, you should spend your time submitting ideas to agents rather than directly to publishers. *Literary Marketplace* and *Writer's Market* list agents and what they are looking for, along with details on how and what to submit.

Most want a proposed table of contents and a one- or two-page prospectus on what the book will be about and how it will differ from competing books. A few want several chapters to see how you handled the material. Publishers will want this too. It is a mistake, however, to write an entire book on speculation without getting a contract. As a free-lance writer, time is money. You simply can't afford to devote the months or years required to do most books—no matter how compelling the topic—without a contract.

A word of caution, however, on submitting material to agents. Some charge a "reading fee" of $100 to $500 per submission. Paying this fee is a mistake because then you start out in the hole. In researching publications for agent names, you will find many who do not charge a reading fee.

Agents typically charge a 10 percent to 20 percent commission on what you earn from your book. That amount is worth it given all the help a good agent provides.

The decision about whether an article has the "legs" to be expanded into a saleable book idea starts with you. Does the idea seem interesting enough to the general public; that is, readers who missed the article when it first appeared? Did you have to leave a lot of material out, given the space restrictions of the magazine? Can you do additional research and reporting to help the expansion? Is the proposed book "doable," that is, do accessible sources exist to interview and can you afford the required travel?

If your answers to these questions are yes, you can probably proceed with the project. Book writing is a rewarding activity. It will enhance your stature as a free-lance writer and, hopefully, fatten your bank balance as well. It is difficult to break into the tight world of trade publishing, but not impossible. "Nothing worthwhile," said a wise person who was probably a free-lance writer, "is ever easy."

21

Law, Ethics, and the Free-Lance Writer

The freedom that free-lance writers enjoy in other areas of their work—whether it be choosing their assignments or setting their schedules—does not extend to two areas of prime concern to everyone in journalism: law and ethics. Even though they may never encounter a legal problem or get into trouble because of an ethical transgression, free-lance writers must be extra careful to avoid both. Their reputations and future livelihood will depend on it. And, perhaps most important of all, they may not have legal and financial resources to support them as they would if they were full-time staff writers.

Law

Most free-lance writers don't give potential legal problems a second thought. Indeed, unless they specialize in investigative articles, the topics they normally cover seldom take them onto shaky legal ground. Being careful with facts and quotes and the spelling of names is normally sufficient.

"In the kind of happy journalism I do, I'm never operating even near to the edge," says Rob Phillips, an Oregon free-lance writer who writes stories about business and aviation. "As a measure of my insecurity when I started free-lancing full-time, though, I looked into libel insurance. At $2,500 a year, I decided I'd just write better." As a means of protecting himself, he shows his copy to sources most of the time.

There are three principal areas of legal concern for free-lance writers: libel, privacy, and copyright.

Libel

Libel is a defamatory statement about a person that is published and thereby injures that person's reputation. Reporters can get into trouble if their words imply criminality or question morals, sanity, or financial stability or if mistakes are made in stating the facts of stories, for example misspellings of names or incorrect addresses. If a reporter, editor, and publication lose a suit for libel, they can then be required to pay for damages.

There are two kinds of libel: civil and criminal. Most libel cases fall into the civil category; that is, a story that constitutes a printed or broadcast defamation. Criminal libel, while rare in the United States, results when something written or broadcast leads to a breach of the peace.

To win a civil libel case, a plaintiff must establish 1) that the item in question was published; 2) that he or she was identifiable by others, even if not named directly; 3) that the plaintiff was damaged by the statement; and 4) that the defendant was at fault—that is, he or she published the item knowing it was false (for public figure), or acted negligently in failing to ascertain that the statement was false (private individuals).

If a publication—or any of its employees—loses a libel suit, it may be ordered to pay damages to the plaintiff. There are three kinds of damages: compensatory or general (awarded to the plaintiff who was named in the published item: the plaintiff need not prove actual injury); special (the plaintiff who can show evidence of particular loss to reputation, well-being, or profession; this kind of damage can be awarded in addition to general damages); and punitive (awarded as a punishment and as an example because the offending publication showed malice in using the libelous item; the plaintiff must show proof of this malice, however).

There are three defenses to a libel charge:

1. *Truth.* To prove in court that what was written is true.
2. *Fair comment and criticism.* To be allowed to make "fair comment" on the performance of actors, sports figures, government officials, and others as long as that comment is without malice and restricted to the person's work.

3. *Privilege*. To use material in stories that is immune to libel action because it is "privileged." Privileged material includes statements by judges, lawyers, and witnesses in court as long as the court is in session; debates in Congress and state legislatures; and public documents.

Over the years, a number of U.S. Supreme Court rulings have pertained to libel law and, thus, have relevance to everyone who writes for a living.

Times v. Sullivan, 1964, resulted in *The New York Times* rule which holds that public figures cannot collect libel damages from journalists unless they can prove that what was written about them was a malicious and deliberate lie and in reckless disregard of the truth.

The *Times* rule was extended to private individuals engaged in matters of general interest in *Rosenbloom v. Metromedia*, 1971.

Since then, as the members of the Supreme Court have become more conservative, the protection of the media from libel suits has ebbed and flowed every few years, dealing with such subjects as who is a public figure (*Firestone v. Time*, 1976); protection of reporters' thoughts, judgments, and newsroom discussions (*Herbert v. Lando*, 1979); where a national publisher can be sued (*Keeton v. Hustler*, 1984); truth as a defense (*Philadelphia Newspapers v. Hepps*, 1986); immunity for statements of opinion (*Milkovich v. Lorain Journal Company*, 1990); and changing the quotes of a source (*Masson v. New Yorker*, 1991) (See Box 21.1).

There are six ways to avoid libel:

1. Be fair and accurate in reporting at all times.
2. Agree to check the facts of any story a person claims libeled him or her; do this politely but without admitting error.
3. Do not discuss the story or the reporting of it with the person who is complaining.
4. Print clarifications willingly and in a prominent place in the newspaper or magazine to explain and clarify the facts that are in question: only in extreme circumstances print retractions which actually admit error and "take back" the original story.
5. Consult an attorney—preferably from the publication for which you are free-lancing so you won't have to pay the cost—from the moment a person complains about an alleged libel.
6. Consult the Reporter's Committee for Freedom of the Press (1735 "I" Street, N.W. Suite 504, Washington, D.C. 20006), a voluntary association of reporters and editors working to protect the interests of journalists; it provides libel defense to journalists in freedom of the press and freedom of information cases.

Box 21.1 *Masson v. New Yorker*
A Libel Case That Hits All Writers Close to Home

In 1991, the U.S. Supreme Court ruled that public figures who sue for libel because a writer has changed their direct quotes cannot collect damages unless they can prove that the meaning of what they originally said was changed significantly.

Along with this decision, however, came the determination that the case that prompted the Court ruling should go to a jury trial. At issue was a lawsuit filed by Jeffrey Masson, a psychoanalyst, against *The New Yorker* and writer Janet Malcolm, charging that he had been libeled by quotations in a 1983 article that were attributed to him that he either never said or that were altered. Malcolm repeatedly denied that charge.

The decision was a victory for the news media because of earlier fears that the increasingly conservative court would come out in favor of the use of altered quotations themselves as evidence for a public figure to win a libel lawsuit. The decision was a great relief to all those who write for a living.

Some writers and journalists had mixed feelings about the victory, however, largely because of who had brought it on (Janet Malcolm) and the subject it dealt with (altered quotes). This was a subject that many would just as soon not see aired at all.

The ambivalence about Malcolm stemmed from another article. She had not exactly endeared herself to many of her fellow writers and journalists in the lead paragraph of her 1989, two-part article in *The New Yorker* on Joel McGinniss, author of *Fatal Vision*:

> Every journalist who is not too stupid or too full of himself to notice what is going on knows that what he does is morally indefensible. He is kind of a confidence man, preying on people's vanity, ignorance or loneliness, gaining their trust and betraying them without remorse. . . . Journalists justify their treachery in various ways according to their temperaments. The more pompous talk about freedom of speech and "the public's right to know;" the least talented talk about art; the seemliest murmur about earning a living.

This view of what writers do was considered mercenary, cold-blooded, and inaccurate by many in the business.

In 1993, the case had been sent back to U.S. District Court in San Francisco for trial before a jury. On June 3, 1993, that jury reached a verdict: it found that Malcolm had defamed Masson by publishing two quotations that she knew defamed him and used them with reckless disregard for the truth. The jury also found that the three other quotes at issue were false, but not defamatory. The magazine was not liable for this because its editors did not know the quotations were false and thus had not acted with "the reckless disregard for the truth" required to show guilt in such cases.

Despite their decision, the jury was not able to agree on damages in the case. The judge will have to decide later whether to declare a mistrial or try to settle the issue of damages separately. This left the legal outcome of this well-publicized case unclear. For all the dirty journalistic linen it aired, the case did not result in a clearcut victory for either side. Indeed, the media as a whole probably lost more than it gained by having the case go to trial in the first place.

Privacy

The foundations of privacy laws have their roots in the U.S. Constitution. Although the word "privacy" does not appear in that document, the Supreme Court has consistently interpreted the Constitution to grant individuals a right of privacy based on the First, Fourth, Fifth, Ninth, and Fourteenth Amendments. Despite this broad support, privacy is an area with few legal precedents, far less well-defined than libel, for example.

As it has evolved over the years, the right of privacy is considered to be the right of a person to be left alone to enjoy life without his or her name, visage, or activities becoming public property, unless he or she relinquishes that right. This privacy—for living persons only—is protected from invasions by newspapers, magazines, books, television, radio, photographs, motion pictures, creditors, and wiretappers.

The laws generally cover invasion of privacy in one of four ways: 1) intrusion (unreasonably intruding upon the solitude of another by physical or other means); 2) publicizing private matters (revealing in print or broadcast something about the private life of a person that offends ordinary sensibilities); 3) publicizing material in a false light (writing something about a person that puts them in a "false light," that is, contrary to the truth); and 4) appropriation (using a person's name, likeness, or personality for advertising or commercial purposes without his or her consent).

There are four defenses in privacy cases:

1. *Consent.* To prove that a person consented to the invasion of his or her privacy. Verbal consent is not enough; the person must give it in writing.
2. *Newsworthiness* (public figures). To show that the person in question is a public figure or public official. Courts have agreed that such a person invites public interest and must accept even unwelcome publicity.

3. *Newsworthiness* (private individuals). To prove that a private individual is involved in a matter of public interest. Unwarranted and unauthorized exposure of the private affairs of a private citizen, offensive to ordinary sensibilities and without legitimate interest to the public, can be deemed an invasion of privacy.
4. *Constitutional privilege.* To show that the alleged invasion of privacy in a "false light" was not carried out with the knowledge that it was false or untruthful. This defense resembles the constitutional proof requirements for public officials and public figures in libel law.

There are far fewer U.S. Supreme Court rulings applicable to privacy than there are for libel. In *Time v. Hill*, 1967, the court said *The New York Times* rule must be applied to privacy cases where the publication is false or fictitious, testing whether the falsehood was intentional and calculated. The court warned the media to watch its careless reporting or face punishment in *Cantril v. Forest City Publishing Company*, 1974. The use of open records in open court hearings was upheld in *Cox Broadcasting v. Martin Cohn*, 1975. In a 1989 case, *B.J.F. v. Florida Star*, the court went on record as favoring privacy laws passed by all 50 states rather than through a national standard.

There are ways to avoid privacy problems:

1. Do not publicize matters about the private life of someone that would be offensive to a "reasonable person," even if what is printed is true.
2. Do not publicize matters that put another person in a false light.
3. Do not physically intrude into a person's solitude or seclusion.
4. Do not appropriate the name or likeness of another person for benefit or advantage. This potential problem for free-lancers who take photographs or arrange for the taking of photos to accompany their articles can be avoided by the use of a model release (see Box 21.2) which needs to be signed by anyone not being photographed in a news situation (where permission is not necessary).

Copyright

Copyright grants its owner the exclusive right to print, publish, or reproduce an original literary, musical, or artistic work for a certain number of years. The federal government has the authority to grant a copyright, which must first be registered by following a set

Box 21.2 Model Release Form

Model Release

Date: ______________________________

Photographer: ______________________________

Address ______________________________

____

For valuable consideration, I hereby irrevocably consent to and authorize the use and reproduction by you, or anyone authorized by you, of any and all photographs which you have this day taken of me, negative or positive, for any purpose whatsoever, without further compensation to me. All negatives and positives, together with the prints shall constitute your property, solely and completely.

I am over 21 years of age. Yes ______ No ______

Model: ______________________________
(signature of model)

Address: ______________________________

Witnessed by: ______________________________
(signature of witness)

(If the person signing is under 21, consent must be given by the parent or guardian.)

I hereby certify that I am the parent or guardian of ______________ ______________ the model named above, and for the value received, I do give my consent without reservations to the foregoing on behalf of him or her or them.

Parent/Guardian: ______________________________
(signature of parent or guardian)

Witnessed by: ______________________________
(signature of witness)

procedure that includes filling out the appropriate form from the Register of Copyrights in the Library of Congress. A new copyright law took effect on January 1, 1978, which extended the duration of a copyright to a term lasting for the author's life, plus an additional 50 years. Under the old law, dating from 1909, the maximum amount of time for a copyright was 56 years.

As a free-lance writer, you have two concerns: 1) will my material be stolen by others; 2) how much of another writer's work can I use in my article or book?

First, protection of your own work should not be a worry. Once you have written an article, it is protected under the copyright law, even before it is published. It must be original and completely written in what the law calls "a tangible form." When a magazine agrees to publish that article, however, it may ask you to sign a contract or agreement which, if you aren't careful, could assign all future rights to the magazine. This is usually called an "all rights" contract. If you don't want to give away these rights for future publication, ask for a contract that calls for "first publication rights" or "first serial rights" only, as explained in chapter 19. This means that the magazine can publish your article once, but you own the article and can collect royalties for reprints and even use it again in another form. Free-lance writers often worry that the ideas in their query letters might be stolen by the editors to whom they are submitted. Since you can't copyright ideas or facts or events—only your writing about them—this might happen. Most editors are too ethical to do so. This is not to say such a thing never happens. It is rare enough not to be a worry, however.

Second, use of the work of another writer in your articles or book is sometimes tricky. The copyright law protects the work of others as it does your own, but it doesn't really specify how much is too much. However, under the concept of "fair use," you can use a limited amount of material without worry. The law does not say what it considers "fair use." The key element is the percentage of the whole that you have used. It is probably permissible to include a few sentences from a 2,000-word article and a few paragraphs from a 400-page book. On the other hand, using even one line from a song without permission could get you into trouble. To avoid problems in copyright, you should excerpt the work of others only when it is necessary, use such material sparingly, and credit the writer prominently, never leaving the slightest impression that what you are including is your own work. As an added precaution, it is wise never to include in your article direct quotes from people who were quoted by the writer whose work you are excerpting. The quote might be inaccurate and you have enough to worry about with the original writer, let alone his or her possibly disgruntled source.

You can use material from another writer without worry in two circumstances. If it is in the *public domain*—that is, if it is an older work and/or you know the author's copyright has run out—you can use as much as you want. You can also secure written permission from the holder of the copyright to use the written material or photograph. In such instances, you get the publisher or writer or copyright holder to sign a permission form and retain it in your files. Sometimes, you have to pay a fee to secure this permission. With all of these considerations, make sure that the material you are trying to get permission to use is worth it. (Box 21.3 shows the permission form used for this book; some publishers have their own pre-printed forms.)

Box 21.3 Permission Form

To: ______________________
____

I am preparing a textbook titled *Free-Lancing: A Guide to Writing for Magazines and other Markets* to be published by Waveland Press in 1994. It will be a paperback edition with approximately 340 pages.

May I please have your permission to reprint in this and future editions the following:

____ Interview material ______________________
____

____ Excerpt from your publication ______________________
____

These rights will in no way restrict republication of your material in any other form by you or others authorized by you. Should you not control these rights in their entirety, would you please let me know whom else to contact. Unless you suggest otherwise, I will use the following credit line:

I would greatly appreciate your consent to this request. For your convenience, a release is provided below and a copy of this letter is enclosed for your files.

Sincerely,

Ronald P. Lovell

____

I (We) grant permission for the use requested above.

______________________ Date: ________

(Signature)

The U.S. Supreme Court has not dealt with copyright as extensively as it has other legal areas, but one case does pertain.

In a 1985 decision, the Court said that federal law prohibits the news media from quoting extensively from unpublished, copyrighted material without permission, regardless of how newsworthy the subject may be. The Court found that *The Nation* magazine infringed a copyright in 1979 by publishing an article using excerpts from the memoirs of former President Gerald Ford. At that time, the book was copyrighted and due to be published in a few weeks. The publishers of the book had sold the rights to serialize the book to *Time*, which canceled its agreement when *The Nation* article appeared and refused to pay the second half of what it had agreed to pay. The Court's decision said the material used by *The Nation* did not fall within the "fair use" exception of the copyright law. It rejected the magazine's argument that the First Amendment guarantee of freedom of press permits the news media to print quotes or excerpts of copyrighted material written by public figures or about public events. This would "expand fair use to effectively destroy any expectation of copyright protection in the work of a public figure," according to the majority opinion. Book publishers at first hailed the decision as a victory for scholars and authors. Media law experts said the decision prevented the public from learning about government decisions unless the decisions were sold to them by former officials.

In the years since, however, that ruling has allowed people to prohibit authors from using excerpts from their unpublished letters in books about them. Although the U.S. Supreme Court has not ruled on this subject again, the U.S. Second Circuit Court said in a 1989 decision that there could be no unauthorized use of unpublished material "even if the work is a matter of . . . high public concern."

In November 1992, a ruling by a U.S. District Court judge in New York once again put writers and publications on notice that someone's private letters are not to be trifled with. The judge found that *Harper's* magazine violated copyright law when it published parts of a confidential letter by author Gordon Lish. The magazine had argued that printing an edited version of the letter was an important journalistic activity designed to inform the public. The judge, who rejected Lish's claim of libel, said *Harper's* violated the author's copyright because the magazine published "an unprecedented" amount (52 percent) of the original letter and because it did so to recreate the author's style. "A journalist is always free," read the opinion, "for example, to characterize and describe Lish's prose or even use brief quotations for that purpose." For that reason, the judge did not think his ruling would hamper journalists in the conduct of their work.

In general, you can avoid problems in copyright if you:

1. Exercise good judgment in using the work of others in your articles so that it qualifies as "fair use."
2. Make sure that any time you use extensive excerpts that the work is in the public domain.
3. Secure written permission to use personal letters, copyrighted written material, or photos taken by others, paying the required fee if necessary.

Ethics

Free-lance writing, like other aspects of journalism, is not governed by a binding and formal code of ethics. Unlike medicine and law, where those who are unethical can be prevented from working, journalism is less rigid and compliance more voluntary. It isn't that journalists are less ethical than doctors or lawyers or other professionals. There is just no formal mechanism to police and discipline them.

Journalistic organizations like the Society of Professional Journalists, along with many individual publications, have codes of ethics that do exert moral pressure on reporters and editors to be ethical at all times. The principles they espouse set high ethical standards in such areas as accuracy and objectivity, fair play, and ethics. But that is all they do. It is up to each reporter and each editor to live up to them. That they do so most of the time—based on their training, experience, and individual consciences—is one of the wonders of journalism. Few other professions exercise such self-restraint and self-policing.

Free-lance writers have to be just as ethical as their staff writer counterparts on newspapers and magazines. They need to be objective; that is, never showing bias or prejudice in their reporting. They need to use good taste in what they write about and how they write. They need to avoid letting their personal relationships with people or ties to organizations or companies influence their writing. They need to be careful not to misrepresent themselves to subjects—whether claiming to be a staff member of a publication when they are only doing a story on speculation or declining to mention they are a writer at all.

Two other ethical concerns are less clear-cut with free-lance writers than with staff members, however. Freebies—a gift to a reporter or editor as a sign of friendship or to influence coverage—

and junkets—trips for reporters where a company or group pays all expenses and hopes for favorable coverage in return—are prohibited for most staff members. Some free-lance writers couldn't do their jobs without them, however.

The best example of this is travel writing. Many Sunday newspapers have travel sections or travel pages each week. Many of the articles contained in them are written by free-lance writers. Neither the writer nor the newspaper could afford to make the trip required to do the reporting unless a hotel, airline, or steamship company paid all or most of the bill. Is the writer compromised in such a situation? All claim not to be and bend over backwards not to seem totally favorable in what they write. The sponsors, if they are smart, avoid blatant attempts to dictate copy. But the common courtesy most people are taught from birth probably precludes a lot of negative comments. This situation persists on most newspapers, with one exception.

Editors of the biggest and most successful travel section, in the Sunday *New York Times*, worry about their writers being compromised by going on junkets. Free-lance writer Susan Hauser was invited on a trip for travel writers around Oregon by the state tourist bureau, and she really wanted to go. But she had just started working for the Sunday *Times* travel section and had heard that even her attendance on a junket she *didn't* write about for the *Times* would disqualify her from writing for the *Times*. She didn't go. The newspaper later paid all the expenses for her first article on the Oregon Trail.

At the other end of the junket spectrum are writers, both staff and free-lance, who write for automobile magazines. According to a 1990 article in *The Wall Street Journal*, writers for *Car and Driver*, *Motor Trend*, *Road & Track*, and *Automobile* regularly receive airline tickets to Japan, free rooms at fancy resorts, gift certificates, clocks, briefcases, and free use of new cars—all courtesy of auto companies. They also assist the ad agencies of these companies by writing special issues for them and even speak for pay at conventions. While others in journalism decry this practice, most of the writers and editors interviewed by the *Journal* said their integrity had not been compromised.

The matter of gifts for free-lance writers is also problematic. Few would see anything wrong, for example, in a book reviewer getting a free copy of the book to be reviewed, along with the payment for writing the review itself. The editorial offices of any publication running reviews regularly are flooded with books and CD's and tapes and passes to movie theaters in the hope of a mere mention—favorable or unfavorable—in a review or column. On the other hand, at most newspapers and many magazines, a reporter and editor cannot accept so much as a cup of coffee from a source.

For a free-lance writer, not bound by such official constraints, refusing a gift is sometimes embarrassing or even rude. "Some of the things I used to teach as a journalism professor don't pertain," says Rob Phillips. "Would I accept a gift from a source? Yes. A model of the Airbus, a book, an umbrella with a company logo, a tie, a hotel room. I'm not above accepting that. I practice corporate journalism."

Ethics for free-lance writers is kind of in the eye of the beholder. Before accepting anything of value, ask yourself, "Can I take this and honestly say that the objectivity and accuracy of my article won't be compromised?" Then, unless the publication you are working for prohibits such acceptance, let your conscience be your guide.

The American Society of Journalists and Authors offers some guidance in its Code of Ethics and Fair Practices. That organization adheres to the code through its Committee on Editor-Writer Relations, which investigates and mediates disagreements brought before it. The code itself deals with such matters as truthfulness, accuracy, editing, sources, ideas, acceptance of an assignment, report on assignment (when a writer decides there is no story), withdrawal, agreements, rewriting, bylines, rights, payment, expenses, copyright, reprints, and agents, along with other things. (Copies of the code can be ordered from the Society at 1501 Broadway, Suite 1907, New York, New York, 10036.)

Glossary of Terms

Advertising/editorial ratio—The ratio of ad pages to editorial pages in a magazine.

Advertising lineage—The amount of advertising included in a magazine over a certain period of time.

Agent—A publishing specialist who, in return for a percentage of sales, arranges book and, on occasion, magazine deals for writers.

Art—Illustrations in a magazine, whether artist's drawings or photographs.

Article—A factual piece of writing on a specific subject; also called a "story" or a "piece."

Assignment—Asking a writer to submit an article by a certain deadline.

Audit Bureau of Circulation—The organization of advertising agencies, advertisers, and the media set up to audit the circulation statements of the media upon which advertising rates are based; also called ABC.

"Back of the book"—The section of a magazine that follows the main editorial section; usually contains regular departments such as "beauty," "health," and the like.

Bind-in card—A card, often used with an accompanying ad, that is bound into a magazine so it can be easily detached and mailed in by readers.

Binding—The last step in the production of a magazine, during which printed pages are folded, collated, stitched, glued, or stapled and trimmed into copies to be mailed out.

Bleed—A photograph or other illustration that goes to the edge of a magazine page to enhance effect.

Book—Another name for magazine.

Breaking the book—The allocation of space in a magazine between articles and ads.

Business magazine—Magazines that serve readers in business and finance.

Caption—The words printed under a photo to identify it.

Center spread—The two pages in the center of a magazine; a highly desirable spot.

Circulation—The total number of copies sold by a magazine through subscription and newsstand sales.

City magazine—A magazine whose editorial content and advertising are targeted to readers in a particular city or region.

Class magazine—A magazine that seeks to attract highly educated, high-income, sophisticated readers with its editorial matter and advertising.

Company magazine—A magazine published by a company or other organization to enhance its image and put forward its point of view; also called public relations magazines.

Consumer magazine—A magazine sold directly to its readers through subscription and/or newsstand sales.

Contract—An agreement between a magazine and a writer that specifies the length of the article to be written, the fee, and the deadline.

Controlled circulation—The circulation policy of most trade magazines wherein only readers in the field covered by the magazine are allowed to receive it.

Copyright—The exclusive right, granted by law for a certain number of years, to make and dispose of copies of a literary, musical, or artistic work.

Cover—The outside front of a magazine; the back and two inside cover pages are highly prized positions for advertisements.

Cover letter—Letter that accompanies a completed article; serves to refresh the editor's memory and to explain any problems or changes since the original assignment.

Cover lines—Headlines or words on the front cover used to attract readers to that particular issue.

Cutline—The information used to identify a photograph.

Deadline—The date when an article is due.

Demographics—The various economic and social characteristics of potential readers (for example, age, sex, education, income level).

Double truck—Editorial or advertising pages that face each other and are designed as one unit.

Fee—The amount of money paid to a writer for completing an article.

Format—The entire "look" of a magazine in terms of size, appearance, content, use of color, etc . . .

Free circulation—Sending a trade publication to everyone in a trade or profession at no cost to them.

Free-lance writer—A writer who works independently for various publications.

"Front of the book"—The main editorial section of a magazine; the first few pages of which contain no advertising.

Galley—A column of type used for proofing before final layout.

Gatefold—An additional leaf of a magazine cover which can be printed as an extension of the cover illustration or as an advertisement.

General magazine—A consumer magazine that is not aimed at any certain audience, but at readers interested in many subjects.

Ghostwriter—A writer who writes books and articles for a fee; however, someone else's name appears on them when they are printed.

"Hot book"—A magazine that sells well on newsstands.

House ad—An ad run by a magazine that extols its own virtues and accomplishments.

House organ—Another name for company magazine.

Kill fee—A percentage of a fee—10 to 25 percent—paid to a writer when an article has been assigned and completed, but is not published.

Layout—The actual placement of type and photos on a page.

Letterpress—A printing process in which ink touches a raised surface (the type); seldom used any more except for special printing jobs.

Magazine—A publication coming out periodically that contains articles, photos, and ads; from the French word, *magasin*, which means "storehouse."

Magazine Publishers Association—The trade organization of magazines that gathers circulation and financial data and promotes interests of magazines.

Makeup—A plan of how elements on a page will look.

Manuscript—The original text of a writer's work.

Masthead—A boxed area of a magazine where information on staff, office address, and subscription is included.

Model release—A written agreement between a person who is photographed and a writer or photographer allowing a photo to be used in print.

Name plate—The name of a magazine on its cover.

Newsletter—An analytical news report distributed regularly for a high fee to special readers; an inexpensive PR publication sent to employees or other special publics.

Offset—The major printing method in use today; a process in which ink does not touch paper directly but instead goes onto a rubber blanket.

Page proof—The final typeset version of a page, used for proofing.

Paid circulation—When most readers of a magazine pay to receive it, as opposed to getting it free.

Payment on acceptance—When a magazine pays a writer as soon as an article has been received and deemed acceptable.

Payment upon publication—When a magazine does not pay a writer until an article is actually published.

Perfect binding—Binding a magazine together with glue; used often by monthlies which have more pages than weeklies.

Periodical—A magazine or other publication issued at regular intervals.

Permission—A written agreement from an individual or publisher allowing a writer to use certain restricted material in an article or book.

Public relations magazine—A magazine produced by a company or other organization as a way to build its image.

Query—A letter written to an editor explaining an idea for an article and a writer's qualifications to complete it.

Rate card—The list of a magazine's advertising rates and publishing schedule.

Reader service card—A card bound into a trade magazine that, if returned by readers, will result in product information being sent to them.

Rejection slip—A printed form sent by magazine editors to writers rejecting their articles or books.

Roundup story—A common type of trade publication story in which the reporter interviews a number of experts in a field and asks them the same questions in order to determine trends; also called a survey story.

Saddle stitch—Binding a magazine together with staples placed at the folding edge; used often by weeklies, which have fewer pages than monthlies.

SASE—Self-addressed, stamped envelope; writers should include one with each query letter and unassigned article submitted to a magazine.

Seed money—Money given by a speculator to start a new magazine.

Sidebar—A short article accompanying a longer article that deals with one element of the same subject but can stand alone.

Signature—A printed sheet folded to page size for binding along with other such sheets, to form a magazine or book.

Side stitch—Binding a magazine with staples placed a quarter inch from the folded edge; used mostly with thick monthlies.

Single copy sales—Newsstand sales of a magazine, used to determine what is a "hot book."

Slicks—Magazines that are printed on good quality paper.

Slush pile—The unsolicited manuscripts received by magazine editors; many are discarded, a few are kept and published.

Specialized magazine—A magazine that aims its content and most of its advertising at a certain audience, from auto buffs to scuba divers.

Subscription—The right to receive a given number of copies of a magazine over a period of time, based on the amount of money paid in advance.

Trade magazine—A magazine aimed at professionals or workers in a specific trade or field.

Type—A letter or character in various styles used to print publications through offset or other processes.

Writer's guidelines—A list of topics acceptable to a magazine and procedures to be used by writers in submitting ideas and articles.

Additional Resources

Biagi, Shirley. *How to Write and Sell Magazine Articles*. Englewood Cliffs, NJ: Prentice-Hall, 1981.

Bly, Robert. *Secrets of a Freelance Writer: How to Make 85,000 Dollars a Year*. New York: Henry Holt, 1990.

Casewit, Curtis. *Freelance Writing: Advice from the Pros*. New York: Macmillan, 1985.

Click, J. W., and Russell N. Baird. *Magazine Editing and Production*, 5th edition. Dubuque, IA: Wm. C. Brown, 1990.

Clurman, Richard. To the End of Time. New York: Simon & Schuster, 1992.

Commins, Dorothy. *What Is an Editor? Saxe Commins at Work*. Chicago: University of Chicago Press, 1978.

Enos, Sandra F. *Breaking Into Article Writing*. Boston: The Writer, Inc., 1988.

Ferguson, Rowena. *Editing the Small Magazine*. New York: Columbia University Press, 1958.

Foley, Martha. *The Story of Story Magazine: A Memoir*. New York: Norton, 1980.

Graham, Betsy P. *Magazine Article Writing*. New York: Holt Rinehart Winston, 1980.

Hamblin, Dora Jane. *That Was the Life*. New York: Norton, 1977.

Land, Myrick E. *Writing for Magazines*. Englewood Cliffs, NJ: Prentice-Hall, 1987.

Mogel, Leonard. *The Magazine*. Englewood Cliffs, NJ: Prentice-Hall, 1979.

Nelson, Roy Paul. *Articles and Features*. Boston: Houghton Mifflin, 1978.

Rivers, William L. *Free-lancer and Staff Writer*, 5th edition. Belmont, CA: Wadsworth, 1992.

Thurber, James. *The Years With Ross*. Boston: Atlantic, Little-Brown, 1957.

White, Jan. *Designing for Magazines*. New York: Bowker, 1982.

Wolfe, Tom, ed. *The New Journalism*. New York: Harper & Row, 1973.

Wolseley, Roland. *The Changing Magazine*. New York: Hastings House, 1973.

Additional Resources

Index